M000250595

LANDSCAPE NARRATIVES

LANDSCAPE NARRATIVES

DESIGN PRACTICES FOR TELLING STORIES

MATTHEW POTTEIGER

JAMIE PURINTON

JOHN WILEY & SONS, INC

New York · Chichester · Weinheim · Brisbane · Singapore · Toronto

This book is printed on acid-free paper.

Copyright © 1998 by John Wiley & Sons, Inc. All rights reserved.

Published simultaneously in Canada.

No part of this publication may be reproduced, stored in a retrieval system or transmitted in any form or by any means, electronic, mechanical, photocopying, recording, scanning or otherwise, except as permitted under Sections 107 or 108 of the 1976 United States Copyright Act, without either the prior written permission of the Publisher, or authorization through payment of the appropriate per-copy fee to the Copyright Clearance Center, 222 Rosewood Drive, Danvers, MA 01923, (508) 750-8400, fax (508) 750-4744. Requests to the Publisher for permission should be addressed to the Permissions Department, John Wiley & Sons, Inc., 605 Third Avenue, New York, NY 10158-0012, (212) 850-6011, fax (212) 850-6008, E-Mail: PERMREQ@WILEY.COM.

This publication is designed to provide accurate and authoritative information in regard to the subject matter covered. It is sold with the understanding that the publisher is not engaged in rendering legal, accounting, or other professional services. If legal advice or other expert assistance is required, the services of a competent professional person should be sought.

Book design by Tenth Avenue Editions, Inc.
for John Wiley & Sons, Inc.

Library of Congress Cataloging-in-Publication Data:
Potteiger, Matthew.
    Landscape narratives : design practices for telling stories /
Matthew Potteiger,   Jamie Purinton.
        p.   cm.
    Includes index.
    ISBN 0-471-12486-9 (cloth : alk. paper)
    1. Landscape design.   2. Landscape architecture.   I. Purinton,
Jamie.   II.   Title.
SB472.45.P68   1998
712' .01—dc21   97-40015

Printed in the United States of America.

10 9 8 7 6 5

CONTENTS

ACKNOWLEDGMENTS

IT TAKES TIME TO KNOW A PLACE AND ITS STORIES. We were only able to understand the value and complexity of the places featured in this book because of the many people who generously shared their experiences of living and working in their landscapes. Don Smith recalled trapping muskrat as he navigated us through the Hackensack salt marsh; the Mississippi couple, picking pepper grass along the side of Highway 61, shared their recipes and invited us for dinner; Ines took us to Xochimilco to hear floating mariachi bands alongside the *chinampas*; Luis Ramos, and many other members of Rincón Criollo welcomed us to listen to music in their *casita*; Carl Alderson led us to the heron rookeries in the industrial Arthur Kill; Jim O'Neal, the owner of Rooster Blues records, and the artist Mara Califf drove us along the back roads of Clarksdale, Mississippi; Marcia Donahue, Tony Darmento, John Hoch, Colonel Johnson, Lorri Davis, Peter Svenson, Richard Register, and Yolanda Garcia all shared their stories of places they knew well.

The ongoing discourse of many landscape architects, artists, architects, geographers, and planners has helped us to define narrative practices. James Wine's book *De-Architecture* explores the narrative potential of architecture and sites. The geographer James Duncan, both an influential scholar and invaluable collague, helped us extend the wealth of post-structural theory to the interpretation of landscape. Lawrence Halprin discussed the current problem of themed landscapes. George Hargreaves', John Hejduk's, and Bernard Tschumi's work challenge traditional notions of narrative. Discussion and correspondence with other practicing landscape architects and artists, including Anthony Walmsley, Frank Edgerton Martin, Katy Wiedel, Lisa Cameron, Dennis Carmichael, Ann Chamberlain, and Paula Horrigan, helped expand our scope of landscape narrative.

The creative inquiries of students at the College of Environmental Science and Forestry at Syracuse and CUNY influenced the way this book developed as a tool for teaching design. In addition, Joshua Sloan, Noriko Maeda, Jen Miller, Gabriela Canamar, Timothy Toland, Barbara Henderson, Helen Wilson and Paul Fritz assisted in research, mapping, and computer graphics.

Many reviewers gave us critical editorial wisdom, raised important questions, and enriched the text. Neill Bogan, an artist with REPOhistory, added his experience with modern theater and public art. Suzanne Nash, professor of Romance Languages at Princeton University, urged us to focus our attention on the uniqueness of the landscape medium—a theme reiterated in the writings of Elizabeth Meyer. Anne McKinnon's editorial skills helped to structure numerous chapters. Alec Finlay, Chris Neville, Ann Uppington,

Peter Jacobs, Kenneth Helphand, Bob Scarfo, Kim Sorvig, and John Stuart-Murray each provoked and challenged us with their readings.

Over the past three years of research and travel, we have relied on generous friends who have shared their homes and meals. We enjoyed crayfish with Ed Blake and Bob Brzuszek in Picayune, Mississippi. Margaret Mori, MaryBeth Pudup, Roger Todhunter, Kim Ackert, Michelle Corbett, and Diane Kane generously offered their homes and studios in San Francisco, Toronto, Rome, Chatham, and Los Angeles. Ines took care of us day and night in Mexico City. In so many untold ways Denise Corbett was an integral part of the story of this book.

We want to thank our editor, Daniel Sayre at John Wiley & Sons for his willingness to support a book that cuts across conventional categories, as well as David Sassian, for maintaining the intentions of the book through production. And most important, our deepest gratitude goes to our friends and families for their constant support and inspiration.

PREFACE

I don't consider myself a storyteller. But if I reach into my coat pockets, I'm likely to find scraps of notes, a ticket stub from a concert, ATM statements, bibliographic references for this book, phone numbers, a map [of Boston] from a spring field trip, a frayed napkin—each piece an unlikely memento recalling a time, an event, or a place. The contents of coats worn less frequently seem to span longer time frames. From this partial anthology, edited as much by chance as by intention, I can begin to reconstruct the various narratives that cohere around this life.
Journal entry, March 17, 1996, M. Potteiger

WE DO NOT USUALLY THINK OF LANDSCAPES AS TELLING STORIES EITHER. Landscape may serve as the backdrop setting or symbol in service to stories told in written texts or verbal performances, but it is rarely conceived as narrative in its own right. Yet, a walk into the woods can initiate narratives of retreat, discovery, interpretation of natural history...and return. And clearing a pathway inscribes these desires and sequences into a more tangible form. In this manner landscape becomes imbricated with narrative.

This book proceeds from the premise that narrative is a very fundamental way people shape and make sense of experience and landscapes. Stories link the sense of time, event, experience, memory and other intangibles to the more tangible aspects of place. Because stories sequence and configure experience of place into meaningful relationships, narrative offers ways of knowing and shaping landscapes not typically acknowledged in conventional documentation, mapping, surveys, or even the formal concerns of design.

Initially, the use of narrative, grounded in lived experience, seems to offer an alternative to both the abstraction of modernism and the simulations of postmodern culture. Yet, even the simplest story raises fundamental issues regarding subjectivity, representation, fiction, and what is taken to be real. The experiences of each character in a story, for instance, introduce shifts in focus and meaning that revise and remap the landscape. It is important then to ask: Whose story is told and why? What systems of belief are established through stories? How does one sort out the many layered (personal, ethnic, regional), multiple, and often contested stories of a place? What are the ethics and politics of telling stories?

Since the early 1980s, narrative has become the focus of a burgeoning number of landscape design projects. As part of the research for this book, we surveyed the scope of narrative design in landscape architecture, architecture, planning, public art, and sculpture. Uncertain at first whether there was enough substantial work to actually write about, we in fact discovered more than expected. We found designers encoding a compendium of narratives from local history to archetypal myths using strategies such as inscribing text in sidewalks, plotting sequences, revealing forgotten histories, writing their own fictions, preserving landscapes associated with stories, retelling tradition in new forms, and inviting people to add their own stories to places. Much of this reflects the ideological and stylistic shift from modernist abstraction and functionalism to the historical, contextual, and referential concerns of postmodernism. But narrative is not bound to any one style or period. There is in fact a long tradition of narrative design, and it can be argued that any design inevitably has its narratives.

From our survey of practice, we found that landscape narratives tend to be conceived primarily in terms of literal storytelling. So many projects rely on signs, icons, and other explicit references to add a veneer of stories to the landscape. While these projects do begin to engage and speak to a public in a more accessible design language, they tend to present already codified versions of stories. These "one-liners" fail to resonate with other dimensions of experience—with the narratives implicit in materials, in processes, and in ordinary practices of drawing boundaries and excavating, preserving, or demolishing landscapes. To extend landscape narrative beyond the literal requires attention to how people read stories in landscape. What are the differences between spatial/visual/ecological narratives and those in verbal or written form? Rather than being something *added to* landscapes, how are narratives implicit in the materials, experiences, and processes of landscapes? What degree of control does the designer have over the reading? What is the role of the reader/participant in constructing the meaning of a story? Besides a few articles or brief references, there has been no sustained, comprehensive investigation into these questions. Narrative is readily evoked in landscape design but often without a critical or theoretical base.

At the same time, narrative has emerged as a central concern not only for literary criticism but across disciplines ranging from art, the social sciences, anthropology, geography, law, and history to the natural sciences. The insights from this rich and diverse field of narrative studies have significant implications for landscape narratives. However, the literature is extensive, and much of it deals with issues and terms particular to written or verbal narratives, as opposed to spatial or visual forms. One of the objectives of *Landscape Narratives* is to relate narrative theory to the particular nature of landscape. We have found that the developments in contemporary narrative theory—the metaphor of landscape as text, the idea of intertextual connections, multiple authorship, and the role of the reader in constructing meaning—open new ways of understanding landscape and suggest potentials for different forms of practice. We can begin to understand landscape narratives not just as literal stories or texts to be read but as integral to the processes that shape landscapes in the first place.

STRUCTURE AND SCOPE OF *LANDSCAPE NARRATIVES*

As the synthesis of landscape and narrative suggests, much of the book is concerned with crossing boundaries between disciplines, between temporal and spatial media, fictive realms and lived experience, and the poetics and politics of stories. And since narrative is fundamental to cultural experience, it is important to look not only at designed narratives but at the routine and extraordinary practices of the naming of places, rituals, journeys, and memories that imbue landscape with stories.

The book is organized in three parts. Part one addresses the primary questions: What are landscape narratives? What forms do they take? How do they construct meaning, and how can they be interpreted? Drawing from contemporary theory in literary criticism, anthropology, geography, and art, as well as significant landscape examples, the two chapters in part one establish a theoretical framework for understanding the elements, processes, and forms of landscape narratives.

Part two defines and illustrates a series of narrative practices: *naming, sequencing, revealing and concealing, gathering,* and *opening.* The practices are applicable across a range of design projects from preservation and heritage planning, public art, and sustainable design to participatory approaches. As ways of constructing meaning, these are common cultural practices found in vernacular contexts as well as design projects at different scales.

Part three applies narrative theory and practices to tell three particular stories: "The Wasteland and Restorative Narrative," "Writing Home," and "Road Stories." As "cultural stories" these narratives are a critical part of contemporary discourse concerning the relationship between culture and nature, the retelling of tradition and community, and the negotiation of differences. We track these narratives in a series of representative projects and places such as the restoration of New Jersey's Meadowlands. These sites and their stories are works in progress in which old tales are revised by very contemporary imperatives. They enable us to see the process of selecting, interpreting, negotiating, and structuring the meanings of contemporary landscape narratives.

Although the arrangement of the chapters in these three parts follows a certain conventional progression from theory to elements of practice, culminating in synthesis, the structure as well as the reading of the text need not proceed in a strictly linear manner. The practices, for instance, do not simply apply narrative theory, they help to further define and elaborate that framework. The process of writing the book between two authors was more iterative, simultaneous, and parallel than linear. In fact, we began from the center, with the practices, and proceeded outward toward the beginning and the end at the same time. Likewise, readers looking for more direct application may start with the practices, while people working with narratives in visual art, geography, or other forms may be interested in the theoretical links with landscape outlined in part one. The organization can be thought of as a spatial narrative, a configuration of stories that map out different relationships and features of landscape narratives, similar to how a set of overlay transparencies reveal different aspects and relationships of landscapes.

The structure and content encourage different readings, combinations, and lines of inquiry for a varied audience. One of the most engaging and encouraging aspects of our research was the appeal of landscape narratives for a diverse group of people: geographers, artists, filmmakers, folklorists, writers, community activists, and professional designers. The people of the places we studied also took an active interest in telling and exchanging stories. We considered it essential to reflect this multiform nature of landscape narratives and their broad relevance across different disciplines and contexts.

The aim of this book is to establish a framework and provide the critical questions for engaging landscape narratives. We do not advocate one particular method or process of narrative landscape design. Narratives can and do relate to the variety of practices. They are just as critical to the designer attempting to refigure culture's relation to nature through sustainable design as they are to the preservationist concerned with maintaining the historic associations of place. And since stories are such a fundamental way of communicating, they offer the potential to be used in participatory and collaborative design methods. As the ideas from this book are taken into design studios, professional practice, communities, and other contexts, we hope the significance and potential of landscape narratives will continue to unfold.

———

Note: The idea that narratives are integral to the making of places was first posed by Matthew Potteiger's master's thesis in Landscape Architecture at the University of California, Berkeley, in 1980. In that project the landscape narratives of the Mission District of San Francisco were developed by collecting oral histories, court transcripts, happenings on the street, scenarios from planning reports, the author's own experience, and reading the physical traces of change in the landscape itself and then overlaying, contrasting, and weaving these narratives into a set of new stories that followed several fictional characters through the district. The inquiry into the storied nature of landscape that began with that project continues through the work of this book.

PART ONE
THEORY

CHAPTER ONE

BEGINNING

NARRATIVE

You stand there at night, you don't see anything. That sound comes to you and there's a beautiful story in it.
Foxhunter listening to the sound of the dogs,
New Jersey Pinelands (Hufford, 6).

WE live within worlds of stories, and we use stories to shape those worlds. In history, fiction, lived experience, myth, or anecdote, stories tell of origins, explain causes, mark the boundaries of what is knowable, and explore the territories beyond. As we remember, interpret, plan and dream through stories they give form to the transience of experience.

Whether they come as the sound of dogs at night, or a human voice at the threshold of sleep, recollected from memory or read from the marks on a page, a picture, or a landscape, stories are only knowable through some form of communication. *Narrative* refers to both the *story*, what is told, and the means of telling, implying both product and process, form and formation, structure and structuration.[1] *Narrative* is thus a more comprehensive and inclusive term than *story*. While every story is a narrative, not every narrative necessarily meets the conventional notions of a story as a well-wrought tale plotted with a sense of clear beginning, middle, and end (Prince, 91). A narrative may be as simple as a sentence, "I went down to the crossroads," or as extensive and complex as the notion of progress. Beyond conscious awareness or inherent in daily actions, it may be as mundane, varied, scripted, or open-ended as our own lives.

Coming from the Latin *gnarus* and the Indo-European root *gna*, "to know," *narrative* implies a knowledge acquired through action and the contingencies of lived experience (Turner, 163). Children develop this very human capacity for understanding narratives at an early age. They can learn complex spatial sequences that will take them from school to home if they are connected to stories (Trimble 1994, 20). We continue to negotiate our way through life with the aid of stories. According to cognitive psychologist Jerome Bruner, narrative is a fundamental way of thinking that is very different from a logico-scientific way of knowing. Instead of searching for universal truth conditions, to follow a story requires paying attention to par-

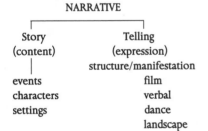

NARRATIVE

Story (content)	Telling (expression)
	structure/manifestation
events	film
characters	verbal
settings	dance
	landscape

The distinctions and relationships between *story* and *narrative*, summarized above, derive from a long tradition of analysis, from Aristotle's *Poetics* to the contemporary interdisciplinary study of *narratology*. (Adapted from Chatman 1978, 26)

Stories do more than explain, which comes from the Latin "to flatten." In his essay "The Storyteller," Walter Benjamin contrasts the power of stories with that of the explanation and information that saturate modern life: "The value of information does not survive the moment in which it was new. It lives only at that moment; it has to surrender to it completely and explain itself to it without losing any time. A story is different. It does not expend itself. It preserves and concentrates its strength and is capable of releasing it even after a long time." (Benjamin, 90)

ticular connections, coincidences, chance encounters. The end cannot always be predicted or deduced (Polkinghorne, 17).

Once in the purview of literature and art, the study of narrative now traverses a broad range of disciplines as part of a shift in the way the world is described in both the humanities and the sciences. Historians, who once attempted to emulate models from the physical sciences by eliminating narrative, now reaffirm its necessity to historical consciousness (Danto: "To exist historically is to perceive the events one lives through as part of a story later to be told" [p. 343]). Thomas Kuhn in *The Structures of Scientific Revolutions* (1960) demonstrated that what passes for progress in science has as much to do with the acceptance and succession of stories as it does with compiling objective descriptions. In addition, Lyotard (1984) argued that science is penetrated by "master narratives" of enlightenment, progress, and nationalism. In anthropology, structuralist theories, most notably those of Claude Lévi-Strauss, established a systematic approach for uncovering the unconscious content of narratives, which in turn helped establish the interdisciplinary study of narrative in the social sciences. Others have applied the insights from narrative theory in areas as diverse as medicine (Coles), policy analysis (Roe), and geography (Duncan). This current interest is not just about how to tell stories, but about understanding the importance of narrative in its archaic sense, as a fundamental means of knowing and representing the world (Mitchell, *x*).

Like a language, narrative is a means of communicating. The selecting and sequencing of events to construct a meaningful story can be homologous to the selecting and sequencing of words to form a meaningful sentence. Changing the order in which events are told in a story changes the meaning of the story. According to Paul Ricoeur, who produced the three-volume study *Time and Narrative*, it is the temporal qualities of existence that reach expression through narrative, and narrative is ultimately a language of time (Ricoeur, 166, 167). The genealogical story of one Pennsylvania German farmer in the Oley Valley illustrates this temporal structuring:

John Hoch

> I'm the eighth generation on the place.
> They came here in 1725. It was Rudolf Hoch.
> He had a son Johannes.
> Then there were two Abrahams, three Gideons
> and then it was me.
>   John Hoch, Oley Valley, Pennsylvania[2]

In just a few lines he is able to encapsulate over two hundred years of events and changes. There is no plot per se, rather, time is structured by the sequence of generations named by each son who inherited the farm. In these ways, by selecting certain events from the flow of time, linking them to make intelligible sequences, or plotting an end in relation to a beginning, narratives shape the sense of time.

In John Hoch's story the biblical references in the names as well as the absence of women's names index important aspects of the social structure of the place. Here too, meaning resides not just in *what* is told but in *how* it is told. The apparent continuity from generation to generation belies the significant sometimes radical changes, reorganization, and modernization that occurred at each transition of ownership. Yet, his narrative style is concise, selective, and without any hint of sentiment. By contrast, an article in the "Lifestyle" section of an area newspaper recast John's life as a nostalgic remnant, an emblem of a better, simpler life that is passing along with the family farm. These differences illustrate that it is imperative to pay attention to narratives, because *they structure the meanings by which people live* (Cohan and Shires, 1).

We can begin to understand narrative, then, as a vital activity coursing through oral tradition, texts, video, and other media, reflecting the diverse motives and contexts for telling stories. Old genres find new expression. Just as oral tradition became codified into epic texts, novels appear on computer screens. Roland Barthes described this multiform and fundamental nature of narrative in his "Introduction to the Structural Analysis of Narrative," noting,

> The narratives of the world are numberless. Narrative is first and foremost a prodigious variety of genres, themselves distributed amongst different substances—as though any material were fit to receive man's stories. Able to be carried by articulated language, spoken or written, fixed or moving images, gestures, and the ordered mixture of all these substances; narrative is present in myth, legend, fable, tale, novella, epic, history, tragedy, drama, comedy, mime, painting (think of Carpaccio's *Saint Ursula*), stained glass windows, cinema, comics, news item, conversation. Moreover, under this almost infinite diversity of forms, narrative is present in every age, in every place, in every society; it begins with the very history of mankind and there nowhere is nor has been a people without narrative. All classes, all human groups, have their narratives, enjoyment of which is very often shared by men with different, even opposing,* cultural backgrounds. Caring nothing for the division between good and bad literature, narrative is international, transhistorical, transcultural: it is simply there, like life itself. (Barthes, 79)

LANDSCAPE NARRATIVES

Narratives are also there in landscapes. They intersect with sites, accumulate as layers of history, organize sequences, and inhere in the materials and processes of the landscape. In various ways, stories "take place."

The term *landscape narrative* designates the interplay and mutual relationship that develops between landscape and narrative. To begin with, places configure narratives. Landscape not only locates or serves as background setting for stories, but is itself a changing, eventful figure and

---

* It must be remembered that this is not the case with either poetry or the essay, both of which are dependent on the cultural level of their consumers." *(Barthes's note)*

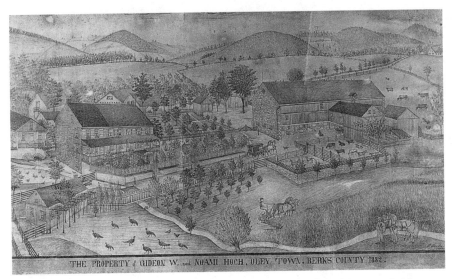

THE PROPERTY of GIDEON W. and NOAMI HOCH, OLEY TOWN, BERKS COUNTY 1882.

The Hoch farm in 1882. The dark shaded roof on the left side of the house marks the "grandparents' addition." Sitting on that side of the porch, John Hoch recalled in 1982: "When I quit farming and sold Mark the place, I said, I don't want to go away. I said, I don't want to move along a highway where there is noise that you can't sit on the porch and talk. We made a deal. I moved over to this end of the house. I can stay here as long as I live. When my Pop was living yet, he died in fifty-six, I used to come over and be with him over here in the evening so he wouldn't sit alone."

The drawing was done by Ferdinand Brader, an itinerant artist from Germany who did similar ones for many of the farms in the Oley Valley. While working on this drawing he also helped with farm work and slept in the straw shed (shown here extending from the middle of the barn).

process that engenders stories. A road establishes a sequence while opening the possibilities of chance encounters. The scale of space becomes the scope of an epic or the confines of a personal drama. Traces in the landscape hold secrets and invite interpretation. Trees, rocks, ground, weather, or any elements can serve as emblems in a narrative. In this manner people map landscapes into the very texture and structure of stories.

In turn, every narrative, even the most abstract, allegorical, or personal, plays a critical role in making places. It is through narrative that we interpret the processes and events of place. We come to know a place because we know its stories. Whether it is an encounter with the edge of a forest or a drive down a suburban street, we know these places through personal experience as well as from books, television, or folklore. Barbara Johnstone writes, "The texture of a familiar neighborhood is a narrative texture, too; when a neighborhood feels like home, the houses and people one passes on its streets evoke stories" (Johnstone, 10). As these stories encode histories and memories, they imbue sites with dimensions of time and associations not readily available to the outside observer.

Besides transforming place through association, the narratives of events, or even fiction and myth, are "written into" the physical form of the landscape, becoming concrete, tangible...real. John Hoch's narrative of genealogy not only structures a sense of time, it is also built into the physical form of the architecture and landscapes. The typical Pennsylvania German farmhouse has a "grandparents' addition." When one generation retires, they move into the addition, making room for the next generation, the next phase of an ongoing narrative. As John and other farmers look out across this valley, each farm marks the site of a specific genealogical story.

The link between landscape and narrative goes beyond shared formal properties of hierarchy, shape, or rhythm. It is more than an analogy such as that made between architecture and music. While there are limits to an analogy, there are untold possibilities when landscape and narrative are seen as intertwined through lived experience. Anthropologist Edmund Leach describes this relationship:

> It is not just that "places" serve to remind us of the stories that are associated with them; in certain respects, the places only exist...because they have stories associated with them. But once they have acquired this story-based existence, the landscape itself acquires the power of "telling the story." (Johnstone, 120)

CROSSING TEMPORAL/SPATIAL BOUNDARIES

There is a tendency to think of narrative primarily as a temporal art and landscape as something visual, spatial, an unchanging background and therefore non-narrative. However, as Ricoeur states, narratives combine two dimensions, one a temporal sequence of events and the other a nonchronological configuration that organizes narrative into spatial patterns. Stories can plot events into lines, create hierarchies, unite beginnings and ends to form circles, or tie knots and design labyrinths. Likewise, through landscape the temporal dimension of narrative becomes visible, and "space becomes charged and responsive to the movements of time, plot and history" (Bakhtin, 84). Landscape narratives mediate this crossing of temporal and spatial experience.

In addition to Horace's notion of *ut pictura poesis* or the evocation of place in literature, there is also a great tradition of visual narratives that solves the problem of how to represent time in spatial form. First, the *single point in time* or "frozen moment" common to realism, photography, the dramatic action of Baroque art, or even the ordinary genre scene frames one episode while implying what went before and what will follow. A second strategy, *linear narrative*, links a series of individual episodes into linear sequences, as in the Bayeaux Tapestry or the ordinary comic strip. A third strategy, *continuous narrative*, represents the passage of time with a series of events, all of which take place within a unified context (Andrews, 126). Medieval depictions of the garden in the Romance of the Rose, for instance, show three different episodes occurring in the same scene. The continuous narrative also uses spatial depth to represent temporal position, with the present occupying the foreground and the past in the distance, or the reverse.

The city consists "of relationships between the measurements of its space and the events of its past: the height of a lamppost and the distance from the ground of a hanged usurper's swaying feet; the line strung from the lamppost to the railing opposite and the festoons that decorate the course of the queen's nuptial procession; the height of that railing and the leap of the adulterer who climbed over it at dawn; the tilt of a guttering and a cat's progress along it as he slips into the same window; the firing range of a gunboat which has suddenly appeared beyond the cape and the bomb that destroys the guttering; the rips in the fish net and the three old men seated on the dock mending nets and telling each other for the hundredth time the story of the gunboat of the usurper, who some say was the queen's illegitimate son, abandoned in his swaddling clothes there on the dock."
(Calvino, 10)

VISUAL NARRATIVES

A Point in Time

Mark Tansey, *The Key*. Oil on canvas, 1984.
(Private collection, courtesy Curt Marcus Gallery.)

This image invites speculation on the circumstances of
what went before and what will follow this moment.
A woman waits impatiently while a man (based on a
self-portrait of the artist) searches for a key to unlock
the gates of a garden (in this case the gates are Lorenzo
Ghiberti's *Gates of Paradise*). Beyond literal aspects of the
scene, the painting suggests allegories of the garden,
gender, art history, and interpretation.

Linear Narrative

Lorenzo Ghiberti, *Gates of Paradise* (east doors of Baptistry,
Florence). Gilt bronze, 1425-1452. (Alinari/Art Resource, N.Y.)

This integral architectural element tells biblical stories of the
Old Testament in a series of framed panels. Like the contemporary Western convention for reading cartoons, the story
begins at the top left panel ("The Garden of Eden") and
proceeds from left to right and from top to bottom.

Continuous Narrative

Lorenzo Ghiberti, "The Creation of Adam and Eve," detail of *Gates of Paradise.* (Alinari/Art Resource, N.Y.)

The first panel of *Gates of Paradise,* "The Garden of Eden," brings together in the same image several episodes spanning a great interval of time. The story can be read from side to side and in successive layers of depth. The foreground tells the creation of Adam (left) and Eve (center) and their expulsion (right). The temptation, the immediate past and cause of the expulsion, is in the middle ground (left). The remote past and eternity recede into the background.

This panel and others on the door were completed with an understanding of linear perspective. While perspective usually represents one moment in time, here it gives a unified context to multiple events in time (Andrews, 117–18).

Continuous Narrative

Garden scene from the *Roman de la Rose.* Late fifteenth-century manuscript in the British Library. (Snark/Art Resource, N.Y.)

A succession of three events, the greeting at the gate, entry, and entertainment by the fountain, is shown here in one scene.

"The city, however, does not tell its past, but contains it like the lines of a hand, written in the corners of the streets, the gratings of the windows, the banisters of the steps, the antennae of the lightning rods, the poles of the flags, every segment marked in turn with scratches, indentations, scrolls." (Calvino, 11)

Similar strategies apply to interpreting the temporal configurations of landscapes. Singular events such as floods, urban renewal, or more quotidian happenstance leave their mark in the landscape. Ensembles formed by one building episode or any site carefully restored to a historic period of significance also tell of one moment in time. The sequence of moving through a series of settings becomes analogous to a linear narrative. In this manner the processions through landscapes recount specific tales (Sacra Monte, which tell of Christ's passion), allegories ("out of the darkness into the light"), or social narratives (routine sequence from public to private realms, or home to work). It is harder to apprehend the landscape itself as a sequence of "slow events" except when process of growth, decay, denudation, succession, gentrification, and so on appear as stages, stratigraphies, or soil horizons. Filled with multiple layers of history and simultaneous events in a common context, landscapes seem most like continuous narratives.

Despite these correlations, there are important distinctions between reading landscape narratives and narratives as spoken or written texts. Unlike verbal narratives, spatial narratives are silent but persistent. With few protocols for reading a landscape from right to left or front to back, the viewer enters at different points, is free to pause, take in the whole image, inspect its parts, or review. This changes the traditional relationship between author, text, and reader where the author exerts control over the *telling*. Instead, the spatial narrative is more about *showing*, relinquishing control to the viewer/reader who must put together sequences, fill in the gaps, and decipher the meaning (Chatman 1981, 124). And since most landscapes are shaped by environmental and cultural processes, they do not have an author or a narrator. In turn the viewer must find the stories and become the narrator.

Rather than a limitation, these conditions offer distinct opportunities for different forms of narratives such as the gathering of past and present into a synoptic view, parallel or intersecting story lines, collages that create nonlinear associations, multiple layers of stories, and narratives open to participants. In fact, the postmodern turn in literature away from 19th-century conventions of realism and notions of linear time employs many of these same strategies. Stories within stories repeatedly interrupt the narrative of Italo Calvino's *If on a winter's night a traveler*. In the short story "The Garden of Forking Paths," Jorge Luis Borges creates a complex labyrinthine configuration of time and space.

FORMS OF LANDSCAPE NARRATIVES

To know landscape narratives involves more than what meets the eye. As protean synthesis of time and space, experience and place, the fictive and the real, they cross boundaries of expressions and representational forms. The following chart outlines this prodigious variety of landscape narratives.

NARRATIVE ARCHITECTURE

Narrative can provide a critical framework for an approach to architecture. However, much of the variety of narrative forms and practices noted above had largely been rejected by modernist design. Not that modernism was totally with-

TYPES	EXAMPLES
Narrative Experiences	
Routines, rituals, or events that represent or follow narrative structures; e.g., festivals, processions, reenactments, pilgrimage, daily journeys, crossing the threshold.	Tours and rituals enact narratives, selecting and organizing the experience of place into temporal sequences. The major tourist route through Prague, from the Powder Tower, to Old Town Square, across the Charles Bridge, and up to the Castle, follows the sequence of public monuments and spaces established centuries earlier by the coronation route of the kings.
Associations and References	
Elements in the landscape that become connected with experience, event, history, religious allegory, or other forms of narrative.	The longevity of trees often serves as a metaphor of the continuity of family genealogy or as a time marker that speaks of the origins of communities. A slippery elm that survived the 1995 bomb blast in Oklahoma City became a symbol and meeting place for survivors and families who protect and water it.
Memory Landscapes	
Places that serve as the tangible locus of memory, both public and personal. This may develop through implicit association or by international acts of remembering (and forgetting); e.g., monuments, museums, preserved buildings, districts, and regions.	The ancient rhetorical practice of delivering long speeches was aided by the mental construction of "topoi," or places organized into spatial complexes or "memory palaces." To remember was to walk through these spaces, noting what was "in the first place," and so on.[3] Likewise, urban design can be conceived as a rhetorical device for activating public memory.
Narrative Setting and Topos	
A setting is the spatial and temporal circumstances of a narrative. It can recede to the background or figure prominently. A narrative topos is a highly conventionalized setting linked with particular events, which is evoked repeatedly in a culture's narratives. In Western culture epiphanies occur on mountaintops, and chance meetings take place on the road.	The pastoral topos is connected with narratives of retreat from the social complexities of the city and a nostalgic return to origins, childhood, and a place apart in harmony with nature. The ideal setting of this story is repeatedly conjured in suburb, park, garden, and campus with just the minimal elements of lawn and trees.
Genres of Landscape Narratives	
Places shaped by culturally defined narrative forms or "genres," e.g., legend, epic, biography, myth.	The settlement of portions of the American West was motivated by legends of a "Great American Garden," a place of utopian harmony and fertility. Photographs sent back from western lands encoded this legend in terms of scale, presence of water, and productive farms (Loeffler).
Processes	
Actions or events that are caused by some agency (wind, water, economics) and occur in succession or proceed in stages toward some end (progress; entropy). Erosion, growth, succession, restoration, demolition, and weathering are visible records of change that inscribe time into landscape form.	On a landfill in the Meadowlands, in New Jersey, designers initiated the process of vegetation succession and separated it into a series of clearly identifiable stages. Walking along a path structures a sequence of interrelated changes in soil fertility, microclimate, vegetation types, and habitat.
Interpretive Landscapes	
Elements and programs that tell what happened in a place. The intent is to make existing or ongoing narratives intelligible.	Besides placing texts in the landscape, interpretation can be achieved through elements of design form. In the early 1800s the foot traffic of traders and pioneers going from Natchez, Mississippi, to Nashville, Tennessee, wore a deep path known as the Natchez Trace. The Natchez Trace Parkway is a modern road that parallels, crosses, and reveals the history of the Old Trace.
Narrative as Form Generation	
Using stories as a means of giving order (selecting, sequencing, etc.) or developing images in the design process. It is not necessary that the story be explicitly legible in the final design form.	To redesign a housing project in France, Lucien Kroll invented what he called "a fairy tale." He imagined a crowd of pedestrians crossing through the area, demolishing and then "remolishing" the monolithic structures in the process. This story helped generate a pedestrian-scale street with more vernacular forms and an evolving program (1994, 45).
Storytelling Landscapes	
Places designed to tell specific stories with explicit references to plot, scenes, events, character, etc. The stories may be either existing literary or cultural narratives or produced by the designer.	Gardens, memorials, and themed landscapes are all designed to tell specific stories.

out narrative content, since the break from the past and initiation of utopian futures were oft-repeated stories with strong moral subtexts.[4] What modernist ideology rejected, postmodernism embraced, and narrative came to epitomize alternative critiques, intentions, and practices. Michael Graves, for example, believed that the abstraction and exclusive formalist exercises of his early work had become increasingly unintelligible to the public. He turned, instead, to a more accessible canon of Western architectural language—pediments, barrel vaults, trabeated columnar porticoes, pyramids, and other classical elements that speak of connection with history and context (at least that of 19th-century cities) rather than rupture (Abrams, 6). In similar manner other architects refer and allude to stories in regional traditions, popular icons such as highway strips (Venturi) or media culture, as in the cyberpunk references of *NATO* (Narrative Architecture Today), started by Nigel Coates. In their design for the Holocaust Museum in Washington, D.C., Pei, Cobb, and Freed demonstrated how space and form can dramatize and exert control over the sequential unfolding of a story. Other designers, most notably John Hejduk and Rem Koolhaas, a former scriptwriter, experiment with writing their own fictions into the fabric of the landscape.

There are important differences about the nature of narrative architecture and its role. The literary or film devices of plotting, foreshadowing, fading, and jump cutting all have their spatial equivalents, which Bernard Tschumi uses to disrupt conventional notions of narrative closure and control of meaning. And even without reference, analogy, borrowed plots, or fiction, a building can reveal its own biography of weathering, histories of use, institutional practices, rituals, growth, adaptation, and decline (Mostafavi and Leatherbarrow, Rakatansky, Wines).

Despite such diverse directions, in all these projects narrative is a means of connecting architecture with landscape. Graves repeatedly depicts his buildings as set within the topos of an "archaic landscape" drawn from memories of afternoons in Tuscany (Abrams, 8, 9), whereas Coates finds his clues for stories in the gaps and gritty reality of marginal spaces, "near railway stations, beneath motorways or on the seventeenth floor of Trellick Tower."[5] And any site holds memory traces that can be extended through new building episodes (Henriquez and Henriquez). In addition to providing the ground of memory or context, landscape narratives also transgress conventional boundaries of built form. In their different ways, Bernard Tschumi and John Hejduk both follow events and characters as they merge with, move, dissolve, disperse, and deform architecture across sites. For Hejduk, characters become buildings that travel "as if" in some medieval miracle play to different cities where they interact with and are changed by these places (Vidler, 209). Aldo Rossi is also interested in event, narrative, and the idea of memory that is dispersed through the forms and institutions of the city. Instead of adding his own story, he uses the analogue of urban design as theater, a setting open to chance encounters, unfolding events, and new stories that arise from the collective experience of the city (Livesey, 115–121). Thus, we can see a range of narrative possibilities from explicit associations with stories to implicit narrative structures and an openness to ongoing social and natural processes.

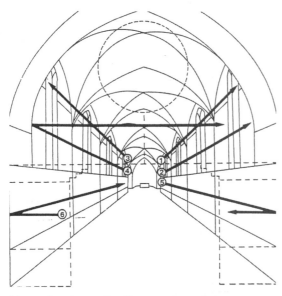

Upper church nave, San Fracesco, Assisi, Italy.

Replete with biblical stories, history, and moral teachings, Gothic and Renaissance cathedrals are some of the most textualized forms of architecture. The narratives continue from the exterior sculptures into the spatial metaphors of the nave, the anagogic function of light through stained glass windows, and the cycles of frescoes. Shown above is an example of the sequence of linear narratives across the interior spaces of Italian chapels and cathedrals mapped by art historian Marilyn Lavin. (From Lavin 1990)

Bernard Tschumi experiments with analogues drawn from literature and cinema. In *Manhattan Transcripts* he transcribes temporal sequences, events, scripts, movement, and other aspects normally removed from conventional architectural representations. The first transcript, "The Park," follows the "archetype" of a murder across twenty-four sheets where "photographs direct the action, plans reveal the alternatively cruel and loving architectural manifestations, diagrams indicate the movements of the main protagonists" (Tschumi, 8). Cinematic framing, sequencing, disjunction, fragments of events, and superimposition were all techniques later employed in his winning entry for the Parc de la Villette competition.

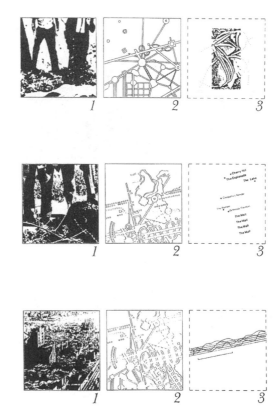

Panel from *Manhattan Transcripts*, "The Park."
(Courtesy Bernard Tschumi Architects)

John Hejduk plots stories instead of programs and functions. Buildings become characters in "masques," allegorical dramas enacted by masked performers popular in 16th- and 17th-century Europe. Like a theater troupe, this architecture is nomadic. "The cast presents itself to a city and its inhabitants. Some of the objects are built and remain in the city; some are built for a time, then are dismantled and disappear." (Hejduk, 15). This is not a frivolous spectacle, however. As Vidler notes, this vagabond architecture resists assimilation into the normal spaces of the city. Like a stranger, it critiques and disrupts the commonplace (Vidler, 214).

"The House of Suicide" and "Mother of Suicide," shown here, traveled with Hejduk from his Lancaster/Hanover Masque in Pennsylvania to the Latvian city of Riga along with ninety-five other buildings/stories. A built version of them remains in Prague.

In the work of Henriquez and Partners, "narrative is used for its power to stimulate the imagination and engage participation... The task is to create narratives that resonate with the history of a specific place—a history that includes both the built and the natural world, the real and fictional pasts, and that enables citizens to project their lives into the future" (Henriquez and Henriquez, 191). Their narratives range from site-specific histories and biblical references to the history of architecture, mythology, ecology, personal stories, and fiction.

Above: John Hejduk, architect, "Gymnasium Male/Female" and "House of the Suicide," Riga. (From Hejduk 1989)

Left: "House of the Suicide" and "Mother of Suicide" on the grounds of the Royal Garden, Prague, Czech Republic.

Of "House of the Suicide" John Hejduk writes:
"Made of steel panels, factory painted white enamel. There is an eye slit in one elevation, a door in the other. The roof is made of vertical volumetric triangular slivers diminishing to a tiny opening at the top. He liked to watch the points of light move along the walls and floor. The Farm Community (in agreement with the family) sealed the door by welding." (Hejduk, 86)

Below: Richard Henriquez, plans and sections for Eugenia Place, Vancouver, 1987. (Collection of the architect)

An invented archaeology and memory traces of the site's history extend from the ground plane to the roof. The landscape, with its sculpted tree stumps, recalls the original forest, while the ground plan incorporates the footprints of the 1940s mock-Tudor apartment building the tower replaces. A single pin oak in the garden on the penthouse roof matches the elevation of the former first-growth forest. (Schubert, 32)

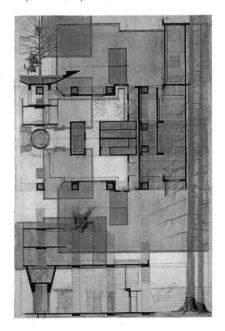

MAKING LANDSCAPE NARRATIVES

As landscape and narrative continue to be primary areas of diverse theoretical inquiry and practice across disciplines, a number of critical questions emerge. Concerns range from the instrumental (How can designers create intelligible narratives? What traditions can be drawn upon?) to the social role of narrative (How can narratives create a shared public realm in a diverse, pluralistic contemporary culture?) and questions of design ideology (What are the potentials and limitations of the designer as author? How does the generation of stories, fictions, or plots challenge and transform notions of function, determinism, and representation?).

EXPLICIT STORYTELLING

Perhaps the most direct way to see the interplay between landscape and narrative is in places designed explicitly to tell a story. Like the Gothic cathedral, the garden is a distinct storytelling site. Here we can see the strategies for translating all the associations and structure of narrative texts into landscape texts. To begin with, a garden becomes a creation story when it attempts to retell the received narratives of a culture's origins in nature. Every garden also initiates its own creation story in the transformation and adaptation to the particulars of site, culture, labor, money, and time.

Stourhead in Wiltshire, England, is a particularly vivid narrative landscape. It derives from a specific story, Virgil's *Aeneid,* a version of the founding of Rome by the Trojan hero Aeneas, which is retold in the landscape with a high degree of authority and control over the means of representation. First, the temporal configuration of the plot becomes the spatial configuration of the gardens, as the story line of the hero's wanderings around the Mediterranean basin unfolds along a stroll around the lake, uniting story and topography. And while it is impossible to reproduce a narrative verbatim in landscape form, it can be effectively alluded to through names, references, associations, and symbols. Along the pathway the scenes, characters, and events of the story are conjured by inscriptions, statues, and identifiable architectural references to ancient Rome (albeit slightly scaled down), includ-

Bottom left: Claude Lorrain, *Landscape with Aeneas at Delos.* Oil on canvas, 1672. (National Gallery London/ Bridgeman Art Library, London)

Bottom right: View of the Pantheon across the lake at Stourhead.

Above: Aeneas journeys into a grotto in search of secrets.

Left: Toward the end of the circuit, the visitor reaches a high point and Aeneas's destination at the Temple of Apollo.

ing the Pantheon, the Temple of Flora, and the Temple of Apollo. This storehouse of images, and the substitution of lake for sea, create a landscape dense with associations for those already familiar with the text.

Yet, clear as this story appears, there is still more to be read. The motivation to create the garden and the selection of this particular story of a hero's great personal loss were influenced by Henry Hoare's own experiences of losing several family members. Virgil's *Aeneid* becomes an allegory that invites the reader to make associations with other stories. In addition to the classical elements, there is a Gothic cottage set against a wooded shoreline, various medieval relics, the salvaged remnant of a Gothic cross from the town of Bristol, and a monument to King Alfred, a hero in the ninth century who played a key role in the founding of Britain (Moore, Mitchell, and Turnbull, 144). All these elements are part of a narrative of a particular British sense of place and history, overlain on the universal story of empire building of Virgil. Therefore, the landscape becomes a multilayered set of narratives.[6]

The desire to tell stories using similar strategies is evident in vernacular landscapes as well. The American front yard is a common narrative tableau, adapting the received traditions of the pastoral topos and its story of rural escapism and leisure to contemporary situations. The lawn and serpentine driveway recall in miniature a version of the pastoral estates of the English gentry. The yard has also shown the capacity to absorb a great mélange of other stories encoded by emblems of national myths (wagon wheels), exotic paradise (pink flamingos), local history (coal chunks displayed on the lawns of Carbon County, Pennsylvania, or bog iron edging yards in the Pinelands, of New Jersey), and ethnic origins (frequency of Blessed Virgin Mary statues marking Italian heritage in Bensonhurst, New York, or elaborate gravel patterns of the Portuguese in South San Francisco).[7]

THE POLITICS OF READING LANDSCAPE NARRATIVES

Telling stories in landscape raises the question "Will they get it?" Henry Hoare's garden in the Stour Valley made sense because of shared knowledge of classical literature and national mythology. Telling this story was a constituent part of creating a shared cultural realm. Even though John Hoch's Oley Valley was settled by Germans, French, Swiss, and English, they were all motivated by a common reading of the Bible forged by the Protestant Reformation, practiced similar farming and building techniques, and spoke the regional dialect of Pennsylvania German. Today development fragments and diffuses what the valley once gathered and stored, introducing greater differences of lifestyles and personal stories. Beyond these particular places, the universal claims of Western classics or the narratives of national identity have been challenged by differences of ethnicity, race, class, and gender. So at the same time that designers are interested in telling stories, the terms of doing so are changing. What are the prospects for landscape narratives when there is a great diversity of readers, few shared texts, and often multiple and competing stories? Because certain symbols and references are context specific, familiar only to certain groups, their use can either include or exclude people from reading the landscape.

CONTESTED MEMORIES

Many designers seem intent on reviving a 19th- and early 20th-century conception of the city as the embodiment of collective memory. But again, what constitutes the collective memory in contemporary culture? One prevalent strategy relies on site-specific references or local emblems such as Martha Schwartz's Blue Crab earth mound for Baltimore's inner harbor to recall the past. While these designs start to reach for meaning beyond the purely abstract visual form, they often remain at a very literal level of symbolism (Cameron, 1996). Another strategy is to create multiple and ambiguous readings that encourage different points of view rather than one correct message.

Two memorials, the Korean and Vietnam Memorials, which lie on either side of the reflecting pool of the Lincoln Memorial in Washington, D.C., demonstrate distinctly different ways of constructing memory in contemporary culture. The very act of constructing these public memories was fraught with the same controversies, questions of purpose, and conflicting interpretations as the wars they commemorate. The process of making these memorials reveals the broader controversies concerning the purposes and approaches to narrative.

Each name on the wall of the Vietnam Memorial evokes a memory, a story—in fact, many possible stories for all those who know the name. As those who make the pilgrimage to the site walk along the wall, they follow a topographic narrative, descending as the wall increases in height. Names accumulate until they reach the apex, where the names of the first and last Americans to die in Vietnam are brought together. The memorial draws much of its meaning from the context of other national memories, as the two ends point to the Washington and

Above: In the Oley Valley, farming practices and religion provide the basis for shared experience. The influence of Calvinist doctrines means there are no explicit religious shrines in the landscape. However, ordinary elements often serve to conjure more extraordinary events. Here, Robert Yorgey opens the door to the root cellar, a typical element of the farms, used to store vegetables, fruits, and root crops. Opening the door and counting the steps as he goes down into "the cave," as he calls it, he also recalls the cave in the biblical story of Lazarus.

Below: The Vietnam Memorial, Washington, D.C.

Above: The Korean Memorial, Washington, D.C.

Below: Themed communities commodify a desire for narrative unity and closure. This desire is evident in an advertisement for Elk River, North Carolina. Elevated physically (4,000 feet) and emotionally ("Follow Your Heart") above the norm, Elk River is pitched as "An Epic Place to Live."

Follow your heart. Out mountain trails or through the exuberant patterns of jumping for show. Either way, you're sitting 4,000 feet in the saddle.

ELK RIVER
North Carolina
AN EPIC PLACE TO LIVE

Exclusive homesites and condominiums in a secure setting. Jack Nicklaus golf course, equestrian center, tennis complex. Call collect, 704-898-9777, P.O. Box 1555, Banner Elk, NC 28604. This advertisement is not an offering to New Jersey and New York residents or where prohibited by law.

Lincoln Memorials and recall the wars associated with the names of those Presidents. The potency of the Vietnam Memorial, however, lies in its rhetorical silence, how it evokes narratives without controlling any specific reading of them and remains ambiguous. Its minimal quality and lack of control over interpretation challenged traditional notions of monument and provoked a storm of protest. As a concession to those who wanted a more traditional (i.e., realistic) memorial, a sculpture of three soldiers posed in a moment of heightened (yet still ambiguous) attention to some invisible action was located nearby.

The winning solution for the Korean Memorial in 1989 also raised controversy, but this time by being too referential. The team of architects and landscape architects from the Pennsylvania State University intended to tell the story of the war in more figurative rather than abstract terms. A group of thirty-eight soldiers (the 38th parallel being the U.N.-designated division between North and South Korea) tells a chronology of the war, from initial surprise and setbacks to a series of victories, ending in an uncertain stalemate. This is accomplished by a sequence of different configurations, facial expressions, and gestures. A conflict developed when the sponsors of the memorial requested changes to the arrangement and expression of figures that the designers felt altered the story to show a single moment of victory. The controversies over this project and the Vietnam Memorial demonstrate that while storytelling is often thought of as a form of entertainment, when it is actualized in any given cultural context it can become a battleground of competing values (Wallace, 8). Whether through abstraction or realism, ideologies inhere in the very means by which a story is told.

THEMING

For very different purposes "themed landscapes" shape and reconstitute memory into clear, controlled narrative tableaux. Disney World's Frontierland, Adventureland, and Main Street epitomize certain selected dramas of a popular American mythos. Beyond the entertainment realm of the theme park, the strategies of theming pervade other enclaves, including festival markets, waterfront redevelopments such as New York's South Street Seaport and Battery Park City, historic districts, tourist areas, resorts, malls, and restaurants. According to geographer Edward Soja, all of Orange County California, where Disneyland is located, is a themed landscape (Soja, 94). In an ironic reversal, even small-town main streets, the originals that Disney simulated, are being rescripted as historic or ethnic caricatures to attract tourists.[8] Like Stourhead, they recover lost worlds. However, as a phenomenon of the late 20th century, the themed landscape serves a more pervasive nostalgia and compensates for a sense of fragmentation and lack of security outside its bounds.

These carefully packaged tales also create a realm for consumption, where people acquire not just single items of clothing, food, or housing, but participation in whole lifestyles and landscapes. As Christine Boyer writes in an essay in *Variations on a Theme Park,* "This subtle form of advertising blurs the distinction between the atmospheric stage-set and the commodities on sale, for its well-constructed historic tableau not only enhances the products on display but locks the spectator into a larger-than-life store/ story" (Boyer, 200). Despite the prevalence of historical allusions of many themed landscapes, the purposes of consumption often require vague remembrance rather than particular accuracy. Boyer notes, for instance, that New York City's South Street Seaport became commercially successful as a "historic" festival market only after the fresh fish (and their odor) were removed (Boyer, 203).

These examples highlight several critical issues for telling stories in landscape. Since there are many possible stories and versions, it is important to consider whose stories are told, and what purposes are served. In addition, what makes for an intelligible story? This requires understanding of cultural contexts, the shared conventions of reading landscapes, as opposed to relying on the approach that "it means this because I say it does."[9] There is also a politics of interpretation to acknowledge. How is it read? Finally, there is the issue of how much control the designer has over the telling and interpretation of a landscape narrative. What role do users/ readers play in interpreting and constructing their own stories? How open is the narrative to change, reinterpretation, participation? By engaging these questions, landscape narratives can go beyond naive storytelling and become a more significant means of making places.

IMPLICIT NARRATIVES

Narrative need not be conceived as an explicit storyline grafted *onto* a site as if it were once a blank slate. Narratives are already *implicit* to landscapes, inscribed by natural processes and cultural practices (Rakatansky, 1992). However, beyond the frame of the garden or the parking lot of the theme park, they may be difficult to read if one is looking for conventional stories. Narratives can reside in very ordinary forms, routine activities, and institutional structures. Behind the uniform setbacks, heights, and materials specified in standard zoning and building codes are social narratives of progressivism and countless adjudications of what determines health, safety, and welfare. As they develop from often competing interests, these landscape narratives often lack clear individual authorship. Constantly in process of being made and unmade, they become open narratives without the closure and clear plot structure of conventional stories. Therefore, understanding narratives on this level requires more than reading a historic inventory or visual survey; it involves special attention, methods, and time to engage the storied texture of a place.

The implicit nature of narratives may be difficult to identify even in cultures which seem to have resisted the fragmentation of modernity. Anthropologist David Guss tells of his search to record the creation epic of the Kekuana in the Venezuelan rain forest. When he got there, he found "no circles of attentive youths breathing in the words of an elder as he regaled them with the deeds of their ancestors." Instead, he gained access to the stories only when he got involved in basket making. Only after spending

Cameron Halkier, model maker; Richard Henriquez, architect; *The Surveyor, Presentation Model for the Bayshore Lands Rezoning Proposal, Vancouver,* 1989. (Courtesy Henriquez and Partners)

In *The Practice of Everyday Life*, Michel de Certeau compares the inscription of lines and boundaries in the landscape with the primary role of stories. Both are *founding* operations that "open a space" and provide a "legitimate theater" for practical actions (124, 125). Architect Richard Henriquez's tripod sculptures derive from their symbolic use in early founding rituals and their instrumental role in marking out the first operations in any building project. In *The Surveyor*, glass sheets suspended from a surveyor's tripod tell the history of the site's development. "Looming heavy in the scaleless sky above the brass outline of the proposal is a sixty-story plumb bob" (Pérez-Gómez, 25).

The new blue silos in the Oley Valley stand out as emblems of either innovation or unsound business risk. As one farmer recalls: "I never will forget, a salesman for these blue silos was around in 1970 and he told me by 1976 I'm gonna be out of business if I don't get one. Well, I thought, I'm gonna go out with something at least. They always call them the 'blue tombstones' because they put so many guys under." The name indicates the conservative orientation of Oley farmers. In other places these silos are refered to as "blue angels."

Right: Madison Backus, *A Memory Painting,* ca. 1982. (Collection of Les LeVeque)

Madison Backus lives in Brooklyn, New York, but he paints scenes remembered from growing up in North Carolina. Houses are depicted as he remembers seeing them from the road. The road itself is a timeline as it changes from a dirt road in the lower left to a paved surface as you travel toward the upper right.

Below: "Les ilettes" found throughout the region of Vercheres serve as a locus of memory. "From the month of March to Easter, it was sugar maple time. Generally, my grandfather spent all of March in the sugar shack in the Vercheres forest. He had to tap about 3,000 maples, collect the sap and boil it, and then conserve it as maple syrup and maple sugar. The sugar festivals took place around Easter. It was an opportunity for family gatherings, to help with the work and to socialize." (Julie Dansereau in discussion with her father, who has always lived in the village)

weeks and months making excursions to gather cane, cutting, peeling, plaiting, learning the motifs of design and usage, and working within the circle of elders at the center of the roundhouse (itself a cosmographic diagram) did he finally learn the complex narrative and its reproduction in experience and objects of the place. He concluded that "to tell a story therefore was to weave a basket, just as it was to make a canoe, to prepare barbasco [a variety of vines used to stun fish by depriving the water of oxygen], to build a house, to clear a garden, to give birth, to die" (Guss, 1–4).

MEMORY LANDSCAPES

As a locus for individual and collective experience, the landscape becomes a vast mnemonic device. Almost any element in the landscape—woodlots, street corners, old trolley tracks, thresholds, or even tools used to shape the landscape—provide access to this memory landscape. Placenames, for instance, become abbreviated histories recording sites of events and activities (Freeport Landing); they mark former landscape features (Wall Street), subjective experience (Desolation Point), encounters with the uniqueness of place (Dancing Rabbit Creek), and specific lives (Washington). While such elements may appear inconsequential on a map, to change or erase them would threaten the structure of shared experience and belief. In a review of community oral histories, Linda Shopes, a historian at the Pennsylvania Historical and Museum Commission, discovered how memory is repeatedly anchored to place. She concluded that "no other topic or way of structuring talk about the past dominates the interviews as extensively, deeply, or consistently as this sense of place" (Shopes, 6).

A recent project for the community of Vercheres, Quebec, by Peter Jacobs and Philippe Poullaouec-Gonidec attempts to reinscribe memory as means of creating a coherent landscape and provide a guide for future growth. Vercheres is one of the six original settlements in Quebec. There are still lines and hedgerows that trace the French Seignieries, long narrow strips

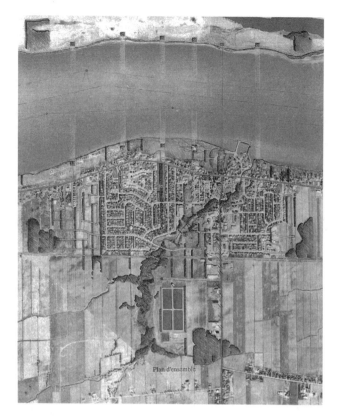

Plan for Vercheres by Peter Jacobs and Philippe Poullaouec-Gonidec showing the reinscription of the landscape structure of hedgerows and "ilettes."

of land, approximately three by thirty arpents, that stretch from the shore across the fertile flood plain to the forest beyond (Jacobs). However, enormous growth in human settlements and in industrial and manufacturing activity over the past twenty-five years has spawned a network of rail, road, and utility corridors that have severed the traditional linkage of river and woods across the agricultural plain.

Their design strategy reestablished the structure of the landscape derived from the biophysical and cultural memory of the region. The connection with the forest is made by "les ilettes" that are found throughout the region, usually associated with changes in topography and soil moisture on an otherwise flat agricultural plain. These clusters of woods serve as visual signals of the once forested plain and will reinforce the memory and presence of what remains of the larger forest of Vercheres farther away. The "ilettes" connect the community to the forest, which is the locus of recreation, the provision of wood, the manufacture of maple syrup in the spring, and romantic encounters in the summer. In addition, the metapattern of linear hedgerows reinscribed across the village through subdivisions will connect the village to the agricultural plain to which it has always belonged. As Peter Jacobs concludes, "By emphasizing the landscape imagery of the region, by tying the village to this imagery, and by projecting it back onto the landscape context of which it is a part, the strata and diversity of the history of the village is encouraged to re-emerge."

Top left: Ann Chamberlain, *Inheritance,* 1993. (Courtesy the artist)

Ann Chamberlain works with processes to evoke stories for people who have a definite need to tell stories: immigrants, former alcoholics, prison inmates. The women in a rehabilitation center wrote memories, habits, and other things they wanted to rid themselves of on teapots and cups. Then, borrowing a tradition from Oaxaca, Mexico, they smashed them. Later they glued them back together and placed them on a mantel. These actions and the process of storytelling become part of the process of recovering their place in the world.

Top right: Visual Books. Paula Horrigan, who teaches landscape architecture at Cornell University, uses visual books as a means to interpret and represent the narrative qualities of landscape that conventional pictoral modes fail to capture. The visual book can be constructed as analogous to the experience of reading a site. Like a site, it is three-dimensional and temporal. Its structure—how it unfolds and changes—can organize sequences, direct perception, and move backward or forward in time.

Professor Horrigan describes the book of her student, Christine Simony, shown top right: "Site images can be slipped out of the book's transparent sleeves or frame structure. At points in the book's unfolding narrative, one was forced to stop and manipulate these frames, changing direction and tempo. This arresting of movement, or freezing frames, derived from her onsite experience, holding a quality which she not only constructed into the visual book, but reinforced in her final design." (Horrigan, 43, 44)

IMPLICIT NARRATIVES OF CONVENTIONAL PRACTICE

Not only is the narrative production of places difficult to apprehend but it is often edited out of and not admitted in conventional representations of landscapes. A map that totalizes the representation of space effectively erases the narrative actions, the journeys of discovery, acts of naming, and daily routines that produced the spatial patterns in the first place. Only the cartouches of certain old maps that depict explorers' ships, travelers, or surveyors hint at this experiential dimension (De Certeau, 121). The challenge is to find new modes of representing and reinscribing narrative into drawings, maps, charts, and other conventional forms.

Yet, as designers shape landscapes they inevitably engage narratives, often without explicit intent. Any clearing of a site is also an erasure of any number of stories, while excavation can unearth and reveal histories. Common practice also employs settings, emblems, and devices so familiar that their narrative associations have been forgotten. The repeated use of pastoral landscapes, for instance, is full of such "dead metaphors." Certain forms of practice, however, are more clearly narrative in their purposes. The interpretation of sites is a common narrative objective of the National Park Service, historic sites and nature centers. In preservation practice alone there are salvage narratives, restorations of one moment in time, or adaptive reuse, which brings the past and the present together into a continuous narrative. There are also narratives of ecology, which employ metaphors to communicate the intricacies of ecological process and extend its principles into the sphere of social action. Restoration ecology constructs narratives of returning to origins, makes propitiations for past environmental mistakes, and perpetuates processes into the future.

ENGAGING PROCESS

Landscape narratives need not be limited to telling what has already happened. They can be an implicit part of daily actions, exchanges, interpretations, and other ongoing processes. For artist Richard Long, walking opens up a geography of stories evoked by placenames, marked by temporary interventions along the way, or plotted on maps and in texts. Narrative is a

Left: Candlestick Point Park, San Francisco. (Courtesy Hargreaves and Associates)

The "tidal garden" at Candlestick Point Park, San Francisco, by George Hargreaves and Associates initiates narratives of the processes of deposition and erosion.

Below: Backyard and springhouse of Hoch Farm.

John Hoch's nephew Mark Hoch maintains the narratives of this landscape through the process of farming. "I don't have that much time to think about the history of the place. Every day I just try to keep the thing going. I'd like to fix up the springhouse but some other things have to be paid first. I can't see sticking money into something just to look at. I figure, if I can keep the place going and if my son would take it, that would be enough." His efforts are supported by a statewide easement program to retain farmland and reduce taxes, as well as changes in the local zoning and a historic preservation initiative. The Oley Valley was selected by the National Trust for Historic Preservation as one of two national rural preservation demon-stration projects. In their study they found that protecting the hydrologic processes of this limestone valley was the most significant preservation strategy.

process continuously moving between a series of interrelated actions. Likewise, narratives emerge from the interplay of natural process and cultural processes. On a tall blank wall of the chapel in the Brion Cemetery, Carlo Scarpa created a gap in the parapet that allowed water to seep through and stain it. This initiated a process of weathering, inscribing time into the life of the building (Mostafavi and Leatherbarrow, 98, 103).

So often the inscription of stories into the landscape ignores the narratives of the medium itself. For instance, Stone Mountain, near Atlanta, Georgia, is the largest exposed granite monolith in the world. Yet, carved into its face is a memorial to Confederate generals (Emanuel Martin, 24). In contrast, the work of an increasing number of landscape architects seeks to reveal the effects of wind, water, and other processes, while also setting up conditions for continuous change and evolution. These actions, interventions, and evocations demonstrate that landscape narratives need not be set pieces requiring prior knowledge and controlled readings for their success. Rather, landscapes offer the unique potential to engage narrative as an integral part of ongoing cultural and natural processes.

SUMMARY

To conceive of landscape narratives means linking what is often treated as a material or visual scene with the less tangible, but no less real, network of narratives. As well as we might already know the various properties of geology, soil, or the social behavior in places, we might also know them within the texture, structure, and processes of narratives. Working within this narrative realm provides access to experience, knowledge, the contingencies of time and other aspects of landscapes not available through other means. In turn, working with landscapes offers the potential for unique narrative forms: spatial stories, continuous narratives, or the anchoring of memories and history to sites. Landscape joins with a very human capacity and penchant for telling stories.

This does not come, however, without challenges as to what constitutes the relationship between reality and fiction, truth and deception. For

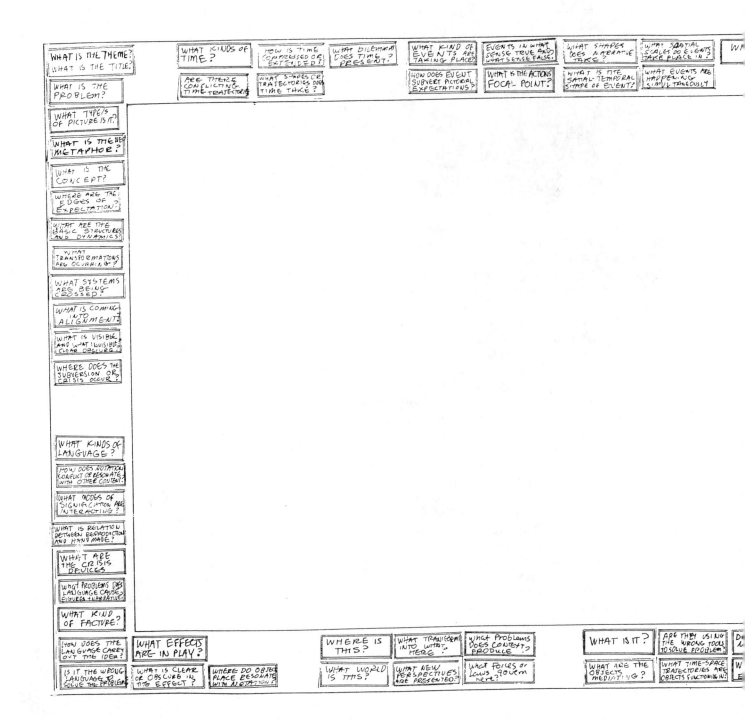

WHAT IS THE THEME?
WHAT IS THE TITLE?

WHAT IS THE PROBLEM?

WHAT TYPE/S OF PICTURE IS IT?

WHAT IS THE NEW METAPHOR?

WHAT IS THE CONCEPT?

WHERE ARE THE EDGES OF EXPECTATION?

WHAT ARE THE BASIC STRUCTURES AND DYNAMICS?

WHAT TRANSFORMATIONS ARE OCCURRING?

WHAT SYSTEMS ARE BEING CROSSED?

WHAT IS COMING INTO ALIGNMENT?

WHAT IS VISIBLE AND WHAT INVISIBLE? CLEAR OBSCURE?

WHERE DOES THE SUBVERSION OR CRISIS OCCUR?

WHAT KINDS OF LANGUAGE?

HOW DOES NOTATION CONFLICT OR RESONATE WITH OTHER CONTENT?

WHAT MODES OF SIGNIFICATION ARE INTERACTING?

WHAT IS RELATION BETWEEN REPRODUCTION AND HAND MADE?

WHAT ARE THE CRISIS DEVICES

WHAT PROBLEMS DOES LANGUAGE CAUSE? FIGURES + NARRATIVE?

WHAT KIND OF FACTURE?

HOW DOES THE LANGUAGE CARRY OUT THE IDEA?

IS IT THE WRONG LANGUAGE TO SOLVE THE PROBLEM?

WHAT EFFECTS ARE IN PLAY?

WHAT IS CLEAR OR OBSCURE IN ITS EFFECT?

WHERE DO OBJECTS PLACE RESONATE WITH NOTATION?

WHAT KINDS OF TIME?

ARE THERE CONFLICTING TIME-TRAJECTORIES

HOW IS TIME COMPRESSED OR EXTENDED?

WHAT SHAPES OR TRAJECTORIES DOES TIME TAKE?

WHAT DILEMMAS DOES TIME PRESENT.

WHAT KIND OF EVENTS ARE TAKING PLACE?

HOW DOES EVENT SUBVERT PICTORIAL EXPECTATIONS?

EVENTS IN WHAT SENSE TRUE AND WHAT SENSE FALSE?

WHAT IS THE ACTIONS FOCAL POINT?

WHAT SHAPES DOES NARRATIVE TAKE?

WHAT IS THE SPATIAL-TEMPORAL SHAPE OF EVENT?

WHAT SPATIAL SCALES DO EVENTS TAKE PLACE IN?

WHAT EVENTS ARE HAPPENING SIMULTANEOUSLY

WH

WHERE IS THIS?

WHAT WORLD IS THIS?

WHAT TRANSFORM INTO WHAT HERE?

WHAT NEW PERSPECTIVES ARE PRESENTED?

WHAT PROBLEMS DOES CONTEXT PRODUCE?

WHAT FORCES OR LAWS GOVERN HERE?

WHAT IS IT?

WHAT ARE THE OBJECTS MEDIATING?

ARE THEY USING THE WRONG TOOLS TO SOLVE PROBLEM?

WHAT TIME-SPACE TRAJECTORIES ARE OBJECTS FUNCTIONING IN?

D

W E

instance, when John Hejduk prefaces *Vladivostok* with the title "As a Matter of Fact," it seems ironic in relation to his proposals later in the book for fictional inventions: "As it was necessary for the highly rational-pragmatic city of 15th century Venice to create masques, masks, masses for its time in order to function; it would appear that we must create masques (programs) for our times" (Hejduk, 100).[10] But if anything characterizes the postmodern landscape, it is this very proliferation of masks, of staged events, simulations, scripted places, invented histories, and escapes to other realities. While there is often deliberate intent to pass off the faux for some notion of the authentic, stories and fiction should not be equated with deception any more or less than photographs or maps are. As representations, they all necessarily mediate reality.[11] Binaries of fact versus fiction, or the visual versus the intangible, have been scrutinized as cultural constructs that serve to privilege the scientific over other forms of knowing (Meyer). The intent here is not to propose narrative as a replacement of or a supplement to rational or scientific modes but as something that crosses, overlaps, and is inevitably inscribed within various discourses.

The real world and a storied world are not mutually exclusive; they intertwine and are constitutive of each other (Jane M. Jacobs, 15). It is important, however, to attend to how this synthesis takes place. While the "Imagineers" of Disney create beguiling fantasies, even histories, these are still framed as simulations. However, in the ordinary landscape there is no frame. The necessary fictions, histories, and myths that people create and use to make sense of their lives become real and "natural" when encoded into landscape. For the designer, then, it is a matter of not only learning how to tell stories in landscapes but developing a critical awareness of the processes and implications of narrative; whose story is told and what values and beliefs inhere in the telling?

Mark Tansey, *Untitled*. (Collection of the artist; courtesy Curt Marcus Gallery)

Mark Tansey frames his work with questions: "What shapes does narrative take? What is the spatial-temporal shape of event? Do objects narrate? What world is this? . . ."

NOTES

1. In narratology, story is usually defined as the content plane of narrative "what" is told as opposed to "how" it is told. Fabula is another term often used for story. Narrative is the expressive plane or "how" a story is told. Discourse is another term substituted for narrative. However, others (Cohan and Shires) argue that this distinction between story and telling assumes that there is a fixed chronology of events that is independent and knowable apart from how they are told. There is no story without its telling. The binary distinctions between story/narrative, content/expression, objective facts/representation, form/process, and system (langue)/usage (parole) become difficult to maintain. The act of telling mediates and constructs the story. Our use of narrative and story derives from this recognition of their reciprocity.

2. This and subsequent quotes are from interviews with a series of farmers conducted in the Oley Valley in 1982, 1992, and 1996 by Matthew Potteiger. Portions of these interviews, "Landscape Narratives, The Oley Valley," were presented at the Conference of Educators in Landscape Architecture, Blacksburg, Virginia, 1982. The author is a descendent of one of the French Huguenot families that settled in what was considered part of the valley in the 1720s.

3. According to Cicero, "Persons desiring to train this faculty (of memory) must select places and form mental images of the things they wish to remember and store those images in the places, so that the order of the places will preserve the order of the things, and the images of the things will denote the things themselves" (Cicero, *De Oratore*, 2.86.351–4. quoted in Andrews, 28).

4. The rejection of narrative was not universal in modernism. Louis Kahn, for instance, sought archetypal stories of origins for institutions of the street, school, or library. His organization of the Exeter Library with the books in the core and the seats and carrels arrayed along the windows sets up the narrative action of "bringing the book to the light." See Alexandra Tyng, *Beginnings: Louis I. Kahn's Philosophy of Architecture* (New York: John Wiley & Sons, 1984), pp. 121–125. (Interview, Christopher Grey, chair, Architecture Department, Syracuse University, April 1997.)

5. The work of Nigel Coates, along with that of Rem Koolhaas, Jean Nouvel, Carel Weeber, and Zaha Hadid, has been described as a genre of "dirty realism." See Liane Lefaivre, "Dirty Realism in European Architecture Today: Making the Stone *Stony*," *Design Book Review* 17 (winter 1989):17–20.

6. The correlation between Virgil's text and the sequence of movement through the garden is clearly demonstrated by Moore, Mitchell, and Turnbull, 136–144.

7. For a fuller treatment of the yard and its narratives, see Girling and Helphand, *Yard, Street, Park* (New York: John Wiley & Sons, 1994).

8. Frankenmuth, Michigan, for instance, has been thoroughly "Bavarianized," while the gas stations and storefronts of Berne, Indiana, bear Swiss chalet motifs. Mira Engler has studied this phenomenon of theming small towns throughout Iowa.

9. From correspondence with Kim Sorvig, Albuquerque, New Mexico, March 16, 1996.

10. In *Delirious New York* Rem Koolhaus uses the interpretive power of myth to understand the material conditions of congestion of New York between 1890 and 1940. He ends the book, however, with a "fictional conclusion," a series of architectural narratives.

11. Artists, writers, and designers may not be lying when they provoke uncertain memories, excavate mythic structures, or explore the fictions that constitute our lives. Vicki Goldberg draws this conclusion in her review of photographers such as Jeff Wall who deliberately stage scenes as if they were real events. ("Photos That Lie—and Tell the Truth," *New York Times*, March 16, 1997.)

REFERENCES

Abrams, Janet. 1995. "Grave's Travels: Giants and Dwarfs." In *Michael Graves: Buildings and Projects, 1990–1994,* ed. Karen Nichols, Lisa Burke, and Patrick Burke. New York: Rizzoli. Pp. 6–11.

Andrews, Lew. 1995. *Story and Space in Renaissance Art: The Rebirth of Continuous Narrative.* Cambridge: Cambridge University Press.

Bakhtin, Mikhail. [1938] 1981. "Forms of Time and Chronotope in the Novel." In *The Dialogic Imagination: Four Essays by M. M. Bakhtin,* ed. Michael Holquist, trans. Carl Emerson and M. Holquist. Austin: University of Texas Press. Pp. 84–258.

Barthes, Roland. 1977. "An Introduction to the Structural Analysis of Narrative." In Barthes, *Image-Music-Text,* trans. Stephen Heath. New York: Hill and Wang. Pp. 79–124.

Benjamin, Walter. 1968. "The Storyteller." In Benjamin, *Illuminations,* ed. Hannah Arendt, trans. Harry Zohn. New York: Schocken Books. Pp. 83–109.

Boyer, Christine. 1992. "Cities for Sale: Merchandising History at South Street Seaport." In *Variations On A Theme Park,* ed. Michael Sorkin. New York: Hill and Wang. Pp. 181–124.

Calvino, Italo. 1974. *Invisible Cities.* New York: Harcourt Brace.

Cameron, Mark. 1996. "Creating a Positive Landscape: Narrative and the Design of Public Space." Paper presented at Council of Educators in Landscape Architecture, Washington State University, Spokane.

Chatman, Seymour. 1978. *Story and Discourse: Narrative Structure in Fiction and Film.* Ithaca, N.Y.: Cornell University Press.

———. 1981. "What Novels Can Do That Films Can't (and Vice Versa)." In *On Narrative,* ed. W. J. T. Mitchell. Chicago: University of Chicago Press. Pp. 117–136.

Chi, Lily. 1994. "'The Problem with the Architect as Writer...': Time and Narrative in the Work of Aldo Rossi and John Hejduk." In *Architecture, Ethics, and Technology,* ed. Louise Pelletier and Alberto Pérez-Gómez. Montreal: McGill-Queen's University Press. Pp. 199–221.

Coates, Nigel. 1985. "Gamma." *NATO* 3:13. Published by Architectural Association, London.

Cohan, Steven, and Linda M. Shires. 1988. *Telling Stories: A Theoretical Analysis of Narrative Fiction.* New York: Routledge.

Coles, Robert. 1989. *The Call of Stories: Teaching and the Moral Imagination.* Boston: Houghton Mifflin.

Danto, Arthur. 1985. *Narration and Knowledge.* New York: Columbia University Press.

De Certeau, Michel. 1984. *The Practice of Everyday Life.* Berkeley: University of California Press.

Duncan, James S. 1990. *The City as Text: The Politics of Landscape Interpretation in the Kandyan Kingdom.* Cambridge: Cambridge University Press.

Engler, Mira. 1993. "Drive-Thru History: Theme Towns in Iowa." *Landscape* 32 (1):8–18.

Freeman, Judi. 1993. *Mark Tansey.* Los Angeles: Los Angeles County Museum of Art.

Gelley, Alexander. 1987. *Narrative Crossings.* Baltimore: Johns Hopkins University Press.

Guss, David. 1989. *To Weave and Sing: Art, Symbol, and Narrative in the South American Rain Forest.* Berkeley: University of California Press.

Hamlet, Russell, and Joseph Schnieders, eds. 1988. "Narrative Architecture." *Oz* 10. Published by College of Architecture and Design, Kansas State University.

Hejduk, John. 1989. *Vladivostok: A Work by John Hejduk,* ed. Kim Shkapich. New York: Rizzoli.

Henriquez, Gregory and Richard Henriquez. 1994. "The Ethics of Narrative at Trent." In *Architecture, Ethics, and Technology,* ed. Louise Pelletier and Alberto Pérez-Gómez. Montreal: McGill-Queen's University Press. Pp. 189–198.

Holliday, Peter J., ed. 1993. *Narrative and Event in Ancient Art.* Cambridge: Cambridge University Press.

Horrigan, Paula. 1996. "Visual Books: Representing Landscapes." In *Selected CELA Annual Conference Papers.* Vol. 2, *Nature & Technology.* Washington, D.C.: American Society of Landscape Architects/Council of Educators in Landscape Architecture, Pp. 35–48.

Hufford, Mary. 1992. *Chaseworld: Foxhunting and Storytelling in New Jersey's Pine Barrens.* Philadelphia: University of Pennsylvania Press.

Jacobs, Jane M. 1996. *The Edge of Empire: Postcolonialism and the City.* New York: Routledge.

Jacobs, Peter. 1996. Correspondence, April 3.

Johnstone, Barbara. 1990. *Stories, Community, and Place: Narratives from Middle America.* Bloomington: Indiana University Press.

Koolhaas, Rem. 1994. *Delirious New York: A Retroactive Manifesto for Manhattan.* New York: Monacelli Press.

Kroll, Lucien. 1994. "Recreating the Image of Luth." *Places* 9(3):44–45.

Lavin, Marilyn Aronberg. 1990. *The Place of Narrative: Mural Decoration in Italian Churches.* Chicago: University of Chicago Press.

Livesey, Graham. 1994. "Fictional Cities." In *Chora.* Vol. 1, *Intervals in the Philosophy of Architecture,* ed. Stephen Parcell and Alberto Pérez-Gómez. Montreal: McGill-Queen's University Press. Pp. 110–122.

Loeffler, Jane C. 1992. "Landscape as Legend: Carleton E. Watkins in Kern County California." *Landscape Journal* 11 (1):1–21.

Lyotard, Jean-François. 1984. *The Postmodern Condition: A Report on Knowledge,* trans. Geoff Bennington and Brian Massumi. Minneapolis: University of Minnesota Press.

Martin, Emanuel. 1991. *Oostamera.* Atlanta, Ga.: Nexus Press.

Martin, Wallace. 1987. *Recent Theories of Narrative.* Ithaca, N.Y.: Cornell University Press.

McHale, Brian. 1993. *Postmodernist Fiction.* New York: Routledge.

Meyer, Elizabeth K. 1997. "The Expanded Field of Landscape Architecture." In *Ecological Design and Planning,* ed. George F. Thompson and Frederick R. Steiner. New York: John Wiley & Sons. Pp. 45–79.

Mitchell, W. J. T., ed. 1981. *On Narrative.* Chicago: University of Chicago Press.

Moore, Charles, William J. Mitchell, and William Turnbull, Jr. 1993. *The Poetics of Gardens.* Cambridge: MIT Press.

Mostafavi, Mohsen, and David Leatherbarrow. 1993. *On Weathering: The Life of Buildings in Time.* Cambridge: MIT Press.

Pérez-Gómez, Alberto. 1993. "The Architecture of Richard Henriquez: A Praxis of Personal Memory." In *Richard Henriquez: Memory Theater,* ed. Howard Shubert. Montreal/Vancouver: Canadian Centre for Architecture and Vancouver Art Gallery. Pp. 9–29.

Polkinghorne, Donald. 1988. *Narrative Knowing and the Human Sciences.* Albany: State University of New York Press.

Prince, Gerald. 1987. *A Dictionary of Narratology.* Lincoln: University of Nebraska Press.

Rakatansky, Mark. 1992. "Spatial Narratives." In *Strategies in Architectural Thinking,* ed. John Whiteman, Jeffrey Kipnis and Richard Burdett. Chicago and Cambridge: Chicago Institute for Architecture and Urbanism and MIT Press. Pp. 201–221.

Ricoeur, Paul. 1981. "Narrative Time." In *On Narrative,* ed. W. J. T. Mitchell. Chicago: University of Chicago Press. Pp. 165–186.

Roe, Emery. 1994. *Narrative Policy Analysis: Theory and Practice*. Durham, N.C.: Duke University Press.

Schubert, Howard, ed. 1993. *Richard Henriquez: Memory Theater*. Montreal and Vancouver: Canadian Centre for Architecture and Vancouver Art Gallery.

Shopes, Linda. 1994. "Popular Consciousness of Local History: The Evidence of Oral History Interviews." Paper presented for the International Oral History Conference, New York, New York.

Soja, Edward. 1992. "Inside Exopolis: Scenes from Orange County." In *Variations on a Theme Park*, ed. Michael Sorkin. New York: Hill and Wang. Pp. 94–122.

Trimble, Stephen. 1994. "The Scripture of Maps, the Names of Trees: A Child's Landscape." In *The Geography of Childhood*, Gary P. Habhan and Stephen Trimble. Boston: Beacon Press. Pp. 15–31.

Tschumi, Bernard. 1981. *Manhattan Transcripts*. New York: St. Martin's Press.

Turner, Victor. 1981. "Social Dramas and Stories about Them." In *On Narrative*, ed. W. J. T. Mitchell. Chicago: University of Chicago Press. Pp. 137–164.

Vidler, Anthony. 1994. *The Architectural Uncanny: Essays in the Modern Unhomely*. Cambridge: MIT Press.

Wines, James. 1987. *De-architecture*. New York: Rizzoli.

Woodbridge, Kenneth. 1970. *Landscape and Antiquity: Aspects of English Culture at Stourhead 1718 to 1838*. London: Clarendon Press.

CHAPTER TWO

THE NATURE OF LANDSCAPE NARRATIVES

Gieseppe Terragni, Paradise Hall, Danteum. (By permission from Princeton Architectural Press)

The Danteum by Gieseppe Terragni is a modern example of translating a literary program into archictectural form. The project's abstract geometry and spiral sequence derive from the structure of Dante's *Divine Comedy* rather than representing specific iconography. Dante's paradise, the "selva antica," becomes a transparent forest of 101 glass columns (there are 101 cantos in the text). The project was conceived under Mussolini as a memorial to Italian identity. See Thomas Schumacher, *The Danteum* (Princeton: Princeton Architectural Press, 1985).

In the middle of our life's path
I found myself in a dark forest,
where the straight way was lost
Dante (*Inferno* I: 1–3)

Following the lead of Dante, Umberto Eco in *Six Walks in the Fictional Woods* uses the forest as the metaphor for narrative texts. "There are woods like Dublin, where instead of Little Red Riding Hood one can meet Molly Bloom." He extends the metaphor of walking in a forest to describe how reading also produces meaning out of the profusion of signs. "Even when there are no well-trodden paths in a wood, everyone can trace his or her own path, deciding to go to the left or to the right of a certain tree and making a choice at every tree encountered. In a narrative text, the reader is forced to make choices all the time" (Eco 1994, 6).

This chapter ventures into various woods including the "barco" of Villa Lante, the successional vegetation of the Indiana Dunes, and the Piney Woods of Mississippi as sites to explore narrative theory. The intent here is to understand what is it about stories and the desire to tell them that seems so natural and universal.

The "nature" in the title of this chapter refers not only to that of narrative but to the particular "natures" that are represented, interpreted, and designed in landscape narratives. Therefore, we are reversing the metaphor of Dante and Eco, turning it over and looking at both sides. The concern is not just how a narrative text is like a forest but how a forest or any landscape is known through narrative. To propose, however, that nature is constructed in stories is not meant to reduce nature to mere conventional symbols that are always in service to something else (passion, virginity, national identity), even though these uses do testify to nature's cultural currency. Rather than reductive, *narratives of nature* whether in myth or ecology are part of ongoing processes of encounter, interaction, and construction of a constantly changing nature that exceeds human attempts to understand and represent it (Hayles, 49).

RE-FORMING CULTURE/NARRATIVE/LANDSCAPE: THE DEVELOPMENT OF NARRATIVE THEORY

Developments in narrative theory have figured prominently not only in literary theory, but across a range of disciplines including anthropology, geography, history, architecture, art, cultural studies, and design. Out of this bountiful, interdisciplinary, often contentious, and evolving field of thought we can identify some critical moves that begin to link landscape and narrative: redescribing narrative and landscape as cultural systems of signification, recognizing the importance of context, and expanding the notion of text and the role of readers in the production of meaning. In reciting these turning points (in very condensed form), we are also directing and adapting them as points of departure for an approach to landscape narrative.

THEORIZING LANGUAGE, CULTURE, TEXT

The common-sense recognition that narratives cross realms of experience and appear in a great variety of forms, including landscape, requires that we reconceive narrative as a *cultural system of signification*. Essentially, narratives construct meaning, or signify, much like the cultural system of language. By combining events in sequences to tell a story, narrative is homologous to the combining of words to construct intelligible sentences. This idea of linguistic system provides a framework for understanding how information, ideas, and experience are transposed from one medium to another (Duncan 1990, 4). Just as language can be communicated in hand gestures, glyphs, or other means besides verbal signs, narratives can be told in almost any means including landscape.

In the metaphor of language as a transparent window or mirror, words or signs allow a direct unmediated representation of things. However, as the story goes, it was Ferdinand de Saussure's famous series of lectures in his *Course in General Linguistics* (1907–11) that undercut the notions of natural or objective language. He posited that there is no one-to-one stable correspondence between a sign (word) and what it signifies. Because words are learned in particular situations, they are conventional and arbitrary—the transparent window of language becomes shaded, more opaque. Likewise, narratives mediate rather than mirror reality.

Structural linguistics is founded largely on Saussure's idea that meaning is relational, produced through combinations and differences. In fact narrative is the central subject of structuralism. The French anthropologist Claude Levi-Strauss examined the great diversity of myths of different cultures in search of constant universal structures operating beneath the heterogeneity of narrative. Thus, when structuralists analyzed a story they were not looking at the explicit content, but were, instead, engaged in revealing universal mental operations, often binaries of dark/light, order/chaos, nature/culture, raw/cooked, that structured them. They asserted that rather than meaning being inherent to things, these structures were inherent in the human mind.

Above: Drawing by Bruce Eric Kaplan. (© 1992. The New Yorker Magazine, Inc.)

Below: Saussure used the example of tree/arbor to demonstrate that a linguistic sign forms the link between a concept ("tree") and a sound pattern (in Latin, "arbor"). The *sign* is the *relation* that holds together the signified with its signifier as a unit of meaning. And that link, according to his first principle of a linguistic system, is arbitrary. For instance, there is nothing inherently treelike in the word for tree. "The consequences that flow from this principle are innumerable" (Saussure: 100/68).

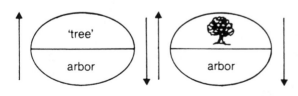

The "literary science" of narratology was an outgrowth of structural linguistics and its attempt to make a science out of the interpretation of texts. This significantly altered the approach to interpreting narrative as well as other signifying systems. By locating meaning in a system of relationships held in culture and language, it also decentered the individual (Duncan and Duncan 1988, 118). Meaning is not so much produced by the individual as it is the product of shared systems that predate the individual (Eagleton, 107). Structuralism also leveled the playing field so that "deep structures" could be found in myths as well as in advertisements, situation comedies, or any form or representation.

The idea of "reading" a landscape or any other object in this manner also relies on an expanded notion of "text." Roland Barthes made the distinction that "the work can be held in the hand, the text is held in language" (Barthes 1977, 157). Accordingly, the production of meaning between author and reader centered around a text can be extended as a metaphor for interpreting gardens or behavior in public spaces as forms of cultural production. Brian Stock, who studied medieval culture, showed that even in an oral culture, a concept of an invisible scripture or text can exist behind everything said, seen, and smelled (Stock 1990, 20).

POST-STRUCTURALISM—ADRIFT ON A SEA OF STORIES

Barthes, originally a structuralist, later rejected its totalizing nature: "There are said to be certain Buddhists whose ascetic practices enable them to see a whole landscape in a bean. Precisely what the first analysts of narrative were attempting" (1974, 3). In a more radical extension of Sausseur's separation of sign from what it signified, Barthes, Derrida, and other post-structuralists asserted that there is no final meaning but rather a network of association. Instead of closure and depth, there is infinite play of meaning across surfaces. Instead of an author's having control of meaning, readers play a significant role in reworking and producing the meaning of a text. In addition, a text, a book, a building, a garden, or "the self" are sites of the intersection or layering of other texts. They become *intertextual*.

Others posit a middle ground between a deep system and infinite relativism. Instead of an autonomous system, Mikhail Bakhtin stressed the importance of interaction with specific contexts that deform, refract, add nuances, or even subtract the meaning of a story according to differences of history, gender, class, place, etc. There is no general language or system separate from specific contexts (Holquist, xxi). Therefore, narrative is not directly homologous to language, but meaning and interpretations are both enabled and constrained within social discourses.

FROM THEORY TO LANDSCAPE

Contemporary theory, as briefly outlined above, enables one to conceive of distinct relationships between culture, narrative, and landscape. In fact the post-structural description of narrative texts and intertextual connections closely resembles the nature of landscapes. This is evident even in certain

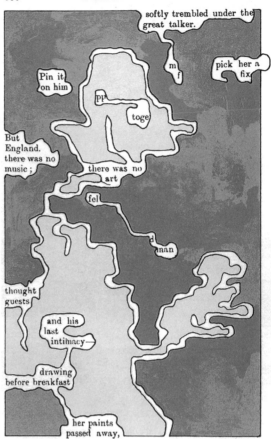

Tom Phillips, *A Humament*. Screen printing on wove paper, 1970. (Courtesy Syracuse University Art Collection)

In 1963 Tom Phillips purchased at random an obscure Victorian novel, *A Human Document*, by W. H. Malloch. His reworking of the text is a somewhat extreme and literal illustration of how readers rework and produce their own meaning from a given text. Phillips describes his process: "*A Humament* is a treated work. A Victorian novel has been taken page by page and altered, adapted and metamorphosed; its text has been excavated for new ambiguities of character and situation and new ironies and paradoxes of utterance. In place of the unused part of Malloch's text an intricate web of visual iconography has sprung up, reminiscent of the varicolored illuminations of Medieval and Oriental manuscripts." (Prince)

organic metaphors, such as the "scattering and gathering of 'semes' (seeds and signs)," post-structuralists use to describe the indeterminacy of meaning (Sartiliot, 3). However, there are also important distinctions and qualifications to make when applying the metaphors of text and reading to landscape.

The key concepts adapted and adopted from contemporary theory establish the context for further exploration of the relationship between landscape and narrative. We proceed then in a sequence of two related discussions. First, we will look at the principal devices or "tropes" for constructing meaning in language and landscape. Then we will discuss three specific landscape narratives as they illustrate relationships between the realms of story, context/intertext, and discourse.

Mark Tansey, *Constructing the Grand Canyon*. Oil on canvas, 1990. (Walker Art Center, Minneapolis, gift of Penny and Mike Winton; courtesy Curt Marcus Gallery, New York)

Mark Tansey engages the issues raised by contemporary theory in a landscape allegory. Taking pages of published texts, underscoring, crumpling, and silk-screening them onto the canvas, Tansey represents the postmodern metaphor of the "world as text," albeit fragmented, eroded, and under [de]construction. People carve, chisel, jackhammer, blast, hoist, erase, and inscribe the meaning of this natural and textual landscape, as the leaders of the Yale School of deconstruction, Harold Bloom, Paul de Man, and Geoffrey Hartman, along with Jacque Derrida (Michel Foucault is perched at the left edge of the painting), stand in the middle ground. It is also a picture that refers to other pictures, including Raphael's *School of Athens* (1506), Courbet's monument to realism, *The Stonebreakers* (1849), and the sublime American landscapes of Frederick Church and Thomas Cole. (Freeman, 30–32)

THE (TROPE)ICAL LANDSCAPE[1]

Tropes are the basic schemes by which people construct meaning in language, narrative, and landscape. They perform the necessary function of relating one thing to another, the known with the unknown. The metaphor of reading the landscape as a text, for instance, is a trope used throughout this book to present difficult and complex ideas in terms of an equally complex but more familiar practice. This ability of tropes to shuttle back and forth from representations in one medium to those in another is especially relevant for transpositions between the verbal and visual, temporal and spatial, narrative and landscape. The etymology of *trope*, which comes from ancient Greek for "turn," "way," or "manner," suggests this relational process (White 1978, 2).

Usually considered special uses of language in poetry or political speeches, tropes are also found in common speech. In fact they are so necessary and ordinary that we are rarely conscious of their use. Their ubiquity is largely due to their persuasiveness. To claim "I see" invokes a metaphor where vision equals understanding, belief, and knowledge; it is a trope used in ordinary conversation, religious faith, and scientific observation. In *Tropics of Discourse* Hayden White analyzes the tropes of nonfiction and history, arguing that rather than distortions of more literal or realistic language, they are necessary means of description in all discourse (White 1978, 2). Tropes are "indigenous to meaning," and we cannot communicate without them (Senecah, 96).

The number of identifiable tropes varies from two to twelve, and in some cases the list extends from "alliteration" to "zeugma" into the hundreds (Mellard, 1). However, we will concern ourselves with what are often regarded as the four major tropes: metaphor, metonymy, synecdoche, and irony.[2] These four figure throughout our treatment of landscape narratives in theory, practices and particular case studies.

METAPHOR

Metaphor derives from the Greek word *metaphora,* to "carry over," to convey.[3] To use a metaphor, the aspects of one object are carried over, or transferred, to another object so that it is spoken of as if it were the first (Hawkes, 1). It operates on the linguistic principles of substitution and similarity. The persuasiveness of metaphor lies in this ability to relate the unfamiliar to the familiar. Metaphors can generate new relationships between elements, but they can also mask qualities of one element with those of another. To call trees "natural resources," for instance, transforms them into raw products that can be detached from their place in an ecological habitat (Senecah, 97).

There are "small" metaphors, the kind that are tossed out in individual utterances, and "big" metaphors of the kind that lie behind research methods, institutions, and lives (Barnes and Duncan 1992, 11). In particular, the extended metaphors employed to comprehend the interrelationships of nature range from that of a complex machine with checks and balances to a self-regulating body, a community of mutual interests, or an economic system. Conversely, the cultural is often turned into the natural as in the use of organic metaphors of nucleated cities or urban blight to explain urban form.

Not only do metaphors convey meanings in a story, but stories also structure the very terms of similarity and substitution that precipitate metaphors. When two elements occupy similar positions in a story sequence or are substituted one for the other, they set up a comparison. The beginning and end of a story, for instance, invite a metaphorical substitution of one state for another.

Top right: Places as Times: The Temporal Trope

Space, distance, and travel become metaphors of time, and the return to origins, to paradise, is a common temporal trope of gardens. At Rousham, William Kent used masses of trees to frame the landscape as one would frame a picture. The foreground is seen against a distant valley and hill in which he placed two follies, The Temple of the Mill and The Eye-Catcher. These refer to a distant medieval past, considered to be the "natural" origin of British freedoms.[4] In a similar manner, tourism is a form of time travel to places that have not changed, or have been restored to some earlier time.

Bottom left: Ian Hamilton Finlay with Sue Finlay and Nicholas Sloan, *Sacred Grove: Five Columns for the Kröller-Müller* or *A Fifth Column for the Kröller-Müller* or *Corot–Saint-Just,* Rijksmuseum Kröller-Müller, Otterlo, Netherlands, 1982. (Photograph © Victor E. Nieuwenhuys; with permission from Rijksmuseum Kröller-Müller)

Classical bases around existing trees transform the trees into columns.[5] Each base bears the name of an individual associated with the French Revolution. Together they allude to the commemorative function of sacred groves of classical antiquity as well as William Kent's Elysian Field and Temple of British Worthies at Stowe.

Top right: Marking Origins.

This lone juniper tree grows beside the grave of the Berber who, it is believed, found this valley in the High Atlas region of Morocco several hundred years ago. Because of this association, the tree has become sacred and the village protects it.

To ecologists the presence of the tree suggests that there was once a whole forest of junipers in the valley that disappeared due to grazing and cutting for fuelwood. This juniper is now a source of seeds for restoration efforts to revegetate the region. (The scientists, therefore, interpret the tree in terms of a synecdoche.) (Photograph by Phillip de Maynadier)

Bottom right: The Blue Line, Adirondack Park, New York

In 1892 blue ink was used on a map of New York State to delineate the boundaries of what was to be preserved as "Forever Wild" in the Adirondack Park. The Blue Line, as it is still called, circumscribes an area of six million acres, making the Adirondacks the largest public park in the United States. In her rhetorical analysis, Susan Senecah argues that drawing this line transformed the landscape, substituting the concept of an uninhabited, aesthetic, and recreational Wilderness Park for what was already there. The Blue Line, therefore, renders those who lived there in 1892 and the 130,000 current residents invisible and out of place. For them it is a metonymy in a contested history. Groups opposed to new park acquisitions and controls take names such as the Blue Line Council and the Blue Line Confederation. They protest with blue balloons and signs, and pin blue ribbons on legislators' offices (Senecah).[6]

METONYMY

A metonymy constructs meaning by *association*. "Where there's smoke there's fire" is a metonymy of *cause and effect*. Through repeated use or memory, one thing can become associated with another so that it can be used as a sign of the other. In this way place-names become metonymies of events (Watergate, Vietnam) or institutions (Wall Street, the White House). This is the original sense of the word derived from *meta* 'change' and *onoma* 'name' (Hawkes, 4).

Contiguity—being next to, on top of, before, or after—is the most basic, yet strongest, form of metonymic relationship. It forms the axis of combination and placement in narrative. Where things or events are placed and combined in a narrative sequence structures their meaning. Hayden White posits metonymy as the favored trope of historic and modern scientific discourse. He cites Darwin's *Origin of Species,* which links the history and diversity all living things to a narrative of contiguity in time and space, known as evolution (White 1978, 131).

Metonymy is also a dominant trope in landscape architecture. The common objective of relating to context, to what is contiguous, or to the site-specific associations is metonymic—as is the semblance of order determined by ecological process. Historic preservation also operates metonymically, preserving the sites *associated with* certain events, periods, people, and styles.

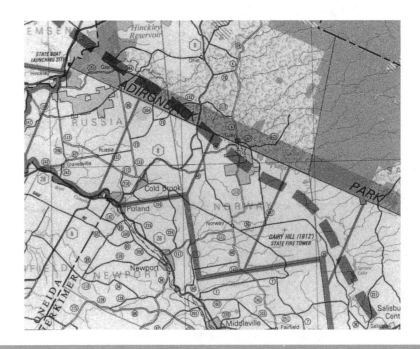

SYNECDOCHE

Synecdoche is the use of a part of something to represent the whole, or of the whole to stand for a part. "Indicator species," for instance, point to the health of a whole ecosystem. Because of this association between part and whole, synecdoche is sometimes confused with or considered a subset of metonymy. White, however, contrasts the sometimes literal or reductive nature of metonymy with synecdoche, which moves toward relating particular phenomena into a more integral whole. For this reason synecdoche is a favored trope of organicist systems which seek to understand the particular as a microcosm of a macrocosmic totality (White 1978, 73).

Synecdoche is a particularly effective device in landscape narrative because it can conjure a whole complex story just by using a piece or fragment from the story. The follies of English garden evoked a field of well-known narratives from classical literature as well as national myths. Also, synecdoche is a way of representing landscape systems, often too vast and complex to grasp. Erratic rocks speak of the power and extent of glaciers, plantings of native species recall whole ecosystems, while arboretums and zoos collect single species as representative of other places.

Left: Buster Simpson, *Host Analog,* Oregon Convention Center, 1991. (Courtesy the artist)

Microcosm of place and process. Buster Simpson relocated a "host" or "nursing log" from an old growth forest near Mount Hood to the city of Portland at the other end of the watershed it came from. While it is a fragment of a larger system, it also becomes a narrative in microcosm as seedlings begin to grow and the host tree rots away. A misting irrigation system simulates the microclimate of the forest from which it was taken. It opens a dialogue between the whole and its parts, in context and out of context, time and change. It also suggests the metaphor of a fallen column. (Simpson, 120–125)

Right: Martha Schwartz, *Splice Garden,* Whitehead Institute for Biomedical Research, Cambridge, Massachusetts, 1986. (Photograph by Alan Ward)

Martha Schwartz was asked to create a garden on a rooftop without soil or water. The garden is drenched in green but all the materials are plastic, dyed, or painted. Splicing French and Japanese traditions reveals different cultural conventions of what is natural in the garden. The splice also refers to the manipulation of nature through gene splice going on inside the building. Through these ironies the work raises questions about conventional notions of gardens and what is natural.

IRONY

Irony derives from Eironia, a character in Greek plays who is caught in a conflict between an unrecognized true identity and a mask that is mistaken for truth. This is the ironic plot in Sophicles' *Oedipus Tyrannus,* when Oedipus calls down a curse upon the killer of Laius, his father, not knowing that this will seal his own destruction (Gibbs, 363–64). We can recognize the "situational ironies" of ordinary life as well. Something is ironic when it presents an *incongruity* or *ambiguity* between expectations and reality, nature and artifice, revealing and concealing, and so on. Oxymora, such as the description of ecology as "discordant harmonies," give names to inherent ironies. Instead of substitution, contiguity, or a part that stands for a whole, the position of irony is in the *in-betweenness* of things. It is an affirmation of both/and, as well as neither completely this nor that.

Unlike the other tropes that work to convince, an ironic position has a sense of detachment that engenders *critique,* including denaturalizing representations themselves. Irony is used as a trope in Enlightenment critique primarily to demystify past dogmas, superstitions, and traditions. In a postmodern culture of relativism and unstable truths, irony is a favored mode that not only unmasks but also masks, splices genres together, juxtaposes fiction and nonfiction, and mixes "high" and "low" culture (Ellin, 121). These strategies often produce the noncommittal attitude of "blank irony," one form of defense against ultrarelativity. On the other hand, irony can open an intermediary space where existing binaries and hierarchies are questioned and reworked to create more hybrid or plural expressions. For example, Charles Jencks identified "double coding" as a way of combining historical tradition with new technologies and ideologies (Ellin, 88,89). At Serling and Wilford's addition to the Staadtsgallerie in Stuttgart, the classically inspired stone cladding (coding history) of the parking garage seems as if it has crumbled at one spot, which reveals the stone as a mask. Yet at the same time this opening provides ventilation (coding function).

The definitions and examples of the tropes cited above demonstrate important ways in which meaning is constructed between both narrative and landscape. While they are necessary to construct meaning in any discourse, it is also important to recognize what tropes are used and how they constitute the ways we understand and explain things, as well as their implications and limits.

The rest of this chapter outlines a framework for applying narrative theory, including the work of tropes, for the interpretation and design of landscapes. Three landscape narratives are used to explore the relationships between story and landscape, author, reading, and the expanded notion of text.

REALMS OF LANDSCAPE NARRATIVE

The "Third Story of the Fifth Day" of Giovanni Boccaccio's *Decameron* tells of two young lovers who run away and end up getting lost in a forest. This story, like all the others in the *Decameron,* is told in a garden. A group of young ladies and lords have escaped to this garden in the hills above 14th-century Florence to tell one hundred stories in ten days to entertain themselves while a plague rages in the streets below. They become authors, audience, and interpreters of stories (stories Boccaccio has them tell) that range from history and cosmography to folklore and geography. This structure of the text of the *Decameron* is known as a frame narrative, a story that frames a compendium of other stories. But the garden is also a frame narrative. The enclosed garden not only frames the real setting for conversation that gives rise to stories, but its allées of orange and lemon trees, frangrances and fountain also recall stories of paradise derived from religious and secular texts. Meanwhile, both garden and story offer a protected realm in the narrative of escape from the plague-ravaged city.

A different sort of crossing between realms occurs in magic realism. In this genre, unique to Latin America, fact and fiction, myth, history, and the present are all penetrated by imagination, resulting in multiple and simultaneous realms (Sorvig, 194). These same qualities are evident in a recent trilogy of parks in Mexico City designed by Mario Schjetnan and Grupo de Deseño Urbano that recover the myth, history, and living connections with the lacustrine past of the region. When the Spanish arrived there, the Aztec city on an island was surrounded by an extensive complex of lakes. The design for Parque Tezezomoc re-creates in miniature the valley and lake of this mythic landscape, which has since been obliterated by massive urbanization. Early in the design, poet Thomas Calvillo suggested making a fiction, evoking something that no longer exists, because the reality is so alienating. For the second project, Culhuacan Historical Park, they designed within the actual physical traces of the myth—the archaeological remains of a pre-Spanish port on the lake exhumed during the construction of a communications tower. The last project in the series, Xochimilco Ecological Park, rescues the last living remnant of the lake culture, a system of canals and *chinampas,* islands that date back to the ninth century when they were created to produce food and flowers. The design restores the hereditary connections as well as the water quality that maintains the ongoing processes. To float through this living anthology, as Mario Schjetnan says, is to "enter a landscape of dreams."

Pietro Boccamazza, fleeing with Agnolella, falleth among theives; the girl escapeth through a wood and is led (by fortune) to a castle, whilst Pietro is taken by the thieves, but presently, escaping from their hands, winneth, after divers adventures, to the castle where his mistress is and espousing her, returneth with her to Rome.
(Summary introduction to the "Third Story of the Fifth Day" of Boccaccio's *Decameron,* a 1925 translation by John Payne. New York: Boni and Liveright Inc.)

Top right: The Myth. The map outlines the early settlements around the original lake in the Valley of Mexico. The present extent of Mexico City is shown in light gray and the remnants of the lake in dark gray. Knowledge of this landscape is maintained in mythic histories.

Parque Tezozomoc at Azcapotzalco uses the illusion of scale to re-create this mythic landscape in miniature. The lake in the park replicates the shape of the original lake. The hills, which surround the lake and help define a separate realm, were created from the soil excavated for the metro line underneath the city. They also repeat the shapes of the mountains that rim the valley. The other two projects by Grupo de Deseño Urbano are located in the original settlements of Culhuacan and Xochimilco.

Bottom left: The History. Culhuacan Historical Park interprets an original Aztec port on the lake. It is also connected to an archaeological museum and monastery built over the site of an Aztec temple.

Bottom right: The Living Landscape. The Xochimilco Ecological Park is part of an effort to restore water quality as well as the cultural links with the *chinampas*, a system of islands created in the lake with willows and dredged soil. These were incredibly productive gardens sustained for thousands of years. They nearly vanished recently because of serious water pollution and invasive plants. The design includes newly created *chinampas* (shown toward the top of the photograph) based on archaeological accounts.

VALLEY OF MEXICO

Ecatepee

Texcoco

Tepeyas
Tlatelolco

Atzcapotzalco
(Tezozomac)

Tenochititan

Chapultepec

Coyoacan

Culhuacan

Tizaran

Chalco

Xochimilco

0 5 10 20 40 Km

North

As these examples demonstrate, stories cross boundaries of different realms. They arise out of conversation or centuries of myth, creating imagined worlds. These fictive realms "take place" and are also "built into" the fabric of "real" places. We will explore these relationships more closely within three particular realms of landscape narratives:

1. The Story Realm
2. The Contextual/Intertextual Realm
3. The Discourse Realm

The story realm is the world of the story itself. The emphasis is on the author's/designer's intentions to create meaning within the structures of story (event, plot, character, point of view, etc.). However, it is important to see how stories relate to contexts and other texts. The emphasis in the contextual/intertextual realm is on the role of readers, community, or memory in the making of landscape narratives. The third realm of discourse requires attention to whose story is told and what ideologies or world views are implicit in the telling.

These relationships are illustrated by three landscape narratives: the Italian Renaissance garden of Villa Lante, the ecological narrative of the Indiana Dunes, and the regional garden of Crosby Arboretum. Each is exemplary of different relationships between realms and between authors, text, and readers. Villa Lante, like many gardens of the Italian Renaissance, is based on Ovid's *Metamorphoses,* a story where all the various forms of life emerge from the same primal matter, shifting shapes in the process. Here, the story is *designed into* the landscape using specific icons, sculpture, topography, fountains, and vegetation. Out on the Indiana Dunes along the shores of Lake Michigan east of Chicago, Henry Cowles developed one of the first narratives of ecological succession at the turn of the 20th century. It is a *found* story recovered from reading the forms and processes of nature, but it was a story nonetheless of origins that eventually led to the preservation of this remnant landscape as a state and national park, a garden. Finally, the Pincote Interpretive Center of the Crosby Arboretum in the Pearl River Basin of Mississippi and Louisiana *synthesizes* the story-shaped garden and the story found in nature. It has been described as "the first fully realized ecological garden in the country" ("Crosby Arboretum," 55). The arboretum design is directly related to an ecological reading of the site, yet at the same time employs storytelling strategies as sophisticated as those in any Renaissance villa. In many ways all three are creation stories.

Above: Diego Rivera, *The Huastec Civilization.* Mural, Palacio Nacional, Mexico City, 1950. The background shows the *chinampas.* (Schalkwijk/ Art Resource; by permission from the Instituto Nacional de Bellas Artes y Literatura)

Below: Willows define the edge of the existing *chinampas.*

1. The Story Realm

The term "story realm" designates the world created within a narrative—its content, *the story,* as well as the means used to shape that world, *the narration* (telling). In this *space* we look at how the narrative units of story, temporal order, place, character, agency, and point of view all work as a system of signification to conjure and sustain a coherent and believable story. The purpose is to conceptualize narrative as an analyzable system whose basic structural components are shared by narratives of all sorts from literary texts to film, paintings, and landscape (Cohan and Shires, 53).

Of bodies changed to other forms I tell:
You Gods, who have yourselves wrought every change,
Inspire my enterprise and lead my lay
In one continuous song from nature's first
Remote beginnings to our modern times.
  Ovid, *Metamorphoses*

...to know how the world came into being. Such an opportunity has
been given on the shores of Lake Michigan, where for centuries new
land has been continually in process of formation and new plant
communities have been developing.
  Summary of the work of Henry Cowles, by George Fuller
  (Engel 1983, 159)

These cosmogenic tales draw boundaries, creating a space for the story to be told. The boundaries act as explicit signs of narration, separating the narration from the ordinary conversation or context and opening up the possible world of the story. They orient readers as to what kind of storied world they are entering—the gates of allegory, personal experience, history, the ordinary, the extraordinary, the scientific, the mythical, etc. (Young, 21). These orientations help to establish different expectations, conventions, and what constitutes truth (or what is believable) within the story.

The signs that mark the opening or closing of the story realm can be verbal ("Once upon a time..."); gestural, as in ritual acts; or spatial, as in the edges, boundaries, and walls that mark the threshold to different storytelling venues— theater, park, garden. The visitor to the garden of Villa Lante is greeted by a wall with statues of the Muses around a pool with a sculpture of Pegasus, whose hoof strikes Mount Parnasus (home of the Muses), creating a spring that inspires creativity (Rainey, 100). This fountain frames the garden narrative in two ways. First, it ushers the visitor into a fictional realm of myth and art derived from another place and time, ancient Rome in particular. However, it also commemorates the real act of restoring water to the site. A poem written in praise of the garden explains that it was this act of bringing fresh water that called the Muses from Pegasus's home on Mount Helicon to inspire the creation of the garden and its stories (Lazzaro 1990, 134). However, narrative frames need not be so intentionally constructed. The realm of shifting sands of the Indiana Dunes was clearly bounded between lake and forest. The amphitheater-like space of a "blowout" also provides a frame for storytelling events such as the grand "Historical Pageant and Masque of the Sand Dunes of Indiana" in 1917.

Agency, Events, and Characters

Within its frame a story begins with an event, a state of existence in time that is then altered, a transition from stasis to process, a metamorphosis. The change may be cataclysmic, as in the struggles of creation stories; a slight shift in routine; or an anomaly barely on the horizon of perception, as in minimalist narratives. The minimal condition for a narrative is a sequence of at least

Below: The Pegasus Fountain at the entry to the garden and park.

Bottom: Aerial view of the Indiana Dunes.

two events, one to establish an existing situation and one to alter it (Chatman, 31, 32).

In the beginning of Ovid's *Metamorphoses* the ideal, timeless state of harmony of the golden age is destroyed by a great flood, after which the humans have to labor to cultivate and perfect nature. At Villa Lante this juxtaposition of a stable, timeless world and a linear historical narrative is structured by the division between the barco (or park), with its oak trees, fountains, and numerous references to life in the golden age, and the formal garden. The Grotto of the Deluge at the upper entrance of the formal garden represents the flood, the event that initiates a story.

On the shores of Lake Michigan the Dunes also display primordial acts of creation and emergence from water. According to geologists and ecologists, twenty thousand years ago the last glaciers receded, and since that event the vectors of wind and the interactions of sand, water, fire, and vegetation have created a series of dunes. The processes continue.

As these stories imply, events only happen as a result of some form of agency or characters. Narratologists (Propp, Greimas) identify six functions of actors or "actants"[7] in relation to events: *subject* (primary performing agency), *object* (serving as a goal of an action), *sender* (initiating or enabling an event), *receiver* (benefiting from or registering the effects of an event), *opponent* (impeding an event by opposing the subject), and *helper* (advancing an event by supporting the subject)(Cohan and Shires, 69). Through the trope of metamorphosis in Villa Lante, gods represent forces of nature that become human and turn into stone sculptures. Cardinal Gambara himself is transformed into a force of nature through the symbol of the crawfish, a play on his name and the Italian word *gambero*. The "water chain" is a stylized cascade contained and controlled literally within the extended "arms" of a crawfish.

In addition to human agency, functions in a story can be performed by objects, abstractions (desire, law), and natural or supernatural forces. On the Dunes wind is both a creative and a destructive force. Cowles gives names for each type of dune that describe their role and function in narratives of advance, retreat, and succession. Others invented characters such as "Duna" to personify the spirit of the Dunes.

Event, agency, and character are the structural elements of story. A story develops through the placement, combination, and substitution of these elements. To substitute one event for another, leave a gap, or in some way alter the sequence of a story changes the meaning of the story. In this respect the structure of story is homologous to the structure of language and the two axes of signification: combination and substitution.

Time, Story, and Narration

Stories do not necessarily form a sequential chain of events lined up in chronological order. Many stories, such as mystery novels, recover a chronology only by working backward. They narrate the process of discovering the actual

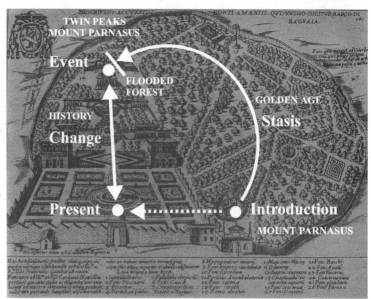

Above: "Plot map" of Villa Lante and the division between park and garden, the golden age and history, stasis and change. Engraving from G. Lauro, *Antiquae urbis splendor*, Rome 1612–14. (Courtesy Dumbarton Oaks, Studies in Landscape Architecture, Photo Archive)

Below: A simulated deluge pours from the eves of the twin pavilions flanking the Grotto of the Deluge at the upper terrace of the formal garden. The two Houses of the Muses represent the twin peaks of Mount Parnasus (home of the Muses), where Deucalion and Pyrrha were saved from the flood.

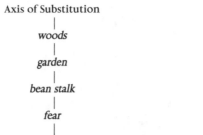

Axis of Substitution

|

woods

|

garden

|

bean stalk

|

fear

|

That very night in Max's room a forest grew and grew and grew, until...

Axis of Combination——placement——sequence——movement———

The axes of combination and substitution structure meaning in language and narrative. The axis of combination also correlates with the trope of metonymy, while the axis of substitution operates as a metaphor. These two axes are also referred to as the syntagmatic and paradigmatic axes of a linguistic system.

sequence of events. A narrative *creates* a kind of virtual space in time, what happened yesterday, last year in Marienbad, or in one hundred years of solitude. Access to and knowledge of this realm is through some form of narration. This is a relationship common to all narratives—a *story*, as a temporal structure, is only available to us through some form of telling or *narration*. Since the narration mediates what events are told and how they are structured, the two must be considered together.[8]

Narration time and *story time* are integral but different. The time represented in a narrative may be one week, a moment, or a millennium, but, the actual time to tell, hear, read, or in some way experience each of these stories may be just five minutes. A lifetime can be summarized in four words, yet in *Remembrance of Things Past*, Proust takes four pages to fully explicate the texture of one moment in time. In stories time can be compressed and expanded, or halted and entered for inspection, as in the freeze frame of the final scene of the movie *The Four Hundred Blows* (Chatman, 119). Gardens perform a similar role by alternately accelerating certain processes (fertilizing) and freezing others (mowing the lawn) or juxtaposing stasis and change to reveal the passage of time.

Events in nature continually test the tolerances of human attention either by happening at such a grindingly slow geologic pace as to appear as a static scene, or by being so infinitely diverse and simultaneous that they appear insignificant and inconsequential. Nature is just a "slow event" that can be retold, organized into epochs, and summarized in story. In Henry Cowles's ecological history of the Indiana Dunes, almost twenty thousand years can be summarized and experienced (read) during an afternoon's walk. As you go from the active, shifting dunes by the water's edge and walk inland, you cross a sequence of dunes and vegetation that increase in complexity and age. The time it takes to walk this route is the *time of narration*, whereas the *story time* is the time of the actual geologic and ecological processes.

In addition, the distance between the time of the story and when it is narrated is critical, making a narrative appear to be historical, mythical, or from direct experience. With telecommunications the distance between events and the report has collapsed, as demonstrated during the Gulf War when televised events appeared as instant replay. While we tend to think of stories and narration as separated in time, direct dialogue and other devices create the semblance of "isochrony," when story time and narrational time appear equivalent. To witness a rare bird returning to the Dunes connects the moment of the observer with the temporality of ecological process.

Sequence, Plot, and Spatial Form

Events do not just happen in a story—they usually happen for reasons. And those reasons, the issues that the story opens up and that ultimately create closure, become bound up with how events and time are presented and organized in the story. The end is always present in each event. In all the wanderings of the *Odyssey*, the hero's desire is always to *get back home again* (Fergusson, 21). All the movement of wind, water, sand, and vegetation works, according to Cowles, toward the ultimate goal of diversity and relative stability of plant communities. "The heath has several origins but one destiny" (Cowles, 367).

As noted earlier, the minimal structure of a story is a two-event sequence, a transition from one state to another. When a story combines more than two events in a sequence, the space of the story expands in scale and complexity. The beginning event opens the space and a range of possible outcomes, while the subsequent events advance and postpone movement toward the ending and closure of the space. The beginning and end are still points of resemblance that function as a metaphor asking the reader to make comparisons (Cohan and Shires, 65, 66).

To talk of story as movement between still points with variations in direction, etc. employs spatial metaphors for the temporal structure of narrative. Indeed, the sequence of a story is often referred to as a story line, and plots take on twists and turns mapping out complex configurations of events. As stories gather events into configurations, temporal order becomes spatialized. Thus we can analyze not just how stories take place, but the placement of events to create the temporal patterns of lines, circles, branching patterns, mazes, and other forms in stories. Bakhtin uses the term *chronotope,* for the materialization of time in space. Figures such as the road, or the garden not only structure events of stories but become central metaphors in the stories (Bakhtin, 250).

A sequence maps out a plot when it can be determined that one event caused another. E. M. Forster illustrated this distinction by explaining, "'The King died and then the queen died' is a story" whereas "'The King died and then the queen died of grief' is a plot" (Forster, 86). The first event provides the conditions that cause the latter events. Notions of causality, whether by divine plan, individual will, or the weather, influence the nature and sequence of events in the plot of a story. But it is important to remember that plot and sequence are not synonymous. In many stories sequences may not be logical or determined by causal relationships, events may lead to wrong conclusions, and sequences may stop without conclusion. "Alice in Wonderland" epitomizes a story without a logical plot structure (Cohan and Shires, 5–8).

MYTH, TIME, STRUCTURE, AND CAUSALITY IN VILLA LANTE

Ovid's *Metamorphoses* sets up the dual structure of the garden as a chronological history set against a timeless golden age. The paths of the golden age of the park lead to the upper end of the walled garden, where the Grotto of the Deluge tells of the flood that destroyed the golden age. In front, the Fountain of the Dolphins recalls Ovid's description of the dolphins that swam between the oak trees submerged by the flood: "and in the woods the dolphins live and high among the branches dash to and fro and shake the oaks in play" (*Metamorphoses* 1. 302–304).

The story of civilization shaping a more perfect nature through the application of art and labor begins at this upper terrace. It is a progressive narrative proceeding terrace by terrace, each one marking a distinct stage in the process and building upon the previous stage. The spatial form, plantings, sculpture, and most important the play of water work together to articulate this process. The upper terrace, for instance, is smaller and

enclosed by a tree canopy with water emerging from its most primal source, a grotto. Each successive terrace becomes proportionately larger, more open and refined. The linear sequence is a continuous narrative along a perspective axis so that from the upper level you can also see below to a glimpse of the final terrace with clipped hedges and flat, placid pools that reflect the sky. The garden telescopes space and time, and gives a clear sense of the direction toward the story's end. However, the visitor never walks directly along this line; there are diagonals and shifts as well as unseen elements that are revealed only in the progression.

The different moments in time are evoked by sophisticated references to classical literature and conventional symbols. For instance, the terrace depicting the age of agriculture is flanked by the statues of Pomona and Flora, gods who produce the gifts of abundance of vegetables and fruit. At the center of this terrace is a long table with a trough of water based on the descriptions of similar elements found in the writings of Pliny. Here the cardinal and his guests could bring the actual fruits and vegetables from the cultivation of land to reenact the garden feasts of ancient Romans. Even the plane trees that flank the space are legendary and evoke associations with antiquity (Lazzarro 1990, 254).

Above: The Fountain of the Moors or the Grotto of the Deluge serve as either the beginning or ending of the narrative sequence.

The events of the landscape narrative are enchained in a chronological sequence in carefully constructed alliances of causality. It is water in all its various manifestations that carries out the trope of metamorphoses.9 It emerges from stone, becomes light and sound, and turns back into flowing stone sculptures. Water becomes actor (River Gods of Tiber and Arno), event, and the cause of events. It is not an anonymous causality; sculptures of Neptune, Venus, the crawfish, etc. all tell how the gods as well as humans play a key role in all of this.

The lowest and final terrace shows the perfect order of nature revealed in geometric form. This is the age of the Renaissance. The plot of the story creates a comparison between this new golden age of the moderns, achieved through labor and art, and that of the ancients. Lante becomes an allegory asking the reader to interpret the actions of the present through the myths and history of the past. By entering the private entrance to the garden at this lower terrace, the cardinal and close associates could look up into the garden and back in time.

Top left: The view from the Fountain of the Dolphins on the upper terrace. The linear perspective and hydrologic chain of connections create a continuous narrative. All the key events are carefully positioned along the visual axis so they can be seen at one moment.

Center left: The outstretched claws of a crawfish ("gambero") directs water to the sprawling River Gods of the Tiber and Arno below.

Bottom left: View from above the Fountain of the Lights overlooking the lower terrace and Fountain of the Moors. (Photographs by Gary R. Hilderbrand)

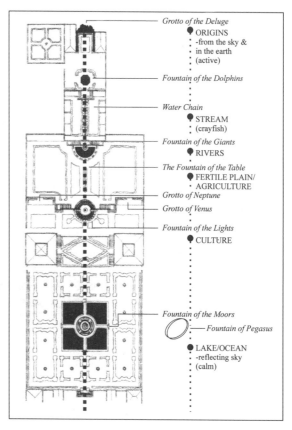

Grotto of the Deluge
ORIGINS
-from the sky &
in the earth
(active)

Fountain of the Dolphins

Water Chain
STREAM
(crayfish)

Fountain of the Giants
RIVERS

The Fountain of the Table
FERTILE PLAIN/
AGRICULTURE

Grotto of Neptune

Grotto of Venus

Fountain of the Lights
CULTURE

Fountain of the Moors

Fountain of Pegasus

LAKE/OCEAN
-reflecting sky
(calm)

Complex Forms

Stories create worlds that operate according to differences in determinism and contingency or chance. The anthem

BIRTH
SCHOOL
WORK
DEATH

by the punk band the Godfathers (1987, Epic Records) is a frustrated send-up of a predetermined life story without creative options in the aftermath of Margaret Thatcher's third election victory. In contrast, in one of the early works on narrative form, Vladimir Propp (1928) analyzed the corpus of Russian folktales to identify a set of all the possible events that could occur at different stages of a folktale. If one event occurs, it shuts down the chance of some other events occurring while opening up a whole series of other possibilities. A story becomes a complex branching structure, a genealogy, as shown in the diagram for "automatic story generation."

Many years later, as he faced the firing squad, Colonel Aureliano Buendia was to remember that distant afternoon when his father took him to discover ice.
    Beginning of *One Hundred Years of Solitude*,
    Gabriel Garcia Marquez

In this opening it is possible for the story to end rather abruptly, yet memory opens a more complex web of possible events. It creates a complex structure of time that is more like a labyrinth or a woods than a straight line. Embedding, opening gaps, and repeating events signify an experience of time that is simultaneous, enfolded, and multiple. In the example above a memory of childhood is "embedded," or inserted into the time of another event, the moment before a firing squad opens fire, so the two events occur simultaneously and they cannot be separated (Cohan and Shires, 57). Likewise the events and structure of time in ecological nature involve simultaneity, embedding, and joining of events to create a complex sense of time and place.

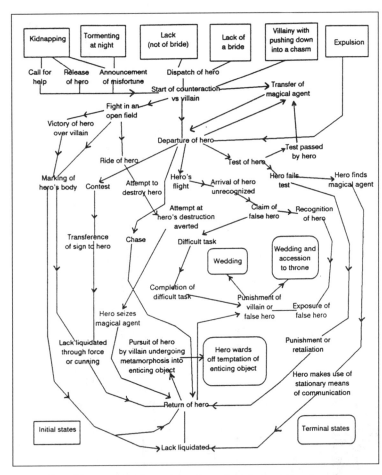

Above: The complexities and contingencies of narrative order. State transition diagram for the generation of Russian fairy tales. (From Ryan 1991).

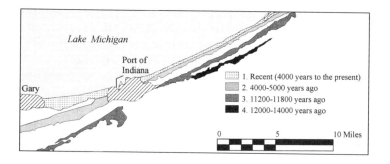

Lake Michigan

Port of
Indiana

Gary

1. Recent (4000 years to the present)
2. 4000-5000 years ago
3. 11200-11800 years ago
4. 12000-14000 years ago

0   5   10 Miles

Left: The temporal structure of the
dunes proceeds from the new and
shifting dunes near the shore to
increasingly older and more
stable formations inland.

Below: Blowing sand near the shoreline.

Bottom: Dunes in the process of being
stabilized by grasses and trees. The pine
forest (left) will eventually be displaced
by oaks (right). (All courtesy Indiana
Dunes National Lakeshore)

TIME AND STRUCTURE IN THE INDIANA DUNES

After glaciers scraped this land, cleared it of all vegetation,
and then retreated twenty thousand years ago, the agencies of
landscape formation—wind and wave erosion, deposition and
succession—began all over again. The instability of the dunes
accelerated the processes of adaptation and succession, which
often take centuries, into just a few years. Henry Cowles found
this story of a "new earth" in the act of constantly being made
and remade, and wrote some of the first papers on the principles of ecological succession. He observed an incessant repetition of this cosmogony: "The advance of a dune makes all
things new" (Cowles, 96).

Out of this shape-shifting landscape, "torn by winds,"
where fleshy fungi become petrified by sand blast action,
Cowles interpreted a narrative with a clear temporal structure. As one walks inland from the beach, one walks backward
in time, crossing a sequence of increasingly older dunes.
Although the transect across time was a common observation,
Cowles worked out a more precise temporal sequence. He
divided the complex of dunes into five sequential stages: 1) the
primitive formation of the beach, 2) the embryonic or sta-
tionary beach dunes, 3) the active or wandering dunes, 4) the
arrested or transitional dunes, and 5) the passive or established
dunes. (Engel 1983, 144). The duration of events in these stages
proceeds from more rapid, unstable changes of uniform material in the early stages to slower changes as the plant societies
approach stable, diverse "climax" conditions.

Unlike that of his contemporary, Clements, who employed
an organic metaphor that was more deterministic and linear,
Cowles's ecology was not a rigid plot. According to Clements,
succession was a narrative of birth, development to a climax,

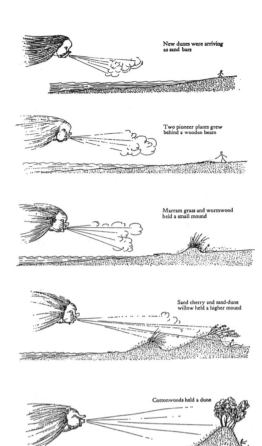

New dunes were arriving as sand bars

Two pioneer plants grew behind a wooden beam

Marram grass and wormwood held a small mound

Sand cherry and sand-dune willow held a higher mound

Cottonwoods held a dune

Reading the landscape. One of Cowles's more well known students, May Theilgaard Watts, went on to write a landmark book using the metaphor of reading to interpret natural process. Her story of dune formation is told as the search for a calm, still place amid shifting sands. In another chapter she tells of the formation of Cowles' Bog between two dune ridges. From May Theilgaard Watts, *Reading the Landscape* (New York: Collier Macmillan, 1975). (Courtesy Erica Watts and Nancy T. Watts)

and eventual death. Cowles preferred the metaphor of plant societies, a community of associations that work toward *relative stability* through mutual cooperation and reciprocity. In his "life histories" of the different dune types, he noted key turning points at each stage where the process might go in another direction (Engel, 145). Established dunes may be "rejuvenated," while old beaches could be "resurrected, though not to life" (Cowles, 104). He found "wandering dunes" that head backward toward the lake. Dunes collide. "Blowouts" cut transects, exposing relic or "fossil beaches." It becomes a whole moving landscape in which all the stages of beginning, climax, and destruction can be seen at once. And it is never finished or concluded. "The dune-complex is a restless maze" (Cowles, 194).

Yet, the regularities of climate and the prevailing winds align these contingencies toward an overwhelmingly historical march inland. Placement and association order ecological and causal relations. The trope is primarily metonymic. The other principal trope is that of synecdoche, where every element is attached to a larger whole. This is the trope Cowles employed in his analysis of a single dune as the archetype of the whole, and he went on to use the complex of dunes to characterize continental processes of succession.

Authority and Belief

A story implies or makes explicit reference to some form of authority. In Villa Lante there is a clear chain of authority of art in service to a patron, who in turn evokes the authority of classical texts in support of the Church. To a large degree the very purpose of telling the story is to establish belief in these authorities. Therefore, the *ideal reader,* who comprehends every allusion and metaphor, works back from the text to construct an image of the *ideal author,* a learned, "magnificent" patron in alliance with other powerful entities. It is through such a compact between author and reader that stories help to establish systems of belief.

An ecological narrative establishes different terms of authorship and belief than the designed garden. Throughout his text, Cowles uses words such as *found,* and *discovered,* implying that he was not imposing a story on the nature of the dunes. Rather, events seem to present themselves to the roving eye of the observer, who describes the "panoramic changes" (Cowles, 95) from the global scale down to internal plant physiology. There is no call to the Muses, no explicit narrating and even the role and the position of the observer are not acknowledged in the first person, "I." The authority of ecology is considered to be the authority of reality itself, apprehended through scientific methods.[10]

As described, however, the fictional realm of Villa Lante also makes appeals to very real authorities. The subject of Nature reveals how narratives mediate the often conflicting desires for the imaginary and the imperatives of the actual and the real (White 1987, 4). This mediation is evident in the ecological design of the Crosby Arboretum. It proceeds from very careful reading of the story found in the site, yet at the same time it employs equally sophisticated means of shaping the site to tell ecological realities.

RETELLING THE ECOLOGY OF MISSISSIPPI'S PINEY WOODS

The sixty-four-acre Pinecote Interpretive Center of the Crosby Arboretum reverses the plot of Villa Lante by restoring the semblance of an original natural order to a site that had been logged, farmed, and abandoned. Healing then is one of the metaphors that structure the plot. The name Pinecote, which is used for the main pavilion, is also a metaphor of the function of the arboretum. It refers to the pine trees that serve as "cote," or home for birds, and resonates with the etymology of *ecology*, from *oikos*, or "home." The egrets that have recently returned to the site have stimulated the regeneration of fish in the arboretum pond by carrying fish eggs that had adhered to their legs from other sites.

This story, however, began with the designers reading of the existing ecological narrative, and "letting the site reveal itself." Ed Blake lived on the site for four years and learned how to read plant signatures, such as how big blue Andropogon indicates drier ground, how sedges begin to predominate as you get into wetter ground, or how certain species extend their range with stolons. He also cut a grid

Signatures in Nature

Carl Sandburg wrote that the dunes "constitute a signature of time and eternity" (Engel 1981, 5). This idea of nature as a signature of something eternal or divine recalls a medieval theophany in which every plant could serve as a religious sign in the book of Nature (Glacken, 167–253).

Cowles, however, reads the dunes as signatures that register the effects of wind and other natural agencies. The symmetry of a dune anchored by vegetation, for instance, changes rapidly without plants producing a gradual windward slope and a steep leeward gradient: "Nowhere can there be a sharper line in nature" (Cowles, 198).

Top: Dr. Henry Cowles standing by exposed roots of cottonwoods on an eroded dune. (National Park Service and the University of Chicago Archives)

Bottom: Aerial view looking north (August 1985) of what had been an old strawberry farm. The clearing for the pond is visible toward the middle left. (Photograph by Ed Blake Jr., courtesy Crosby Arboretum/ Mississippi State University)

Top Left: Grid lines were overlain on the site to map the subtleties of moisture and vegetation patterns. (Ed Blake Jr.; courtesy Crosby Arboretum/ Mississippi State University)

Top Right: Grid line, a straight path through the woods. As the site matures, most of these lines will disappear and only the points of intersection will remain marked on the ground. Pinecote Pavilion is aligned with one of the grid lines, which serves as a path. (Photograph by Ed Blake Jr.; courtesy Crosby Arboretum/Mississippi State University)

through the vegetation as a device for revealing how these subtle changes occur along a "moisture gradient."

The design then retells the region's ecology by reestablishing the structural combinations of plants in relation to processes. As at Villa Lante, bringing water to the site sets it all in motion. Here, instead of myth, a pond was invented "as if" a beaver had dammed a meandering stream in a possible ecological world. This wetland zone forms part of a mosaic of interlocking ecotones. They gather, compress, and reconfigure the patterns found in the larger landscape into a comprehensible whole, making the garden a synecdoche of the region. Each of the zones is managed to reflect different stages of ecological succession. In the savanna habitat, for instance, fire is used to suppress the growth of certain species while encouraging others. Ed Blake and the staff of the Arboretum learned that by shifting the burning to different times of the year, they could alter the flowering patterns. In other zones the process of succession toward diversity is "nudged," or accelerated, by planting native species that had disappeared from the site over the last one hundred years. By these means, the zones become metaphors of different times, some reflecting the recent past, some telling of first contact with this nature as a landscape that "represents the dominant pinewoods which the early European settlers encountered" (*Pinecote,* 7).

The series of "journeys" that structure the narrative sequence weave through the zones, juxtapose edge with edge, move back and forth through different stages of succession, or follow a transect along the moisture gradient in order to develop themes and break down the complexity and build it back up again into an understanding of the whole. Rather than explaining in words, these design devices structure ways of reading signatures and signs in the landscape, replicating the ways Cowles and other ecologists read the landscape. Meanwhile

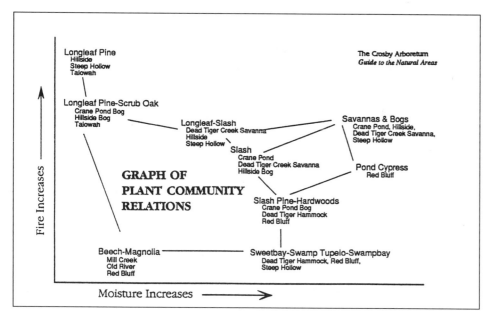

GRAPH OF
PLANT COMMUNITY
RELATIONS

Fire Increases →

Moisture Increases →

Longleaf Pine
Hillside
Steep Hollow
Talowah

The Crosby Arboretum
Guide to the Natural Areas

Longleaf Pine-Scrub Oak
Crane Pond Bog
Hillside Bog
Talowah

Longleaf-Slash
Dead Tiger Creek Savanna
Hillside
Steep Hollow

Savannas & Bogs
Crane Pond, Hillside,
Dead Tiger Creek Savanna,
Steep Hollow

Slash
Crane Pond
Dead Tiger Creek Savanna
Hillside Bog

Pond Cypress
Red Bluff

Slash Pine-Hardwoods
Crane Pond Bog
Dead Tiger Hammock
Red Bluff

Beech-Magnolia
Mill Creek
Old River
Red Bluff

Sweetbay-Swamp Tupelo-Swampbay
Dead Tiger Hammock, Red Bluff,
Steep Hollow

Left: A "plotting" of the complex relationships between water, fire, and plant communities. These relationships can be found on different sites dispersed throughout the Pearl River Basin and miniaturized in the design of the Pinecote Interpretive Center. (Ed Blake Jr. and Crosby Arboretum/Mississippi State University)

Below: A page from the *Pinecote Master Plan* describing "the Savanna Journey," one of a series of thematic journeys. In the graphic design, pitcher plants become background texture. (Courtesy Crosby Arboretum/ Mississippi State University)

the site is in the process of becoming a complex, braided, and evolving narrative of ecological time: "As it matures, its [the pond's] open, youthful expanse will condense to expanding and shrinking ribbons of light which follow the meandering, channel-like bottom framed by a towering perimeter of largely deciduous trees leaning out over the water" (*Pinecote*, 9).

Above: The Pinecote Pavilion overlooking the pond. The stepped edge of the roof imitates the density and gradations of the forest edge. (Ed Blake Jr.; courtesy Crosby Arboretum/Mississippi State University)

The weir in the foreground dividing the water between the pond and the slough registers (as in the function of "receiver" in a narrative) the three variables of a storm event: intensity, duration, and frequency. The flow from a long-duration, low-intensity storm would gradually rise over the widely spaced registrations on the right side. Yet, in a different storm the water may rise higher and faster, resulting in flow over registers on the left side of the weir (Blake 1996).

THEMATIC JOURNEYS

The Savanna Journey

The theme of this 1.6-mile loop circling the Savanna is fire: an awesome, destructive force which can be a constructive, creative one as well. Crossover walks will delineate eight major Savanna ecotones. The Pitcher Plant Bog Walk is presently in place.

The Pinecote center miniaturizes and gathers the diversity of 1,700 acres of natural areas dispersed throughout the Pearl River Basin. Standing near the pavilion, Ed Blake explains the microcosm of the arboretum: "Just as you would look at mountains, piedmont, and coastal plain, those things exist here in a miniature version, in a smaller scale. This is a mountainous ridge where we are right here, and then this ridge deadends into a depression, which is one of the wettest areas. We're standing on an escarpment revealed in a more dramatic way with the pavilion cantilevered out over the water" (Blake 1996).

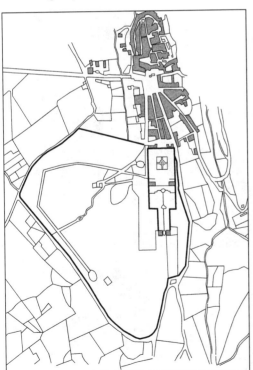

Context of Villa Lante in the town of Bagnaia and property boundaries. The owner of the villa also commissioned the design of the three streets that extend from the piazza to key points of the garden. (Source: Catasto Plan of Bagnaia)

Closure and Control of Meaning

The pleasure and power of stories lie in their ability to create coherent and believable worlds. This is achieved by the play of "narrativity'—the units of story: frame, events, characters, plot, space, authority, etc. All these aspects work to produce and control meaning within a closed system of signification. The character traits and events and their causes in a story make sense within the structure of this system, assuming there is a reader who participates in and believes in the possible world created in the story. We can enter the various spaces and times of stories—myth, natural history, magic realism, etc.—only to the extent that we let their conventions determine what we look for and do in them.

2. The Contextual/Intertextual Realm

Despite the illusion of closure, stories are necessarily interrelated with aspects outside their control. They contain multiple references and traces of other stories by many different authors, and they are interpreted from multiple points of view in different contexts.

The terms—contextual and intertextual—designate a realm of narrative where meanings cross boundaries between the story and sites outside them. Instead of bringing closure, the contextual/intertextual realm opens a story to multiple readings, references, associations, and constellations of stories. The control of meaning shifts from the intentions of the author to the role of the readers within particular cultural contexts.

Context

There are both intentional relationships between the story realm and its context, and unintentional ones that influence meaning.

A story simultaneously carves out a specific realm of events as well as the context for those events—the events of The Odyssey plot a map of the Mediterranean, Faulkner's stories construct the imaginary geography of Yoknapatawpha County, Mississippi. Thus, the context, like the other aspects of narrativity, is actually integral to the structuring of meaning inside the story, and conversely, the story reveals much about the context. The relationships between story and context are strongest in realistic novels of the 19th-century. In this genre the story is a "natural" outgrowth of the circumstances and milieu of the time and place. As causes are linked to environment, they reflect the prevailing ideology of environmental influence and determinism of the 19th century.

Villa Lante creates its own context of the golden age of the park, acting as foil for the linear narrative framed within the wall of the formal garden. However, since it is built on land once belonging to the Commune of Bagnaia, a name that referred to the ancient baths in the vicinity, the park become linked to the history of the town. The act of restoring the aqueduct, bringing water to the garden and the town, not only called the Muses to the site but recalled the history of the locality (Lazzaro 1990, 243). Drawings of Villa Lante that show only the formal garden edit out a significant part of the story.[12] The Crosby Arboretum, on the other hand, is called a "regional garden" because the ecological relationships of the region it sits within become the content of the story.

In the various design ideologies of contextualism, regionalism, ecological design, historicism, etc., the story is about connecting to some larger frame of reference. In the English school of landscape gardening the illusion of the garden blending with the landscape is created by selectively framing views, hiding boundaries, and even changing the context to incorporate it into the narrative of the garden. The direction of development in contemporary contextualism is often from the outside in, starting with the broader patterns and then bringing them into and through the specific site.

The intelligence at work in contextualism is mimetic. The stepped edges of Fay Jones's Pinecote Pavilion imitate the effect of filtered light through the tree canopy. The forest of columns inside the pavilion are notched to link them with the segmented bark of the slash pines, the angles of the bracing just under the pavilion canopy correspond to the angles of the upper branches of the pines, and the brick floor blends with the red clay of the region exposed in the pathways (Johnson and Frankel, 185).[13] The dominant trope is metonymy. Story space and contextual space are contiguous, linked in a sequence or influenced by the same processes.

Synecdoches also help to connect sites with their context by bringing pieces, fragments, or miniaturized representations of the context into the space of the story. The regional garden of the Pinecote Center interprets in miniature the patterns and process found in eleven "dispersed sites" throughout the Pearl River Basin. As mentioned earlier, Henry Cowles found the dunes to be a natural microcosm of continental diversity where "species of the most diverse natural regions are piled together in such abundance as to make the region a natural botanical preserve" (Engel 1981, 6). The view of the dunes as microcosm was supported by geologists' descriptions of the four great elements (earth, water, fire, air) shaping the dunes, geographers noting the region as the epicenter of the continent, Jensen describing the plant associations as botanical melting pot (Engel 1981, 6), and ornithologists studying the convergence of birds from all directions.

Context of this nature can be a very sophisticated blending of story realm and the world it is immersed in. It is important to recognize, however, that it is still a highly selective structuring of context in relation to story.

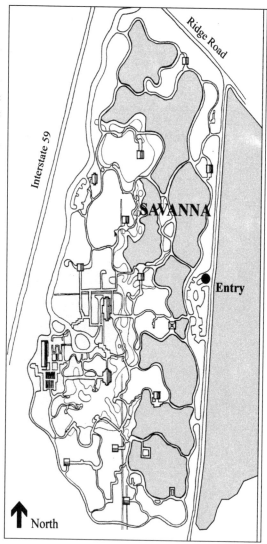

The savanna area within the Pinecote center reflects the landscape immediately adjacent to the entry. (Fritz, SUNY, ESF. Source: Crosby Arboretum Master Plan)

Intertext

"Every text is constructed as a mosaic of quotations, every text is absorption and transformation of another text"
(Julia Kristiva, cited by Ellin, 254)

Despite the ability of stories to create a sense of closure as well as to carefully position their meanings in relation to a context, stories are necessarily related to aspects outside their control. The devices used in a story to bring closure—metaphor, metonymy, etc.—also have the potential to open other associations, references, and codes beyond the intentions of the author. Metaphors have "entailments," extra connotations that come inadvertently with their usage.

In addition, multiple authorship of landscape narratives increases plurality and complexity of meaning. Who is the author of Villa Lante? The architect, the successive owners who made changes, or the Lante della Rovere family, who maintained it for almost three centuries and whose name we now attach to the place? Should Ovid get some credit? And how much attribution should go to the fountain engineer and the "iconographer"? How much can we trust the visitors to get all the references? Likewise, the Crosby Arboretum is shaped by the collective work of the designer, consultants, a board of directors (local, national, of different professions), the Crosby family, marketing consultants, and an implied public audience.

The difficulty of controlling meaning inside a story arises not only from inadvertent associations, multiple authors, or a lack of precision in the use of language but, as post-structuralists argue, from the very nature of language itself. Meaning as structured through language is relational, produced by differences between one thing and another, resulting in a constant deferral or slippage of meaning without a final "transcendental signifier" (such as nature).

To demonstrate the migrating, plural, textured quality of narrative, in *S/Z*, Barthes took a realistic novel by Balzac and fractured it into what he called "lexia," the smallest units of meaning. Proceeding one fragment at a time, he showed how each piece—sometimes one word, sometimes a paragraph—was intersected by codes, citations, and knowledge found outside the text. What he demonstrates is that not only is there a potentially limitless network of meaning beyond the work, but within the work itself there are gaps, silences, and an array of meanings that can disassemble the sense of unity of the work.

A story, then, is intertextual in two senses: 1) the layering of texts and references to other texts within the work itself that are considered relevant to its meaning and 2) the dissemination of meaning from the work across a network of other texts, contexts, genres, and forms (writing, speech, visual images, social behavior, landscape). These relationships are evident in Villa Lante, which is constructed from references not only to Ovid but to Pliny, Virgil's Georgics, other descriptions of a golden age, the historical events of the Counter-Reformation, and the narratives told in other gardens. Today its images are also dispersed through design and art texts as well as tourism. Likewise, the pattern of water features at the Crosby Arboretum is a collage of the straight lines of existing drainage ditches that became the source for the new curvilinear pond. Its ecological narratives are based on Cowles's work, other ecological texts, and Japanese and English design traditions. In addition, the narrative of restoration resonates across a global network of other restoration projects. In Mississippi, restoration also parallels a narrative of the emergence of "the New South," which aims to regain national economic and cultural significance with its own regional distinctiveness.

Reading the Landscape as an Intertextual Practice

In their article "[Re]reading the Landscape," geographers James and Nancy Duncan recognized the significance of the text and intertextual metaphors for reading the landscape. They note that this conception aptly describes the nature of landscapes, "because landscapes are usually anonymously authored: although they can be symbolic, they are not obviously referential, and they are highly intertextual creations of the reader, as much as they are the products of the society that originally constructed them" (Duncan and Duncan 1988, 119).

Yet, while agreeing that meaning is unstable, they criticize the notions that the interaction of texts is autonomous and that meanings can be freely construed by any individual reader. Such thinking leads to solipsism and the potentially dangerous position of extreme relativism where any story is as good as the next. Instead, the Duncans assert that while meaning *is* unstable and plural, it is not infinite, because texts also interact with social contexts that work to enable and constrain the range of interpretations (Duncan and Duncan 1988, 120).

The intertextual realm of dispersed and unstable meaning can then be grounded in specific social contexts where meaning is not only dispersed but also gathered. Social groups from a nation-state to a subculture form around shared stories as well as common interpretations of those stories. In fact, part of the strength of narratives lies in how extensively they become imbricated or woven into the fabric of a community.

The term *interpretive communities* designates the context of social practices in which narratives are interpreted and produced.[14] This concept maintains the plurality and fluidity of meaning but identifies limits to the endless play of signification. An interpretive community is a group of people who hold a shared reading/interpretation of a set of narratives. They share not only the stories but the interpretive frameworks that make them intelligible and tellable. Thus, they are familiar with a set of codes, genres, the structures of stories, the references, and the appropriate uses of the stories.

It is the interpretive community of the friends and society of Cardinal Gambara to which the garden story is addressed and who, as "learned men" familiar with a set of classic texts and competent in allegorical readings, could follow the complexities of the story. Gambara and his iconographer encoded messages for the reader who was equipped with the keys to unlock their meanings. The garden held narrative potential if the reader did the work to find the stories.[15]

The Crosby Arboretum faces the different problem of how to develop shared readings of the site when the concept of a garden or an arboretum for many is a ring of azaleas around a pond (Brzuszek). Visitors coming with such expectations are likely to miss complexities and larger ramifications of ecology. Henry Cowles and the community of social reformers, artists, the Prairie Club, Jens Jensen and others who shared an interpretation of the special nature of the Indiana Dunes faced a similar situation. One means of communicating their narrative of the Dunes to the larger public was through storytelling events; ritual pilgrimages to the dunes; poetry; novels; public speeches; painting; pageants; and masques, such as "The Spirit of the Dunes," staged in 1913 as part of the dedication of the Prairie Club's Beach House near Mount Tom. Jensen tried to develop popular support for a national park and considered the dunes overlooking the lake to be the ideal spot for the public ritual of story-telling around the fire of a council ring (Engel 1981, 201)

Landscape and Memory

Reading relies on remembering, and memory is an intertextual realm. It is dispersed among individuals, yet shared to create collective identities. Memories cut pathways and networks across time and are often anchored in place by association with events or explicit commemorative practices. The whole landscape can be woven into the texture of memory. Any element—a doorstep, a tree—may provide an opening into this realm. To alter landscapes often erases the locus of shared memory. As Robert Pogue Harrison cautions in *Forests: The Shadow of Civilization,* the destruction of the world's forests not only means the loss of habitat and biodiversity, but it obliterates a landscape of thousands of years of cultural myth and memory (xi).

The masque of "The Spirit of the Dunes," 1913, where Duna is hailed as Queen of the Dunes to help create a mythic geography of the dunes. This was part of the dedication ceremonies for the Prairie Club's Beach House on the dunes. Jens Jensen encouraged the production of similar events in his work with the Chicago park system to help communicate the narratives of nature to a larger community. (Courtesy Prairie Club Archives, West Chester Public Library)

Memory, or Mnemosyne, was one of the most important Muses, inspiring all the arts. Villa Lante clearly courts this Muse with all its explicit references from Western culture's collective memory of classical antiquity. It is part of a tradition of "emblematic" gardens that evoke very particular memories with sculpture, inscriptions, follies, etc. Most contemporary visitors, however, do not have the specific memory for reading these emblems. Instead of imposing specific readings, an "expressive garden" encourages more direct, immediate sensations and short-term memory. It is still narrative, however, with sequences of dark to light, closed to open, etc., which become metaphors of a Romantic notion of consciousness evolving through direct sensations of the world. This is the narrative implicit in much of the Crosby Arboretum.

But memory can also be evoked in contemporary culture through synecdoches of more regional or local contexts. The name Crosby, first of all, recalls the patronage of the family that shaped much of the area. Fay Jones's design for the Pinecote Pavilion also works much like a folly in an English garden. Like his other designs for chapels inspired by vernacular forms, it refers to an American vernacular religion whose setting was often camp meetings and groves. The woods alone are a rich intertextual realm of memories. Carol Franklin, one of the designers of the Crosby Arboretum, notes that all of the design components came together once the designers made the associations with the "Piney Woods"—a landscape with a thick, variable stock of stories and local memory specific to southern Mississippi and Louisiana.[16]

Opening the Text

To some degree all stories are open to various readings. Umberto Eco notes that every text, is "a lazy machine" asking the reader to do some of the work:

In building a world that comprises myriad events and characters, it [a text] cannot say everything about this world. It hints at it and then asks the reader to fill in a whole series of gaps...What a problem it would be if a text were to say everything the receiver is to understand—it would never end.

(Eco 1994, 3)

Meaning depends on the readers' particular frames of reference, their familiarity with a set of stories, the degree of focus on those stories, and the practices used to interpret them.

Another way to open the realm of intertextual relationships is to stimulate a diversity of associations rather than attempt to control one specific reading. In one of his earlier books, Eco identified the "open work" as a particular interest of contemporary writers and artists. According to Eco, the open work encourages the participation and creativity of the reader.[17] A work is opened through strategies of ambiguity, disjunction, and multiple points of view. Eco notes that the enduring interest in the Bible is due in part to the disjointedness among its authors. This creates complexities for constant interpretation and exegesis (Eco 1994, 128). The Crosby Arboretum uses the indeterminacy of ecological processes to create an open narrative that develops over time.

The Piney Woods of Mississippi and Louisiana, early 1900s, Great Southern Lumber Company. (Photograph by Sidney Steator; courtesy Forest History Society, Durham, North Carolina)

Significance

In the intertextual realm we can track how narratives can be discovered and recovered in a variety of forms and practices outside the discrete frames of a story. Locating the intertextual realm within social practices enables one to see both the multiplicity of meaning as well as how narratives become a constitutive part of the very texture of landscapes and experience. It is connective and integral. In the realm of the intertextual, readers make stories their own, through experience, interpretation, memory, and landscape.

It is important for designers to understand these relationships. First, recognizing that the reader actively produces a given narrative avoids a naive approach to symbolism. Designers often create an elaborate iconography—"the narrow passageway is the 'artery' of the body."—without a sense of how such references might be read by an individual or a community. Second, designers can begin to engage the process of landscape narrative as connected to social practices. This means discovering the existing social frameworks of intelligibility and looking at the landscape as interwoven with a set of narratives dispersed throughout a community.

3. The Discourse Realm

In August 1579 Pope Gregory XIII canceled the annual pension of Cardinal Gambara (Coffin 1979, 340). The following year the powerful Cardinal Carlo Borromeo visited Gambara's villa and reprimanded Gambara for the money he had sunk into making a garden instead of helping "those poor Hungarian, Bohemian and Flemish Catholics, wickedly driven out of their houses by the enemies of the Holy Church" (Adorni, 95). At issue was not only money, but the differences between a humanist's narrative of nature and history, and that of the Counter-Reformation. The contention over this garden points to the significance of landscape narratives as a discursive realm for negotiating and structuring values, beliefs, and ideologies.

A discourse is a "social framework of intelligibility" that influences all practices of signification, including narrative and landscape (Duncan 1990, 16). Discourses are found and produced within social institutions such as law, medicine, economics, art, biology, the family, the church, the office, the nation, and so on. Within these frameworks, discursive practices generate and invent relationships as well as impose conventional restraints on meaning.[18] But as Duncan emphasizes, discourses are not rigid, deterministic frames, but fields where ideas are "communicated, negotiated or challenged" (Duncan 1990, 16).

Discourse, in this sense, is more than the moral of a story. Attention to discourse focuses on the uses of stories, the purposes to which they are put, and the institutions and the worldviews they create and sustain. Since narratives help to establish systems of belief and authority, they reproduce relationships of power in a society. Often dominant groups tell their story in the landscape, controlling interpretations as well as preventing others from making history (Parker, 20).

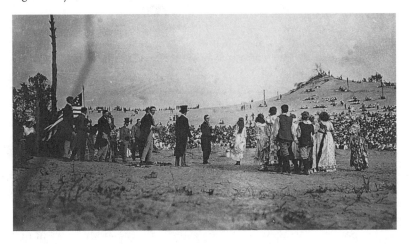

The Historical Pageant of the Indiana Dunes, May 1917. The pageant was staged as part of the campaign to generate support for purchase of the dunes as a national park. Thousands came to an amphitheater created by a blowout in the dunes to witness what was hailed at the time as the largest outdoor drama in American history. It retold history from Native American creation stories to explorers and the new episode of democracy that the creation of a park would represent. In this narrative the place is the hero, and the development of the community is the plot (Engel 1983, 11–42). (Photograph by Arthur E. Anderson, collection of James C. Fisher; courtesy Calument Regional Archives, Indiana University Northwest)

THE DISCURSIVE SPACE OF THE INDIANA DUNES
Like the Renaissance garden, the Indiana Dunes are a discursive space that focuses contesting ideologies of nature, culture, identity, and history. From the first proposals to preserve the dunes by Jensen and then by Stephen Mather (a Chicago native and the first director of the National Park Service) to the 1960s and the present, the narratives of this nature fuse with certain social narratives. Jenson noted that "trees are much like human beings and enjoy each other's company." But it was Cowles who established the metaphoric link between ecology and society by naming plant associations as communities.[19] Further, his

science documented a near epic struggle as these communities moved toward greater diversity, creativity, and abundance through collective, nonhierarchical, and reciprocal relationships. Jensen extended the implications of these "inherent" qualities by asking: "And is not this the true spirit of democracy?" (Engel 1981, 7).

Jane Adams, Thomas Allison, and other leaders of Chicago's social reform movements made the link, as well, between plant communities and a vision of social democracy. The residents of the dozens of "settlement houses" not only established the first public playgrounds and other social programs, but they also sponsored ritual hikes to the dunes and led preservation efforts. The connections were even metonymic. Allison's settlement house stood where, he said, a sand mountain once existed. He referred to it as a piece of "Dune Country" in the city, and the dunes, in turn, as a "settlement house" in the country (Engel 1983, 115). These connections were also evident in the architecture, literature, and art of the "Chicago Renaissance," which exsposued an ideology of regionalism. Its proponents stressed, as Engel describes, the contextual connection between the "democratic community of artists building a civilization in continuity with, and in response to, the democratic community of natural artistic processes of the native landscape" (1981, 9). These uses of nature as a democratic metaphor countered social Darwinists' laissez-faire attitude toward competitive survival, and contrasted with the exclusionary use of "native" and "exotic" metaphors adopted by National Socialists in Germany in the 1930s (Groening and Wolschke-Bulmahn).

Hikers on their way to the top of Mount Tom, the highest dune. 1915. (Collection of James C. Fisher; courtesy Calumet Regional Archives, Indiana University Northwest)

Organizers of settlement houses, the Prairie Club, and others made regular pilgrimages to the dunes and spoke of them in sacred terms, as a limnal space and a microcosm of natural order. Mount Tom, the highest dune in the area, became the center of this special realm, an *axis mundi*. An early president of the National Dunes Park Association said, "Here is the center, all things considered" (Engel 1983, 110).

The example of the dunes illustrates how discourses interrelate. The metaphors and analogies from one discourse, such as the metaphor of community, are available for other discourses. Nature in particular is consistently constituted within religious discourse. As J. Ronald Engel describes the dunes' ecological creation story in *Sacred Sands*, the sense of timelessness, their reflection of the macrocosm, and other qualities described scientifically were closely interrelated with the discourse of a civic religion that saw the dunes as a sacred space. As mentioned, a similar connection between religion and nature is suggested by Fay Jones's Pinecote Pavilion at the Crosby Arboretum.

Naturalizing Discourse

There is a tendency to consider the examples above as ideological distortions of facts or the result of not enough information. But facts do not speak for themselves. It is how they are put together and used within discourses that they gain their authority and status as facts (White 1978, 125). And metaphor and narrative are a necessary part of these discursive practices.

These practices are difficult to apprehend, however, because they are effectively embedded in the ordinary, the commonplace, and the very means of telling a story, from selecting metaphors to structuring time. It is below this horizon of critical awareness that ideologies become "naturalized." As Eagleton states: "It is one of the functions of ideology to 'naturalize' social reality, to make it seem as innocent and unchangeable as Nature itself" (Eagleton, 135). In their study of the town of Bedford, an affluent residential suburb of New York, geographers James and Nancy Duncan demonstrate how discourses of nature and history naturalize the social practices that maintain the community. The town historical society asks people to celebrate history as part of their heritage. But this linking of the past to heritage invokes the discourse of biology, of breeding. Here the cultural is transformed into the natural and vice versa. (Duncan and Duncan, forthcoming).

In a sense, instead of the landscape functioning as a locus of memory, it can also be a site of "cultural amnesia." The landscape is replete with "dead metaphors" sites where the original conjunction of meaning is taken-for-natural. The metaphors and values of a pastoral landscape, for instance, reproduced in lawn, park, suburb, and campus have become totally naturalized.

Denaturalizing Discourse

Occasionally a discursive space is opened during critical moments of change and controversy, as in the repeated battles over preservation and development of the dunes. However, conflict can also reinforce and polarize ideological positions without involving a critical examination of the conditions they derive from.

Because landscapes materialize beliefs, yet become so taken-forgranted, denaturalizing is an important and critical act (Duncan and Duncan 1988, 125). There are several strategies for opening the discursive space of narrative. One need only to locate discourses in history and place to show that they emerge and change in relation to changes in societies. Donald Worster in *Nature's Economy: A History of Ecological Ideas,* for instance, describes the changing discourse of ecology from community and organic metaphors to metaphors derived from physics, economics, and mathematics. Each of these discourses has different implications for actions.

Another method is to examine how a narrative is used, who uses it and why, who benefits from its use, and what authority and institutions are reinforced or subverted by its use. What appears convincing and natural in dominant discourses can be challenged by alternative readings. Irony, in particular, is an effective trope for unmasking and denaturalizing. Deconstruction is a more radical form of denaturalizing that seizes an inevitable point of contradiction within a work and then works this point of contradiction through to dismantle the whole. While effective, the endless interrogation, subversion, and play of differences become an untenable position for critique. Deconstruction also has its own narratives and embedded ideologies.

The Discourses of Ecological Design
at the Crosby Arboretum

In both the interpretation and the design of the arboretum, the discourse of ecology is primary, including the metaphor of plant communities. Carol Franklin, a principal with Andropogon Associates, the landscape design consulting company for the project, in effect paraphrases Jensen: "Plants, like people, live and develop as communities with characteristic companions" (Franklin, 271). She eschews conventional, formalist design as arbitrary, capricious, and inconsequential (273). Instead, all the design interventions—the extensive "native" plantings, controlled burning of the savanna, and accelerated processes—are authorized within an ecological discourse. The most dramatic intervention, the creation of the pond, was cast not as arbitrary, but as something that could have occurred ecologically or historically. The water level of the pond is regulated by a small dam that simulates the water fluctuation created by a beaver dam (Johnson and Frankel, 179). Ecology also serves a discourse of scientific management that judges decisions according to "energy inputs" (mowing grass is inefficient) and functional relationships. But unlike engineering, ecological design has an aesthetic ideology as well. Here again, aesthetics are not considered cultural conventions imposed on the site, but coevolve with the site's ecology: "Grass and sedge meadows occupy ephemeral shallows bordering deep water with adjacent woodlands maturing as an arched canopy mirrored in black water" (*Pinecote Master Plan*, 9).

The religion, history, social class, and ethnicity of residents of Picayune, Mississippi, produce their own discourses on nature that in various ways may contrast, overlap, compliment, and conflict with the nature of the arboretum.

The environmentalist's narrative of crisis, however, creates the imperative for ecological design. As Carol Franklin describes their mission: "We don't have time to debate about styles, about fashions. They are irrelevant to the survival of the diversity of life on our planet... Passion should come first in putting systems back together, reconnecting us spiritually and functionally to the earth" (Johnson and Frankel, 181).

As this quote indicates, the ecological narrative of the site is also an allegory, a means for telling other morally charged stories of restoration, the emergence of a New South, and the continuity of enlightened paternalistic control of the land. It is also important to ask whose stories these are and whose ecology is represented here. The difference between nature as presented inside the arboretum and that of many of the local residents of Picayune is probably as pronounced as that between the Humanist cardinal of Villa Lante and the leaders of the Counter-Reformation. The educational mission of the arboretum is largely about changing the commonly held discourses through an ecological [re]reading and design of nature.

Finally, the nature of a discourse is understood by the comparisons it makes to differentiate it from other discourses. Ecological design, as following natural order, is often contrasted with highly geometric and, therefore, artificial or arbitrary designs. Renaissance gardens such as Villa Lante are posed in opposition to ecological design. From an ecological point of view they represent the "domination of man over nature." However, it was not until the 20th century that Italian Renaissance gardens were described in this gendered term. Lazzaro found that in the 16th-century discourse of gardens, instead of domination, power, and conquest, the relationship was seen as a reciprocal one between nature and art. Nature was emphatically identified

with the feminine and repeatedly paired with art. The principal act of the artist or garden designer was not subduing but revealing the order inherent in nature—similar to the objective at the arboretum (Lazzaro 1991, 71–113).

The discursive issues raised by the Crosby Arboretum exemplify a more pervasive issue for the designer engaged in making places. On the one hand, narratives structure the values people live by. On the other hand, their strength lies in their fictions. As Hayden White argues, this situation is unavoidable since tropes and narratives constitute the way we understand and explain the world. It is an ironic position.

However, it is also an important critical position. An understanding of the role of discourses within narratives enables one to identify the positions from which a story is told, examine the values that inhere in the telling, and constantly test how different positions interrelate, compete with, or compliment one another in the shaping of the landscape and culture.

A CONCLUSION AND A POINT OF DEPARTURE

This chapter does not cut a straight path through the woods of narrative theory or establish a singular method for its application. As Robert Scholes writes, the role of theory is "not to lay down laws but to force us to be aware of what we are doing and why we are doing it" (Scholes, 88). Therefore it is important to name the multiple realms of landscape narratives, track their interrelationships, and understand how we engage them. The power of the story realm lies in the devices that create a coherent sense of closure, an ordering of event, time, and place created and controlled by the intent of the designer. The vector of meaning created by the alliance of designer and reader is centripetal, inward toward determined meanings. Yet, that inner world is necessarily related to and draws its meaning from worlds outside of the story. A narrative is brought to life and proliferates in the multiple and "real" contexts of its readers. A web of relationships working centrifugally outward from a narrative creates interpretive communities, and the landscape provides multiple openings for stories and memories. By definition, landscapes and narratives are intertextual creations. Finally, the discourses inscribed in both the story and its contexts reveal the necessary fictions for creating and maintaining social worlds. Discourse requires critical understanding of the positions from which a story is told, as well as constant testing of the metaphors and tropes used to construct that reality against other descriptions of the world. This is an initial framework for understanding the implications and potentials of the stories we tell and the landscapes we make.

Fay Jones's design for the Pinecote Pavilion.

1. This play on terms derives from James S. Duncan's "Me(trope)olis: or Hayden White Among the Urbanists," in A. King, ed., *Representing the City* (New York: Macmillan, 1995).

2. Theorists differ on the relationships between these tropes. For instance, Terence Hawkes identifies metaphor as the fundamental trope of figurative language that transfers meaning from one object to another. In this system simile, synecdoche, and metonymy are categories of metaphor. Others make increasingly fine distinctions that begin to be overly reductive. Our aim is simply introductory.

3. In the Athens airport, the conveyor belt at the baggage claim area is called a *metaphorae.*

4. This temporal metaphor is constructed through the use of synecdoches.

5. This metaphor is established through a metonymic relationship of placement of one thing next to another.

6. Senecah refers to the Blue Line as a metaphor, using *metaphor* as a general and inclusive term, rather than making the distinction between metaphor and metonymy.

7. In Griemas's model the term *actant* avoids the confusion between human actors and functions in a narrative that are played out not only by human actors, but also animals, things, forces, etc. Further, different actants can be represented by one actor.

8. Our distinction differs from many narrative theories that pose a knowable chronology against what is told. Instead, chronology cannot be separated from the telling, because it is the telling that creates, names, and structures events. Any single named event can be broken down into a series of other actions, and there is an infinite number of possibilities between any two events.

9. According to one conception of the hydrologic cycle in the Renaissance, water returned to mountains via underground passages. See Yi Fu Tuan, *The Hydrologic Cycle and the Wisdom of God: A Theme in Geoteleology* (Toronto: University of Toronto Press, 1968), pp. 50–53.

10. We are applying, here, Hayden White's characterization of historical discourse. Historical accounts evoke the authority of reality while at the same time endowing it with "the formal coherency that only stories possess...they give to reality the odor of the ideal. This is why the plot of a historical narrative is always an embarrassment and has to be presented as 'found' in the events rather than put there by narrative techniques" (White 1987, 20–21).

11. The grid acts much like what is referred to as a *focalization* in a narrative, the perceptual position from which events are rendered. Thus, events in a story may be seen focused through one character's perception, or through the omniscient gaze of the author (Gerald Prince, 31–32).

12. The context of the park is often edited out of representations of Villa Lante, including Geofrey Jellicoe's water color and Norman Newton's depiction of the garden. From Gary Hilderbrand "Modes and Motivations of Travel," lecture, State University of New York, Syracuse, February 1993.

13. The clay-fired bricks over a bed of sand at the pavilion also mimic the soil structure of the site. Above a layer of sand, there is a layer of clay that is responsible for the perched water table across the entire site.

14. This term is a variation on Brian Stock's *textual community* (Stock 1986).

15. Until recently the major history textbooks in landscape architecture, such as Newton's *Design on the Land* did not explicate the narrative aspects of Villa Lante, concentrating instead on its formal spatial qualities.

16. The first series of lectures of the "Crosby Memorial Lectures in Mississippi Culture" (1985) explores various aspects of the Piney Woods: pioneer culture, the various ethnic groups who identify the woods as home territory, black labor in the forest industries, the folk life of "Sacred Harp" singing, the novelists who told its stories, and the natural history of the vegetation. These essays are collected in *Mississippi's Piney Woods: A Human Perspective*, ed. Noel Polk (Jackson: University Press of Missippi, 1986).

17. Barthes calls the type of text that invites the reader to rework it or write it over again a "writerly text." A text that controls the reading he refers to as a "readerly text" (Barthes 1974, 4).

18. This use of *discourse* as a framework of intelligibility, linked to ideology, differs from the use of the word to describe the presentation of an orderly argument (Descartes' *Discourse on Method*) or any verbal exchange—although these uses do suggest the structuring of ideas or values through a dialogic process. In narratology *discourse* is also used as another term for narration, or how a story is told.

19. Cowles often employed the language of historical epic where plant societies are subject to great natural forces: "The slightest change in the physical conditions is often sufficient to bring about the destruction of a coniferous society...Fig. 22 shows a plant society that is being destroyed mainly by gravity" (Cowles, 375–377).

REFERENCES

Adorni, Brunao. 1991. "The Villa Lante at Bagnaia." In *The Architecture of Western Gardens: A Design History from the Renaissance to the Present Day*, ed. Monique Mosser and Georges Teyssot. Cambridge: MIT Press, 91–95.

Aristotle's Poetics. 1961. Trans. S. H. Butcher. New York: Hill and Wang.

Bakhtin, Mikhail. 1981. *The Dialogic Imagination: Four Essays by M. M. Bakhtin*, ed. Michael Holquist, trans. Caryl Emerson and Michael Holquist. Austin: University of Texas Press.

Barnes, Trevor J. and James S. Duncan, ed. 1992. *Writing Worlds: Discourse, Text and Metaphor in the Representation of Landscape*. New York: Routledge.

Barthes, Roland. 1974. *S/Z*, trans. Richard Miller. New York: Hill and Wang.

———. 1977. *Image Music Text*, trans. Stephen Heath. New York: Hill and Wang.

Blake, Edward L., Jr. (designer in collaboration with Andropogon Associates and former director, The Crosby Arboretum). 1996. Interview, March 25.

Brzuszek, Robert (curator of Pinecote, Crosby Arboretum). 1996. Interview, March 25.

Carruthers, Mary. 1990. *The Book of Memory: A Study of Memory in Medieval Culture*. Cambridge: Cambridge University Press.

Chatman, Seymour. 1978. *Story and Discourse*. Ithaca, N.Y.: Cornell University Press.

Coffin, David. 1979. *The Villa in the Life of Renaissance Rome*. Princeton, N.J.: Princeton University Press.

Cohan, Steven, and Linda Shires. 1988. *Telling Stories: A Theoretical Analysis of Narrative Fiction*. New York: Routledge.

Cowles, Henry Chandler. 1989. "The Ecological Relations of the Vegetation on the Sand Dunes of Lake Michigan." *Bontanical Gazette* (February): 95-117; (March): 167–202; (April): 281–308; (May): 361–391.

"Crosby Arboretum." 1991. *Landscape Architecture* 81(11):55.

Crosby Arboretum. 1990. *Pinecote Master Plan*.

De Certeau, Michel. 1984. *The Practice of Everyday Life*, trans. Steven Rendall. Berkeley: University of California Press.

Duncan, James S. 1990. *The City as Text: The Politics of Landscape Interpretation in the Kandyan Kingdom*. Cambridge: Cambridge University Press.

———. Forthcoming. "Deep Suburban Irony: The Perils of Democracy in Westchester County, New York." In *Visions of Suburbia*, ed. R. Silverstone. New York: Routledge.

Duncan, James S., and Nancy G. Duncan. 1988. "[Re]Reading the Landscape." *Environment and Planning D: Society and Space* 6:117–126.

Eagleton, Terry. 1983. *Literary Theory: An Introduction*. Minneapolis: University of Minnesota Press.

Eco, Umberto. 1989. *The Open Work.* Cambridge: Harvard University Press.

———. 1992. *Interpretation and Overinterpretation.* Cambridge: Cambridge University Press.

———. 1994. *Six Walks in the Fictional Woods.* Cambridge: Harvard University Press.

Ellin, Nan. 1996. *Postmodern Urbanism.* Cambridge, Mass.: Blackwell Publishers, Inc.

Engel, J. Ronald. 1981. "Sacred Sands: The Civil Religion of the Indiana Dunes." *Landscape* 25(1):1–10.

———. 1983. *Sacred Sands: The Struggle for Community in the Indiana Dunes.* Middletown, Conn.: Wesleyan University Press.

Evernden, Neil. 1992. *The Social Creation of Nature.* Baltimore: Johns Hopkins University Press.

Fergusson, Francis. 1961. "Introduction." In *Aristotle's Poetics,* trans. S. H. Butcher. New York: Hill and Wang. Pp. 1–25.

Forster, E. M. 1927. *Aspects of the Novel.* New York: Harcourt, Brace and World.

Franklin, Carol. 1997. "Fostering Living Landscapes." In *Ecological Design and Planning,* ed. George F. Thompson and Frederick R. Steiner. New York: John Wiley & Sons. Pp. 263–287.

Freeman, Judi. 1993. *Mark Tansey.* Los Angeles: Los Angeles County Museum of Art.

Gibbs, Raymond W. Jr. 1994. *The Poetics of Mind: Figurative Thought, Language, and Understanding.* Cambridge: Cambridge University Press.

Glacken, Clarence. 1967. *Traces on the Rhodian Shore: Nature and Culture in Western Thought from Ancient Times to the End of the Eighteenth Century.* Berkeley: University of California Press.

Greimas, Alan J. 1987. *On Meaning: Selected Writings in Semiotic Theory,* trans. Paul J. Perron and Franck H. Collins. Minneapolis: University of Minnesota Press.

Groening, Gert, and Joachim Wolschke-Bulmahn. 1992. "Some Notes on the Mania for Native Plants in Germany." *Landscape Journal* 11(2):116–125.

Harrison, Robert Pogue. 1992. *Forests: The Shadow of Civilization.* Chicago: University of Chicago Press.

Hawkes, Terence. 1972. *Metaphor.* New York: Routledge.

Hayles, N. Katherine. 1995. "Searching for Common Ground." In *Reinventing Nature? Responses to Postmodern Deconstruction,* ed. Michael E. Soule and Gary Lease. Washington, D.C.: Island Press.

Holquist, Michael. 1981. "Introduction." In *The Dialogic Imagination: Four Essays by M. M. Bakhtin,* ed. Michael Holquist, trans. Caryl Emerson and Michael Holquist. Austin: University of Texas Press. Pp. xv–xxxiii.

Hufford, Mary. 1986. *One Space, Many Places: Folklife and Land Use in New Jersey's Pinelands National Reserve.* Washington, D.C.: American Folklife Center, Library of Congress.

———. 1992. *Chaseworld: Foxhunting and Storytelling in New Jersey's Pine Barrens*. Philadelphia: University of Pennsylvania Press.

Hunt, John Dixon, and Peter Willis. 1988. *The Genius of the Place: The English Landscape Garden, 1620–1820*. Cambridge: MIT Press.

Johnson, Jory, and Felice Frankel. 1991. *Modern Landscape Architecture: Redefining the Garden*. New York: Abbeville Press.

Lazzaro, Claudia. 1990. *The Italian Renaissance Garden*. New Haven, Conn.: Yale University Press.

———. 1991. "The Visual Language of Gender in Sixteenth-Century Garden Sculpture." In *Refiguring Woman: Gender Issues in the Italian Renaissance*, ed. Marilyn Migiel and Juliana Schiesari. Ithaca, N.Y.: Cornell University Press. Pp. 71–113.

Martin, Wallace. 1986. *Recent Theories of Narrative*. Ithaca, N.Y.: Cornell University Press.

Mellard, James M. 1987. *Doing Tropology: Analysis of Narrative Discourse*. Urbana: University of Illinois Press.

Mitchell, W. J. T., ed. 1981. *On Narrative*. Chicago: University of Chicago Press.

Ovid. 1986. *Metamorphoses*, trans. A. D. Melville. Oxford: Oxford University Press.

Parker, Ian. 1992. *Discourse Dynamics: Critical Analysis for Social and Individual Psychology*. New York: Routledge.

Pinecote Master Plan: A Guide for Long Range Development. 1994. Picayune, Miss.: The Crosby Arboretum.

Platt, Rutherford H. 1972. *The Open Space Decision Process: Spatial Allocation of Costs and Benefits*. Chicago: University of Chicago, Department of Geography. Research Paper no. 142.

Polk, Noel, ed. 1986. *Mississippi Piney Woods: A Human Perspective*. Jackson: University Press of Mississippi.

Polkinghorne, Donald E. 1988. *Narrative Knowing and the Human Sciences*. Albany: State University of New York.

Prince, David. 1997. "Every Picture Tells a Story: Don't It?" Exhibit description, Syracuse University Art Collections.

Prince, Gerald. 1987. *A Dictionary of Narratology*. Lincoln: University of Nebraska Press.

Propp, Vladimir. [1928] 1968. *Morphology of the Folktale*, trans. L. Scott, rev. Louis A. Wagner. Austin: University of Texas Press.

Rainey, Rueben. 1981. "The Garden as Myth: The Villa Lante at Bagnaia." *Union Theological Seminary Review* 37(1–2):91–114.

Roskill, Mark. 1997. *The Languages of Landscape*. University Park: Pennsylvania State University Press.

Ryan, Marie-Laure. 1991. *Possible Worlds, Artificial Intelligence, and Narrative Theory*. Bloomington: Indiana University Press.

Sartiliot, Claudette. 1993. *Herbarium Verbarium: The Discourse of Flowers.* Lincoln: The University of Nebraska Press.

Schama, Simon. 1995. *Landscape and Memory.* New York: Knopf.

Schjetnan, Mario (principal, Grupo de Dese-o Urbano). 1996. Interview, March 27.

Scholes, Robert. 1989. *Protocols of Reading.* New Haven, Conn.: Yale University Press.

Senecah, Susan. 1996. "Forever Wild or Forever in Battle: Metaphors of Empowerment in the Continuing Controversy over the Adirondacks." In *Earthtalk: Communication Empowerment for Environmental Action,* ed. Star A. Muir and Thomas L. Veenendall. New York: Praeger. Pp. 95–118.

Simpson, Buster. 1995. In *Sculpting with the Environment—A Natural Dialogue,* ed. Baile Oakes. New York: Van Nostrand Reinhold. Pp. 120–125.

Sorvig, Kim. 1990. "The Magical-Realist Landscape." In *The Avant-Garde and the Landscape: Can They Be Reconciled,* ed. Patrick M. Condon and Lance Neckar. Minneapolis, Minn.: Landworks Press. Pp. 189–206.

Stock, Brian. 1986. "Texts, Readers, and Enacted Narratives." *Visible Language* 23 (summer):294–301.

———. 1990. *Listening for the Text: On the Uses of the Past.* Baltimore: Johns Hopkins University Press.

———. 1993. "Reading, Community and a Sense of Place." In *Place/Culture/Representation,* ed. James Duncan and David Ley. New York: Routledge. Pp. 314–325.

Thompson, J. William. 1994. "Aztec Revival." In *Landscape Architecture* 84(4):61–65.

Todorov, Tzvetan. 1984. *Mikhail Bakhtin: The Dialogical Principle,* trans. Wlad Godzich. Minneapolis: University of Minnesota Press.

Warnke, Martin. 1995. *Political Landscape: The Art History of Nature.* Cambridge: Harvard University Press.

White, Hayden. 1978. *Tropics of Discourse: Essays in Cultural Criticism.* Baltimore: Johns Hopkins University Press.

———. 1987. *The Content of the Form: Narrative Discourse and Historical Representation.* Baltimore: Johns Hopkins University Press.

Worster, Donald. 1977. *Nature's Economy: A History of Ecological Ideas.* Cambridge: Cambridge University Press.

Young, Katherine Galloway. 1987. *Taleworlds and Storyrealms: The Phenomenology of Narrative.* Dordrecht, Netherlands: Martinus Nijhoff.

PRACTICES

In part two we extend narrative theory into the practices of designing place and story. Take, for instance, the idea that each reader enlivens a text with his or her own experiences and understandings and that the meaning of text is therefore multiple and fluid. This concept is realized in the street that becomes the shared creation of an entire neighborhood or in the design of a park intentionally left unfinished so that those who use it engage in the perpetual reshaping of its form.

We chose the notion of *practices* because it reaches beyond the working processes of design to include cultural practices of daily life, rituals, and interpretation. The five chapters in part two, *Naming, Sequencing, Revealing and Concealing, Gathering,* and *Opening,* were selected from a larger group of practices (including recycling, referencing, inscribing, and registering) as the most fundamental to narrative. Each chapter goes back and forth between looking at the designed landscape and the vernacular landscape because designers will better understand how every site has its own stories by understanding how narrative practices inhere in the ordinary landscapes. Every practice is also a literal means of physically communicating narrative as well as a metaphor for narrative. *Gathering,* for instance, is both the literal pulling together of parts as well as the joining of collective memory and social ideals. It is fundamental to narrative because stories *gather* time, event, and place.

We begin with the simplest way that stories are anchored to place—na*ming.* Names are abbreviated stories of discovery, biography, and identity. *Sequencing,* the ordering of names, trees, paths, and other elements, events, and characters, structures meaning, for every part is understood in terms of what comes before and what follows. *Concealing and revealing* information, whether in a decipherable sequence or all at once, creates drama, suspense, or surprise that engages the reader with a story. Narratives are also a way of *gathering* or drawing together broader experience into a tangible and cohesive place. Finally, *opening* involves ways of creating places responsive to cultural and natural processes.

All of these practices cross and intersect; some of the richest and most complex work engages many practices at once. These five chapters articulate and define ways of making landscape narrative. They also intend to inspire new practices for telling landscape stories.

CHAPTER THREE
NAMING

TO name something is as much a creative act as giving it form is. The act of giving a name to a newborn child bestows an identity; it is an attempt to illuminate an essence that has yet to develop. Rarely a description of what is, the name creates a continuity with the past, the family line, or cultural memory while projecting future hopes and aspirations of who the individual will become. Naming both situates things within narratives and marks the beginnings of narratives.

Naming is also an act of possession and a desire to fix the unpredictability and indeterminacy of a child's life within a system of cultural values. The name borne by a body, the proper name, also implies a proper place

Children's names scrawled on a wall in Boston's North End.

within the social life of a community. The names of Puritan children, for instance, read like explicit moral injunctions: "Roger Clapp's children were named Experience, Waitstill, Preserved, Hopestill, Wait, Thanks, Desire, Unite and Supply" (Ragussis, 7).[1] However, a name is rarely a fixed and transparent icon of character. There is constant tension between the name and the referent it is attached to—the body, life, will, and identity of the individual. Unlike an object or a platonic ideal, the child's nature is unpredictable, willful, and often resistant to the identity willed by the parents.

Naming raises questions of identity that generate the plots of stories. In *Acts of Naming*, Michael Ragussis analyzes how actions in novels resolve around the search for true identity or the recovery of a name. For example, in *Tess of the D'Urbervilles*, Thomas Hardy reverses the standard plot of searching for a true family name. In the beginning of the novel, Tess discovers that the true noble origins of her family were purchased as a title by an impostor. It is the deception of names and the attempt to sacrifice first to the name of the family and then to that of her love that have tragic consequences. In *The Last of the Mohicans*, Nathaniel (Natty) Bumpo goes through a series of name changes, Straight-Tongue, Pigeon, Lapear, Deerslayer, and Hawkeye, earning each one through deeds and actions. In this sequence of multiple names, Cooper outlines an American naming plot where identity is achieved in a landscape of freedom in the New World, as opposed to the fixed inherited identity of the Old World. The earned name, considered a natural name, arises out of the primacy of experience, as opposed to the artifice of tradition (Ragussis, 231).

Glass towers of the Boston Holocaust Memorial etched with the numbers of over six million individuals whose names were taken away. (Photograph by Richard Purinton)

In life as well as fiction, names are caught up in the plots of family narratives, local identity, national history, and gender roles. People may go through many name identities, acquiring names in one context and changing them in another—nicknames, childhood names, professional names, stereotypes, married names, hyphenated names, epitaphs, and so on. People try to live up to a name, make a name for themselves, or achieve their desires by means of a pseudonym. While a name serves as a stable sign of identity, there is always the potential for new association, change, loss, disruption, and deception of names. In the process a name becomes a rich multivalent sign, bearing the trace of original aspirations, as well as the history of its use and acquired associations. "That we find ourselves when we find our name and lose ourselves when we lose our names, that we can control another by knowing their name and escape by hiding our names is part of the mythology of Western culture" (Ragussis, 218).

NAMES AS MEMORIAL

The five glass towers of the Boston Holocaust Memorial are etched with over six million numbers, marking the attempt to erase the identity of a people by erasing their names. Names were central to Hitler's plot of genocide. Beginning in the 1930s, a series of Nazi name decrees required Jews to adopt "Jewish-sounding" names, usually from the Old Testament, while true Aryans employed "native" German names. Certain popular names of Hebrew origin, such as David, Joachim, Anna, and Eva, were allowed because they had become "typically German" and in a sense naturalized. Working on the principle that a person's name belied his or her identity (racial, ethnic, sexual, national, familial), the name decrees began the process of singling the Jews, as well as foreigners, out from the masses of Germans with whom they shared language and space, a process that eventually led to the erasure of prisoners' names with tattooed numbers and the "final solution" (Rennick, 69). At one entrance to the Boston Holocaust Memorial a stone bears the Jewish name for this tragedy, "Shoah," which has both biblical and modern interpretations.[2]

Each of the 57,692 names inscribed on "the wall" of the Vietnam War Memorial evokes multiple memories and stories for those who in some way knew the named as a family member, friend, high school alum, or soldier. Instead of listing the names alphabetically, as the telephone directory does, the chronological list emphasizes the individuality of each name, each unique story of loss. The words of the prologue and epilogue inscribed at the ends of the V-shaped wall are no larger, nor more important, than any individual name. Collectively, the names of the Vietnam War Memorial give a name to a war that was never officially declared. This simple use of names as a memorial as opposed to more explicit symbolism or an allegory of a heroic war story set a precedent for other memorials.

Growing from one stitched cloth panel with the name of one victim of AIDS, the quilt of the NAMES project continues to expand panel by panel, name by name. Like the replica of the Vietnam War Memorial wall that travels to communities, the quilt has traveled from San Francisco to the Capitol

Mall to various gymnasiums, convention centers, and football fields throughout the country. The unfolding and display of the quilt is accompanied by the ritual reading of the names.

On the streets of the Lower East Side of New York, a series of memorial walls mark the "epidemic" of street violence that has increased since the late 1980s. The name of the victim is the center-piece on these walls, which are often near the place where the vic-tims lived, died, or hung out with their friends. And it is their friends who commission graffiti artists to do a memorial wall. Unlike sub-way graffiti, however, where the "tag name" of the artist is in the "wildstyle," memorial walls speak to the general public with the names in legible script (Cooper and Scioria, 39).

Whether the names are etched in granite, quilted in cloth, spray painted on a wall, or replaced by numbers etched on glass, these memorials demonstrate the power of names to evoke narratives. As words that acquire multiple stories, names resonate in ways sometimes more effectively than crafted eulogies or a single story line.

While the names serve as a locus of memory, the memorials give the names a tangible place. The walls of the Lower East Side often mark the spot or the street where someone actually lost his or her life, the Vietnam Memorial brings what was distant and foreign back home to the center, and the AIDS quilt can be unfolded in any city or neighborhood. The connec-tion between names, memory, and place is noted directly in the Boston Holocaust Memorial. The first gateway states the memorial's objective—to be "a place to give them an everlasting name."

NAMING PLACES: TOPONYMY

Naming is a fundamental strategy of making places, transforming undiffer-entiated, raw space, mass, objects, land, rocks, trees, and streets into known places. The "name cover"[3] of a map as a collection of signs is rarely direct-ly inscribed in the physical material of a landscape, nonetheless it is funda-mental to the making of places. Without altering a leaf, stone, street, or anything physical, to name a ragged coast New Hebrides, a fron-tier community in Indiana New Harmony, or a sandy hill in Australia's outback Mount Misery completely changes the semantic register of these places, fixing them within a system of values.

The named site also becomes a storied place. Each name inad-vertently carries the trace of its own inception (Eureka!), the story of how it got its name, legend, exploration, settlement history, anec-dote, or rumor. In 1700, Frenchmen heading up the Mississippi passed a boundary marker between two tribes, a red-stained pole they named Baton Rouge (Stewart, 137). Place names become abbre-viated narratives of various types:

☙ **Name and Memory**
Commemorating individuals, events, and experiences with a named place is one of the most common narrative practices. Ordinary streets, hills, or

Above: Numbers and text inscribed on one of the Boston Holocaust Memorial towers. (Photograph by Richard Purinton)

Below: Memorial wall on the Lower East Side of Manhattan.

Nothing belongs to us anymore.
They have taken our clothes,
our shoes, even our hair.
If we speak, they will not listen to us.
And if they listen, they will not understand.
They have even taken away our names.
My number is 174517. I will carry the tattoo
on my left arm until I die.
—Primo Levi, Survivor

Above: Calle Cinco de Mayo, Mexico City, commemorates the victory of Mexican forces over the French army in the 1862 Battle of Puebla. May 5 is a day for celebrating national sovereignty and self-determination.

Below: Virginia Place, Glasgow, refers to the historic connection between Scotland and the colony of Virginia that developed through the tobacco trade. (Photograph courtesy John Stuart-Murray)

buildings serve as memorials to the famous or simply the first to settle on the spot. In Latin America, using dates of important events for street names and other features is a common practice. In Asunción, Paraguay, the streets read as a calendar of thirty-four historic political moments, battles, and religious events including "31 de Enero" (the 1866 Battle of Corrales, 1866, a Paraguayan victory over Argentina), "23 de Octubre" (which commemorates the deaths of student protestors, 1931), and "14 de Mayo" (the date of independence of Paraguay, 1811) (Aschmann, 147). Placenames also serve as the memorials of other places, as reminders of where people came from or places they wish they could re-create.

☞ Stories that Create Names
Stories may precede and be the cause of a placename. Runaway Pond, near Glover, Vermont, marks the site of what was known as Long Pond before June 6, 1810, when residents, attempting to change its outlet to divert water to a series of mills down by Mud Pond, inadvertently caused a large breach. It took just over an hour for the whole pond to "run away" causing a flood that demolished the mills downriver (Hobson, 299).

☞ Names that Acquire Narratives
Like nicknames, placenames acquire new stories and layers of association over time. Because placenames are difficult to dislodge, on the one hand they serve as the secure locus of shared memory. On the other hand, as places and cultures change underneath the cover of the name, names can acquire associations that diverge from the original appellation. The coincidences of historic event and place can permanently re-story a name. Gettysburg, Bay of Pigs, Watergate, Pruit Igoe, lend their names to histories that have significantly altered the meaning of each place. Likewise narratives of personal memories refract the associations of names. Michel de Certeau describes the instability of name meanings that "slowly lose, like worn coins, the value engraved on them, but their ability to signify outlives its first definition....These names make themselves available to the diverse meanings given them by passers-by: they detach themselves from the places they were supposed to define and serve as imaginary meeting-points on itineraries" (De Certeau, 104).

☞ Placenames as the Cause of Stories
Stories not only create placenames, but placenames can even be the cause of stories as people try to explain through folktale and anecdote how places such as Bird-in-hand, 96 or Dead Tiger Creek Hammock got their curious and enigmatic names. The 1947 USGS topographic quadrangle for Reading, Pennsylvania, still showed an old logging road from the previous century leading back into a valley labeled Nigger Hollow. The word meaning is clear, but how it got that name still provokes speculation. One story maintains that the farm at the base of the valley was owned by abolitionists and supporters of the underground railroad. The remote notch at the upper end of the valley was thought to be a hiding place for escaped slaves, a place where

the smoke from their fires would dissipate before it could be seen above either ridge (Ewald). In the 1968 revision of the topographic quad, the name was deleted. Yet, older residents still refer to the place by its former name, fully aware of its racial connotations, as well as its imagined history.

Names that Encode a Narrative Topos

Taken together, names can construct a highly conventionalized setting linked to the narratives of a culture—a narrative topos. Arcadia was a real place in ancient Greece, a region of pastoralists and hunters, whose ancestors claimed to be older than the moon. It became a place associated with retreat from the complexities of the city (Bell, 23–28). The naming of elements in English gardens of the 18th century strategically evoked the Arcadian narrative topos by borrowing the names of its famous inhabitants and toponyms: the river Styx, Hermes, his son Pan, Artemis, and Callisto. The names of contemporary suburban communities, cemeteries, or vacation homes evoke their own versions of this narrative topos but with references to other mythologies, histories, leisure activities, and imaginative literature.

Names as Metonymies and Metaphors in Narratives of Place

When Ian Hamilton Finlay first came to the place where he would spend decades creating a garden, it was a rough, barren Scottish upland infested with thistle as a result of overgrazing. He called the place "Stony path," a description of what he found—a metonymy of association. As he began transforming the site, the metaphoric use of names became one of his principal strategies for encoding narrative and making a garden. On a hill under one of the few trees on the site, he placed a stone tablet inscribed with the name "mare nostrum." The allusion is to the Roman term for the Mediterranean sea, "our sea," connecting to a place and time far removed from this landlocked site in Scotland.[4] Likewise the making of "the New World" of America was achieved by substituting place-names of the Old World, borrowing histories and imaginatively transforming what Native Americans referred to as Turtle Island.

THE DISCOURSES OF PLACENAMES

There is power in naming places and the elements that constitute them. Therefore, it is important to know who has the authority to name—who are the namers of places? Is a placed named by those who live there, by the selectmen of a town, by a centralized planning body, by the designer? Does the name come from the top down or emerge from the bottom up? What role does the mapmaker play in editing, spelling, including, and excluding names?

The language of names is not neutral. Even descriptive names are bound up within narrative discourses. As much as they describe any objective reality, names mirror intentions of observers and how they view the landscape. Descriptions are enticements (Sweetwater,

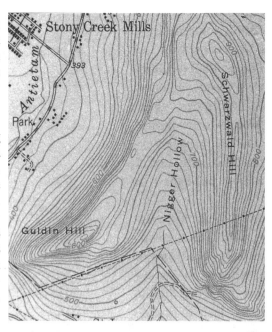

Above: Birdsboro, 1947, USGS topographic quadrangle.

Below: 1968 map showing the deletion of the name.

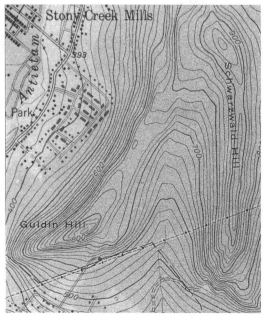

Encoding a narrative topos.
The self-named cottages in the Adirondack State Park, New York, carve out a vivid realm
of individualism and escapism within a designated wilderness park.

Florida, Greenland) as well as warnings (Skull Mountain, Dismal Swamp, Spector Range). They reference the namers' experience (Spanish Conquistador, Apache, Developer) and their way of organizing and categorizing the world. In Western culture the language of visual fact is often privileged over other modes of experiencing and knowing a place. Describing apparent fact, the namers of the American West used numerous anthropomorphic metaphors (Grand Tetons, Squaw Valley), usually from the perspective of a male gaze focused on finding available resources (Rudnick, 10–26). The descriptive categories of biology employ metaphors from human social systems (kingdom, family) and the Latin terms of Linaen nomenclature link new worlds with those of classical Greece and Rome (Seddon, 11).

It is also important to see names not just as individual words but as social practices that attempt to fix identity within a system of values. Names are drawn from distinct referent systems—history, politics, science, mythology, art, etc. Paris street names show a preoccupation with artists and writers, whereas American grid streets have rationalized systems of numbers, letters, or trees (Ferguson). What types of names are considered appropriate, what categories of elements they are attached to, and what metaphors are employed are all choices organized around a range of discourses including individualism, nationalism, locality, race, and gender. It seems natural in Western culture, for instance, to honor individuals by giving places their names. Status often corresponds with the size and location of the element or place (mountains become presidents, the most important streets in a city reflect systems of social status). In research on the commemorative uses of John F. Kennedy and Martin Luther King, Jr. Roger Stump found that political and racial ideologies shaped the selections of who was honored and what type of place got the individual's name. Fewer schools in the South bear the name of King, reflecting the controversies of the civil rights movement, which often centered around the desegregation of these institutions, considered critical for maintaining social values. In turn, commemorating King's legacy with street names is less controversial and is more common in the South than in the North (Stump, 203–215).

Place names reveal a culture's relationship to locality, land, and natural processes. At issue is the degree of intimacy with place. For instance, the whole idea of honorific naming for individuals is foreign to Native Americans, whose place names, instead, reflect patterns of use usually keyed to natural processes, events, and mythic origins. Cronon argues that the cultural ecology of Indians in colonial New England can be inferred from the names they attached to places, such as "clam bake place," "small island where we get pitch," and "the end of the fishing place," which marked the inland limit of the spring spawning runs. In this manner the great density of names reflects an intimacy with a very localized ecology (Cronon 1983, 65, 66).

Such "auto chthonic" names, which seem to spring from an indigenous contact with the realities of a place, are often held as an ideal set against cultural practices that are seen as more superficial or alienated from nature. Imported European names or the vague topos of the contemporary

Environmental historian William Cronon recites the names Americans have given to the Great Plains since 1880—the Land of the Buffalo; the Great American Desert, the Wheat Belt, the Dust Bowl—and notes that "these are not simply names or des-criptive phrases. Each implies a different possible narrative for environmental histories of the region, and different possible endings for each of those stories. Narrative is thus inescapably bound to the very names we give the world."
(Cronon 1992, 1375–76)

Meadowdales or Forest Hills seem to obscure the native. In a studio exercise on renaming the Forth Valley of Edinburgh, Scotland, Professor John Stuart-Murray found that students had difficulty in naming the ridges, hills, marshes, and meanders of the region. They seemed out of practice with naming places determined by natural processes. He suggests this as evidence of a broader cultural disengagement and lack of intimacy with the nature of a region (Stuart-Murray 1995, 39, 40). This desire to name things according to some true nature is a long-standing concern in Western culture, evident in Adam's nomenclature in the Garden of Eden, as well as in Plato's critique of naming in the "Cratylus."

This discourse is critical in the ongoing process of the naming of places by designers. Decisions by designers and planners help to shape this toponymy in a variety of ways: by creating new names as the driving metaphor of the design, attempting to reveal the nature of a site through names, recycling existing names, transplanting a name from one place to another, overlaying, erasing, and renaming. In this manner names become linked to the narratives of creating, maintaining, revealing, or reclaiming the identity of place. Three of these narrative plots are discussed below: naming the empty spaces, interpreting the palimpsest of names, and renaming/reclaiming places.

NAMING THE EMPTY SPACES

The unnamed places beyond the margins of experience are perceived as voids without structure or history—an anxious geography of fear ("here be dragons"). Historically the places without proper names, the "terrain vague," "waste," "heath," or "wilderness," have been the refuge of those without a proper place and outlaws (whose proper names were disguised in folktales by nicknames such as Robin Hood and Swamp Fox) as well as the sites of obscene activities. In the late 16th century a lawless territory which neither England or Scotland wished to claim as their own was called "the Debatable land" (Stuart-Murray, 1997). More recently, over 1,300 square miles of virtually uninhabited Nevada desert was treated as a moral vacuum. Unnamed, unknown, and unprotected, this area provided the cover of anonymity for the government's clandestine bombing rehearsals for nuclear war from the 1940s to the 1960s (Solnit, 5–7). Unnamed places are also landscapes of opportunity, places imagined to have unclaimed wealth ("here be resources"), and territory for expanding nations, cities, and suburbs. Naming is a means of taking control of both the threat and the opportunity of the unknown.

In narratives of discovery, colonizing, and settlement, naming is the first act of "taking place," of taking possession of the empty spaces on a map. Coming from stable, named places and facing the chaos of the unknown, the unsignified, naming repeats original acts of creating an ordered world, remaking new worlds in the likeness of an original model. The very first act Columbus performed on newly discovered land was an extended naming ceremony, as Indians witnessed the drafting of a deed of possession (Todorov, 28). On repeated voyages he brought whole worlds into European consciousness simply by sailing by and naming them after biblical stories, medieval travel narratives, imaginative literature, and images of paradise. The Virgin Islands, for instance, are so named because the numerous islands reminded him of a story of a thousand martyred virgins. He believed, however, that names must correspond to the nature of things, and for his own name he chose the more ancient term "Colon," or Colonizer, and "Christopher," Bearer of Christ, which when taken together attested to what he saw as his divine purpose (Todorov, 26).

In exploration and discovery the journey itself becomes a narrative—the line of movement becomes spatialized history (Carter, 102). The events in these narratives become the line of names on maps. Columbus was concerned with the proper chronological sequence of the first five places he "discovered" and named them in a hierarchy beginning with the Savior (San Salvador), followed by the Virgin Mary (Santa Maria de la Concepcion), the King (Fernandina), the Queen (Isabela), and the Royal Prince (Juana) (Todorov, 27). The patterns of names appear as sketchy outlines along coasts, tracks along rivers, and forays into the interiors of continents. These tentative and partial descriptions of place reveal the temporal experience of gradually *coming to be* located, of uncertainty and moments of discovery in an *as yet* unorganized environment. Eventually, the process of exploration produces a map, a total spatial representation, concealing the temporal qualities and narratives that produced them in the first place.

In the narratives of exploration, naming is critical for exercising the rights of discovery. In America the various colonial powers waged a veritable naming war, competing to be the first to name, or asserting newly acquired power by renaming what had already been claimed by another. Such a "right" existed in the discourse of European power, irrespective of Native American cultures whose places were being renamed (Simpson, 187). The claiming of this right was the first step in a much larger global story of colonial competition. Names became symbols in narratives of empire as nations acquired sovereign territory, laying claim to the resources therein and the future planting of colonies. These first names provided the framework for appending future names of trade and settlement.

The naming strategies of the first colonial settlers to follow discovery belie the aspirations of their mission. Confronting the vicissitudes of the American wilderness, religious colonists on the East Coast saw their task in terms of the ancient Hebrews wandering in a wilderness in search of a promised land. This metaphor was encoded in the places they named after Old Testament places—Canaan, Gilead, Goshen, Hebron, Palestine, Sharon, or the sacred center of the Christian world, Jerusalem (which in its clipped form became Salem, Massachusetts) (Leighly, 303). As settlement traveled westward with the course of empire, new metaphors continued to transform the frontier. In the early years of the Republic, classical placenames, Ithaca, Rome, Troy, Syracuse, Homer, Ovid, Marcellus, Camillus, and so on march across "upstate" New York. Geographer Wilber Zelinsky observed that even a cluster of houses in the wilderness had visions of being a new Athens or Rome. In an effort to settle vast territory quickly, Americans

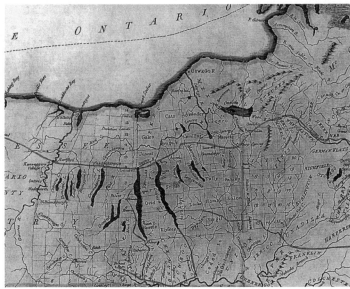

Top left: "A Mappe of Coll. Römer his Journey to ye 5 Indian Nations going from New Yorck to Albany." Wolfgang Römer's 1700 map of his journey shows only the names of the Mohawk River, two of the Finger Lakes, Oneida Lake ("Onydea"), Lake Ontario ("Cadraggua"), and the Niagara River ("Iagera"). It designates Lake Erie as simply "Large Lake." (Courtesy New York State Archives)

Top right: Portion of a 1796 map of the State of New York. At the end of the 1700s and in the early 1800s, inscribing a toponymy of ancient Greece and Rome helped to civilize this landscape of upstate New York in the late 1700s. (Courtesy Syracuse University Special Collections)

invented a landscape by using a rich toponymy of other places, exotic realms, imaginative literature, and hybrids (Zelinsky, 296).

LAST FRONTIERS AND COMPETITION FOR SHRINKING SPACE

Rather than limiting exploration, discovery, and colonization to historical epoch, they can be understood as an ongoing process of claiming territory. Similar episodes occurred in the 20th century. The exploration and naming of much of Alaska, America's "last frontier," occurred early in the century. In 1929, Robert Marshall, a leader of the wilderness movement and the U.S. Forest Service, discovered an unmapped region in the central Brooks Range of northern Alaska. Marshall loved the blank spaces on the map and idealized adventures into these unknown places, as exemplified by Lewis and Clark; he was just a hundred years too late. However, his discovery enabled him to bestow one of the largest groups of names (169) by any one person on such a vast scale (15,000 acres) in the 20th century. He believed that only local people connected to the place, living residents who had actually seen the mountains, should be attached by name to those features.[5] For the most part he used the native Inapaiq language to describe what he discovered in names. These were not in most cases the actual native name but rather translations of his own descriptive names into the native language—Alapah (cold) Mountain, Binnyanaktuk (superlatively rugged) Creek, Kinnorutin ("you are crazy," in reference to an initial mistake in the direction of its course) Creek (Cole, 99–115). Ironically, his naming helped to fill in those blank spaces he so loved.

In the vast territory of the Amazonian rain forest, various groups, including the indigenous peoples, compete for space in a closing frontier. In Brazil, missionaries, gold seekers, industrialists, cattle ranchers and government planners percieve the Amazon basin, an area over 1½ million square miles, as a "demographic vacuum." Each group has left a trail of names. The rivers, often named after Catholic saints, bear the oldest colonial names. Since the 1950s, government-sponsored capitalist expansion and encouragement of resettlement to reduce pressures for land reform have followed highways. Dozens of settlements (Km 95, Km 139, etc.) are simply named after the distance markers along the new highways. The naming reflects the rationality of military centralized planning. Towns are named according to a hierarchy of their functions from large to small (Ruropolis, Agropolis, Agrovilla). Meanwhile, squatters actively rename these sites and claim space on the margins by inscribing their own names (Roberts).

THE UNNAMING AND DISPLACING OF A NATIVE TOPONYMY

Of course the concept of the tabula rasa is one of point of view, that of the colonial power (in its various manifestations) that sees only open, unclaimed land without history or rights of ownership. The places newly named were often renamed, replacing those known by native inhabitants for hundreds of years. Columbus was well aware of Indian names. As noted in one of his letters, what Columbus christened San Salvador the Indians called Guanahani (Todorov, 27). Only a small percentage of native names were ever mapped because of language differences and an indifference to acknowledge these names and their claims on space. The irony is that the indigenous names, which derived from an intimate knowledge of place, often guided the routes of discoverers. The discoverers relied on local knowledge and toponymy while supplanting it at the same time (Simpson, 179).

Often what appears as empty, uninhabited, and without claim of names is actually crisscrossed by a network of names, albeit unofficial and undocumented on a map. Various groups claim these voids with names derived from their own use and experience. Vacant lots, the ragged edges of suburbia, or the adjoining "open spaces" are continually named and renamed by children. The diverse recreational uses of open land create nomenclatures particular to each activity. "Spelunkers" know the underside of the landscape by name as well (Stuart-Murray 1995, 37–39).

To discover these "hidden" names requires time and a recognition of the value of use and symbolic "ownership" that maps very distinct sets of narratives. For most people the Pinelands is an uninteresting stretch of wilderness to pass by on the New Jersey Turnpike on their way to the shore. However, generations of locals and newcomers have shaped and named it as their home, as environmental psychologist Nora J. Rubinstein discovered.

Nora J. Rubinstein, Ph.D., has spent years discovering the undocumented nomenclature of place which gave her access to past experience, social patterns, uses of the land, and stories of the New Jersey Pinelands. Her ongoing work in the Pine Barrens began with her thesis and continues with her research and teaching in environmental psychology and theory at Rutgers University.

J. Timmons Roberts documented the ongoing process of naming the Amazon and the contests between the government and the squatters competing for a piece of the closing frontier. "I also observed a series of urban land invasions in June and July of 1990 aimed at opening up new neighborhoods because rents exceeded the incomes of most residents. A political candidate had bought an enormous ranch on the edge of town which he intended to distribute before the elections in order to gain votes. Because he delayed in distributing lots, hundreds of families invaded the ranch on an afternoon in July of 1990. Within 48 hours, over 2,000 lots were demarcated. A number of names were being tossed about for the new neighborhood. Some thought it should be named 'Neilandia' to commemorate the man who had lost millions of cruzeiros with the invasion. Another consideration was 'Faisalandia' after the mayor who moved in and registered all invaders and others seeking land in the town....In the end the mayor named the site Barrio da Paz 'Neighborhood of Peace' in keeping with his earlier naming of the town's new plaza after Mahatma Gandhi. The name has stuck, but many towns people think it ironic." (Roberts, 174)

Even the very use of Native American names can mark the alienation of natives from their former places. The first Europeans to actually enter the Yosemite valley on March 27, 1851, was an army battalion chasing the Yosemite Indians out of the valley to open it up for future American interests, first in resources and later in scenery. The first night around the campfire the battalion named the valley after the very Indians they were chasing.

The Yosemite's name for their valley, "Ahwahnee," was later transposed to

(Continued overleaf)

(continued)

the famous lodge for tourists. Just as native peoples were displaced, so too were their names displaced, misplaced, misspelled, and misused to map a native toponymy that never existed. The Yosemite never named features for important people, but "Tenaya," the name of the chief, was given to a lake by Lafayette Bunnell. "Tioga" names a pass, a peak, a lake, and one of the early mining districts. One of the mining promoters from the East imported this name from Indians living in New York and Pennsylvania. (Browning, xi, xii)

In the Pine Barrens, the place-names on regional maps fall into three very broad categories, which I will call *real, rhetorical and remembered*. *Real* places exist both on the map and in the location indicated. These may still locate thriving historical communities or they may be newly created by the planning process. Some identify tourist or commercial centers, while others may be less developed, but remain significant to some subgroup of residents or planning officials.

The second broad category of place-names, the *rhetorical* places, which remain as artifacts on the map, but no longer exist on the land. They suggest the region's history and culture, but today these places may neither support, nor be supported by, local or regional institutions or use patterns. Cultural historians paint detailed portraits of the villages of Washington Forge and Martha Furnace, but little remains other than the stone foundation blocks and partial walls of the furnaces. Washington's nineteenth century iron forge is located along a "paper" road and surrounded by chain link fence, and in an oddly symbolic gesture, Martha Furnace, founded in 1793, was both fenced and buried to protect it from relic seekers.

Even ecological features may become rhetorical devices in the Pines. For years I had searched unsuccessfully for the two highest points in the Pine Barrens—the Forked River Mountains and Apple Pie Hill. It should have been easy enough to spot the 184 foot high "mountains" in the flat pine and hardwood landscape, but eventually I enlisted the help of Jack Cervetto, who had spent some seventy years in the Pine Barrens when he died in 1995. With his wife, Pearl, who can trace her own family roots in the place to the Revolutionary War, we drove for hours in the scrub pine. We climbed the local fire tower and scanned the horizon; we spotted rare plants as we wandered along the edges of fire breaks, until eventually we realized we had been driving in circles, and had come no closer to the elusive landmark.

"Well, I guess we've been around Jake's Barn," Jack said, using an old phrase that signified both that we had been lost *and* that we found what we sought. Like "not seeing the forest for the trees," to be there and to be lost were not juxtaposed concepts. The Forked Mountains had been beneath our feet, but we had not seen them, for the lack of structure or signage or the lack of a vista.

There are still other places, whose names are now entirely lost to the mapmakers and planners. Some of these *remembered* places exist only in the memories of the old-timers, while others are part of the daily use patterns of local residents, and may be located either by ecological features or by consensual experience. Many were named without great symbolism, for a stand of trees near the road or the family that owned the land. These place-names may have never appeared on any maps but those of the local surveyor as he designated the next parcel for sale, or they may have been no more than a local convention in conversation, used to designate the area where the water stood deep at the bend of a road in summer, or where the red berries grew thick enough for a good grave blanket. But some of these remembered place-names carry the history of land use and meaning of place. In some cases they are the only remaining trace of the old families, occupations or events.

The Clarks' graves still lie deep in the woods beside Clark's Landing Road. They bear a 1752 date on their inscribed surfaces, but only muskrat trappers are likely to be able to find these stones, for even the road they gave their name to has now been changed to County Route 539. It is still possible to hear these place-names when listening to the police scanner. "There's a fire back of the Eslow house," one member of the volunteer fire company may say to another. The Eslow family hasn't lived in the Pine Barrens for decades, but the old-timers still know where they can find the hand hewn beams and the fireplace mantle. And there are echoes of the old place-names if you listen to the kids talking about where they're going hunting. "I'll meet you over at Oak Island." Although technically outside the political boundaries of the Pine Barrens, Oak Island was the location of a self-sufficient farm. The house still stood the last time I went to visit, although you could see sky through what is left of the roof and there were few walls remaining, but Oak Island does not exist on any map I have seen. It has been swallowed up by the lagoon community of Mystic Island and exists on a spit of undeveloped land between two growing Pine Barrens communities, and has been bypassed by the major state road—perhaps protected by its very anonymity.

These places are part of the pattern of life of the local residents and in many cases may have been handed down for generations. One day, as I sat in his living room, Jack Cervetto gave me a list of the old place-names that he said had been given to him by "the old-timers." That list contains the names of places that must now be more than a hundred years old. Some, like Hog Wallow, are still used among locals. Others, like Coffin Board Hollow and Indian Jack, may no longer be located. Many were close to being lost when Jack gathered them some forty years ago, and a few were identified by using other more familiar place-names or by triangulation. Bennet Mill is near New Egypt as is Head of Snag and Hurricane Brook. Apple Pie Hill is the sandy ridge north of Tabernacle and Mary Ann Furnace is three miles east of Browns Mills, and Mt. Misery is two miles from Mary Ann Furnace. Nor are the place-names the only history that is being lost. Jack is gone now, along with Fred Brown, Jr., and Leo Landy. They were three men whose knowledge of the Pine Barrens will never be replaced, and there may be few people left who remember these places or can mark them on a map or can find their way around "Jake's Barn."

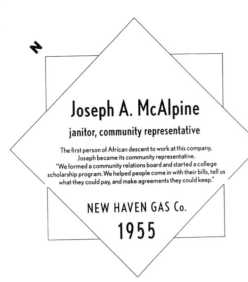

Joseph A. McAlpine

janitor, community representative

The first person of African descent to work at this company,
Joseph became its community representative.
"We formed a community relations board and started a college
scholarship program. We helped people come in with their bills, tell us
what they could pay, and make agreements they could keep."

NEW HAVEN GAS Co.
1955

Sheila Levrant de Bretteville, stone inset
for *9th Square Public Art: Path of Stars*.
New Haven, Connecticut, 1993.

In 1993, when Sheila de Bretteville began
her project, the 9th Square area of New
Haven, Connecticut, faced an uncertain
future. It was perceived as "unprofitable"
and "blighted." Many white residents had
left the area, while the use of "eminent
domain" emptied the area of many elderly
and retired residents. The documentation
for the National Register of Historic Places
also contributed to the sense of vacancy of
the present by naming only the architects
of the 19th and early 20th century who
designed the distinctive buildings.

In an effort to repeople this place with
the names of those who have made and
continue to make this place their community, de Bretteville set out to find "who
was in the back room." To honor the
everyday lives she found, she developed a
series of stars in the sidewalks that reveal
names and their stories. These include not
only the oldest names or the first to live
there, but current residents such as the
manager of a single-room-occupancy
boarding house, the clientele who stopped at Colonel Lip's restaurant and bar,
and a dressmaker who taught fashion
design in the back room of her shop.
These names on the sidewalk help to
counter the loss of stories that
accompanies the emptying of names.

ERASING NAMES TO RESTORE THE EMPTINESS OF WILDERNESS

In a recent story by Ursula Le Guin, "She Unnames Them," an unamed Eve
("she") frees creatures in an Edenic landscape by her power to unname:
"Most of them accepted namelessness with the perfect indifference with
which they had so long accepted and ignored their names. Whales and dolphins, seals and sea otters consented with particular grace and alacrity, slid-
ing into anonymity as into their element." Her story illustrates the long-
standing desire in Western culture for a space in nature outside the control
of humans. The freedom of escaping to nature is also the freedom of escaping from the cultural confines of names. However, as in Le Guin's story,
there is irony in unnamed space being created by a human act of erasure. To
create the fantasy of a pristine Eden in real places like Yosemite, any names
marking human presence, possession, or history had to be removed. Thus,
the Yosemite Indians were removed from their valley. This idea of wilderness is maintained in the present by continued unnaming and erasing of
names. Overcrowded parks and wilderness areas are also crowded with
names. The U.S. Board on Geographic Names states that "a fundamental
characteristic of elemental wilderness is that features are nameless..."
Hence it developed a policy of no new names in designated wilderness areas
and initiated the systematic removal of names that have not been published
and are considered to have no administrative or other function (Cole, 113).
This practice restores an imagined state of nature that never existed on
these sites, while at the same time erases the realities of historic experience
associated with the names.

THE CLEAN SPACES OF DESIGN AND PLANNING

The plots of naming the empty spaces are not limited to historically or
geographically remote episodes, but occur in ordinary professional practices. In fact design and planning often repeat the acts of unnaming,
replacing, displacing, and erasing names to create a "clean space." A blank
slate, without the history, memory, or authority of a name, allows designers, developers, or planners to assert their own authority. The semantic
emptying of landscapes can be subtle, as well, inherent in the language of
common practice. A recent historic preservation report for the 9th Square
area of New Haven, Connecticut, for instance, focused on the names of
building designers in the 19th and early 20th century without mentioning
those who presently live and work in them. It contributed to a strong sense
of vacancy in the present as a result of flight to the suburbs and urban
renewal. The language of modernism, in particular, with its borrowing of
scientific discourse, emptied places of their traditional associations,
replacing them with names denoting functional hierarchies, zones, and
often a utopian topos. And just as the line of explorers' names opened territory for global competition for resources, future trade, and settlement,
new names for development realign histories and integrate sites into new
social, economic, and political systems.

INTERPRETING THE PALIMPSEST OF NAMES

As new names are added to the old, some stick, providing the framework for daily lives, while others are forgotten or erased. In this manner a map becomes a palimpsest of names, a temporal collage marking various episodes of origin, discovery, conquest, settlement, resettlement, abandonment, and change. The persistence, accumulation, and reworking of names create unexpected juxtapositions of different times and stories. In Mexico City the corner of Reforma Avenue and Arquemedes Street brings together a Mexican sociopolitical event of the 19th century, revolution and reform, with a Greek sage of the third century B.C.

Instead of treating the landscape as a blank slate to be crosscut by a line of new names, designers may engage in the continuous layering of names. Working within this collage recognizes the past, the authority of the local, and the diversity of values encoded in names. The first step is interpretive, an investigation into etymology, history, geographic processes, and values embedded in placenames. Interpretation provides a critical position for a range of alternative naming strategies that continue to shape the collage.

INTERPRETING THE STORIES OF CHANGE

The stories encoded in the collage of placenames require an act of recovery to make them intelligible. This is partly because names are "opaque"—their meanings as words are not transparent. Linguistic change (divergence, syllabic combination, back-formation, etc.) leaves curious and odd-sounding words embedded like fossils in the map. Meanwhile names derive from other names, transforming places through reference to other places, individuals, or histories that happened elsewhere. As a result, each name is an intertext, a locus of intersecting histories and places. The inquiry, then, into "what this placename means and where came it from" involves an investigation into its origins as a word, as well as its history as a name. The inquiry is both etymological, relating to the study of word origins, and onomastic, relating to the study of names as a special use of language in particular contexts. It involves unearthing the temporal depth of names as well as mapping their spatial narratives.

Etymology is a narrative of linguistic origins that seeks to recover the forgotten histories of words. W. F. H. Nicolaisen, who spent a lifetime interpreting the names of the Scottish landscape, cites several examples of the attempt to recover the meaning of placenames by tracing their linguistic origins. The name Hawick, for instance, was first recorded as Hawic in 1165 and goes back to a compound formation of two Old English words, *haga* and *wic*, or "hedgefarm." *Wic* has dropped out of common usage to designate a farm, but *haga* still survives in its cognate form as *hedge*. The case of Hawick, now a town with no evidence of hedges or farms, illustrates that while language changes and words drop out of use, names often survive because they become meaningful as names (Nicolaisen 1976, 4).

Names persist because they can function as names even when they no longer make sense as words. They have name value, which is distinct from common word value. Nicolaisen uses the analogy of geology for visualizing

Gaelic name and its English transformation on the Isle of Skye, Scotland.

how the persistence of names reveals layers of linguistic change. He cites places such as Melrose, a Gaelic name from the eighth century, which survived the death in that part of Scotland of the very language that formed it. This "fossil" from a "deep" layer of the linguistic strata continues to function as a name in the most contemporary stratum of use. However, the linguistic processes are complex and varied over space. In other parts of Scotland, Gaelic is not fossilized, but still a vital part of naming places (Nicolaisen 1976, 6).

When a name is not transparent, when it does not make sense as a word in the current usage, stories are created to explain the anomaly. So-called folk etymologies attempt to recover the meaning of a name that no longer makes sense in order to make it transparent again. Pluckemin, New Jersey, according to some, comes from the custom of a local innkeeper who solicited his customers by standing on the road to "pluck 'em in." Another explanation traces its origin to an Indian word for "persimmon" (Hobson, 283). Stories of these types often explain a rupture in meaning in terms of a chance utterance or the miscommunication between strangers, cultures, or languages.

The object of name interpretation extends beyond the recovery of word meaning to the recovery of the use of a name in its spatial context. In addition to their dimensions and layers along a vertical axis of time, names also have a horizontal distribution across space, which can be read as narratives of settling, migrating, or claiming landscapes. The name Hawick, for instance, relates to Berwick, Birswick, Bothwick, Fenwick, Heatherwick, etc., and the distribution of these placenames across the land gives a picture of early phases of Anglian settlement in Scotland (Nicolaisen 1976, 40–45). In the landscape of North America, where European settlement is only several centuries old, the etymology of individual names is less significant than the spatial narratives of the names.

Learning to read the complex spatial narrative of a map goes beyond the individual or curious names, to interpreting the larger history of inhabitation, and the cultural processes of settlement, possession, con-

Richard Long, *Desert Flowers*.
Eight-day walk in and around the Hexie Mountains,
Joshua Tree, California, 1987. (Courtesy the artist)

Richard Long's art takes the form of walks, marked sometimes by ephemeral arrangements of stones and twigs, or by names. He walks in both inhabited places as well as empty spaces. In parts of Scotland, every path, wall, and field has a name. His walk calls out this litany of names, each with their own histories and associations. Exploring more remote regions, his personal impressions and experiences become the markers of time and space. The names have a sense of immediacy and necessity, "animal holes," "riverbed sleeping-place," recalling both indigenous inhabitation and the transience of exploration. The map of names becomes a spatialized history of the walk.

flict, accommodation, or diffusion reflected in the spatial pattern of names. While the physical forms of early settlement may have vanished, the names that persist still speak of the symbolic life of the community, their metaphors, who was honored, and how people organized their world. Interpretation begins to sort through the layers, juxtapositions, and sequences of names in this rich collage in order to find many possible stories.

Designers shape this collage in various ways. Preservation seeks to retain or even restore existing names considered historically significant. For a new park in Mexico City, Mario Schjetnan restored the original names of the lacustrine basin now covered by the world's largest city. New designs either build upon existing systems, or replace them wholesale with names that cohere, internally, to a consistent theme. Discursive naming practices insert or juxtapose names to reveal histories and values. Sasaki Associates' master plan for Ohio State University employed several strategies of naming. Starting from the traditional center of campus, which generations knew as "the Oval," the designers proposed new spaces with similar nomenclature, "the Field" and "the Stadium Green," as opposed to unnamed open space. The Waterman Farm on the north side of campus commemorates the local heritage, while the expanding research park on the south side is yet to be named (Baur).

RECOVERING THE EARLIEST LAYER OF NAMES
In the early 1500s, long before Mexico City became the world's largest city, it was a landscape of settlements around an extensive lake. The Aztec and other indigenous names mark these origins, which are practically submerged in the matrix of the contemporary city. For a new park located in an expanding industrial and housing area, Mario Schjetnan and the Grupo de Diseño Urbano evoked the origins of this landscape through a series of obelisks bearing the placenames of the early 1500s. Each obelisk includes the story of the name, an evocation of the place in literature, and a map showing its location in the valley. The park's name, Tezozomoc, refers to the former Aztec king of the area known as Azcapotzalco, where the park is located. Together, the sequence of obelisks tells the story of the Aztecs' movement around the lacustrine basin up to the moment of contact with Cortéz.

Following is a translation of the story of one place name:

"Azcapotzalco: In the Anthill"
Since the times of the God's city, Teotinuacan, Azcapotzalco was a populated and important place on the shore of Lage de Texcoco, which was also named Meztliapan, the Lake of the Moon.

In the beginning of the 13th century, the Tepanescas arrived to the shores of Lago de la Luna (Lake of the Moon), coming from Chicomostoc. Xolotl, the chief (master) of the Chichimecas, married

BEINN A'CHAIT
BEINN DEARG
ELRIG'IC AN TOISICH
BEINN GHARBH
BEINN BHREAC
AN SLIGEARNACH
MEALL ODHAR
ALLT DAMH DUBH
LEATHAD AN TAOBHAIN
CARN AN FHÌDLEIR LORGAIDH
SRÒN NA BAN-RIGH
CAOCHAN DUBH
RIVER FESHIE
ALLT A'CHAORAINN
SCARSOCH BHEAG
CNAPAN GARBH
BYNACK BURN
BRÀIGH COIRE CAOCHAN NAN LAOGH
CARN GREANNACH
AN SCARSOCH
SRÒN NA MACRANAICH
ALLT A'CHAORAINN
LEACHDANN FÉITH SEASGACHAIN
CARN EALAR
MEALL TIONAIL
GLAS FÉITH BHEAG
SRÒN GHARBH
GLAS FÉITH MHÓR
MEALL TIONAIL NA BEINNE BRICE
LOCH MHAIRC
CARN A'CHIARAIDH
BEINN MHEADHONACH
FÉITH AN LOCHAIN
AONACH NA CLOICHE MÒIRE
BRÀIGH NAN CREAGAN BREAC
BRÀIGH CLAIS DAIMH
CARN A'CHLAMAIN
BRÀIGH SRÒN GHORM
SRÒN DUBH
MEALL DUBH-CHLAIS
TARF WATER
FÉITH UAINE MHÓR
MEALL TIONAIL
CONLACH MHÓR
BRÀIGH COIRE NA CONLAICH
AN SLIGEARNACH
TARF WATER
CNAPAN NAN LAOGH
AN SGARSOCH
BYNACK BURN
CNAPAN GARBH
SCARSOCH BHEAG
ALLT A'CHAORAINN
MEALL TIONAIL
RIVER FESHIE
LEATHAD AN TAOBHAIN
CARN EALAR
LEACHDANN FÉITH SEASGACHAIN
BRÀIGH SRÒN GHORM
AONACH NA CLOICHE MÒIRE
CARN A'CHLAMAIN
BRÀIGH NAN CREAGAN BREAC
FÉITH AN LOCHAIN
BEINN MHEADHONACH
CARN A'CHIARAIDH
ELRIG'IC AN TOISICH
BEINN DEARG
BEINN BHREAC
BEINN DEARG
BEINN A'CHAIT

Richard Long, *Ten Days Walking and Sleeping on Natural Ground*.

134-mile meandering walk, Scotland, 1986. (Courtesy the artist)

In Tezozomoc Park the pattern of early placenames of the Valley of Mexico is reproduced around a miniature representation of the original lake complex, obliterated by subsequent growth of the city. Obelisks mark the name, location, and stories of the ancient communities that once surrounded the lake. The park is located at the former settlement of Azcapotzalco.

his eldest daughter, Cuetlaxochitl, with Acolhua, chief of the Tepanecas, and he gave them Azcapotzelco for their new home.

From this marriage Tezozomoc was born; he transformed the city of Azcapotzalco in the capital of the Tepaneca empire, which, during the 14th century, developed a model for political organization that the Aztecas would later follow.

Tezozomoc exercised a strong dominion that expanded across the valley to his neighbors, the Mexicas, on which he imposed high tribute. The monarch of the Mexicas, Huitzilihuitl, married one of Tezozomoc's daughters, Ayauhcihuatl, who asked her father to help the Mexicas when she gave birth to their first son. Tezozomoc, in need of more friends than enemies, reduced the tributes from the village of Hutzilopochitli and persuaded them to join him in his next conquest.

In 1418 Tezozomoc murdered Ixtlixochitlel, chief of Texcoco, subordinating the Acolhicas. Nezahualcoyotl, son of Iztlixochitlel, hid, and in his unhappiness he wrote a song:

> Bitterness has come and grown,
> next to you and beside you, Giver of life.
> I only seek,
> to remember our friends.
> Will they come again?
> Will they live again?
> Just once we die,
> just once here on the land.
> Don't let your hearts suffer!
> next to and beside the Giver of Life.

(from the manuscript of *Romances of the Lords of the Nuevo Espana*, translated by Miguel Leon Portilla)

In the early morning of one of the last days of 1426, when the morning star came out, Tezozomoc dreamed that Nezahualcoyotl was transformed into an eagle that scratched his face and pulled out his heart. He dreamed the same later, but this time, he was a tiger that destroyed his feet with his claws.

Tezozomoc's dreams were filled with premonitions.

Sitting in a basket filled with cotton, due to his old age, he contemplated the destiny of his empire from the shore of the lake of Texcoco. In 1427 Tezozomoc, chief of Azcapotzalco, died. His son Maxtla usurped the power from his brother Tayauh, who was designated by Tezozomoc to succeed him, and precipitated with his cruelty and inefficiency the fall of the Tepaneca empire.

In 1428, Itzcoatl and Nezahualcoyotl, in command of the Mexicas and Tezcoanos, defeated Maxtla and destroyed Azcapotzalco. The surviving Tepanecas moved to Tlacopan. The Mexicas decided to transform the city of Azcapotzalco into a slave market.

(translated by Gabriela Canamar)

Naming strategies also reflect ongoing professional and cultural discourse on history, locality, and nature. Using names that are "thick" with local history or describe a significant natural feature attempt to maintain a "sense of place" in the face of trends that erase place identity. On the other hand, local historic names can also be used as a strategy to simulate the past and disguise current realities of development.

OLMSTED'S TOPONYMIC STRATEGIES

Olmsted's deployment of names in his designs was as carefully crafted to create the same kind of complex landscape narrative as his manipulations of the physical elements of landform, roads, and vegetation that carry the names. In Franklin Park, part of his "Emerald Necklace" of parks for Boston, the name cover encodes a set of narratives that draw from local history, a passing event in the Revolutionary War, Indian use, and honored individuals. The name Schoolmaster Hill commemorates William and Ralph Waldo Emerson, who taught school in the area and lived on the east side of the hill. By attaching the site to stories through the strategy of naming, Olmsted gave the park an expanded temporal dimension.

In his report to the Boston Parks Department, Olmsted stressed the metonymic relationship of names to place. Through research he recovered names that were directly associated with the site—original homesteaders, Indians, and the Revolutionary War lieutenant and captain who both lived there and rested their army there (thus the name "the Resting Place" in the park). Olmsted then selected certain names for their particular associations and stories. In effect he simulated the kind of temporal depth and associations of a rural landscape that evolved over time.

The names that seem to originate from the place also construct the metaphors central to the park's Romantic landscape. The local names create the metaphor of rootedness and indigenous rurality; meanwhile names such as the Playstead, or the Steading encode reference to the topos of a pastoral ideal constructed centuries earlier on English estates. Olmsted grafted this Englishness to the local. At the same time, there were erasures. From rock-strewn meadows farmed by several generations, Olmsted had to "remove what is inconsistent, develop and expose elements favorable" to a picturesque Romantic landscape (Olmsted, 1886, 63). Local farmers were removed from the land by eminent domain, and only those names consistent with a romantic topos were honored in the plan.

In Olmsted's other projects, he employed similar sophisticated naming strategies. Even while evoking a sense of the region and local history, he

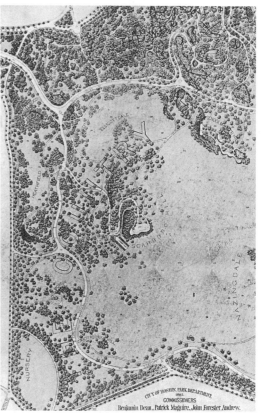

Portion of Olmsted's plan for Franklin Park, Boston. 1885. (Courtesy Olmsted Lithograph Collection, National Park Service)

added an English toponymy to the American landscape. In his recommendation for a suburban enclave to be built in Berkeley, California, he offered detailed advice on how to Anglicize the landscape. However, he also offered the local Spanish names as a more appropriate alternative. He also used names didactically to explain the moral purpose of his parks. In New York City's Central Park, the Bethesda Fountain refers to a biblical placename associated with a story of healing—an apt metaphor for the role of the park in the city. Meanwhile, the erasure of names, such as Seneca Village, a viable African-American community in what became Central Park, helped to mask the race and class issues of land acquisition and the exercise of power through eminent domain (Blackmar).

Place Names for California: excerpts from a letter by Frederick Law Olmsted Sr., to the acting president of the College of California. Olmsted had been requested to offer suggestions for the name of a new college town just north of Oakland.

Bear Valley, California
July 25, 1865
Rev. J. H. Willey
My dear Sir:

I propose to offer you a few thoughts upon the question of a name.

I think the best way to form an English name is to find a word signifying something characteristic of the place to be named, or the name of the person, event or quality which would be satisfactorily associated with it, and if the word or name is not sufficiently agreeable in itself, complete it with some of the old English terminations of names of localities, such as —

stay	beck	croft	lynne	burg
yard	bourne	combe	worth	worth
caster	brook	hill	rise	dene
chase	mede	burne	val	grange
ley	ming	hoke	thorpe	side
sey	stock	mead	mere	ing
field	cot	lea	brig-bridge	

Of persons I have heard you mention but two (not connected with the faculty) as having had any association with your enterprise, Dr. Bushnell and Mr. Billings. Either would make a good name for a locality by itself. Bushnell has a particularly Saxon local association and I should like it best alone. For a combination, Bushnellwood, Billingsley, Billinsbrook, are easily turned.

Lincolnwood or Lincolnwold sounds well.

I don't think water should be the characteristic quality, since your water becomes insignificant, if it does not wholly disappear, in the more important points of the ground in summer...

Two kinds of trees are prominent, the Oak (or Ilex) and the Laurel. The Saxon for the evergreen Oak is Holm or Holms, which is a capital word by itself. Oak you can't well use, except on some novel combination, from your vicinity to Oakland and its triteness, but Holms, the Holmes, is not trite in America. Ilex is hardly English, and combines with nothing English... Of Laurel: Laurella, Laureller, Laurelee, Laurelea, Laurel wood, Laurel hill, the latter trite and not of cheerful associations, the others rather weak and un-English.

Your sheltered condition from wind gives another suggestion: Leewood, Leeroads, Leepaths, Leesides, Leecombe, Leeley, Hurstlee, Shelterwood, Shelterdene, Shelter, Harborwood, Havendene, Havenwood, Blythehaven, Havenhurst.

The gap in the mountain behind you gives another, but neither gap nor any of its synonyms, gate, notch, port, ravine, defile, etc., suggest any thing very pleasant to me that is not trite. Glen is the best to build on perhaps but your gap is hardly a glen.

In fact all English words having any local applications and which are simple and natural and particularly agreeable are likely to have been appropriated too frequently to be quite satisfactory for your purpose. It seems just and proper to fall back on Spanish at this time in California; it has already given us so many euphonious, and to English ears entirely original, proper names. I give you the following assortment; a little study would find more: Villa, I may remark is Spanish as well as Italian for a country seat, but it is applied as a generic designation of a certain class of towns, generally honored with a residence of some royal or notable person. You will find a larger list of them—many in Mexico—in "Webster's Unabridged". It is more appropriate for application to your combination of village, villas, and villa or pleasure ground roads, than "park" or the unfortunate French "ville". If you could hit upon some very short Spanish adjective which would be descriptive at all, it would probably make a good proper name coupled with villa.

Villarosa	of roses or red, sunny.
Villabrecha	of the springs or flowing water or beach.
Villaverde	green.
Villa-feliche	happy
Villabrena	of the thickets or brambles.
Villavega	of the mead or meadow (appropriate enough as your public ground will take that character).
Villalaurino (Vilaurino)	of the Laurels.
Villabarranca	of the ravine.
Villafronde	leafy.

I believe your property was formerly included in the ranch of Peralta or owned by Senor Peralta. If this name has not been appropriated to designate any other locality, it would be natural and proper to take it, and it is not bad.

If I have misunderstood or taken unjustifiable liberties with any of the Spanish words, Mr. Billings can set you right.

Please let me know when you have hit upon anything that suits you, as I may want a name for use.

Yours respectfully,

Fred. Law Olmsted

(*Source*: Manuscript Division, Library of Congress)

The trustees, however, did not follow Olmsted's recommendation. Instead they chose the name Berkeley, after the philosopher George Berkeley, who wrote, "Westward the course of empire takes its way," expressing the narrative of manifest destiny (Ranney, 410).

OF SETTLEMENTS AND SUBDIVISIONS

The issues of locality, history, nature, and simulation are reflected in the naming strategies of recent settlements, or subdivisions. From World War II to the present, the mass initiation of new landscapes has erased old names while overlaying new and different toponymic strategies. Differences in names highlight discourses of local tradition and mass culture, the increasing commodification of place images, and the changes in who has the power to shape and name the landscape. Looking at these placenaming events, we can observe the actual process of reworking the collage of names.

In the Oley Valley in southeastern Pennsylvania, near the city of Reading, the changing name cover tells the story of a traditional farming community now being subdivided and renamed by developers. "Oley" originally comes from the native Lene Lenape, meaning "kettle," describing the bowl-shaped limestone valley. This landform contains both a natural and a cultural watershed, where traditions are stored. Oley still bears the distinct imprint of a diverse groups of immigrants— German, French, Dutch, Swiss and English—who established farms here in the early 1700s. Much of the material culture in the form of barns, houses, spring houses, and field patterns. persists, as well as the names that first shaped the land: Bertolet, Kiem, Yoder, DeTurk, Levan, and Hoch.

-Mark Hoch
-John Hoch
-Gideon Hoch
-Gideon Hoch
-Gideon Hoch
-Abraham Hoch
-Abraham Hoch
-Johannes Hoch
-Rudolf Hoch

Hoch Farm and family cemetery, Oley Valley, Pennsylvania. Genealogy runs like a vertical axis of time through the farmsteads of the valley.

The names of the valley derive from use and associations with the people who made the landscape over a long time. They are metonymic. Road names map patterns of use—Blacksmith Road, Limekiln Road, Bieber Mill Road. And curious names such as Yellow House or Black Bear Hill recall actual experiences. Yellow House was named for the color of a turnpike tavern that still exists, and Black Bear Hill was named after the inn that kept a tame bear for patrons' amusement.

But it is the persistence of family names that encodes the ethnic identity of the original settlement. The names are attached to local roads and small nodes of settlement—Griesmersville, Spangsville—and most important, the specific farmsteads.

The farmsteads are the primary landmarks of the valley's life. They also locate one of the most important narratives that have sustained the traditions of this place—genealogy. The sequence of generational names runs like a vertical axis of time through each farmstead. It is a narrative of continuity closely linked to the economic life of the valley. Even when the line of generation ends, and a farm passes out of a family narrative (often to be picked up within another genealogy), places continue to be referred to by their original family name. Family cemeteries, thirty-six of them, provide immediate physical access to the genealogy.

In the 1920s, extensions of streetcar lines outward from Reading to the edges of the Oley Valley began the process of subdividing. However, these early subdivisions continued a metonymic use of names. New streets were given the names of residents in the vicinity—Ganster Street, Trout Street, Levan Street.

Subdivisions since the 1950s have introduced different kinds of names and obliterated the local usage. In 1978, across from a line of streetcar-era houses, on what was the old Levan Farm, a sign for "Lenape Acres" marked a new subdivision adjacent to the 1950s section. While the name referred to the original Native Americans of the region, the sign showed an Indian wearing a headdress associated with western tribes. The original design for the cul-de-sac streets included the names of an exotic tree, "Teak," and the developer's wife. Besides introducing new names, these developments erased landmarks that were known informally as "the lane," "the bend," "the meadow," and "the creek."

Along Bertolet Mill Road, leading (inevitably) past Bertolet Mill (still lived in by a Bertolet), the new development of Charmingdale appears. The streets are named Dale Drive, Wagon Way, Carriage Circle, Shay Lane, Surry Court, and Coach Lane, in an attempt to evoke a vague nostalgia for rustic transport technology and a rural landscape that Charmingdale helps to erase. At the other end of the valley, a development called Morning Mist includes streets named Misty Lane and Meadowlark Road to conjure a soft-focus, lyrical countryside. Rather than continuing the specific metonymies associated with the Oley Valley, the developers selected names with the potential for wider circulation and consumption. The conflation of images and vagueness is a consequence of this strategy.

Entrance to subdivision in the Oley Valley, Pennsylvania.

Differences in naming index real differences in experience. There is a wide gulf between those who continue to farm and those who live in the developments. Mark Hoch, a farmer working land that has always borne his family's name, every day looks out to a line of new houses at the edge of his property, yet he cannot name any of the people who live there. He considers his neighbors to be the other farmers in the valley, and he knows the names of the original families for each of the farms.

How such a place is named highlights the larger ideological issues of traditional landscapes versus commercial and commodified landscapes. In the ideology of regionalism, the local name is favored over the import. Randall Arendt et al. prescribe in their book *Rural by Design* (1994) that developers be encouraged to name streets after natural features or local historic names. In addition,

> terms such as "road," "lane," "street," or "way" should be used rather than suburban words such as "drive," "circle," "place," "court," "view," "vista," "manor," or "terrace." ...Personal first names should be strongly discouraged ("Barbara Road," "Robert Circle," e.g.) unless they are also readable as surnames ("Douglas," "Leslie," "Tracy," "Thomas," etc.). (Arendt, 190)

As they describe, locality is clearly signified by distinct naming strategies. Likewise, a suburban topos is clearly conjured by its own set of toponyms. Perhaps, however, this distinction between the Hoch Farm and Charmingdale is useful to reveal the new layer of change. Unless naming is connected to a series of other decisions to maintain the local cultural landscape, the attempt to mimic local names in new development could, instead, mask the changes in social and economic life. Using local names may memorialize former people and uses, but it also marks the real loss of the traditional use of the land. One farmer, when asked about this approach, considered it almost as an insult to have his name appended to a street that bears no relation to his labor and family tradition. It also ignores the fact that even rural landscapes, prosaic as the names may seem, include a range of naming systems including names from literature, religious narratives, and references to other places. To prescribe one strategy for naming would seem to be contrary to the diverse collage of names on the land.

RENAMING/RECLAIMING PLACES

Because naming is such a fundamental gesture that marks the symbolic presence in and possession of a place, name changes are at the center of plots to contest, control, or reclaim places. Saint Petersburg, renamed Petrograd, then Leningrad, only to be restored to Saint Petersburg, indexes the tides of Russia's political conflicts. In Paris, as the succession of governments sought to repudiate the past and legitimate the present, they replaced the names of old heroes with new ones. Place Louis XV became Louis XVI, 29-Juillet, and finally Concorde (Ferguson, 391). Other episodes of renaming occur as demographics shift, formerly distinct places merge into a larger region, or new immigrants gain economic and political status.

Renaming is an effective strategy for claiming space by groups traditionally without power. Informal or slang designations mark the symbolic appropriation of places cutting across the names of historic patrimony, official designations, and rational but semantically flat designations. Residents in the public housing on the lettered streets in one area of New York City renamed the area Alphabet City; in the Brighton Beach section of Brooklyn, there is an area known as Little Odessa because of the concentration of Russians there. As groups gain political power, they often assert their iden-

Avenue C in Manhattan was renamed Loisaida Avenue after the Puerto Rican pronunciation of "Lower East Side."

tity and history by claiming space with official name changes. The Hispanic[6] who now live in Manhattan's Lower East Side know it in their own pronunciation as the "Loisaida." Avenue C is now officially designated as Loisaida Avenue. A nearby garden on Fourth Street is dedicated to Bimbo Rivas, the Puerto Rican poet who coined the name for the area (Zeitlin). Renaming, then, whether by decree, developers, or referenda, is an exercise in claiming identity and power. It raises issues of whose history is inscribed in the landscape, how diversity is included within previous discourses of selection and exclusion, and how renaming reclaims the loss of place identity.

Above: REPOhistory sign marking the entrance to the area of Atlanta once known as Buttermilk Bottom. (Photograph by Frank Niemeir)

Below: Map showing the former extent and present-day pattern of Buttermilk Bottom after urban renewal. (Jim Costanzo)

WHERE'S BUTTERMILK BOTTOM? PUTTING A COMMUNITY BACK ON THE MAP OF MEMORY

Under the guise of urban renewal, whole communities and countless individuals were erased from the map in the United States in the 1960s. Designated as "slums" these areas were treated as places without a history (or at least as places with history considered shameful, one to be edited out), without status, and without claims to certain rights of possession of urban space. All the differentiated places, landmarks, streets, and houses were cleared to make a blank slate for the modern vision of the city. If one looks at any of the Sanborn maps prior to demolition, there is a wealth and diversity of names that "disappeared" with "urban removal."

In Atlanta, the Fulton County Stadium, Civic Center, Georgia Power headquarters, public housing, large parking lots, and stylish Rio Shopping Center, with Martha Schwartz's frogs paying homage to a large globe, occupy the site of what was once an African-American community. The area, a low, poorly drained and sometimes foul-smelling district created by segregation, was designated a "slum" and cleared of shotgun shacks and juke joints to make way for a version of the "New South." However, it was also a vibrant community of African-American-run schools, churches, and businesses known as Buttermilk Bottom.

The former residents were dispossessed and dispersed. The city leveled and cleared 90 percent of the district. Streets were realigned or removed. The transformation was so extensive that most people had even forgotten that there had ever been a place called Buttermilk Bottom.

Mark O'Brien, an Atlanta artist living in New York City and working with a group known as REPOhistory, however, remembered the place and the name. This became the kernel for initiating a project to reclaim the history of this site in 1995, thirty years after the events of its destruction. As their name suggests, REPOhistory is an artists' collective engaged in repossessing, or reinscribing, absent, suppressed, or forgotten narratives through site-specific public art. Their intention is not to substitute their own version but to provoke multiple readings of sites in relation to other histories. Working with Atlanta artists and former residents of the Bottom, REPOhistory began a project to put "Buttermilk Bottom" back on the map. They documented the forgotten names, events, and experiences in the Bottom

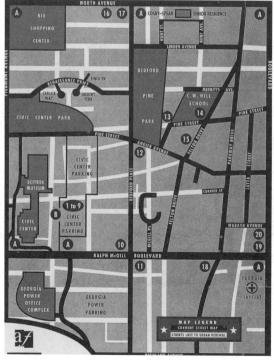

There are different versions of how Buttermilk Bottom got its name. June Mundy recalled a story, which, like many "folk etymologies," resolves around a chance event:

"Well, I'm not sure, but there are several stories out about how the name Buttermilk Bottom came about, and the one that comes to me most, which was really a long way before my time, I believe it was in the area of about probably horse and buggy days... there was a milk truck. It wasn't really a truck, then, but it was a wagon. And this person was trying to outrun the police and somehow ran upon this mule wagon, horse wagon, and startled the milkman and turned over the milk, the buttermilk truck, so there was this big ... buttermilk ran down there a long time. But that's one that comes through the grapevine."
(REPOhistory, 1995)

and then remapped them by marking sites, including painting former footprints of a house on a current parking lot and locating a series of signs throughout the area. They also organized a reunion of former residents.[7]

The artists started by asking how the area got this curious name. There were several versions ranging from tales of a chance event to James Malone's belief that it was associated with an African-American preference for buttermilk. It may also have derived from a sparsely used creek bottom called The Butler Street Bottoms, where this black housing district began and which it followed as it grew northward (Bogen).

Whatever its origins, its use became part of the racial discourse of the city. Emory Searcy remembers that this place name was also used as a racial epithet.

The word "nigger" has a negative connotation depending upon who's using it. You know, it's just like, I can curse my brother or my sister, but you better not. So the word "Buttermilk Bottom" had positive and negative connotations depending upon who was using it. For instance, people would joke among themselves, but then as it relates to people talking about somebody or something in the Bottom, you resented that, simply because you had friends there, that you cared for, that you had a great deal of respect for.
So there was a resentment but yet you could use it internally....So it's just like that word, you know.

Street names played a role in the segregation practices that created the Bottom. While the streets and boulevards passed through the city, when they reached the black portions of the town that included the Bottom, the names changed to keep the distinctions between white and black clear. Ra Khabeer

Betti-Sue Hertz and Tom Klem paint "School Street" back on Buttermilk Bottom.

remembered the name changes: "Ponce Boulevard changed to Monroe. White people did that deliberately so there would be no connection. They didn't want that continuity like we lived on the same street so the name was changed." Thad Olive also noted this peculiarity of Atlanta's streets: "Here you can just go through a traffic light and for no reason at all, I mean, I know the reason, but the average person is not aware of the reason how come the street changes name...it was really a racial thing." And Emory Searcy was not aware until he was an adult that the namesake of the main street in the Bottom, Forrest Avenue, which passed Nathan B. Forrest school, was a Confederate general and a founding member of the Ku Klux Klan. However, an earlier generation who shopped and worked along this street would have been well aware of the association, since Nathan B. Forrest Klavern Number 1 (Atlanta was the headquarters of the national Klu Klux Klan) was well known around the country (Bogen). The street name has subsequently been changed to Ralph McGill, after a moderate journalist and editorialist.

Based on interviews with former residents, REPOhistory artists attempted to reconstruct aspects of the life of the now dispersed community tied to vanished streets, houses, and other landmarks. The project, entitled "Entering Buttermilk Bottom," which opened as part of the 1995 Arts Festival of Atlanta and continued through the 1996 Olympics, told the story of the birth, life, and destruction of the Bottom through a series of markings laid over the rebuilt physical and social landscape. First, a series of official-looking signs with the words "Entering Buttermilk Bottom" designated the former boundaries of the area and gave status to what was formerly an unofficial name.[8] It also spoke a name created by systematic practices of segregation at all levels, from real estate development to city planning.

A series of signs located within the Bottom reclaimed the names of sites, events, people, and history of the district. The sign "Shermantown" recalled a former name for the area just south of the Bottom, a result of Sherman's march to the sea and the stream of freed African-Americans who poured into the cities of Richmond, Washington, and Atlanta, only to occupy the unclaimed or marginal real estate. Other signs recalled the names of specific institutions, such as Ingram Temple, and noted significant events (residents' meeting, 1965) as well as daily routines.

By calling out the forgotten names, the project reclaimed memory and space in the urban landscape. Without nostalgia, it raised the questions and issues of naming in the plotting of city space. One sign provoked comparisons by substituting the name Olympic Redevelopment for Urban Renewal.

The project challenged the tendency to stereotype people and the history of places by naming specific individuals, places, and experiences. At one of the early working meetings, James Malone pulled out an old crumpled photograph of his mother when she lived in the Bottom. This image became the sign:

> Mrs. Sara Lena Echols MALONE raised her family on 267 Pine Place, Apt. #3 in the early thirties.

Placed back on that site, it reclaimed space for one name out of the many that were removed from the Bottom.

RECLAIMING INDIGENOUS NAMES

Names figure in narratives to restore a lost relationship to place. The "salvage toponymy"[9] of Buttermilk Bottom is a strategy used in other places by groups seeking to reclaim a lost identity and place in history following episodes of industrialization, colonization, or other significant displacements. Describing efforts to restore Irish names, Catherine Nash writes:

> The placename in Ireland carries cultural connotations that are being employed in a post-colonial exploration of identity, in which the

Top left: "Segregation on the Map." This sign reveals how racism was embedded in the changes in names as the streets continued out of the Bottom. (By Neill Bogan and Irene Ledwith, courtesy REPOhistory)

Top right: The sign by Atlanta artist James Malone, and REPOhistory's Tom Klem reclaimed the place where Malone's mother lived in the Bottom. The Georgia Power building is in the background. (Photograph by Frank Niemeir)

The back of the sign noted a series of significant named people and places: "Mrs. Sara Lena Echols MALONE was a resident of 267 Pine Place, Apt. #3, in the early thirties. She was a member of Elder Henry Ingram's Church of God in Christ located on Buchanon Street near Currier Street. Mrs. Malone, homemaker, was born on September 4th, 1908, in Athens, Georgia. She was the wife of Ralph Malone and mother of two sons, Ralph Jr. and James. Surviving family member James Hiram Malone is a professional artist who now lives on North Avenue NW in Atlanta, Georgia, 30318."

placename carries the burden of a history of colonial subjugation, resultant loss of the Irish language, loss of population due to emigration, and colonial Anglicization of placenames during the 19th-century British mapping project. (Nash, 239)

Likewise Native American placenames contain similar narratives of colonization, loss of language, and loss of place. Efforts to restore Native American names are part of a broader effort to restore a different relationship to place. In the 1920s a group of Anglo women writers in the Southwest sought an alternative relationship to land they believed could be found in the original Native American experience. Mary Austin, in *The Land of Journey's Ending,* rejected Anglo names and used the original Indian and Hispanic designations, which she believed reflected a respect for the land, a communal sense of shared identity, and an intimate knowledge of place gained from living with the land and waiting for "its occasions," versus a dominant position of discovery, mastery, and private possession. However, despite such sympathies, the attitudes of Austin and her friends represented a European desire to return to what was imagined as timeless, and more authentic (Rudnick, 10–26). Thus, they inadvertently reinforced colonial stereotyping of the indigenous group as close to nature, and therefore more intuitive, feminine, naive, and childlike.

Despite these associations, renaming can be a strategy for remembering the violence of colonialism and recuperating lost identity without resorting to the discourses that served to disrupt an indigenous culture in the first place. The proposal in 1992 to rename the streets that intersect Junipero Serra Boulevard in San Francisco with the names of the tribes that once lived in the region linked the Spanish missions established by Fra Serra to the decimation of the indigenous population. There is also concerted effort to reclaim placenames by Native Americans themselves. By restoring placenames, they restore their history. Rather than a nostalgic exercise, this act is linked to other actions to reassert land claims, preserve sacred sites, and restore economic and legal status. For instance, the 1,672 places in the United States with *devil* in their title, including Devils Tower, Wyoming (of *Close Encounters* fame), and Devil's Lake, North Dakota, were named by Europeans because they seemed hellish in origin. However, most of these sites were sacred areas for Native Americans, who now seek to restore their spiritual significance (Brooke).[10] The restoration of names helps to protect sites from further change, yet certain places must be left unnamed and unmarked to retain their sacredness.

"LEARN THE NAMES OF ALL THESE PLACES"

Anthropologist Keith Basso discovered the bond that develops between names, places, and stories. In attempting to interpret the culture and landscape of the Western Apache, he puzzled over statements such as "The land is always stalking people. The land makes people live right." At one point his Apache friend and consultant, Nick Thompson, advised him to "learn the names of all these places." What he found was a landscape dense with names in the form of complete descriptive sentences: "water flows downward on top of a series of flat rocks" or "white rocks lie above in a compact cluster." These name pictures are evoked at the beginning and end of oral narratives ("It happened at men stand above here and there") and serve as "mnemonic pegs" on which to hang their histories (Basso, 44). They are also highly moral stories. The names and their stories are directed at individuals, and as Benson Lewis says, they "go to work on you like arrows," conveying very specific social criticisms, injunctions, and teachings (Basso, 21). The names provide a collective social memory so that "even if we go far away from here to some big city, places around here keep stalking us....The names of all these places are good. They make you remember how to live right, so you want to replace yourself again" (Basso, 42)

In Cibecue, Arizona, and other places, it is critical to learn the names and their stories, since connections to both place and society are constituted by the institution of names. They carry the voice of people speaking, sometimes in languages that have died. In their abbreviated form names tell who lives there, what happened, who or what is honored, the important metaphors, and their aspirations. Not only are there narratives *in* names, but names figure in the narrative plots surrounding questions of identity: giving presence to the unknown, taking possession of space, interpreting and remembering the past, erasing claims, and reclaiming connections to place, history, and nature.

NOTES

1. Descriptive character traits of figures acquire names that reflect discourses. Chatman notes that each epoch characterizes human qualities in relation to concerns of the times. *Devotion, pity,* and *patience* are presumed to be human traits observable through the ages, but these terms were not established until the Church articulated them as Christian virtues. "Other sources for our trait-names are astrology (*jovial, saturnine*), Galenian medicine (*good-humored, cold-blooded*), the Reformation (*sincere, bigoted, fanatic, self-assured*), Neoclassicism (*fatuous, callous, countrified*), Romanticism (*depressed, apathetic, diffident*), psychology and psychoanalysis (*introverted, neurotic, schizoid*), etc." (Chatman 123). Trait names for the natural features of landscapes reflect similar discourses.

2. The term *Shoah*, which designates what happened to Jews under the Nazis, has a complex history and meaning. In the biblical references the term implied divine judgment and retribution. However, the connotations shift in modern Hebrew usage to designate "metaphysical doubt, reconsideration of the validity of man's rational faculties, sometimes even personal indulgence in despair." From Uriel Tal, "Excursus on the Term *Shoah*," *Shoah: A Review of Holocaust Studies and Commemorations* 1(4):10–11.

3. Wilber Zelinsky coined this term in his various studies of names in the landscape, many of which are collected in his book *Exploring the Beloved Country: Geographic Forays into American Society and Culture* (Iowa City: University of Iowa Press, 1994).

4. Following a series of "battles" with authorities over the tax status of the property, Finlay renamed the site Little Sparta in keeping with the subtext of warfare throughout the garden.

5. He did, however, refer once to a place from his own biography, naming a peak Whiteface Mountain because it resembled a peak in the Adirondacks where he began exploring wilderness as a teenager.

6. The name *Hispanic* actually erases differences of Chicanos, Cubans, Puerto Ricans, etc., ignores indigenous heritage, and emphasizes a Spanish link. The term *Latino* is preferred as the more inclusive term (Lippard, 1990).

7. The artists who collaborated on this project included Donna Kessinger, Jenny Hoffner, Betti-Sue Hertz, Flash Light, Tim Arkansaw, Sarah Vogwill, James Malone, Tom Klem, Paul Menair, Jim Costanzo, Lisa Maya Knauer, Stephanie Basch, Chris Neville, Neill Bogan, Tony Bingham, Marie Cochran, Jim Williams, Anne Cox, Irene Ledwith, Eddie Granderson, Cynthia Anderson Liesenfeld, George Spencer, and Ed Woodham.

8. The "Entering Buttermilk Bottom" signs were directed at an audience traveling in automobiles. Other aspects of the project, the specific signs and

the map superimposed over the parking lot, were intended to be read from a pedestrian viewpoint.

9. The term is derived from anthropologist James Cliffords' term *salvage paradigm.*

10. One response of the National Parks Service to the issue of restoring Native American names is to create a dual naming system, preserving both the European name and the indigenous name.

REFERENCES

Arendt, Randall, with Elizabeth A. Brabec, Harry L. Dodson, Christine Reid, and Robert D. Yaro. 1994. *Rural by Design: Maintaining Small Town Character.* Washington, D.C.: American Planning Association.

Aschmann, Homer. 1986. "Calendar Dates as Street Names in Asuncion, Paraguay." *Names* 34(2):146–153.

Basso, Keith H. 1984. "'Stalking with Stories': Names, Places, and Moral Narratives among the Western Apache." In *Text, Play and Story: The Construction and Reconstruction of Self and Society,* ed. Edward M. Bruner and Stuart Plattner. Washington, D.C.: American Ethnological Society. Pp. 19–55.

Baur, Kim (program chair, landscape architecture, Colorado State University; former associate, Sasaki Associates). 1996. Interview, February 22.

Baxter, Timothy M. S. 1992. *The Cratylus: Plato's Critique of Naming.* Leiden, Netherlands: E. J. Brill.

Bell, Robert E. 1989. *Place-Names in Classical Mythology: Greece.* Oxford, England: Clio Press Ltd.

Blackmar, Elizabeth. 1996. "Preserved Narratives, Recovered Stories, and Forgotten Politics: Central Park in New York City." Presentation, Yale University, March 2.

Bogen, Neil (member of REPOhistory). 1996. Correspondence.

Brooke, James. 1996. "What's in a Name? An Affront, Say Several Tribes." *New York Times,* November 17.

Browning, Peter. 1988. *Yosemite Place Names: The Historic Background of Geographic Names in Yosemite National Park.* Lafayette, Calif.: Great West Books.

Carter, Paul. 1990. "Plotting: Australia's Explorer Narratives as 'Spatial History.'" *Yale Journal of Criticism* 3(2):91–107.

Chatmon, Seymour. 1978. *Story and Discourse: Narrative Structure in Fiction and Film.* Ithaca, N.Y.: Cornell University Press.

Cole, Terrence M. 1992. "Placenames in Paradise: Robert Marshall and the Naming of the Alaska Wilderness." *Names* 40(2):99–115.

Cooper, Martha and Joseph Sciorra. 1994. *R.I.P.: Memorial Wall Art.* New York: Henry Holt.

Cronon, William. 1983. *Changes in the Land: Indians, Colonists, and the Ecology of New England.* New York: Hill and Wang.

———. 1992. "A Place for Stories: Nature, History, and Narrative." *Journal of American History* (March):1347–1376.

De Certeau, Michel. 1984. *The Practice of Everyday Life.* Berkeley: University of California Press.

Ewald, Barry (borough supervisor, Saint Lawrence, Pennsylvania). 1996. Interview, March 13.

Ferguson, Priscilla Parkhurst. 1988. "Reading City Streets." *French Review* 61(3):386–397.

Hobson, Archie, ed. 1985. *Remembering America: A Sampler of the WPA American Guide Series.* New York: Columbia University Press.

Hoch, Mark (farmer, Oley Valley, Pennsylvania). 1996. Interview, March 13.

Hufford, Mary. 1986. *One Space, Many Places: Folklife and Land Use in New Jersey's Pinelands National Reserve.* Washington, D.C.: American Folklife Center, Library of Congress.

Koegler, Karen. 1986. "A Farewell to Arms: The 'Greening' of American Apartment." *Names* 34:48–61.

Large, Arlen J. 1994. "All in the Family: The In-House Honorifics of Lewis and Clark." *Names* 42(4):269–277.

Le Guin, Ursula. 1985. "She Unnames Them." *The New Yorker,* January 21.

Leighly, John. 1986. "Biblical Place-Names in the United States." In *Names and Their Varieties: A Collection of Essays in Onomastics,* ed. Kelsie B. Harder. Lanham, Md.: University Press of America.

Lippard, Lucy. 1990. *Mixed Blessings: New Art in Multicultural America.* New York: Pantheon.

Miller, J. Hillis. 1995. *Topographies.* Stanford, Calif.: Stanford University Press.

Nash, Catherine. 1994. "Remapping the Body/Land: New Cartographies of Identity, Gender, and Landscape in Ireland." In *Writing, Women, and Space: Colonial and Postcolonial Geographies.* New York: Guilford Press. Pp. 227–246.

Nicolaisen, W. F. H. 1976. *Scottish Place-Names.* London: B. T. Batsford Ltd.

———. 1984. "Names and Narratives." *Journal of American Folklore* 97(385):364–377.

———. 1988. "The Toponymy of Remembered Childhood." *Names* 36(3&4):133–142.

Olmsted, Frederick Law. 1865. Letter to J. H. Willey. Library of Congress, Manuscript Division. Reprinted in *Landscape Architecture* 13(1):40–42.

———. 1886. *Notes on the Plan of Franklin Park and Related Matters.* Boston: Department of Parks.

Ragussis, Michael. 1986. *Acts of Naming: The Family Plot in Fiction.* Oxford: Oxford University Press.

Ranney, Victoria Post, ed. 1990. *Papers of Frederick Law Olmsted: The California Frontier, 1863–1865.* Baltimore: Johns Hopkins University Press.

Rennick, Robert M. 1970. "The Nazi Name Decrees of the Nineteen Thirties." *Names* 18(1):65–88.

REPOhistory. 1995. "REPOhistory 'Entering Buttermilk Bottom': Video interviews conducted by Lisa Maya Knauer and others."

Roberts, J. Timmons. 1993. "Power and Placenames: A Case Study from the Contemporary Amazon Frontier." *Names* 41(3):159–181.

Rubinstein, Nora. 1996. Correspondence with authors.

Rudnick, Lois. 1987. "Re-Naming the Land: Anglo Expatriate Women in the Southwest." In *The Desert Is No Lady*, ed. Vera Norwood and Janice Monk. New Haven, Conn.: Yale University Press.

Scruggs, Jan C., and Joel L. Swerdlow. 1985. *To Heal a Nation: The Vietnam Veterans Memorial*. New York: Harper & Row.

Seddon, George. 1995. "Words and Weeds: Some Notes on Language and Landscape." *Landscape Review* 2:3–15.

Simpson, Charles. 1994. "Mapping an Extreme Landscape: The Cultural Meanings of British Arctic Exploration between 1769 and 1835." In *Re-Naming the Landscape*, ed. Jurgen Kleist and Bruce A. Butterfield. New York: Peter Lang.

Solnit, Rebecca. 1995. *Savage Dreams: A Journey into the Landscape Wars of the American West*. New York: Departure Books.

Stewart, George R. 1945. *Names on the Land*. New York: Random House.

Stuart-Murray, John. 1995. "Unnameable Landscapes." *Landscape Review* 2:30–41.

———. 1997. Correspondence with authors.

Stump, Roger W. 1988. "Toponymic Commemoration of National Figures: The Cases of Kennedy and King." *Names* 36(3&4):203–216.

Todorov, Tzvetan. 1982. *The Conquest of America: The Question of the Other*. New York: Harper & Row.

Zeitlin, Steve. 1995. "So What's in a Name? Plenty!" *New York Newsday*, May 24.

Zelinsky, Wilber. 1994. *Exploring the Beloved Country: Geographic Forays into American Society and Culture*. Iowa City: University of Iowa Press.

CHAPTER FOUR

SEQUENCING

INTRODUCTION

A story begins with an event, a state of existence in time that is bound to change. The change may be sudden or cataclysmic or it may be a barely perceptible shift in routine. Any two events can make up a narrative sequence, one to establish an existing situation and one to alter it. This may be as simple as bringing the old into direct contrast with the new, compressing otherwise gradual and unobservable changes of a landscape into a clear moment of contrast. This happens everywhere there is change.

Drivers along U.S. Route 1 in Freeport, Maine, pass a complex of buildings that tell the familiar regional story of connected barns developed over generations.[1] Once off the main road, however, instead of finding the expected white clapboards, one sees the new glass walls, signage, and bright colors of a retail shopping center behind a small preserved cemetery. By juxtaposing the agricultural landscape against the commercial landscape, fieldstone against glass, earth tones against primary colors, and old against new, the architects Mitchell/Dewan and Teas Feeley and Hingston reveal how Freeport has changed from a rural village to a mecca for outlets and mail-order shopping. The contrast of beginning and end creates speculations about what happened, for between the juxtaposition of two events lies a story.

Although events may be independent, the suggestion of causality once those events are placed in a sequence is powerful. For instance, "the forest caught fire and young plants grew vigorously" is a series of two events that makes a cohesive story. From experience or scientific knowledge, we implicitly understand that the vigor of growth results from the nutrients left by the fire. Even if the order is reversed, or the plot structure is changed, the causal order, which may be independent from the narrative order, is understood. In fact, the reader tends to make sense and connect the given events of a narrative. Philosopher Paul Ricoeur discusses how sequences create a sense of "connectedness" despite the realities of independent events, the unexplainable, freak disasters, or sudden chance. The reader assumes that because one event in a story takes place *next to* another, there is a causal relation. In the often repeated example "the king dies and the queen dies of grief," the reader implicitly assumes that the queen's grief is caused by the king's

Top: Along Route 1, Freeport Crossing, appears to be a typical vernacular farm with barns extended by family additions over time.

Above: Off the local road, Freeport Crossing appears as a shopping center behind the local cemetery.

James Wines of the environmental design firm SITE takes an ordinary experience, the sequence from the parking lot to the shopping mall, and surprises you. Once close to the building, the visitor sees the soil of the region through the glass facade. Instead of finding a gleaming bright showroom, once inside the BEST store the shopper meets a woodland.

death, although it is possible that the events are independent.[2] In the landscape, assumptions regarding causal relations are often made based on spatial proximity. Trash dumped on abandoned lots in the South Bronx, for instance, is often considered to be the fault of the community's low-income residents, despite the fact that the dumping is done by outsiders arriving by truck. The suggestion and presumption of causality by proximity means that narratives are constantly and unconsciously evoked in the landscape.

Narrative sequences
one word after another in a sentence
one event after another in a story
one element after another in a landscape

Narratives can be suggested by the simplest juxtaposition and do not necessarily require either a conscious ordering or defined causal relation. Chronicles, diaries, walks, and routes are types of sequence that are without plot yet are narrative. In both the Vietnam Memorial and the Yale University Women's Memorial, for instance, the architect and artist Maya Lin created a chronicle suggesting numerous narratives that are open to interpretation and explanation. The number of soldiers who died each year of the war and the number of women enrolled at Yale since 1701 each tells a story of change. Although routine trips are less consciously ordered or less well defined around themes than these memorials, they also gain narrative associations over time. A trip from New York City to Long Island, for instance, may to some reveal the history of suburban development or to others be a collection of evocative place names, Kew Gardens, Valley Stream, Freeport, Babylon, Eastport, Hampton Bays, Montauk Point. For the commuter, repeated trips over time build associations: where an accident was witnessed, where traffic tends to jam, where stops are made for food or flowers, where a radio station may be received. Although in the first sequence the destination of Montauk Point may correlate with the end of the physical island, most sequences end in the middle. Hayden White considers chronicles to be narrative without storylike closure: he writes that a chronicle does not "so much conclude as terminate. It starts out to tell a story but breaks off *in medias res*, in the chronicler's own present; it leaves things unresolved, or rather it leaves them unresolved in a storylike way" (White, 5). The order of experience rather than the physical composition gives meaning to the sequence.

Familiar routes gain layers of association because of the many events that take place along them over time. Every Memorial Day weekend for at least thirty-five years the Davis family has traveled from Florida, Georgia, North Carolina, Virginia, New York, and Ohio to meet in Clay, West Virginia. Lorri Davis describes a family tradition kept alive by her father's side of the family, which starts at her father's birthplace:

"The family members begin arriving sometime around noon at the Clay house, where my father was born and raised. Everyone brings food...which is another story altogether. Anyway...some or most of the food is consumed and then the journey begins.

"At least three pickup trucks will be on the premises (not the least out of place for Clay, West Virginia), and we all pile in the back, making sure the young ones will sit up close to the cab. The truck caravan drives along the Elk River for three miles or so, then it takes a right up a hill. The climb up the hill is quite slow—parts of the road are missing and we don't want to lose anyone out the back. Along the way up the hill we pass small, makeshift houses. The people seem sad and poor and the truck usually becomes silent. The same people seem to be there year after year.

"We finally arrive at an abandoned one-room schoolhouse where the road no longer exists. We pile out of the truck to walk the rest of the way to the cemetery. We used to picnic at the cemetery but that tradition was slowly outlawed since it was difficult for the women to trudge up the mountain with food and children. Once we arrive at the graveyard, we sit around on the gravestones and talk for an hour or so.

"We then walk back to the schoolhouse and pile into the trucks. After we pass the mountain inhabitants, the trucks stop suddenly and the men jump out of the trucks and scramble around in the woods. They return proudly with branches and limbs of birch. The women all reach out gleefully with hands and mouth to chew the birch bark. Where this tradition comes from defies my imagination.

"Almost home, one more stop. We return to the main road and all the children scream, 'Go across the bridge! Go across the bridge!' The bridge is a very narrow and rickety steel cable suspension bridge that only one vehicle at a time may cross. Crossing it is very scary and very fun.

"Every year every single step is the same."
(Davis)

Plots, on the other hand, are more ordered arrangements that give meaning to events and actions. Beginnings establish the potential for change, frame the scenes that follow, and create a mood. What is known in advance affects the reader's understanding and interpretation of events that follow.

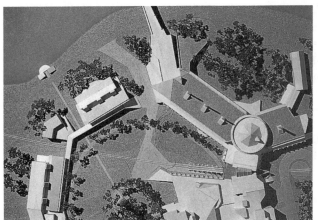

It is proposed that each spring graduates from Trent University's Environmental Sciences Program in Peterborough, Ontario, perform a ritual procession through their campus. The architects Richard and Gregory Henriquez structured the sequence so that "individuals would be able to perceive the historical evidence of their daily actions" (Henriquez, 198). Two graduates, one female and one male, proceed with an oak sapling and a vessel of water, respectively. From a river footbridge they enter the rotunda of the Environmental Science Building, then ascend stairs that take them to a railcar that will descend into a "spiral forest." Other students control the descent of the railcar with ropes. Once they are off the railcar, the vessel is filled with water from the Otonabee River, and then the graduates plant and water the saplings. Each year, for 350 years, a tree will be added to make a continuous spiral. The ceremony ends with the lifting of the railroad car to the trestle, where it is bolted into place until the next year's ceremony.

On the other hand, endings enclose the story and define the meaning of past events. With a plot, every event is in the story for a reason, even if it is meant to throw the reader off from the main plot. The dynamics of a plot are created by establishing tensions that pose and move toward resolution.

The events of every story can be ordered in an unlimited number of ways, each conveying a different meaning. All histories or stories worth telling have more than one interpretation or version of the order of events (White, 19). The historian William Cronon, in his article "A Place for Stories: Nature, History, and Narrative," analyzes the multiple narrative versions of the midwest dust storms of the 1930s. Historians with similar knowledge of the subject matter differ in their interpretation of this event. These differences appear in the sequences of their stories—in particular where the stories begin and end. Yet meanings and morals lie in the changes that occur from a story's beginning to end. A story that starts with a scene of productive and peaceful Great Plains Indians and ends with the dust bowl as the product of devastating frontier agricultural practices conveys a different meaning than a story that starts with brave frontier people establishing communities in the Great Plains and ends with them persevering and flourishing despite the drought. Cronon concludes with an essential observation about narrative itself: "where one chooses to begin and end a story profoundly alters its shape and meaning" (Cronon, 1364).

Even the most ordinary event can take on an extraordinary meaning depending on its placement within a sequence. A traffic light changing from green to red is an ordinary event, but when it happens after Luke is shot at the end of *Cool Hand Luke*, the traffic light becomes a powerful metaphor for Luke's tragic end. He is being taken to the prison hospital instead of the emergency room, and the viewer knows he is going to die. In usually more subtle ways, when planners and designers order movement and the sequence of events they are also affecting meaning beyond formal terms. In designing a pedestrian sequence through the Brooklyn fishing community of Sheepshead Bay, landscape architectural students at City College were asked to think cinematically about ways of entering, destinations, and routes. One student's concept to connect the community with the life of fish and fishing was realized by creating a wall of fish in the subway station as an "opening scene."[3] Other students built a more gradual sequence toward the water that climaxed at a community waterfront park.

Film is perhaps the closest medium to landscape design in terms of potential means for structuring plot. Flash-forwards, flashbacks, and as the literary theorist Nelson Goodman coined, "flash-betweens" are some of the time-altering devices that structure plot and order our discovery of meaning by giving the reader the power of hindsight and foresight not always possible in the experiences of real life.[4] Although many conventional narrative structures present stories chronologically or logically around an idea

with the use of flashbacks and flash-forwards, some narratives follow neither a chronological nor apparently logical sequence.

EXAMPLES OF TIME-ALTERING DEVICES FOUND IN THE LANDSCAPE

jump cut	Outside the city a farm may jump-cut to suburban development or the streets of Manhattan north of Sixtieth Street may jump-cut to Central Park.
flashback	In the book *On This Site* by Joel Steinfeld, photographs of the scenes of past crimes are placed next to the description of the crime. The viewer imaginatively flashes back to the crime that is described in the accompanying text. This is a common experience in historical landscapes, where the visitor imagines *what happened here.*
flash-forward	As the visitor circulates around a picturesque garden, glimpses of the future and final destination are given. Or along a road way, signs flash-forward the places that are ahead.
flash-between	The insertion of billboard advertising for sneakers, gum, or blue jeans along a scenic drive is a flash-between, or something that happens between two events that does not belong there. Agricultural field–sneakers–hedgerow.
fade	Many gardens fade, or create gradual transitions, from the urban environment to pastoral or from formal to informal.
blackout	The tunnel acts as a blackout between one side of the river or mountain and the other.
freeze-frame	Historic landscapes such as Colonial Williamsburg are frequently interpreted according to one historic period. These places seem frozen in time.
slow motion	The careful selection of ever-blooming plants and the development of new hybrids that bloom later or earlier than usual may create the sense of a spring in slow motion.

Multiple sequences through the same landscape structure different meanings depending on where people are coming from and where they are going. These differences are made evident in the Cumberland Valley, a section of the Appalachian Trail in Pennsylvania. Those hiking along the 2,000-mile range from Maine to Georgia experience a sequence from wilderness to agricultural and suburban growth when entering this distinct valley. On the other hand, those entering the trail from the new suburban community experience a sequence from the suburban streets and homes to a relative natural oasis.[5] What is an interruption or a perceived *decline* to some may be considered an improvement by others, suggesting that the meaning of sequences is relative to the context of what lies before and after.

Running north and south, across the "grain" of the sedimentary layers, is an intrusive igneous rock that is more resistant than the surrounding rock and therefore forms a low ridge that the Appalachian Trail follows. The east-to-west cross section reveals the progressive development of sedimentary rock. The design team, led by Thomas Yahner of The Pennsylvania State University, considered how different geologic and ecological stories are understood by hikers, depending on how they approach and move along the trail.

The amusement park ride is a unique case where the narrator controls the strapped-in rider. Brenda Brown, while teaching landscape architecture design at the University of Illinois, asked her students to design ride sequences in part because they "provide some extremely fine-tuned examples, even models, of how sequential multi-sensorial landscape experiences may be composed" (Brown, 23). Her studies of contemporary rides at Orlando, Florida's Universal Studios and Walt Disney World illustrate ways that sound, sight, and movement combine to create memorable sequences. Splash Mountain at Walt Disney World's Magic Kingdom is, for instance, a plotted tour through mountains, swamps, bayous, and caverns based on *Tales of Uncle Remus* and *Song of the South*. Brown describes the rider's experience:

"Riders plummet, splash into, and cruise around the briar patch; they slowly climb, and then slither into the joyous strains of 'How DO You DO' and gently curve through a domestic, outdoor, momentarily unpopulated high-altitude landscape; they drop, splashing into a colorful 'outdoor' landscape within the mountain, profusely populated by singing animals;...and in a portion devoid of music, they take the long climb up the hill to Brer Fox's den, the ride's kinesthetic and dramatic climax, before the by far steepest and most thrilling chute, down through and under the briar patch and into freedom and the landscape beyond." (Brown, 2)

In contrast Space Mountain creates a more visceral and disorienting experience because movement is more primary than visual imagery or a clear story line: "One enters the spacious darkness of the main part of the ride with a plunge. The spaceship's accelerations and decelerations, its gravity-powered plunges and rises, its banks and straight-aways, its rhythmic clickety-clacks, take place in a blackness broken only by small bright stars, shooting comets and the occasional passing iridescent glow of another ship." (Brown, 10)

Brenda Brown rides Disney's Splash Mountain, a thrill flume ride, to experience how movement is synchronized with scene, musical tempo, and the plot of the Uncle Remus story.

fast motion	Most interpretations of ecological successions are presented in fast motion, making the otherwise slow and unperceivable processes of nature visible. At the Crosby Arboretum the juxtaposition of ecological stages of succession enables the visitor to walk by in a few minutes what would take nature hundreds of years to transform.
in medias res	Landing by plane into a foreign country or a distant city is a way of entering in medias res, or in the middle of the activities of a distinct space.

Plots are often formulated and follow definite patterns of movement. We know, for instance, that the events of a tragedy will decline as the story progresses, while the events of a romance or a comedy will probably end well for the lead characters. In Cronon's analysis of the dust bowl, he classified stories in which "the plot line eventually falls towards an ending that is more negative" as tragic or "declensional stories" and stories that progress toward a more hopeful ending as "progressive." Knowing these previously experienced formulations enables the reader to understand and make sense of what will happen for any new story. These are conventional ways of ordering time that extend from literature to ordinary life. The designed landscape typically tells romantic or progressive stories of hope, explained in part by those who have the authority to tell these stories, such as the commercial

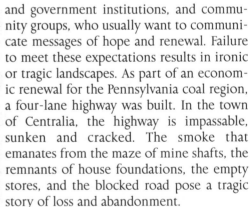

and government institutions, and community groups, who usually want to communicate messages of hope and renewal. Failure to meet these expectations results in ironic or tragic landscapes. As part of an economic renewal for the Pennsylvania coal region, a four-lane highway was built. In the town of Centralia, the highway is impassable, sunken and cracked. The smoke that emanates from the maze of mine shafts, the remnants of house foundations, the empty stores, and the blocked road pose a tragic story of loss and abandonment.

Another fundamental concept related to the ordering of events is that story time and narration time are independent variables in the making of landscape narratives. The time it takes to move through the landscape or to experience a sequence or change, analogous to the time it takes to read or tell a story, is narration time. Story time, on the other hand, refers to the imagined time span of the story. Unlike in film, narration time in the landscape is rarely controlled by the designer, for visitors may choose to pause or pass by selected parts of the landscape at their own pace.

Narrative sequences in the medium of the landscape differ from those in other mediums because the participant moves through the medium itself at his chosen speed while potentially engaging in various activities. Conversely, the medium is also constantly undergoing change as a result of human interaction and natural processes; each time one returns to the landscape it has changed in subtle or obvious ways. Bernard Tschumi, in a chapter titled "Sequences" from *Architecture and Disjunction,* identifies three factors—space, movement, and event—that may be subject to sequencing in architecture or landscape architecture (Tschumi, 162). The sequencing of *space* includes formal and physical aspects of the space—whether it is light or dark, inward or outward, linear or curvilinear, open or closed, narrow or wide, horizontal or vertical. These factors are often included in landscape and architectural design texts such as those of Lynch and Simonds. These same texts also discuss the sequencing of *movement,* including aspects of rhythm and speed. Lawrence Halprin found original ways to articulate and interpret movement through the landscape by borrowing from the choreography of dance. He distinguished open scores from closed scores based on the potential for improvisation. And *event* relates to what happens—the program, or the actions such as running, sitting, eating, listening to music, and reading—that take place in space through various movements. The placement of a "skating rink through the piano bar" or " the pole-vaulter in the catacombs" (Tschumi, 158) illustrates that in Tschumi's landscapes the program/event may be indifferent to spatial sequences, reinforce spatial sequences, or work against spatial sequences. We would add that a continual sequence of events—climatic, physical, and biological—alters the landscape itself. Together these factors of space, movement, and event consummate sequential and narrative experiences.

The following discussion begins with a sequence that happens or is experienced from the perspective of a static viewer, moves to increasingly complex sequences (from those that follow lines to those that open and branch), and concludes with sequences that are about the all-at-onceness or simultaneity of surrounding events. We start with processions through the landscape and end with processes that are part of the landscape.

THE PANORAMIC POSITION

In the landscape, the panoramic view—a superior position from which the viewer sees all that passes before or comes ahead—is analogous to the position of a reader with all the information about plot and motives. The designer takes this position by working over plans and aerial photographs and constructing perspective views. This way of looking at landscape leads to structured or planned sequences, whether formal or informal. The

Although story time and narration time usually differ, Umberto Eco describes George Perec's attempt to make the writing and reading of the story last as long as the live happenings the reader witnesses:
"The great literary trickster George Perec once nurtured the ambition of writing a book as big as the world. Then he realized he couldn't manage it, and in *Tentative d'epuisement d'un lieu parisien* he more humbly tried to describe 'live' everything that had happened in the Place Saint-Sulpice from October 18 to October 20, 1974. Perec knew perfectly well that many things have been written about that square, but he set out to describe the rest, what no history book or novel has ever told: the totality of everyday life. He sits down on a bench, or in one of the two bars of the square, and for two whole days writes down everything that he sees—the buses that go by, a Japanese tourist who photographs him, a man in a green raincoat; he notices that the passersby have at least one hand occupied, holding a bag, a briefcase, the hand of a child, a dog's leash; he even records seeing someone who looks like Peter Sellars. At two P.M. on October 20, he stops."
(Eco, 59–60)

A plot sequence can be shaped and reinforced by physical space. The downfall of Lily Bart in Edith Wharton's *The House of Mirth* is felt by the gradual sense of confinement represented by a series of places. The story begins in the open grounds of Rhinebeck, goes to the smaller house at Roslyn, then to a hotel room, followed by a boarding room, and finally ends in a narrow bed where Lily Bart dies (Lutwack, 73).

Right: Visitors stand for ten minutes in the dark center of the Cyclorama at Gettysburg National Park while the narrator interprets the sequence of events of the Battle of Gettysburg which are depicted in the surrounding painting by Paul Philippoteaux.

Below: Driving through the eighteen-mile loop of the battle site.

Bottom: The National Park Service Official Map and Guide of Gettysburg directs the visitor to tour the site by automobile.

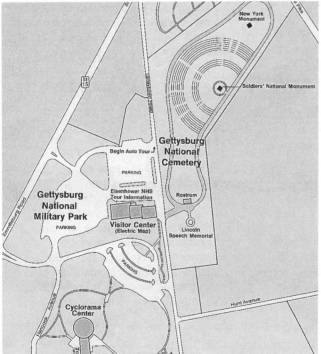

Visitors can take the self-guided tour through the National Park at Gettysburg by way of their car or a bus:

The tour begins at McPherson Ridge the morning of July 1 at 8:00 A.M. where Union and Confederate soldiers first met and fighting began. Five hours later in battle time and one stop more in story time marks the place where Confederates attacked with a force that pushed Union soldiers southeast toward town to McPherson and Oak Ridge. Here stands the Eternal Light Peace Memorial.

The events of July 2 are described at Seminary Ridge, where Confede-rate forces were positioned to face the Union troops occupying Culp and Cemetery Hills. The next stop is the Virginia Memorial, where the view across the field to the High Water Mark acts as a flash-forward to the climactic events of the following day. At Devil's Den, we park the car and climb the rocky hill to view the "Valley of Death." Taking such a position makes it possible to imagine the perspectives of the Union soldiers who once occupied this spot. Little Round Top, the Wheatfield, and the Peach Orchard describe a peaceful agricultural landscape where the tide begins to turn and the Union "bombards" the Confederates with fatal and bloody consequences.

The third and last day of battling takes place in the largest field. The Angle in the stone wall marks the furthest point a Confederate soldier trod before he was captured or killed. The field was named the "High Water Mark" at the end of the Civil War when it was known that this would be the furthest point north that the Confederate troops reached during the Civil War. The Confederate troops met their doom with their last uphill charge through an open and unprotected field facing the firing Union troops.

panoramic view is a visual representation that also conveys a distinct way of interpreting and representing history from a superior position where one understands the events of the past, the lay of the land, and the sequence of events.

The complex historic events of the Battle of Gettysburg are presented from this kind of clear and superior position at the National Park Service Visitor Center. Here a panoramic landscape painting by the French painter Paul Philippoteaux depicts the events of the battle. The audience stands elevated and in the middle of the 360-degree painting for a narrated sound and light show that presents a series of "causal events" building up to Pickets Charge. The show climaxes with a fully lit surround painting of the landscape filled with thousands of fighting, wounded, and dead soldiers. In contrast to moving through the landscape, the panorama collapses an entire sequence into one single place. In this "continuous narrative" representation of the sequence of events, the observer of history becomes central to both the tiny painted soldiers and the encircling landscape.

Reenactments open up the interpretation of what happened by giving the visitor his or her own personal experience of an event. These experiences usually bring the participant down from a superior position to a more empathetic position (Which is analogous to the dichotomy of one who is lost within a maze versus the designer or person who gazes down upon the maze).

"At the site of Pickett's Charge, a group of fourth graders charged across the field. One boy stuck his hat on a stick as General Armstead had held his hat on a sword. As the screaming children met the Angle, which marks the furthest point the Confederates charged, a few fell to the ground. One child was trampled in the stampede and had to be helped back to the school bus."

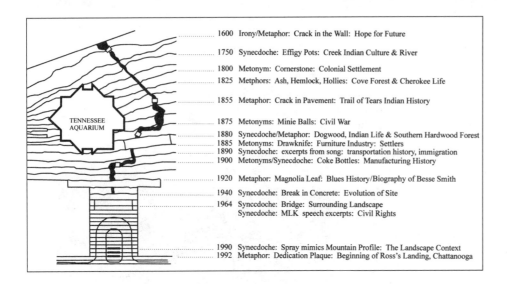

1600	Irony/Metaphor:	Crack in the Wall: Hope for Future
1750	Synecdoche:	Effigy Pots: Creek Indian Culture & River
1800	Metonym:	Cornerstone: Colonial Settlement
1825	Metphors:	Ash, Hemlock, Hollies: Cove Forest & Cherokee Life
1855	Metaphor:	Crack in Pavement: Trail of Tears Indian History
1875	Metonyms:	Minie Balls: Civil War
1880	Synecdoche/Metaphor:	Dogwood, Indian Life & Southern Hardwood Forest
1885	Metonyms:	Drawknife: Furniture Industry: Settlers
1890	Synecdoche:	excerpts from song: transportation history, immigration
1900	Metonyms/Synecdoche:	Coke Bottles: Manufacturing History
1920	Metaphor:	Magnolia Leaf: Blues History/Biography of Besse Smith
1940	Synecdoche:	Break in Concrete: Evolution of Site
1964	Synecdoche:	Bridge: Surrounding Landscape
	Synecdoche:	MLK speech excerpts: Civil Rights
1990	Synecdoche:	Spray mimics Mountain Profile: The Landscape Context
1992	Metaphor:	Dedication Plaque: Beginning of Ross's Landing, Chattanooga

(Label inside diagram: TENNESSEE AQUARIUM)

Above: The design of Ross's Landing is structured according to the chronological history of Chattanooga represented symbolically by metaphor, synecdoche, and metonym. Drawing by Paul Fritz.

Below: The view of Ross's Landing looking across the break in the concrete and the bridge toward downtown Chattanooga.

CHRONOLOGICAL PLOTS THAT ORDER A DISORDERED WORLD

A clearly ordered plot about the actually chaotic events of the battle is also represented by the National Park Service's "Official Map and Guide" auto tour that describes the three-day Battle of Gettysburg in chronological order. The eighteen-mile loop through the landscape starts with the first confrontation described in terms of the advancement from the southeast by the Confederate soldiers and ends at the National Cemetery, the site of Lincoln's Gettysburg address.

Although the auto tour maps a clear sequence of military events that led to the "climax" at the High Water Mark, the interpretation of this—as of any other historic event—clearly depends on one's position.[5] In contrast to the National Park Service interpretation of events, the firsthand accounts of soldiers and townspeople included in the Ken Burns television series on the Civil War are filled with images of chaos, "groping in the landscape," "air filled with lead," "being hit simultaneously from many directions," and "perfect hell on earth." The asphalt road that gently loops through the fields and woods does not feel like a "perfect hell on earth." Its ordered plot represents a fundamental need to bring clarity and unity to a life that is often disordered and unexplainable.

Many designs overlay upon the land an ordered version of what happened and treat the landscape as a scene upon which events take place. The linear structures of roads, paths, and streams become ordering devices for a sequential experience as well as a place from which to view the landscape. The Gettysburg asphalt road, like many interpretive trailways, heritage corridors, and themed landscapes, provides a *yellow brick road* that structures a story's development.[6]

The man-made stream at Ross's Landing designed by EDAW and James Wines of SITE also structures a chronological plot—that of the history of Chattanooga, Tennessee. In contrast to the Gettysburg auto tour, where a plot structure is overlaid on an existing landscape of accumulated events and memories, the plaza at Ross's Landing reconstructs and gathers the history of Chattanooga on one plaza. The stream leads the visitor in fast motion back through the history of Chattanooga from the 1992 construction of the plaza to the pre-1600 Indian settlement. Thirty-five increments of time are demarcated by colored bands of pavement. Along the way references to Martin Luther King, Jr., Bessie Smith, Coca-Cola, the development of the railroad, the Civil War, and the Trail of Tears recall the events, characters, and themes of this city.

Lines in the pavement separate years and events. Disjointed but adjacent information makes for a pastiche of events that are connected more geographically than causally. One event jump-cuts to another. Because the events are organized on a flat plaza along a linear grid of time, they all seem to have equal importance. The positivistic grid of time acts as a frame, open to the placement of diverse information such as the singing of Bessie Smith, the founding of a Coca-Cola plant, or the words of "Chattanooga Choo Choo." The clean and clear sequences of demarcated years do not reflect the actual overlaps of historic events, which are more often simultaneous or discontinuous.

The changing grid also conveys ideas about changing relationships between culture and nature. As the visitor walks toward the river and back in time along the stream, the grid becomes increasingly curvilinear. As in stories such as *Huckleberry Finn* that use the distinct location of the river and the shore to reinforce the meaning of events, at Ross's Landing being near to town or near the river also conveys the polarities between past and present. Although an elevated parkway separates the plaza from the river, the designers cracked the wall that runs along the parkway to convey a hope of breaking the city's separation from the river. Here is a progressive and romantic plot structure that ends with hope for a closer relationship with nature.

In all landscapes where layers of events have taken place, a story is a way of untangling the layers into sequences that make sense. Although not as dramatic as Gettysburg or as comprehensive as Ross's Landing, the everyday sequences of people's lives—their rituals of traveling from home to work or their journeys through their yard or neighborhood—are a way of making sense of the landscape.

Robert Henry's watercolor painting titled *Country Wanderings* maps his daily route from his studio to his house. He writes about how his habitual detours are communicated in the painting: "At the extreme right-hand side is the trunk of an oak that is two panels high. This is a sort of detour that I frequently make. I often walk right up to the tree, and then turn and go to the house, so it is quite large within the painting" (Henry, 47).

Whether one arrives by trolley, foot, or car, the plaza begins at Second Street with a 1992 dedication to its construction. Straight ahead and on an axis, water jets create a mountainous profile, a miniature of the surrounding Elder and Signal Ranges of the Smoky Mountains. Atop the bridge, arching east to west, are excerpts of Martin Luther King, Jr.'s speech delivered in Washington, D.C., in 1963 that refer to Chattanooga: "Let freedom ring from Lookout Mountain." From this bridge the entire layout of the plaza and the banks across the Tennessee River may be viewed. Plantings of birch and ash replicate the ecology of the surrounding mountains.

For the year 1920, imprints of magnolia leaves pay tribute to Bessie Smith, who grew up several blocks from Ross's Landing in Blue Goose Hollow. For 1900, the concrete mix on the floor of a footbridge includes crushed Coca-Cola bottles and the actual bottoms of green glass bottles stamped "Bottled in Chattanooga" in recognition of the site of the Coca-Cola company's first bottling plant. Next, the stream crosses railroad tracks that curve through the bands representing 1910 through 1880. The words of Glenn Miller's "Chattanooga Choo Choo" inscribed in the pavement recall the journey from New York to Tennessee: "I've got my fare and just a trifle to spare...You may leave the Pennsylvania Station bout a quarter to four, read a magazine and then you are in Baltimore."

At the entrance to the Tennessee Aquarium, the pavement banding shifts alignment from the gridded streets of Chattanooga to the natural eroded edge of the Tennessee River, marking a symbolic change in culture's relations with nature. For the year 1885, concrete cast coiled ropes and a draw knife refer to the docking of river barges at Chattanooga and the prosperous local furniture industry. Sweet gums, hollies, basswood, dogwoods, Carolina allspice, jasmine, and mountain laurels represent a southern hardwood forest. Engraved quotations in the cracked pavement from leaders, including Cherokee Phoenix, document the outrage and suffering of the Trail of Tears, the forced removal of 14,000 Cherokees from Ross's Landing. Concrete castings of effigy pots and necklaces convey the Cherokees' active trading along the limestone-bluffed banks of the Tennessee River. The plaza is abruptly interrupted by the granite block wall of the elevated Riverfront Parkway, which separates Chattanooga from its riverfront. The stream appears to penetrate the wall in order to make its way to the river and the site of the original Ross's Landing.

Top: "Chattanooga Choo Choo" is about traveling by train from the northeast cities to Chattanooga.

Center: Ross's Landing: the coiled rope as a metonym representing the life of the traders and settlers who arrived by the Tennessee River.

Bottom: The crack in the pavement signifies the pain associated with the Trail of Tears, the forced removal of the Cherokee Indians from Chattanooga.

PERIOD AND PROCESS

The plot and narrative of entire biographies or histories are frequently organized around selected and conceptual periods. A biography of a person, for instance, is more coherent if personal events are organized around themes that reveal character rather than by a straight chronicle of events. A periodization requires the author to analyze and synthesize facts and information, while a chronicle requires the reader to interpret meanings and make connections. Preservationists and landscape architects who restore properties and gardens to "a period of significance" use periods as a way of interpreting and communicating history. This approach makes sense, for landscapes are rarely understood in terms of one single moment but rather around a series of events. The desire to make landscape adhere to a period is taken to an extreme degree at the Lincoln Homestead in Illinois, where the National Park Service repeatedly replants an American elm sapling so that it remains the size that corresponds to a specific photograph of people gathered around Lincoln's house the day his coffin came home (Blake). Likewise, Sagamore Hill on Long Island is preserved to the period when Teddy Roosevelt lived there.

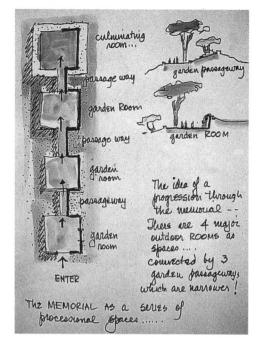

It is more rare and difficult to structure landscapes in terms of a transect across a greater span of time, yet in part this is what Lawrence Halprin did by connecting different periods into his design for the Franklin Delano Roosevelt Memorial in Washington, D.C. Halprin's design is structured according to episodes in the political and personal life of Roosevelt. Each of the four "rooms" represents a period of his presidency and is framed by connecting passages along a continuous 800-foot granite wall with plantings. The structure of the sequence works on a number of levels: four terms in office, the four freedoms he espoused (freedom of speech and worship and freedom from want and fear), four geographic areas of the country, and four stages of life. Multiple sculptures and murals embedded in the wall expand the biography of Roosevelt to include the social and political life of the country.

During the design process, hundreds of images of Roosevelt and the country were tacked along a wall to structure a storyboard or a conceptual sequence that the sculptors and architects could then experience by rolling along on a dolly. From these images the designers wrote the narrative, which starts with Roosevelt's leadership during his first term, when he launched the New Deal; proceeds to the difficult times and his heroic efforts during the Great Depression; then moves to the chivalry, violence, and hatred of World War II; and ends with his sudden death during a period of significant achievements in terms of world peace.

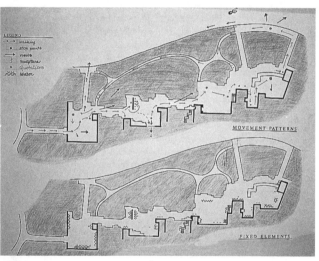

Top: The four rooms of the FDR Memorial structure a progression that parallels the life of Roosevelt and the social times of the country.

Bottom: The "Movement Patterns" in the FDR Memorial's series of rooms create a rhythm between in and out and stillness and movement. (Plan and sketch by Lawrence Halprin)

Water syncopates the route as it changes back and forth from quiet pools to waterfalls. It is the connective thread and the dynamic experiential factor that gives each room its mood. It also personally relates to Roosevelt, who acted as secretary of the navy, vacationed by the ocean, and sought the therapeutic powers of mineral pools because of his polio. Through the use of water, plantings, and sculpture, as well as the movement of people,

Right: Fairmount Park is composed of a series of stations that each represent a chronological period in the history of Philadelphia. According to Anthony Walmsley's design, history moves forward in time along the flow of the Schuylkill River.

As with Ross's Landing, the "Water in the Life of the City" at the Fairmount Waterworks in Philadelphia represents a "progressive story" that is structured along the flow of the Schuylkill River. Six consecutive wayside stations, designed by Anthony Walmsley, interpret the development of Philadelphia in relation to the Schuylkill River in this order: The Lenape Indians live in harmony with the river, settlers establish prosperous communities along the river, manufacturing grows, the river suffers, and the environmental movement returns the river to its former health.

"At the last station, the path returns to the river and metaphorically to the 20th century, where the water is celebrated with 'a renewal of pride and pleasure.' An asphalt walkway embedded with a bronze inlaid school of alewives, shad, white perch, and crappies, fish that populate the river today, leads us to a human-scale cast bronze fisherman mounted on the river's rocky bank. The cast still scenes are meant to evoke the drama: the sound of horns blowing, boats moving, fish being caught. History and events are frozen. Although a scene may be a still setting, it figures in the plot's movement, for the scene is an arrested process or implied sequence where action takes place."

Right: The Depression Breadline, by George Segal, creates the entrance wall to Franklin Delano Roosevelt's second term

Halprin scores a processional and synaesthetic experience where "we will be able to feel, touch, hear and smell, and in other ways, connect with a time that once was" (Tuchman, 103).

Nature, the pools and plantings, frame the entire procession. Halprin wrote that he "set out to design not an object but an experience over time," and he uses the processes of nature to communicate this experience (Gabor, 106). Natural sequences and processes, such as upstream to downstream, birth to death, order to entropy, dry to wet, lowland to highland, or early to late are some of the many devices Helprin uses to structure narratives. These processes become not only key players in the plot but also build the content of the story.

Although we tend to see landscape as a static and permanent scene, a superabundance of small events and gradual changes characterize landscapes. Invisible grinding, erosion, and decomposition, as well as the visible flow of water and seasonal changes, are potential figural unifiers that structure sequences. The natural processes also become metaphors that expand the meanings of the narratives. In *Spiral Jetty*, Robert Smithson uses entropy and erosion as a means of returning to the beginning of evolution; Anthony Walmsley at the Fairmount Waterworks uses the flow of the Schuylkill River as a metaphor for the passing of time in the history of Philadelphia; Lawrence Halprin uses the ecological succession of the California landscape as a metaphor for personal discovery; and R. Terry Schnadelbach at the Parc de Techniques in the Saar Valley of France uses the filtration of water in a vegetated stream as a metaphor for healing the polluted environment in a postindustrial age.

In Parc de Techniques, the visitor's sequence is defined by industrial and natural processes. The visitor first crosses a network of railroad tracks, then enters the historic research facility, proceeds to the production and shipping areas, to the mine shafts that drew the ore, to the terraced hillside stripped bare of trees used to fire the furnaces, and finally climbs the mound of overburden. The path up a slag heap cuts into the hill to reveal actual industrial debris: mining bits, extraction tools, and rolling mills. The designer intended to create and preserve an "archaeological cross section through history" that would contrast with the recently restored surrounding landscape that tends to hide the industrial history (Schnadelbach 1996).

Parc de Techniques conveys an ambiguous idea of industrial "progress"; production results in a slag heap marked by romanticized yet dysfunctional remnants. The rusty mill, mine, and laboratories contrast with the bright and clean modern tourist facilities. The mound of debris is both a monument to the past and a place to begin anew. Ironically, the formal path zigzagging up the terraced toxic hill refers to opulent French estate Renaissance gardens. At the top, instead of meeting Hercules, visitors find a restaurant and view of both the industrial processes and the surrounding valley, severely impacted by the steel industry.

The climax of this industrial story, the top of the mound of overburden, is also the threshold of a transformation. It is a place where the visitor sees the expanse of the industrial past below and begins a journey down a natural stream. A hyper-accumulator pond with sedges and rushes will begin to extract the toxic compounds and residues of the steel-making process. Following the winding path down the stream, the water gradually becomes more pure as it passes through filtering vegetation. In this narrative, nature is the powerful purifier that heals the wounds of the industrial past.

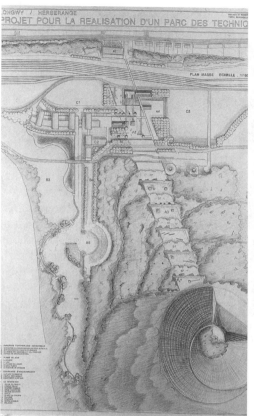

Top left: Plan of Parc de Techniques, designed by Terry Schnadelbach.

Top right: Looking along the grottos across the sloping lawn towards the statue of Hercules.

Above: View looking up the terraced hill to the climactic mound of overburden.

TWISTED TALES

In some narratives the past does not lead to the present nor the present to the past. Time is indefinite or cyclical. Events may be overlaid, simultaneous, and open to infinite interpretations. Twisted, crossed-over, and forked paths, as well as spirals, labyrinths, mazes, open fields, or vast forests, present plot potential for open sequences that involve exploration. *The Wizard of Oz*, for instance, contrasts the association of progress and movement along the linear yellow brick road with the associations of being lost and intoxicated in the field of poppies. These open landscapes don't necessarily lead to a center or an end and are analogous to the modern mystery story. "The Garden of Forking Paths," by Luis Borges, in which the order of events makes no sense and there is more than one possible ending.

As an inspiration for his design for many urban plazas, Lawrence Halprin followed the course of the water, beginning in the glaciated mountains of the High Sierras, moving down into the canyons, into the meandering streams, and through the floodplains en route to the sea. The mountain falls of the High Sierras are placed in the costal city of Seattle in Freeway Park (above). In San Francisco's Levi Plaza scenes of the High Sierra waterfalls, foothill rivers, and meandering streams burst through the pavement, juxtaposing upstream with downstream, the origins of life with a developed urban society, and the ideal with the real. Halprin connects the mountain streams to origins of life:
"Up high above timber line the lichens, earliest pioneers, dissolve the rock into tiny beginnings of soil which fill the split rock crevasses and form footholds for the later alpine flowers. As the water from melting snow rushes down the slope it carries the soil into the small tarns, they fill gradually, and slowly planting invades the water....
It is a garden of movement in static form, whose outlines imply movement and the process of change."
(Halprin 1970, 104)

"We descendants of Ts'ui Pen," I replied, "continue to curse that monk. Their publication was senseless. The book is an indeterminate heap of contradictory drafts. I examined it once: in the third chapter the hero dies, in the fourth he is alive. As for the other undertakings of Ts'ui Pen, his labyrinth..."
(Borges, 24)

These multidirectional structures merit multiple reading or multiple visits to understand the meaning of their stories. Mazes and forking paths are a metaphor for an elaborate plot where a spy, Yu Tsun, is lost in a plot that lies inside yet another plot. The finding of a manuscript written by the spy's grandfather, Ts'ui Pen, becomes a clue to the events to come. The manuscript is the maze and the maze the manuscript, as realized by the spy: "Everyone imagined two works; to no one did it occur that the book and the maze were one and the same thing" (25). In the indeterminate chaotic structure of the maze and manuscript, the forked paths represent an infinite possibility of outcomes within both the plot of the manuscript and the story by Borges.

He creates, in this way, diverse futures, diverse times which themselves also proliferate and fork. Here, then, is the explanation of the novel's contradictions. Fang, let us say, has a secret; a stranger calls at the door; Fang resolves to kill him. Naturally, there are several possible outcomes: Fang can kill the intruder, the intruder can kill Fang, they both can escape, they both can die, and so forth. In the work of Ts'ui Pen, all possible outcomes occur; each one is the point of departure for other forkings. (26)

In this plot of infinitely possible outcomes, the main character has the power to create his own story. Borges's spy controls the ending of the story. The reader writes the story.

In Seymour Chatman's discussion in *Story and Discourse* of chronological deviations or anachronisms, he states:

Playing with sequential ordering is not just a literary convention; it is also a means of drawing attention to certain things, to emphasize, to bring about aesthetic or psychological effects, to show various interpretations of an event, to indicate the subtle difference between expectation and realization, and much else besides.
(Chatman, 52–53)

The artist and architect Maya Lin plays with sequential ordering and creates a circular chronology in the Vietnam Veterans Memorial. Each end of the wall starts in the middle of war, and the beginning and end of the war collide at the vertex of the chevron wall. By walking along the wall, one metaphorically descends back and forth into time. The meeting of two time frames puzzles and poses questions of why and how the war began and ended and conveys an ambiguous sense of the war. This memorial interprets history differently than, for instance, the Gettysburg auto tour, where the visitor's sequence parallels the order of events. The sequence along the wall engages us in a way that a clear and unified sequence does not. Ehrenhaus contrasts the conventional methods of giving "an indisputable and reassuring version of the past" that "blocks alternative interpretations of the past, of our community and our place in it" with the Vietnam Veterans Memorial, which involves the audience in a discourse about what happened (Carney, 212).

In Maya Lin's memorial the mounting of 58,000 names, located by the time of the soldiers' death, structures the memorial procession made by millions of visitors. The pilgrimage includes the private experience of traveling to the wall, the public experience of meeting strangers or comrades at the wall, and the search for the remembered name. The journey from the private realm of the home to the public realm of the national government parallels stories of leaving home for the war. The pilgrimage memory and the over 48,000 items left at the wall that have been collected by the National Park Service (*The New York Times Magazine,* Nov. 12, 1995) are part of the infinite number of stories that crisscross the physical lines of the wall. One letter left with a dollar bill on Veterans Day describes one of many personal experiences associated with walking along the wall:

> On Nov. 12, 1994, my dad and I walked down the brick path past the increasing rows of names on the black wall of the Vietnam Memorial. He stopped at a panel and pointed to a spot between two names. "That is where my name would be." I didn't know what to say, I just stood there silently, selfishly realizing that if he had died that day I would not have been born.

Above: Visitors to the Vietnam Veterans Memorial in Washington, D.C., progress downwards toward the apex of the wall, where both the beginning and the end of the Vietnam War come together.

Below: Cancer Survivor's Park in Maryland.

CIRCLES

Without beginnings or endings, the circle represents a nonlinear concept of time and a joining of past and present. A circle is a form without hierarchies, for everyone standing in a circle takes an equal position.

Cancer Survivor's Park in Maryland

In the Cancer Survivor's Park in Towson, Maryland, a sequence of ascending circular places relates to the process of healing. According to the landscape architects Mahan Rykiel Associates, Inc.,

> Level one is the Circle of Life. Highly ordered, clear and simple, this level is, metaphorically, life before cancer. Level Two is a passage through a maze-like configuration of large evergreen walls and benches arranged for contemplation and meditation. This area

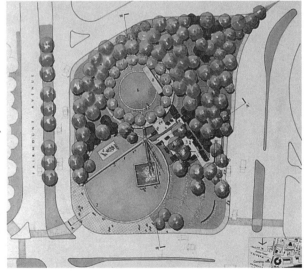

Above: Kelly Ingram Park in Birmingham, Alabama. (Plan by Grover Harrison and Harrison)

Below: Shakopee Correctional Institute. (Hammel Green and Abrahamson, Inc. Landscape Architecture Group in collaboration with artist Gary Dwyer)

represents the process of getting well, a time when the future is unclear and when support and inspiration are essential. It is here that the Positive Attitude Walk begins. As part of the maze, the visitor can derive strength from the success stories of others. Raised above the other two levels, the Summit is a serene landscape with a view of the park's centerpiece, the Beacon of Hope.

Kelly Ingram Park

Kelly Ingram Park commemorates the civil rights demonstrations that took place in Birmingham, Alabama, during April and May of 1963. The recent renovations to the park by landscape architects *Grover Harrison and Harrison* included the addition of a circular path superimposed on an existing axial layout. The circular Freedom Walk intends to reconcile the turbulence and pains of segregation. The walk passes through the events of the demonstrations, portrayed by bronze sculptures of attack dogs and fire hoses like those Bull Conner's police turned on demonstrators. According to Colonel Johnson, civil rights activist, union representative, and body guard for the Bethel Baptist Church preacher, "once upon a time you and myself couldn't walk here. They would put us in jail. They would put you in jail and me too." So to simply walk together black and white on the same path means a great deal.

MAZES

The floors of many Christian churches include mazes that symbolize journeys to attain belief or salvation. They were also intended for those who were unable to make the pilgrimages to sacred sites. Nigel Pennick in *Mazes and Labyrinths* discusses the forms and symbols of the Christian labyrinth: "Clearly the unicursal labyrinth has always been recognized as a kind of pilgrimage, with its twists and turns first bringing the pilgrim close to the 'goal' then taking him or her away before finally the center is reached" (113). The forking paths of mazes are associated with brave trials and tribulations. Theseus's clever escape from the labyrinth, for instance, was rewarded by the offer of Ariadne's love and marriage.

Shakopee Correctional Institute

The maze, a passageway that poses choice and complexity, is, according to the landscape architect Gary Dwyer, "emblematic of the confusion of ordinary life." It is the structure he chose for the garden at the Shakopee Correctional Institute in Minnesota. When a prisoner is awarded work-release status, she is allowed to walk the passage from the main prison through all the phases of the garden on her way to life in the community. The procession begins with the Agricultural Maze (composed of the dominant row crops of the regional landscape), then forks through the "pathway of decisions" (based upon the Ojibway legend of seven great choices in life), and ends with the narrow paths at the Forest Knoll where final decisions are made regarding future life. This processional ritual is witnessed by other prisoners and has become a "tradition of hope" (Dwyer).

The Story Garden, Portland, Oregon

In a play area designed by Macy and Kirkland for the Portland, Oregon, Waterfront Park, a maze of cobblestones and grass includes riddles, puns, and stories etched on 150 granite blocks. The center of the maze features questions such as "What is your sadness?" and "What is your joy?".

SPIRALS

Spiral Jetty: Time Contracts

Spirals are metaphors for growth and evolution whether reeling clockwise or counterclockwise. In his film on the making of Spiral Jetty, Robert Smithson spirals counterclockwise back into primordial time. He fights the whirling wind of the helicopter over the uneven surface of the rock jetty to metaphorically return to the past. The salty, blood-red lake and the industrial earth-moving equipment refer to the primordial past of crystal life-forms and dinosaurs. The film juxtaposes the present, experienced by the wind and salt sprays and movement, with the past. According to Hobbs: "The Spiral Jetty, located in a lake called 'America's Dead Sea,' is an image of contracted time: the far distant past (the beginning of life in saline solutions symbolized by the lake) is absorbed in the remote past (symbolized by the destructive forces of the legendary whirlpools in the lake) and the no longer valid optimism of the recent past (symbolized by the Golden Spike Memorial). All these pasts collide with the futility of the near present (the vacated oil rigging). All appear to be canceled, made useless: all are a result of the essential universal force of entropy."

(Hobbs, 193)

Above: Story Garden, Portland, Oregon.

Bottom left: Robert Smithson walking the Spiral Jetty. (Photograph by Gianfranco Gorgoni, courtesy John Weber Gallery.)

View of Memorial Entry (looking Northwest)

View of Vortex (looking Northwest)

Liberty Walk

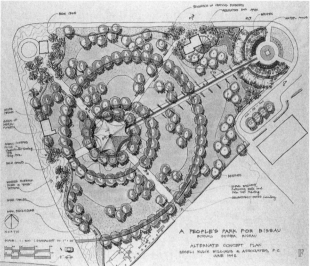

A PEOPLE'S PARK FOR BISSAU
BISSAU GUINEA BISSAU
ALTERNATE CONCEPT PLAN
MICELI KULIK WILLIAMS & ASSOCIATES, P.C.
JUNE 1992

AIDS Living Memorial, New Jersey

A combined spiral and maze is a place for "healing, remembering, and revival" in the AIDS Living Memorial in New Jersey. According to the designers, Wallace Roberts and Todd, a marker stone covered by reflective water stands in the vortex to "symbolize the point at which visitors are isolated from the community and must turn inward" (Wallace Roberts and Todd).

People's Park for Guinea-Bissau, Africa

The spiral form conveys, according to the designer, Miceli Kulik Williams and Associates, the idea of "rapidly changing local life" and the loss of tradition in Guinea-Bissau. The center of the spiral is on axis with an existing memorial that refers to the past, while the form "looks toward the future."

Top left: AIDS Living Memorial in New Jersey.

Top right: People's Park in Guinea-Bissau.

SUMMARY

Structures that deviate and play with chronological ordering closely represent our experience of life in its disorder, happenstance, detours, and unnecessary information. Life rarely follows an established chronological sequence, that is then reordered by narrators. Rather, the events of life may be as twisted as the stories that arise from life.

Bakhtin did not think of "conventional time" and "real time" as distinct. In his interpretation of Bakhtin, Holquist writes, "Time in real life is no less organized by convention than it is in a literary text" (Holquist, 18). Our understanding of both the events of real life and the mediated telling of those events is structured by culture and cognition. John Berger explains that a "change in the mode of narration" arises out of a modern world whose modes of communication reach rapidly across economic and cultural boundaries.

It is scarcely any longer possible to tell a straight story sequentially unfolding in time. And this is because we are too aware of what is continually traversing the storyline laterally. That is to say, instead of being aware of a point as an infinitely small part of a straight line, we are aware of it as an infinitely small part of an infinite number of lines, as the center of a star of lines. Such awareness is the result of our constantly having to take into account the simultaneity and extension of events and possibilities.

(Berger, 40)

Every place, from the intersection of a busy street to a clearing in the woods, represents the junction of a "star of lines," or a star of stories. Even in a single spot, a constant sequence of events has unfolded and continues to unfold. And even the still person viewing the panoramic landscape witnesses all the implied past and future changes in flux in that passing moment. The landscape is always more than a static backdrop, and efforts to clip, trim, prune, restrain, divert, or otherwise control it only slow down otherwise inevitable changes or cause a new web of events to follow.

The content of the landscape narrative cannot be separated from the ongoing processes of the medium itself. George Hargreaves talks about setting the site in motion. His designs engage both the visitor's movement through the site and the site's movement through time. At Candlestick Park in San Francisco, the rise and fall of tides bring regular deposits of debris revealed along the levied shoreline. At Guadalupe River Park in San Jose, the constructed berms that run parallel to the river are shaped by flooding and the accretion of debris and seeds left by the water flow. In these landscapes, Hargreaves changes the mode of narrating the landscape by considering the "simultaneity and extension of events and possibilities" (Berger, 40). What was perceived as distinct in the picturesque garden—figure and scene—instead becomes integrated. The ongoing events, actions, and qualities of figure and ground make up the content of the narrative.

Places are shaped by the ethnic, religious, and economic groups who rework old patterns. To tell the sequence of change that is woven into a neighborhood in Roxbury, Massachusetts, the artist Will Holton wrote four letters "as if " new immigrants were writing back home. The letters, written to rural Maine in the 1830s, Ireland in the 1880s, Poland in the 1920s, and Georgia in the 1960s, parallel the sequence of immigration in this community. A series of changes, from the condition of housing to treatment of immigrants to the quality of the landscape, may be deciphered from the letters, all sent from the same place. Each letter also anticipates upcoming changes in transportation and media. Inscribed on granite slabs, the letters have become part of the current changes associated with the restoration of an industrial and transportation corridor.

"Our apartment is on Ruggles Street near Westminster Street in Lower Roxbury. The roof leaks in heavy rains. There are vacant apartments, and some wooden houses nearby are empty....Change is coming. We hear that two big highways will be built and join at the corner of Ruggles Street and Columbus Avenue. Our building will probably be torn down in a few years for the Inner Belt Highway. We hope we can find a better place," writes Charlie Robinson in "Four Letter Home," by Will Holton.

Top left: Byxbee Park, Palo Alto, California, in the spring.

*Top right:*Byxbee Park in the fall.
(Both courtesy Hargreaves Associates)

The integration of figure/plot and ground/story represents a significant change in the way landscape is understood and interpreted. An ideal sequential ordering does not exist separate from the story; rather the retelling fundamentally shapes the story. Through the constant revising, reinterpreting, reenacting, retelling, and reshaping of the narrative, the landscape is set in constant motion. The landscape as ground becomes figured through story.

NOTES

1. The book *Big House Little House Backhouse and Barn* is about the connected farm buildings found in the vernacular architecture of New England.

2. The novelist E. M. Forster used this example to differentiate plot from story. According to him, "The king died and the queen died" is a story and "The king died and the queen died of grief" is a plot.

3. The proposal to include a wall of fish in the subway station was made by David Oettinger.

4. In many cultures, including that of the Australian aborigines, spiritual leaders are believed to have the hindsight to know what has happened in prehistory and the foresight, through dreams and premonitions, to know what will happen. In *The Last Wave*, directed by Peter Weir, for instance dream time becomes a part of real time.

5. A study team at the Department of Landscape Architecture at the Pennsylvania State University developed a design and management plan for the trail corridor in the Cumberland Valley for the Appalachian Trail Conference that negotiated differences between suburban growth and the wilderness experience and revealed and highlighted sequential changes along the trail.

6. For example, the High Water Mark was understood as a climax only in hindsight, once the Civil War was over.

7. The National Park Service is currently airing a sponsor announcement with the State of Virginia to tour through Virginia and "the Life of Thomas Jefferson." Biography becomes a landscape journey.

REFERENCES

Berger, John. 1974. *The Look of Things.* Middlesex, England: Penguin Books.

Blake, Larry. 1997. Interview with authors from the National Park Service's President Abraham Lincoln Homestead.

Borges, Luis. 1984. "The Garden of Forking Paths." In *Labyrinths: Selected Short Stories and Other Writings,* ed. Donald A. Yates and James E. Irby. New York: Random House.

Branigan, Edward. 1992. *Narrative Comprehension and Film.* New York: Routledge.

Brown, Brenda. 1996a. Letter to authors, June.

———. 1996b. "Landscapes of Theme Park Rides: Modes and Media of Knowing." Draft Paper for presentation at Dumbarton Oaks, May.

———. 1997. Interview with authors by telephone, June.

Burns, Ken. 1989. *The Civil War.* Alexandria, Va.: PBS. Videocassettes.

Carmichael, Dennis (principal at EDAW). 1995. Interview with authors in Alexandria, Va., September.

Carney, Lora Senechal. 1993. "Not Telling Us What to Think." *Metaphor and Symbolic Activity* 8(3):211–219.

Charlesworth, Michael. 1989. "On Meeting Hercules in Stourhead Garden." *Journal of Garden History* 9(2): 71–75

Chatman, Seymour. 1978. *Story and Discourse.* Ithaca, N.Y.: Cornell University Press.

Cronon, William. 1992. "A Place for Stories: Nature, History, and Narrative." *Journal of American History* (March):1347–1376.

Davis, Lorri (landscape architect). 1996. Letter to authors in New York City, January.

Dwyer, Gary. 1997. Letter to the authors, June.

Eco, Umberto. 1994. *Six Walks in the Fictional Woods.* Cambridge: Harvard University Press.

Ehrenhaus, Peter. 1988. "Silence and Symbolic Expression." *Communication Monographs* 55:41–57.

Faris, Wendy B. 1988. *Labyrinths of Language: Symbolic Language and Narrative Design in Modern Fiction.* Baltimore: John Hopkins University Press.

Forster, E. M. 1927. *Aspects of the Novel.* New York: Harcourt, Brace, and World.

Gabor, Andrea. 1997. "Even Our Most Loved Monuments Had a Trial by Fire." *Smithsonian* May/June.

Greiner, Virginia. 1992. "A Garden to Walk through with Your Eyes." *Landscape Architecture,* February.

Halprin, Lawrence. 1970. *RSVP Cycles.* New York: George Braziller.

———. 1997. *Smithsonian,* May/June.

Hara, Mami. 1984. "News Items." *Landscape Architecture* 84:4.

Harbutt, Charles (photographer). 1995. "The Things They Leave Behind." *New York Times Magazine,* November 12.

Harrison, Lois S. (partner at Grover, Harrison and Harrison). 1995. Interview with author in Birmingham, Ala., October.

Henriquez, Richard and Gregory. "The Ethics of Narrative at Trent." In *Architecture, Ethics, and Technology,* ed. Louise Pelletier and Alberto Pérez-Gómez. Montreal: McGill-Queen's University Press.

Henry, Robert. 1987. "Country Wanderings." In *The World is Round,* ed. Alan Gussow. New York State: The Hudson River Museum.

Hobbs, Robert. 1981. *Robert Smithson: Sculpture.* Ithaca, N.Y.: Cornell University Press.

Holquist, Michael. 1989. "From Body Talk to Biography: The Chronology Bases of Narrative." *The Yale Journal of Criticism* 3(1).

Johnson, Colonel. 1985. Interview with authors in Birmingham, Ala., October.

Lutwack, Leonard. 1984. *The Role of Place in Literature*. Syracuse, N.Y.: Syracuse University Press.

Lynch, Kevin. 1960. *The Image of the City*. Cambridge: MIT Press. P. 96.

Macy, Kirkland. Firm Project Portfolio. 1995.

Mahan Rykiel Associates, Inc. 1996. *Cancer Survivor's Park Portfolio Sheet.*

Miceli Kulik Williams and Associates. 1995. Firm portfolio and letter to authors.

National Park Service, U.S. Department of the Interior. 1990. *Gettysburg: Official Map and Guide.*

Pennick, Nigel. 1990. *Mazes and Labyrinths*. London: Robert Hale Limited.

Rainey, Reuben M. 1994. "Environmental Ethics and Park Design: A Case Study of Byxbee Park." *Journal of Garden History* 14(3):171–178.

Ryden, Kent C. 1993. *Mapping the Invisible Landscape*. Iowa City: University of Iowa Press.

Schnadelbach, R. Terry. (chairman of University of Florida at Gainesville). 1995. Interview with author in New York, April.

———. 1996. Letter to authors, October.

Scholes, Robert, and Robert Kellogg. 1975. *The Nature of Narrative.* London: Oxford University Press.

Steinfeld, Joel. 1996. *On This Site*. San Francisco: Chronicle Books.

Tilley, Allen. 1992. *Plot Snakes and the Dynamics of Narrative Experience.* Gainesville: University Press of Florida.

Tschumi, Bernard. 1994. *Architecture and Disjunction*. Cambridge: MIT Press.

Tuchman, Phyllis. 1986. "The Franklin Delano Roosevelt Memorial." In *Lawrence Halprin: Changing Places*. San Francisco: San Francisco Museum of Modern Art.

Walker Macy Landscape Architecture and Urban Design Planning. 1995. Firm portfolio and interview by phone with authors.

Wallace, Roberts and Todd. 1995. Firm portfolio and interview with authors.

Walmsley, Anthony (partner of Tourbier and Walmsley). 1995. Interview with authors, spring and fall.

White, Hayden. 1987. *The Content of the Form: Narrative Discourse and Historical Representation*. Baltimore: Johns Hopkins University Press.

Yahner, Thomas. 1990. The Appalachian Trail Corridor concept plans.

———. 1996. The Appalachian Trail Corridor in the Cumberland Valley: Designing with Landscape History. Presentation at OnSite/Insight: Nature, Humanity and Time.

CHAPTER FIVE

REVEALING AND CONCEALING

INTRODUCTION

THE designer, like Hermes the messenger, interprets the embedded layers of change when deciding to conceal or reveal certain histories and meanings.[1] She highlights or dramatizes the effect of hidden meanings and makes underlying dimensions transparent. And so the designer engages the reader in a process of discovery or revelation by posing questions and enigmas. She builds suspense to activate the reader's desire to pursue the mystery. Roland Barthes, who called this basic code of storytelling the hermeneutical code, described its components as follows: "all the units whose function it is to articulate in various ways a question, its response, and the variety of chance events which can either formulate the question or delay its answer; or even, constitute an enigma and lead to its solution" (Barthes 1974, 17). In *S/Z*, where he outlines and applies the hermeneutical code along with four other codes of narrative practice, he writes: "The dramatic narrative is a game with two players: the snare and the truth"(Barthes 1974, 188).

This chapter approaches the practice of revealing and concealing by exploring three fundamental ideas connected to landscape narratives: first, the idea of *secrets* or hidden information; second, the idea of *transparency*; and finally, the idea of *masking* and *unmasking* information, identity, and meaning. Secrets, transparency, and masking/unmasking each create specific relations between the author and the reader. Secrets imply that something is known yet deliberately concealed for various purposes ranging from affecting emotion to holding power to creating suspense. A reader engages in the narrative to uncover and decipher the secrets. In the case of transparency, the author, by opening up the information to the reader, invites the reader to figure out the processes and structures at work. Masking and unmasking goes back and forth to open up the paradoxical space *between* what is hidden and what is seen. This tricky practice emphasizes the role of the designer to construct complex images, and the role of the reader to inquire about the mask and what lies beneath it.

These three practices apply to the interpretation of landscape narratives. Natural and cultural processes hide layers of change and expose underlying structures. Erosion, for instance, may lay bare a steep hillside and its geologic history as it also hides former contours by deposing soil at the base. Vincent Crapanzano's description of the role of the ethnographer is aptly extended to the role of the landscape interpreter and designer as one who understands the interplay of masking and unmasking:

> The ethnographer is a little like Hermes; a messenger who, given methodologies for uncovering the masked, the latent, the unconscious, may even obtain his message through stealth. He presents languages, cultures, and societies in all their opacity, their foreignness, their meaninglessness; then, like the magician, the hermeneutic, Hermes himself, he clarifies the opaque, renders the foreign familiar, and gives meaning to the meaningless. He decodes the message. He interprets.
> (Crapanzano, 43)

Physical forms and processes, metaphysical ideas, associations, hopes and fears, and political ideologies are all embedded in the landscape and wait to be deciphered.

SECRETS

THE CASTLE OF OTRANTO AND THE PICTURESQUE GARDEN

The Castle of Otranto, the 18th-century Gothic novel written by Horace Walpole, begins with a mysterious "ancient prophesy" and the violent and phantasmal death of a young man, Conrad, on his wedding day. The ancient prophesy states that "the Castle and Lordship of Otranto should pass from the present family whenever the real owner should be too large to inhabit it" (Bleiler, 27). In the beginning of the story, the young groom is "dashed to pieces" by an "enormous helmet, a hundred times more large than any casque ever made for human beings, and shaded with a proportionable quantity of black feathers." From this odd and enigmatic spectacle begins a story whose secrets gradually unravel. Conrad's death jeopardizes the right of his father, Manfred The Prince of Otranto, to continue as owner of the castle, and so the father attempts to marry his son's bride, Isabella. Isabella flees in disgust and fear. The pursuit of Isabella is followed by murders based upon mistaken identities, the discovery of lost family members, and unrequited romantic love. In the end the supposed servant Theodore is found to have a noble heritage and gains the right to inherit the castle.

The Castle of Otranto, considered a precedent for an entire genre of Gothic romance and the later detective novels, was written by an amateur picturesque gardener, Horace Walpole, in the 1760s at the height of the picturesque movement in England. This novel established certain Gothic conventions that influenced later authors such as Ann Radcliffe, Charles Maturin, Matthew Gregory Lewis, and Edgar Allan Poe.[2] These familiar conventions include setting the story in the Middle Ages, creating scenes in a castle, solving a mysterious crime, deciphering mistaken identities, and using the influence of supernatural powers, such as ghosts, or hermits (Bleiler, xiv).[3] But it is the concealing and revealing of identities and actions

From *The Castle of Otranto* by Horace Walpole:
"The lower part of the castle was hollowed into several intricate cloisters; and it was not easy for one, under so much anxiety, to find the door that opened into the cavern. An awful silence reigned throughout those subterraneous regions, except, now and then, some blasts of wind that shook the doors she had passed, and which, grating on the rusty hinges, were re-echoed through that long labyrinth of darkness. Every murmur struck her with new terror; yet more she dreaded to hear the wrathful voice of Manfred, urging his domestics to pursue her. She trod as softly as impatience would give her leave, yet frequently stopped, and listened to hear if she was followed. In one of those moments she thought she heard a sigh. She shuddered, and recoiled a few paces. In a moment she thought she heard the step of some person. Her blood curdled; she concluded it was Manfred. Every suggestion that horror could inspire, rushed into her mind..."
(Bleiler, 35–36)

that is key to the engagement of the reader and the making of suspense in both the Gothic novel and the romantic narrative of the picturesque. These picturesque ideas, which originated in the middle of the 18th century, continue to be firmly engrained in the practice of landscape architecture.

The fundamental metaphor of the picturesque landscape movement is that the designer, like the painter, can control what is seen and what is hidden in order to make the best picture.[4] In the same way that painters such as Salvator Rosa or Claude Lorrain played with the contrasts of light and dark to create mystery and a sense of hidden places in their paintings, landscape designers of the period were also controlling for effect what gets seen in the landscape. For instance, Humphrey Repton's Red Books *improved* landscape scenes by revealing picturesque views to pastoral fields and distant waters and concealing unsightly views to butcher shops, beggars, or service yards.[5] The practice of controlling what gets seen and what gets hidden continues to be a fundamental part of the landscape architect's picturesque approach to the analysis and design of a site. Typical service areas, utilities, and roads, or other more threatening elements such as nuclear power plants, are disguised by planted "screens."

The Castle of Otranto is set in a Gothic castle with a gallery, a round tower, and a great cloister fitting the description of Horace Walpole's own property in Twickenham named Strawberry Hill. At Strawberry Hill in view of the Thames, Walpole turned a small farm cottage into an English Gothic "castellino" with a refectory, a round tower, cloisters, and a cabinet. The eclectic interior decorations included artifacts, furnishings, and paintings from the Middle Ages—some of which appear in the story. The plot unfolds through the castellino's labyrinthine underground passages, towers, and gallery and the nearby woods and dark caves. The characters escape, meet unexpectedly, chase one another, and gradually discover the truth about relations and identities in the dark and winding passages. Similarly the compositional elements of the picturesque garden, its grottoes, hermitages, and cabinets, create emotions, moods, and allegorical associations that surprise, mystify, and in some cases terrorize.

Horace Walpole wanted to create an effect of "gloomth" at Strawberry Hill. The Gothic ornamental features of his house included battlements, the Gothic "ogee," quatrefoil windows, and finials, or pinnacles (Iddon, 6–7). (Courtesy Anthony Miller)

BUILDING SUSPENSE

Creating secrets and a sense of mystery builds suspense and creates opportunities for personal revelation as well as revelation of the spirit of place (genius loci). By beginning with an unexplainable and fantastic event, *The Castle of Otranto* creates an enigma that pulls the reader into the story. The plot unfolds by gradually making sense of the puzzles it begins with. Many historic picturesque gardens also created suspense by building a series of revelations that would sometimes climax at a high point with an overall view. At Stourhead, for instance, a winding path around the lake reveals in stages distant temples, grottoes, artifacts, and other visual climaxes. Or at Painshill in Surrey, where a visitor, Elizabeth Montagu, in 1755 remarked that "the art of hiding is here in such sweet perfection"

(Griswold, 69), a circuit walk through thick woods progressively reaches a Gothic tower, a Gothic abbey (now ruined), a Gothic temple, Roman mausoleums, and Roman baths. As remarked by the garden writer Mac Griswold, "like characters in a play, the little temples, the water, and the hills disappear and reappear, carrying the wordless action of the garden forward to a different mood," and the suspense builds to a "grand finale, in a visionary burst" where many of the events seen along the way are viewed simultaneously (Griswold, 70).

Like the half-finished sentences, enigmatic clues, or escapes of *The Castle of Otranto,* the picturesque garden's serpentine paths, forked sequences, partially obscured views, darkened woods, and sculpted land build a suspenseful journey. At Painshill, the narrow path that leads to the hermitage threatens the visitor with the chance of falling into the River Mole. Suspense in the picturesque garden is an experiential process where the pleasure is in finding one's way in and out of dark woods or imagining that one is lost or in danger.

There is a distinction between suspense and surprise, as Alfred Hitchcock, the master creator of sublime terror, pointed out. He believed the effect of suspense, unlike that of surprise, could be experienced repeatedly and was therefore more enduring (Chatman, 59). A surprise, once experienced in a film or a garden, can be predicted, thus losing its power of repeated effect. Suspense is much more about experiencing the process of exploration or detection than it is about reaching the end, finding one's place, or solving the crime. Hitchcock's films sustain thrill and terror because the viewer, more than a passive and distant observer, experiences what is happening to the characters.

Top: View of Painshill landscape. From the Gothic pavilion visitors can look over much of the garden at Painshill.

Above: The mausoleum at Painshill frames the view to the next folly—the Brahman Waterwheel.

"Twenty Rules for Writing the Detective Story" (S. S. Van Dine) and rules of the Picturesque:

"The reader must have equal opportunity with the detective for solving the mystery. All clues must be plainly stated and described." (Haycraft, 189–193)

"Deception may be allowable in imitating the works of nature. Thus artificial rivers, lakes, and rock scenery can only be great by deception, and the mind acquiesces in the fraud after it is detected; but in works of art every trick ought to be avoided. Sham churches, sham ruins, sham bridges, and everything which appears what it is not, disgusts when the trick is discovered." (Repton, 69)

"No willful tricks or deceptions may be placed on the reader other than those played legitimately by the criminal on the detective himself."
(Haycraft, 189–193)

"There must simply be a corpse in a detective novel, and the deader the corpse the better."
(Haycraft, 189–193)

From Joseph Spence (1751):
"To conceal the bounds of your grounds everywhere if possible. This is done by grove-works, sunk fences, and what they call invisible fences, as being but little discernible to the eye."
(Hunt and Willis, 270)

"Display the natural beauties and hide the natural defects of every situation. Studiously conceal every interference of art making the whole appear as a production of nature only."
(Loudon, 84)

In the design for the Bloedel Reserve, Bainbridge Island, Washington, Richard Haag reveals the site's history of logging and the consequent ecological disturbances. Remnant stumps and fallen tree trunks scarred by logging are made visible in the forest floor by the selective clearing of the understory. Elizabeth Meyer, in a comparison of Gas Works Park in Seattle, Washington, and Bloedel Reserve Gardens, writes about how Haag creates a modern sublime landscape:
"Haag's selective editing of the sites surrounding the stumps and the alder grove renders the invisible more visible by exploiting the physical characteristics of disturbance through changes in scale, spatial structure, and surface characteristics. These changes create an aesthetic that vacillates between beauty and horror, between pleasure and pain. Disturbance is implied, not masked. The surfaces are exposed, the scars not healed."
(Meyer, 4)

The escape of Isabella, the mysterious murder of Conrad, and the presence of giants all keep the reader of *The Castle of Otranto* in a state of terror (Mehrotra, 11). Terror is also an emotion of the sublime landscape of immense waterfalls, cragged rocks, steep banks, and broken ruins. Edmund Burke in *A Philosophical Enquiry into the Origin of Our Ideas of the Sublime and Beautiful,* written in the mid 18th century, distinguished the sublime from the beautiful. He associated the beautiful with softness, fragility, sweetness and cleanliness, and the overall emotion of "pleasure." In contrast he associated the sublime with "mystery," "darkness," "fear," terror, and secrets (Andrews, 323; Haddad, 48–56). Simon Schama in *Landscape and Memory* writes about where the landscape of Burke's sublime could be discovered: "So it would be in the shadow and darkness and dread and trembling, in caves and chasms, at the edge of the precipice, in the shroud of the cloud, in the fissures of the earth, that, he insisted in his *Inquiry,* the sublime would be discovered" (Schama, 450). *The Castle of Otranto* incites the imagination and causes the reader to conjure explanations by the secret meetings in subterranean passages and undisclosed identities of those met in the dark. The romantic garden similarly engages the imagination in its boundless edges, dark grottoes, and winding turns. Both romantic narratives emphasize engaging the reader in the pleasure of the imagination. Fear and terror become pleasurable for they are solely imagined and realistically unthreatening. The picturesque gardens, as well as picturesque travel, vicariously engage visitors in imagined fear. An intent to create imagined fear finds contemporary expression in the making of modern amusement and adventure parks where dangerous heights and speeds simulate experiences with the *real* dangers of waterfalls, rapids, mountain faces and dark caves.

Creating mystery, which is key to the romantic narrative, continues to be a fundamental means for engaging the reader and a key criterion for evaluating the success of design in engaging the participant. Kaplan and

"She condemned her rash flight, which had thus exposed her to his rage, in a place where her cries were not likely to draw anybody to her assistance. Yet the sound seemed not to come from behind; if Manfred knew where she was, he must have followed her: she was still in one of the cloisters, and the steps she had heard were too distinct to proceed from the way she had come. Cheered with this reflection, and hoping to find a friend in whoever was not the prince, she was going to advance, when a door that stood a-jar, at some distance to the left, was opened gently; but e'er her lamp, which she held up, could discover who opened it, the person retreated precipitately, on seeing the light." The Castle of Otranto.
(Bleiler, 36)

According to Simon Schama, the dark opening of *The Source*, by Gustave Courbet, relates both to natural origins and to female sexuality.
(Schama, 373)

Kaplan, in *The Experience of Nature*, hypothesize that the motivation for exploration is contingent upon mystery. They define mystery as "a promise of further information" or the "inference of alternate hypothesis" (Kaplan and Kaplan, 55–56). Similarly in *Townscape* the urban designer Gordon Cullen defines mystery as: "where anything could happen or exist, the noble or sordid, genius or lunacy," and so enlivens the romantic narrative by engaging the reader's imagination.

SECRETIVE PLACES OF REVELATION: THE UNDERGROUND

The idea that nature's wonders and processes hold the key to understanding truth about our lives appears throughout literature and history. In *The Castle of Otranto*, the hermit's cave in the forest is the site where the fleeing Isabella seeks refuge, meets her guardian Theodore, and discovers her father. In the picturesque gardens, unique natural wonders are also the sites of personal revelation, an idea that is not unique to the picturesque but is one shared by others from romantic poets and philosophers such as Wordsworth, Coleridge, and Rousseau to transcendentalists such as Emerson and Thoreau, surrealist artists and writers, and contemporary landscape architects. Both Lawrence Halprin and George Hargreaves have expressed experiences of personal revelation, for Halprin in the High Sierras and for Hargreaves in the high peaks of Machu Picchu during the natural disaster of the recent Hawaiian hurricane (Beardsly, 48). The current environmental movement continues the romantic's and transcendentalist's belief that nature holds the key for finding and understanding our most authentic personal and social identities.

The grotto, for instance, is a symbolic natural element in the picturesque garden connected to personal discovery. It is both the entrance to the underworld and the entrance to subconscious desires. Dido and Aeneas's love was consummated at Stowe in "Dido's Cave." Pope's grotto at Twickenham is the "hermit's cave" or the "philosopher's den" and "the domain of the contemplative life" (Miller, 77–78). At Stourhead, the grotto is the "home of the nymphs"

and also the location of the River God statue. Here, the grotto is the symbolic source of the Stour River and the source of life. All these grottoes share romantic notions and link mysterious natural forms and the dark entrance to the idea of spiritual and personal revelation. In Gaston Bachelard's phenomenological study of the architecture of the house, *The Poetics of Space,* the cellar holds similar associations. As the darkest and most subterranean part of the house, it is the location of unconscious fears and buried memories. Bachelard extends the associations of hidden and secret places into the upper levels of the house where drawers, chests, and wardrobes are the model containers of intimate knowledge and past memories. He writes: "Wardrobes with their shelves, desks with their drawers, and chests with their false bottoms are veritable organs of the secret psychological life" (Bachelard, 78).

The grotto at Stourhead.

In *The Mole People,* Jennifer Toth tells the stories of people living in New York City's underground tunnels, abandoned subway stations, and unfinished subway lines. This is a hidden culture, both physically, in its deep underground existence, and politically. Although the New York City Health Department and the mayor's office have conducted studies that estimate that between five thousand and six thousand people are living underground, these studies are kept internal and unpublished. Toth reveals this hidden culture through the experiences of numerous people such as Bernard Isaacs, who worked as an editorial assistant at CBS before he started dealing drugs. A difficult separation with his girlfriend over six years before caused him to live in the tunnels. Toth writes about how our culture's negative associations with the underground keep New York City from offering help to these hidden homeless people.

"Frightening philosophical and psychological notions of the underground, which have been passed from one generation to the next in our culture, color our perceptions of the region and the people who live there. For centuries, the depths have been depicted in literature and history as a nurturing environment for evil and madness. It is the perfect dark, unknown and foreboding terrain on which imaginations avidly feed.

From these images, the subterranean environment in Western culture has evolved metaphorically as a mental landscape, a social environment, and an ideological map. The underground has been portrayed as a threatening underside of aboveground society. Although the symbolic significance has changed dramatically over the centuries, recurring metaphors in social and literary history have spawned widespread and enduring connotations, damaging prejudices, and a simple but deep fear of the dark—all resulting in serious obstacles to helping the underground homeless. Fortunately,

Alleged tunnel entry known to residents of the Mian Khan *haveli* (residential compound) and *hammam* (baths) in the walled city of Lahore, Pakistan. (Courtesy James Wescoat)

scholars are recognizing and exposing this cultural inheritance—the first step towards ridding ourselves of its pernicious effects."
(Toth, 169, 170)

James Wescoat, Michael Brand, and Naeem Mir researched the legends/stories associated with the now disappeared tunnels said to link the Mughal gardens, shrines, and forts of Lahore, Pakistan. The researchers mapped these stories to make physical connections between imagination, memory, history, and the physical landscape. As a result of their interviews with longtime residents, they identified six narrative themes forming a "valuable reservoir of collective landscape memory"—giving coherence to the Mughal, landscape which continues to be threatened by war, migration, and social trauma (Wescoat, Brand, and Mir, 3).

Under the theme of the "modesty and passion of royal woman" are the stories of secret romantic meetings. Other narrative themes connected to the tunnels relate to conquest, escape, romance, supernatural powers, and fantasy.

"Not all tunnels protected the modesty of women. Some served as secret passageways linking the house of a lover with the chambers of his beloved. One thinks of the "thief of love" stories in Bengali literature, as well as in the Hasht Bihisht of Amir Khusrau.... In each case lovers with extraordinary intelligence and passion were separated by insurmountable barriers which could only be circumvented through a tunnel. One person in Lahore suggested that the princess Zebunnisa "must have" met her lover in the harem of Lahore Fort via a tunnel. Others argued that the death of the lover occurred near her tomb on the Multan road, and that no tunnel was involved. Neither account is substantiated by contemporary Mughal or European texts. Instead they represent a large genre of stories about errant lovers who somehow found their way into the royal harem and rarely exited alive. For more humble lovers, who do not dare to meet in secret, tunnel stories continue to fuel unfulfilled romances and passions. Fantasies of this sort abound in popular Urdu films and literature, where the tragic "Anarkali" escapes her awful fate through a tunnel. In this case and many others like it, tunnel stories involve human encounters that are risky or impossible on the surface. They link imaginary landscapes of passionate freedom with historical places or times."
(Wescoat, Brand, and Mir, 11)

The picturesque iteration of the idea of genius loci implies that a landscape holds hidden spirits or qualities waiting to be discovered. Alexander Pope articulated this idea in 1731.

To swell the Terras, or to sink the Grot;
In all, let *Nature* never be forgot
Consult the *Genius* of the *Place* in all,
That tells the Waters to rise or fall...
    (Hunt and Willis, 212)

Pope modeled his concept of the genius loci from the Latin poets of the Augustan period who spoke about some mythical time in the past when there was greater harmony between man and the spirits of nature. Much like the romantic narrative references to Gothic castle architecture of the Middle Ages, genius loci refers longingly to spirits of the past animated by legend. This idea, rekindled during the picturesque movement, continues to be important to landscape architects and other interpreters of the landscape who believe that there is more to understanding a site than recording grades, viewsheds, drainage, and functional use. For them each place has a residing invisible spirit and an underlying natural order that must be revealed, searched for, listened to, felt, or understood by careful observation.

SECRETS AND INTERPRETIVE INQUIRY

Sydney K. Robinson structures his contemporary book *Inquiry into the Picturesque* in the mode of the picturesque so that "partial concealment of possible implications" engages the reader and spectator in a probing inquiry. Although the constructed and orchestrated concealment of secrets was integral to the picturesque, secrets are fundamentally connected to narrative structures before and beyond this genre. In an article titled "Secrets and Narrative Sequence," Frank Kermode writes that stories are capable of infinite interpretations and hence that the text of every story always contains secrets that are revealed through the process of interpretation (Kermode, 82). In this dialogue between the text or the landscape and the interpreter, the interpreter unlocks the secrets and hidden meanings based upon distinct knowledge, approach, and experience. Kermode identifies the "abnormal" reader as one who examines minute details of the narration, who reads between the lines of the text or between the forms of the landscape. This acute interpreter attentively and slowly hunts for undisclosed information, and in the process opens the text to multiple readings and disrupts the "order, sequence, and message" of the literal narrative (Kermode, 84–85).

Robinson concludes his chapter entitled "Artifice" by evaluating concealment in terms of whether the "concealment, deception, and manipulation are considered benign or threatening" (Robinson, 115). Although picturesque theorists debated about what should be revealed and concealed in the landscape, modernist and postmodernist theorists and designers have more thoroughly challenged the artifice of representation by either stripping away surface treatments or playing more consciously and ironically with the surface. In Robinson's postmodern interpretation, he measures the success of the picturesque in terms of whether it prompts the participant to probe beneath the artifice:

The Picturesque worked when the artifice successfully posed a question about its status. To make its presence unmistakable or completely concealed is to leave out the primary experience of actively probing and questioning what one sees.

(Robinson, 108)

In the late 1980s when Peter Svenson first walked the Virginia farmland where he would build his house, he felt that there was something indescribably compelling about his land that "held secrets that would eventually be brought to light" (Svenson, 9). Before he uncovered the history of the Civil War's Battle of Cross Keys, which took place on his property, he sensed "the pulse of a battlefield," as he describes in his book *Battlefield: Farming a Civil War Battleground:*

"The thing I sensed was that people had been here before, en masse. At times I have noted a comparable intimation after a public auction, when the last item of furniture has been carted off and the last pickup truck has driven away. The grass is patterned with tire tracks and footprints. The buzz of the crowd, the auctioneer's warble still echo in my ears. A sniff of humanity lingers, a subtle indefinable something, but it is not an olfactory sensation. It too, is an echo, a reverberation of the auction-goers who were convened an hour earlier. A similar presence lingered in these pastures a hundred and twenty-three years after the battle. After that length of time, I would not have thought it possible to stand at the heart of a battlefield and pick up its living pulse."

(Svenson, 39)

As he tills, mows, and rakes his fields or digs into the earth to make a pond or the foundation for his house, he makes sense of the events of one overlooked day during the Civil War, a day that figures so prominently in the spirit of his property. Svenson developed a

Bottom left: Peter Svenson analyzes the military moves of the Civil War troops during the Battle of Cross Keys over his property in the Shenendoah Valley of Virginia.

Bottom right: Peter Svenson's painting *The Battle of Cross Keys.*

desire to protect the invisible subterranean history, the genius of place, manifested in the buried secrets, from the mining of the land by Civil War buffs or the historicizing of the site by developers. He thought the Civil War "hounds" who detected and dug up the bullets, buttons, and cannonballs were thieves who stole the meaning of the land, for "as insignificant as these artifacts may be, surely they lose their final iota of meaning as soon as they are lifted from the soil" (Svenson, 16). The keeping of buried memories versus the exhibition and collection of unearthed remnants to him represents a way of respecting history as enigmatic and partially concealed. In the same way that the order and regularity of the Civil War gravestones do not reflect the horror, pain, and chaos of battle, a greater respect may be paid to history by leaving the land quiet and alone (Svenson, 40).

TRANSPARENCY

In contrast to romantic and picturesque ideology, which provokes the imagination with a sense of mystery, modernism emphasizes laying bare underlying truths and order. The dark and hidden passages of the Gothic architecture embraced by English romanticism contrast with the open and light structures embraced by modernism. Corbusier's idea of creating "a single indivisible space" or Vidler's metaphor for modernist ideology as the "glass house of the soul" (Vidler, 218) (in contrast to Saint John of the Cross's "dark night of the soul") broke open separations between the inside and the outside, nature and culture, the private and the public, the conscious and the subconscious. These breaks challenged ideas about what should be hidden. The modernist exploration of transparency crossed art forms. Cubist painting flattened perspective and dissolved lines between images; Brechtian theater woke the audience from unconsciously entering a state of fiction by calling attention to the actors as actors and the audience as audience. All of the arts engaged in a more conscious use of their medium, so that painting would be about painting, theater about theater, buildings about buildings, and landscape about landscape.

In Madelon Vriesendorp's *Freud unlimited* painting, from Rem Koolhaus's *Delirious Manhattan*, Manhattan wakes up in the bed of the Empire State Building above the infrastructure of the city. (Courtesy the artist and Office of Metropolitan Architecture)

Part of what is made transparent in the modernist landscape is the medium itself: the drainage patterns, plant ecology, erosion, geologic formation, and other natural processes as well as the man-made infrastructures controlling water, energy, and waste that are often kept out of sight. A body of current work in the ecological movement shares the intention to reveal fundamental natural and engineering systems, such as where the garbage goes (Flow City in New York City, 27th Avenue Solid Waste Facility in Phoenix, Hackensack Environmental Center in New Jersey), drainage patterns (Berkeley Streams in California, Holt's Catch Basin in Toronto, Gary Strang and Daniel Solomon's Chapel and Cemetery in Houston, Steve Martino and Jody Pinto's Papago Park in Phoenix), water use (Pottenger's water tunnel #3 in New York City), energy systems (Gary Strang's proposals to mark gas lines), and erosion processes (Hargreave's Byxbee Park in Palo Alto). By portraying the gritty, everyday cir-

Top left: The aqueduct walls, shaped in the
form of a branching tree, at the Papago
Park City Boundary Project, designed by
artist Jody Pinto and landscape architect
Steve Martino, collect and distribute
water into retention basins.

Top right: The bridge for the Elgin
Riverwalk in Illinois (designed by EDAW)
reveals the underwater world to bikers
and pedestrians crossing the river.

cumstances of life, these projects seek to demystify romantic notions of nature
and challenge the clean images that dominate the landscapes of early modernism. Thus they begin to bridge relations between culture and nature.

EMPHASIS ON PROCESSES AND INTEGRATION

Although the picturesque movement was interested in selectively revealing
the power and beauty of nature, modernist and postmodernist landscape
architects such as Richard Haag and George Hargreaves rework the themes
of the picturesque by revealing nature not as a captured spectacle but as a
dynamic evolving process. They make the slow and invisible processes of
nature apparent. Exposing the underlying structure of building or natural
systems or making transparent what was once concealed is connected with
the idea of integrating nature and culture and making people more aware of
their actions and their use of resources. What is in sight will become in
mind; however, the familiar also becomes invisible over time.

The "daylighting" of Strawberry Creek in Berkeley, California, in the
early 1980s began a movement of uncovering natural drainage systems in the
East Bay Streams as well as other culverted and covered streams across urban
and suburban North America. This small grassroots community effort is symbolic of a larger movement toward creating more visible and viable connections between culture and nature. Strawberry Creek, one of several natural
streams that carry water from the Berkeley Hills to San Francisco Bay, was
covered up in the early 1900s by the development of a railroad freight yard.
Like those of many other streams, its natural meanderings were straightened,
hidden, and channeled underground through culverts and concrete; it had
not seen the light of day since 1904. Although many people, including the
leading environmentalist David Brower, who played as a child in an uncovered portion of Strawberry Creek, remember the local waterways, this and
other creeks have been buried by the development of roads, housing, and
industry, making the holistic drainage pattern barely perceivable.

In the early 1980s landscape architect Douglas Wolfe proposed that a
200-foot-long stretch of Strawberry Creek crossing a four-acre park be lifted
from its underground channel buried twenty feet below the surface. After
years of rallying community support, the idea was realized and what was

once called SUDS Neighborhood Park was renamed Strawberry Creek Park for its naturalized meandering streambed. Not only was the stream revealed but a diversity of former life reappeared, including trout, crawfish, dragonflies, frogs, bees, and mud daubers.

Over the decade after the reclamation of Strawberry Creek, a number of other creeks, streams, and rivers were lifted from underground or revitalized with natural channeling including Walnut Creek, Santa Rosa Creek, and Guadelope River in California; Boulder Creek in Boulder, Colorado; Woonasquatucket River in Providence, Rhode Island; and Garrison Creek in Toronto. Each reminded its community of their connection to a distinct ecosystem.

At Codornices Creek, just a few blocks from Strawberry Creek, local volunteers—with the help of the East Bay Citizens for Creek Restorations, Urban Ecology, the Coalition to Restore Urban Waterways, and the designer Gary Mason—dug up an asphalt parking lot and removed concrete culverts to re-create an earlier meandering streambed. Richard Register, the founder of Urban Ecology, negotiated a deal with the owner of the adjacent Southern Bank and gained permission from the University of California to re-create the creek. It required time-consuming negotiation to gain the support of community members, who objected to the liabilities of an open stream and hesitated to live with the mess and inconveniences of a long-term construction project.

Above: Water flowing through the culvert at Strawberry Creek in Berkeley, California.

Below: Volunteers meet on a Saturday to reconstruct the streambed of Codornices Creek in Berkeley, California.

For over a year more than two hundred volunteers from around Berkeley and San Francisco worked nearly every Saturday to plan the course of the stream; dig the bed by hand; build up and reinforce the edges with recycled pavement, gabions, and woven willow facimes, and plant the shores with a diversity of plants including edibles. Although the cost of using heavy machinery may have been comparable to the cost of reconstructing the creek by hand, Register believes that doing it by hand developed a constituency of community support that will ensure the long-term viability of the creek (Register). By working together, the community also recollected shared memories of their landscape.

Revealing this small creek is part of larger ecological and cultural narratives about restoring neighborhoods and creating healthier communities. The natural streambed reduces flooding, supports a diversity of wildlife, and improves local pollination, flowering, and songbird populations. Educational opportunities for the community—particularly schoolchildren—to learn about ecology now exist along this wildlife corridor. The open and vital creek is a cleansing "connective tissue" attached to a social story of creating viable, integrated communities with better child care, drug rehabilitation, and community centers. Reestablishing local and distinct waterways is an important means for establishing and celebrating local identity.[6]

REVEALING INFRASTRUCTURE

Gary Strang, a landscape architect who has actively advocated that infrastructure systems be revealed, believes that designers have been in a state of denial regarding their relationship to infrastructure:

Above: Gary Strang's proposed steam temple for the Lower East Side in Manhattan varies with the seasons according to the temperature differential above and below ground.

Bottom right: The Mostra d'Aqua in Rome marks the terminus of the ancient aqueduct.

Paula Horrigan and Margaret McAvin's visual book and design *(above and below)* for Clute Memorial Park in Watkins Glen, New York, reveals an active mining site that lies beneath the picturesque waterside park. The reader may read the book and the landscape "at their own pace, in part or whole, in or out of order." In other ways the form of the book is analogous to the interpretation of and interaction with the landscape: "This is a landscape created by water: the inland sea, the glaciers, the canals, the water pipes that flush out salt as brine. When closed and tied, the book/site presents a cover of green land and silver water. Over this landscape we impose a grid of exploration or of subdivision. Each page/layer is a map order that prevails as surface. Within each page/layer, we can open windows into the past. We turn pages/layers and open/close windows creating permutations. The grid deepens and fragments. Our universal and superficial understanding of the landscape becomes local and circumstantial." (Horrigan and McAvin 1994b)

> Designers have most often been charged with hiding, screening, and cosmetically mitigating infrastructure, in order to maintain the image of the untouched natural surroundings of an earlier era.
> (Strang, 11)

The idea of creating an *untouched* natural surrounding is part of an enduring picturesque ideology that romanticized and aestheticized nature. The picturesque landscape created an illusion of pastoral leisure by concealing the property bounds, the service side, or the infrastructure. What was hidden also related to divisions between economic and social classes. At Claremont in Surrey, England, for instance, Capability Brown hid the service entrance from guests of Lord Clive by raising the ground level and creating a gentle mound, despite the difficult consequences for drainage (Turner, 117). The restoration of Strawberry Creek both romanticizes nature by re-creating a winding streambed and lays bare the drainage system and a community's relationship with nature.

Strang thinks that the "masking" of infrastructure systems is not only misleading but impractical, for it "multiplies the task of maintenance and renovation beyond com-

prehension" (Strang, 12). He proposes that "significant sources, paths and transition points of our collectively owned resources should be made legible in the landscape" (Strang, 12). In one of his proposals, he marks the presence of a submerged gas line with a sequence of eternal flames. Although these proposals are part of a modern ecological movement, there are many historic examples of celebrating engineering accomplishments and human achievement related to urban infrastructure and civic progress. For instance, the major aqueducts in Rome are announced by monumental sculpted arched fountains that reveal the flow and volume of water through the city.

Robert Thayer in *Gray World Green Heart* writes about how the concealment of technological features implies a certain dishonesty, denial, and guilt. Scenic management practices that conceal visual "problems" may mislead the public by disguising the origins of the real problem. Thayer points out that the practice of blending and softening clear-cuts in the national forests is "unethical cosmetology" that makes society ignore the consequences of its consumption. This and other cited examples raise the fundamental questions: Should the surface reflect the core, and should the symbology of the surface correlate with the symbology of the core? (Thayer, 77). Thayer writes that we are reaching an "ideological path in our profession which, in essence, may force us to choose between two competing paradigms: simulation or sustainability" (Thayer, 218). He concludes that transparency is key to sustainability: "The movement towards a sustainable world must include the peeling away of intervening images between landscape *function* and landscape *experience*" (Thayer, 222). If Thayer would respond to Robinson's inquiry regarding the value of concealment, he would find the concealment of infrastructure as "threatening rather than benign." Thayer advocates the unmasking of "intervening images" and thus challenges the centralized powers that control key life support systems. As Thayer notes: "Opacity and fakery in the landscape ultimately only serve to perpetuate the unsustainable status quo" (Thayer, 311). He suggests that transparency and truth will give communities the power to make more responsible decisions.

Top left: Gary Strang's design proposal for Herman Park in Houston reveals the annual flooding of Houston's bayous. In the wet season the basin fills with water and in the dry season the pools recede, revealing a series of gardens composed of native plantings. Basin in dry season with gardens at the base of the cypress trees.

Top right: Basin in flooded winter season with bald cypress trees.

Instead of associating underground passages with mysterious secrets, performance artist and carpenter Marty Pottenger reveals the working stories of constructing New York City's water system. In her performance piece titled *City Water Tunnel #3*, she describes the details and processes of digging and drilling the shafts, valve chambers, and tunnels for the city's third major water tunnel. Based on her interviews with the drillers, blasters, project managers, and engineers, she reenacts their stories of working in the tunnels. Her performance brings New Yorkers down into the earth and makes them aware of what supports their everyday needs to shower, drink, clean, and cool off. Pottenger retells the story that one of the tunnel workers, or "sandhogs," told her about finding a leak:

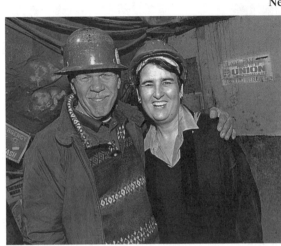

Tommy Selkirk with Marty Pottenger 600 feet below ground in shaft 23B of the New York City Water Tunnels. (Photo by Brittain Stone)

"Once we were down in a tunnel, must've been up at Highbridge, and we couldn't get this leak to stop. Water was coming in pretty good, underground stream, we get them all the time. We tried everything, stuffing it with oakum, caulk and concrete. After a bit, whatever we put in would come right out with a rush of clean water behind it. Finally we got some oatmeal and stuck that in there. Oatmeal swelled up and gave us just enough time to fill it in with a chemical grout. Water stopped and we finished, packed up and left. About a year later we had to come back to check on something. As we walked to where the leak had been, there was something growing all along the floor of the tunnel, two, three feet high. The chemical grout we had used was nitrogen based, so the nitrogen had fertilized the oatmeal and since there wasn't any sun, this was 700 feet down, the oats came out albino. White oats."

(Pottenger, 1996)

In *Flow City* Mierle Laderman Ukeles makes New York City's garbage removal system transparent so that residents appreciate the daily maintenance involved in keeping the city clean and realize the outcome of their consumption. Her project brings people into contact with a system that is normally removed and disguised from them. (Most current landfill reclamation projects include "capping" the landfill and concealing the contents with vegetative cover.) Typically New Yorkers only realize what it means to have their garbage removed when sanitation workers go on strike and the trash builds up on the street. This project enables visitors to comprehend the process for handling the volume of trash that is generated by the city each day. Ukeles puts garbage in sight and in mind. As noted by the writer Robert Morgan, Ukeles' emphasis on trash maintenance "challenges the embedded notion of refuse as a despicable sign, as matter which can not be appropriated psychologically or environmentally" (Morgan, 53).

People enter *Flow City* at the Marine Transfer Station located on the shore of the Hudson River and 59th Street through the Passage Ramp—a corridor made from recycled glass, aluminum, newspaper, rubber, and other thrown-away materials. Along the corridor is a glass wall that looks out on the collection trucks entering the facility. Next the visitor crosses the Glass Bridge, which looks out on the surrounding city and down to the "tipping floor," where the garbage is transferred from the trucks to the barges. At the south end of the Glass Bridge is the Media Flow Wall, where video monitors convey information about waste disposal, the Hudson River's tidal changes, and other regional environmental issues. Ukeles says that she wants *Flow City* to reveal the interconnections between the natural and human environments. The idea of flow connects the cleansing powers of the river to the urban maintenance system:

> "I kept thinking that the transfer station is an intersection between the waste flow and the water flow, and if we could just make the waste flow as wise as the water flow, we would understand how to fit into the real systems of life."
>
> (Yung, 26)

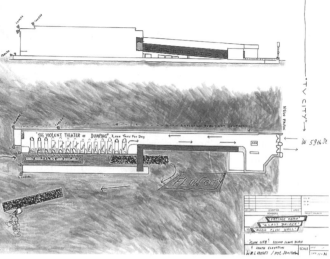

Above: Ukeles' plan for *Flow City* showing the passage ramp leading to the Violent Theater of Dumping.

Below: The competition presentation for *De-Code/Re-Code Atlanta* by Conway and Schulte included rewriting the zoning regulations pertaining to public space districts.

THE PARADOX OF TRANSPARENCY

Although making energy and waste systems more apparent can effect a greater awareness about culture's interconnections with ecology, there is a certain irony to the fact that what becomes visible and familiar often becomes invisible over time. What we see the most we may appreciate the least. In other words, there is more to change than simply exposing the problems; however, revealing the problem may be the first step toward collectively solving it. Attached to the physical form of the landscape are deep-seated cultural values and political systems, which are more difficult to expose and reform.

A project in downtown Atlanta, Georgia, illustrated how a challenge to underlying political and legal systems met formidable resistance, greater than what might have been prompted by an effort to merely expose. The project *De-Code/Re-Code Atlanta* makes apparent the otherwise inaccessible written regulations and government processes that determine the form of public space and the streetscape. In response to a call for new ideas for public space, the architects William F. Conway and Marcy Schulte marked the locations of street restrictions such as view corridor restrictions, access zones, and the setbacks for parking lots, buffer zones, and signage.

The architects went beyond making the codes apparent, because they believed that to make substantive change, the fundamental struc-

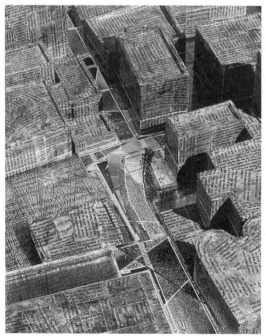

Excerpt from the rewritten zoning ordinance by Conway and Schulte:

Section 16-18.005. Permissive uses.
A building, area or premises may be used for, but not limited to, the following purposes (not subject to the procedures as specified in Section 16-18.005):
(1) Broadcasting services, line-of-sight relay devises for telephone, radio or television communication.
(2) Literature distribution.
(3) Children's and school activities.
(4) Religious activities.
(5) Recreation uses and places of assembly and similar uses which may typically be constructed within fully enclosed buildings.
(6) Eating, drinking, and the distribution of food/meals for free.
(7) A first aid center and clinic for the distribution of condoms, other birth control, needle exchange/cleaning programs, blood donor stations and information distribution on health concerns.

(Continued opposite)

Seating and social spaces in the traffic island, defined as a pedestrian circulation zone, for Conway and Schulte's project *De-Code/Re-Code Atlanta.*

ture or text of the city needed to be changed. In fact, their original competition proposal for the project included only an orange line, which delimited the site, and their rewritten ordinance for public spaces. They treated "language as infrastructure." They challenged the idea that the design of physical space must conform to invisible norms by *re-coding* or rewriting the code rather than designing to the code. They also broke regulated divisions between public and private space by "encouraging engagement between private lives in public space" (Conway and Schulte). "Rather than limiting the ordinance to the definition of what is *not* possible on private property, the rewritten text offered the definition of possible actions on public property" (Conway and Schulte). The space was designed so that people would appropriate it with their uses. Seating, for instance, has been designed to occupy the pedestrian circulation zone defined by the existing city zoning ordinance. Limiting regulations that treat the street as a "residual space of circulation for a passive public" are rewritten to "allow consensual action, experience, and debate" and the involvement of individuals and the community in the "establishment and maintenance of a safe, empowering and expressive public life" (Conway and Schulte).

Although Conway and Schulte's proposal was chosen by competition, the client, the Corporation for Olympic Development in Atlanta (CODA), finally rejected the specific rewriting of the Atlanta Municipal Zoning Ordinance, insisting instead that the architects provide something physical. Their resistance to changing the legal structure may have been caused by a complex set of factors including lack of time with the oncoming Olympics, lack of a sense of authority for changing the code, and also probably a sense that the more fundamental change posed by the architects would require more than their typical project involvement. The architects revised their plan by using the language of the existing ordinance that defined a pedestrian circulation zone to locate new programs for use within the space of the streetscape. They created social and sitting spaces both along the sidewalk and out on the intermediary traffic island. "Fugitive text" etched into the walls and benches provides a "rich legacy of urban occupation" (Conway and Schulte). By defying the common blankness of over-regulated public spaces, this project raises questions about the validity of the unseen text that determines the life of public space.

Anthony Vidler writes that the modernist "myth of transparency" is "uncanny," for the very familiar may become strange. He uses the metaphor of glass to illustrate the paradox of transparency, for this highly transparent material is so reflective that it obscures views into it. According to him, reflective surfaces create a "state of anxiety" because the architect or author "allows us neither to stop at the surface nor to penetrate it..." The mirror transforms what is familiarly seen into a "strange" projection (Vidler, 222–223). He presents truth as an illusion, in keeping with other postmodernist theorists. Colin Rowe also writes that transparency, as a formal characteristic of contemporary architecture, is "clearly ambiguous" (Rowe, 161). Ambiguous because the superimposition of forms and ideas that "intersect, overlap, and interlock" create double entendres and complexity of interpretation. By making the stratification and overlapping layers of change transparent in the landscape, a deeply complex and ambiguous text is revealed.

MASKING AND UNMASKING

Postmodern or post-structural theory of representation posits that there are always structures that mediate perception or representation. It questions the idea of creating a transparent window on reality. Authenticity or realism is challenged by the idea that what appears as "natural" often conceals historical contingencies and ideology, and inhibits negotiation and contestation (Duncan). The *search for depth* has been criticized as naive, nostalgic, or often conservative. So instead, postmodern design plays with surface, denies depth, and deemphasizes a privileged perspective. Sometimes this means a free play of surfaces without the intention to penetrate the surface. Sometimes postmodernism may simulate depth, like at Kentlands in Maryland or other neotraditional landscapes where veneers, symbols, and inscriptions of historic fabric mask and blur distinctions between the historic and the new, the "real" and the simulated.

Masking and unmasking open a middle position between a total relativism that negates truth and the desire to find truth and so create a *provisional* truth shaped by multiple perspectives. Masking is a way of accepting the unknowns, doubts, and necessary fictions of life, and unmasking is a way of seeking more complex answers to questions.

Revelation often follows concealment. The dynamic between masking and unmasking is illustrated by a "ritual of reversal," called mumming, which took place in small fishing communities in Newfoundland, Canada, in the late 19th and early 20th centuries. During the twelve days of Christmas, people would disguise themselves in costumes that would conceal their identities. All their well-known features—their hands, face, and body—were made unfamiliar by gloves, masks, and body padding. These masked people would then visit their usually familiar neighbors as if they were strangers. As disguised persons, they would behave with more openness, saying things normally considered socially unacceptable, making sexual gestures, and behaving outside the normal social code. The neighbors would try to detect and guess their identity.

The anthropologist Don Handelman notes that in this ritual the masking of the "personhood" was followed by the revealing of the "selfhood." In other words, in the daily familiar life the "personhood" is a mask (or hood) of social values and expectations. When the people explicitly donned a physical mask, the social norms were suppressed and the "selfhood" that had been concealed was revealed. By concealing what is familiar (and in Duncan's terms naturalized), the mask reveals the *unheimlech*, or that which cannot be repressed.

In the landscape, the characteristics of nature may be masked but not completely concealed. In formal gardens, clipped hedges, axies, allées, monocultures, and channeled waterways mask the underlying diversity, growth, and wildness of nature. Even an ordinary mowed lawn acts as a mask. Nature's potential for uncontrolled growth is implicit in the artificial

(Continued)
(8) Clothing and bedding/linen distribution centers.
(9) Display or posting of political bills and information.
(10) Hiring hall/area for day workers as well as longer term employment.
(11) Temporary markets (flea, clothing, food, etc.).
(12) Music, theater, dance, cultural presentations. Other uses which may be inappropriate or not permitted in other districts and adjoining district may be permissible here given that these activities are defined as consensual uses.

Section 16-18X.006. Consensual uses.
In addition to permissible uses some activities may be permissible in the Special Public-Interest Space District given that they are negotiated and agreed upon by mutual consent and agreement among involved parties.

Weather and age peel away the thin postmodern surface of Piazza D'Italia in New Orleans by Charles Moore.

Above: For *Camouflage History* by Ericson and Zeigler, Reverend John Hamilton's house is painted in military camouflage.

Below: 5-27, The porch railing of *Camouflage History* calls out the names of Dutch Boy Paint's "Authentic Colors of Historic Charleston."

restraint of growth. In contrast to the formal garden, which celebrates its artifice, the picturesque garden disguises its artifice to reveal the landscape as more purely "natural." But, as Robinson asserts, the picturesque garden can be more than a set of conventions and may challenge divisions between nature and artifice by its ambiguity and undecidedness. The appearance and disappearance, the masking and unmasking, or the hiding and seeking of nature in both picturesque and formal garden, create dynamic tensions as well as openings for critical interpretation of the values that inhere in representations or artifice and the ideologies of nature.

The designer may play the role of the trickster who in order to interpret embedded ideologies, goes between unmasking and masking the familiar and the strange. Two artists, Kate Ericson and Mel Ziegler, played the role of the trickster by revealing the inherent ideology and invisible preservation codes in Charleston, South Carolina. Their piece titled *Camouflage History* comments on the community's telling of their history, a history "that is constructed and constantly reinvented in the wake of restoration" (Jacobs, 177). Ericson and Zeigler painted a single-room-wide house owned by Reverend John Hamilton at 28 Mary Street in the "nonhistoric" and predominantly African-American community of East Side. This house faces the more gentrified neighborhood of Mazyck-Wraggborough. The East Side community decided that it did not want to be a designated historic district, because residents believed gentrification would threaten their security and push them out of their neighborhood, as it had done in other African-American neighborhoods in Charleston (Jacobs, 179). The artists painted the house in a military camouflage motif using Dutch Boy Paint "Authentic Colors of Historic Charleston." Their "authenticity" masks social and racial hierarchies. According to the company's paint chart, these colors represent "events from U.S. History, Charleston's History and Architectural Styles of the Era." Paint names such as Huguenot Deep Brown, Plantation Red Brown, Promenade Pineapple, Aiken Light Pumpkin, and Peninsula City Red act as synecdoches for histories associated with certain families and places. The selected historic period is 1660 to 1900, or the period of European settlement, thus omitting Native American settlement as well as subsequent changes. Sites of the American Revolution and the Civil War are part of the tourist tour, but the currently active Charleston Naval Base and Weapons Station is not. Ericson and Ziegler's project comments on what gets omitted from history by the designated districts, periods, and paint colors, which also tend to demarcate racial lines.

Although camouflage is typically used to hide the presence of a stranger or an attacking soldier in a foreign landscape, here camouflage has the opposite effect. This camouflage makes the familiar strange and more apparent, like the masks of the mumming ritual in Newfoundland. This familiar architecture is pulled out of the context of all the other single-room-wide houses by the camouflage, which is double coded with the language of the elite preservation movement and the current military operation based in Charleston.[7] Here, masking and unmasking decodes and questions embedded ideologies about race, history, and identity.

Masking and unmasking is not just a game of tricks but a necessary means for denaturalizing and decoding as well as recoding and encoding meaning. Crapanzano writes about how the messenger must "disrupt the prejudices and pre-understandings of his interlocutors and break the frames in which these prejudices and pre-understandings are held" so that the message is heard (Crapanzano, 3). Both *Camouflage History* and *De-code/Re-code* "break" the social "frames." In these cases underlying social codes are unmasked by placing the language or the form (the preservation paints or the street bench) that typically masks code into a new context. These projects use masking and unmasking to elicit a critical questioning of psychological, ideological, and social structures.

SUMMARY

Revealing secrets or that which is hidden for political or cultural reasons often results in conflict, pain, and hostility. The architects and artists who unearth forgotten or hidden artifacts are often surprised by the political conflicts that follow. We conclude with an instance of how the physical excavation of the land led to the unearthing of repressed conflicts and the reconsideration of *normal* values.

The excavation for the foundation of a Federal Court Administration building in the City Hall district of lower Manhattan led to political conflict between the African-American community and the federal General Services Administration (GSA). Despite the marking of this burial site on 18th-century maps as the "Negroes Burial Ground," and the Historic Conservation and Interpretation reports that noted the presence of the burial ground on the construction site, the land was purchased because it was assumed that all significant archaeological remains had already been destroyed by the excavations for building foundations in the 20th century. Six months after the land was purchased by the GSA, in May 1991, archaeologists found human bones. The excavation of the skeletons then proceeded without the approval of the black community or the office of then mayor David Dinkins, who together insisted that greater respect be paid to this sacred site. After a backhoe operator working on the building's foundation was seen accidentally digging and lifting up jawbones, leg bones, and arm bones, activists blockaded the site and demanded that construction cease until better provisions were made to preserve the area. They also demanded that archaeologists familiar with the culture and history of African-Americans be included in the research team and that the site be commemorated with a museum and memorial.

The discovery of these bodies that had been buried for two centuries raised conflicts about what happened, how to represent what happened, and who has the power to research and tell history. As noted by Michael L. Blakey, a Howard University anthropologist and the director of the African Burial Ground archaeological research group, the conflicts that arose around this burial ground were a "microcosm" of broader issues of racism and economic segregation (Harrington, 30). Conflicts over the burial ground revealed a deep-

According to Howard University's archaeological research on the bones removed from the New York City African Burial Ground, the brutal wear of the back and shoulder bones, and fractured skulls and spinal columns are the result of extreme axial loading and forward bending. The condition and chemistry of the bones reveal poor health (rickets and other infectious diseases) and poor nutrition. Over half of the four hundred skeletons removed from the site were those of infants who died when they were under two years old.

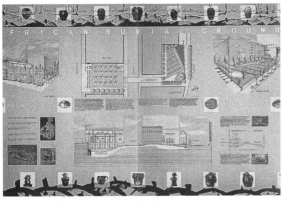

Above: Paula Horrigan and Margaret McAvin's proposal for the African Burial Ground Memorial.

Below: Karen Bermann and Jeanine Centuori's proposal for the African Burial Ground.

seated distrust between government and community interests and between whites and blacks. The desire to commemorate the site became part of a larger story to reclaim heritage and retell forgotten or disregarded history.

In response to the demand to involve African-Americans in the research and representation of the burial ground history, the artifacts and bones were transferred from Lehman College in New York to Howard University in Washington, D.C. These bones tell stories about the diet, health, labor, customs, and relationships of African-Americans living in New York in the late 17th and early 18th centuries. Although it is commonly believed that blacks were free workers with far better conditions in the northern cities than on southern plantations, the condition of these bones reveals severe hardship and suffering.[8] Ironically, what is now the center of government and the justice system was in the late 17th and early 18th centuries outside the city limits—unclaimed wetland and "potter's field," a place African-Americans were buried because they were not allowed to be buried with white European descendants in the lower Manhattan churchyards.

Uncovering the African-American bones and traditional burial customs inspired the telling of a whole set of stories of African culture and history. The cowrie shells found on some of the buried women are believed to be part of a West African burial tradition and symbolize a return in the afterlife to Africa. African-American drummers, dancers, artists, and storytellers gathered at the burial ground to call forth political power, celebrate culture and pay respect to ancestors. In August 1995 a delegation from Ghana visited the African Burial Ground to offer libation and mourning. A Yoruba priestess performed private ceremonies that reenacted West African burial customs. Other ceremonies will be held when the four hundred bodies taken to Howard University are reinterred in the burial ground.

In January 1994, 164 designers and artists submitted designs for the African Burial Ground Memorial competition. The designs varied from proposals that created mystery around the buried secrets to ones that attempted to make more transparent previously untold or forgotten African-American history. In Paula Horrigan and Margaret McAvin's proposal, water flowed from hollow clay pots across a shelled surface and disappeared underground. They wrote that "the entire realm is haunted by sound: the whistle of the wind over the tops of the open clay vessels and the unseen voices and feet on the Pot Yard floor." Another haunting proposal inscribed "THE AFRICAN BURIAL GROUND WALKING AMONG AFRICAN GRAVES/SPEAKING THROUGH THE GROUND" on manhole covers within the historic district.[9] The Luke proverb "Nothing is covered up that will not be revealed" becomes ambiguous by a glass room "which one can observe but not enter," placed in the center of the memorial site.[10] What appeared to be an unmasking of the truth was instead displayed as a void. In contrast, other proposals made transparent previously hidden histories by digging underground, exhibiting artifacts, and telling hard facts.

Many of the designs treated the landscape as a palimpsest of layers of history to conceptually and physically unearth. In Rachel Frankel's, twelve borings of the earth containing archaeological remnants, encased in plastic

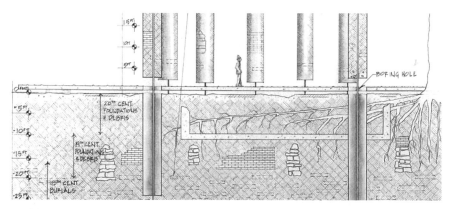

and lit at night, stood united in a circle as a representation of history in terms of sedimentation and gathered depth.[11] Others connected the past with the present by commemorating current African-American social activists. Sequences from the current ground surface down to the level of the former burial ground or sequences from the contemporary city grid to the former layout of the potter's field signified the passing of time in depth and form. One of the winning designs, by Chris Neville, connected the present surface and everyday lives of office workers with the buried past by the inscription "You are now suspended above the African Burial Ground" placed in the many elevators within the historic district. The artist wrote, "Filled with constant motion, these elevator shafts loom like secret, animate headstones, connecting our lives here on the surface with the histories that lie buried beneath us" (Kaufman, 32). This proposal was powerful because it did not physically change the site yet conceptually altered or unmasked what was normally understood.

All of these design responses used devices of revealing and concealing to tell the many stories surrounding the African Burial Ground. The designers peeled and plastered the thick layers of experience, history, and memory and engaged the visitor in the interpretation and representation of place. What becomes hidden or displayed tells the story of cultural values, myths, and ways of knowing. Designers do not necessarily have to bring symbols to the site, for stories to be told are already there, lying in place.

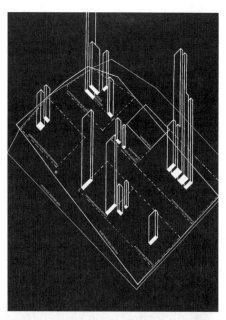

Top: Rachel Frankel's design for the African Burial Ground.

Above right: Chris Neville's plan showing elevator banks within the National Historic Site District.

Right: Chris Neville's proposal for the elevators in the National Historic Site of the African Burial Ground.

NOTES

1. Crapanzano (1992) compares the ethnographer to Hermes the messenger.

2. Today *The Castle of Otranto* seems not to be taken seriously in part because it is interpreted as being formulaic—in terms of the setting, language, and plot (relying upon supernatural events). It is for this same reason that this story is also important to the understanding of the genre. Furthermore, as far as the authors know, there has not been a thorough study of this novel in relation to conventions that Horace Walpole also established as a landscape designer.

3. Michael Bakhtin identified the "castle" as a chronotype used in the Gothic novel and closely connected to the historical past, a time of lords, and hereditary rights. He cites *The Castle of Otranto* as one of the first Gothic novels to use the castle to conjure all these associations. Ancestral rights to the castle is the main theme of this story.

4. Hunt and Willis (1988) present the writings of various picturesque landscape theorists who vary greatly in their comparison of landscape and painting.

5. Knight thought that more of the landscape should be revealed and countered Repton's tendency to control too much that which is concealed (Robinson, 101).

6. Restoration projects such as Strawberry Creek and Codornices Creek have affected political and legal change. Today in Berkeley, a Creek Preservation Ordinance requires that a public hearing be held in the event of proposed creek coverings.

7. The Desert Storm operations used this military disguise for equipment and dress.

8. Prior to the American Revolution, New York City had the highest population of enslaved African-Americans of any English colonial settlement besides Charleston, South Carolina.

9. Design by Karen Bermann and Jeanine Centuori.

10. Design by Richard Scherr.

11. Design by Rachel Frankel.

REFERENCES

Andrews, Malcolm. 1991. "The Sublime as Paradigm: Hatod and Hawkstone." In *The Architecture of Western Gardens*, ed. Monique Mosser and Georges Teyssot. Cambridge: MIT Press.

Bachelard, Gaston. 1969. *The Poetics of Space*. Boston: Beacon Press.

Bakhtin, M. M. 1981. "Forms of Time in Chronotype in the Novel." In *Dialogic Imagination: Four Essays by M. M. Bakhtin*. Austin, Tex.: University of Texas Press.

Barthes, Roland. 1974. *S/Z*. New York: Hill and Wang.

———. 1975. *The Pleasure of the Text*. trans. by Richard Miller. New York: Hill and Wang.

Beardsley, John. 1995. "Poet of Landscape Process." Landscape Architecture 85(12):45–51.

Bleiler, E. F., ed. 1966. The Castle of Otranto *by Horace Walpole,* Vathek *by William Beckford,* The Vampire *by John Polidori: Three Gothic Novels*. New York: Dover.

Boyer, Christine M. 1996. *The City of Collective Memory*. Cambridge: MIT Press.

Burke, Edmund. [1759] 1990. *A Philosophical Enquiry into the Origin of Our Idea of the Sublime and Beautiful*. Oxford: Oxford University Press.

Calvino, Italo. 1972. *Invisible Cities*. San Diego, New York, London: Harcourt Brace.

Chatman, Seymour. 1978. *Story and Discourse Narrative Structure in Fiction and Film*. Ithaca, N.Y.: Cornell University Press.

Conway, William F., and Mary Schulte. 1996. Design documents for the *De-Code/Re-Code* Atlanta Project. Unpublished.

Crapanzano, Vincent. 1992. *Hermes' Dilemma and Hamlet's Desire: On the Epistemology of Interpretation*. Cambridge: Harvard University Press.

Cullen, Gordon. 1961. *Townscape*. New York: Reinhold.

Griswold, Mac. 1987. "A Painshill Progress." *Garden Design* 6(1).

Haddad, Laura. 1996. "Happening: Paradigms of Light a Blaze (A Dialectic of the Sublime and the Picturesque)." Landscape Journal 15(1):48–57.

Hargreaves, George. 1995. Talk given at S.U.N.Y. School of Environmental Science and Forestry.

Harrington, Spencer P. M. 1993. "Bones Bureaucrats: New York's Great Cemetery Imbroglio." *Archeology* (March/April):28–33.

Haycraft, Howard. 1946. *The Art of the Mystery Story, A Collection of Critical Essays*. New York: Simon and Schuster.

Horrigan, Paula, and Margaret McAvin. 1994a. In *Reclaiming Our Past, Honoring Our Ancestors: New York's 18th Century African Burial Ground & The Memorial Competition*, ed. Edward Kaufman. New York: The African Burial Ground Competition Coalition.

———. 1994b. Sedimentary Site: Project Description of Clute Memorial Park Project.

Hunt, John Dixon, and Peter Willis. 1988. *The Genius of Place: The English Landscape Garden, 1620–1820.* Cambridge: MIT Press.

Iddon, John. 1996. *Horace Walpole's Stawberry Hill: A History and Guide.* Saint Mary's University College.

Jacobs, Mary Jane. 1991. *Places with a Past: New Site Specific Art at Charleston's Spoleto Festival.* New York: Rizzoli.

Kaplan, Rachel, and Steve Kaplan. 1989. *The Experience of Nature: A Psychological Perspective.* Cambridge: Cambridge University Press.

Kaufman, Edward, ed. 1994. *Our Past, Honoring Our Ancestors: New York's 18th Century African Burial Ground & The Memorial Competition.* New York: The African Burial Ground Competition Coalition.

Kermode, Frank. 1980. "Secrets and Narrative Sequence." In *On Narrative,* ed. W. J. T. Mitchell. Chicago: University of Chicago Press.

Loudon, John Claudius. 1840. *The Landscape Gardening and Landscape Architecture of the Late Humphry Repton, Esq.* London: Longman

Mehrotra, K. K. 1934. *Horace Walpole and the English Novel.* New York: Russell and Russell.

Miller, Naomi. 1982. *Heavenly Caves: Reflections on the Garden Grotto.* New York: G. Graziller.

Meyer, Elizabeth. "Seized by Sublime Sentiments: Between Terra Firma and Terra Incognita: Gas Works Park and Bloedel Reserve Gardens." Unpublished version of paper sent to authors.

Morgan, Robert C. 1986. "Touch Sanitation and the Decontextualization of Performance Art (1979–80)." *Kansas Quarterly* (Spring):41–54.

Neville, Chris. 1994. "You Are Now Suspended above the African Burial Ground." In *Reclaiming Our Past, Honoring Our Ancestors: New York's 18th Century African Burial Ground & The Memorial Competition,* ed. Edward Kaufman. New York: The African Burial Ground Competition Coalition.

Pottenger, Marty. 1996. *City Water Tunnel #3.* Performance script, Unpublished.

Register, Richard. 1987. *Ecocity Berkeley: Building Cities for a Healthy Future.* Berkeley, Calif.: North Atlantic Books.

———. 1996. Interviews with authors. Berkeley, Calif., fall.

Repton, Humphrey. 1907. *The Art of Landscape Gardening.* Boston: Houghton, Mifflin.

Robinson, Sidney K. 1991. *Inquiry into the Picturesque.* Chicago: University of Chicago Press.

Rowe, Colin. 1993. *The Mathematics of the Ideal Villa and Other Essays.* Cambridge: MIT Press.

Ryden, Kent C. 1993. *Mapping the Invisible Landscape: Folklore Writing and the Sense of Place.* Iowa City: University of Iowa Press.

Schama, Simon. 1995. *Landscape and Memory.* New York: Knopf.

Scherr, Richard. 1994. *Reclaiming Our Past, Honoring Our Ancestors: New York's 18th Century African Burial Ground & The Memorial Competition,* ed. Edward Kaufman. New York: The African Burial Ground Competition Coalition.

Strang, Gary. 1996. "Infrastructure as Landscape." *Places.* 10(3):9–15.

Svenson, Peter. 1992. *Battlefield: Farming a Civil War Battleground.* Winchester, Mass.: Faber and Faber.

Thayer, Robert. 1996. *Gray World Green Heart.* New York: John Wiley & Sons.

Toth, Jennifer. 1993. *The Mole People: Life in the Tunnels Beneath New York City.* Chicago: Chicago Review Press.

Turner, Roger. 1985. *Capability Brown and the Eighteenth-Century English Landscape.* New York: Rizzoli.

Vidler, Anthony. 1992. *The Architectural Uncanny: Essays in the Modern Unhomely.* Cambridge: MIT Press.

Wescoat, James L., Jr., Michael Brand, and Naeem Mir. 1991. "Gardens, Roads and Legendary Tunnels: The Underground Memory of Mughal Lahore." *Journal of Garden History* 17:1–17.

Yung, Susan. 1996. "Mierle Laderman Ukeles: All Systems Flow." *Appearances* 23(February):26–29.

CHAPTER SIX

GATHERING

INTRODUCTION

THE first botanical gardens of the 16th and 17th centuries represented within the confines of their walls the imagined Garden of Eden. Plants found in the discoveries of the four continents were brought back to places like the town of Padua, Italy, to re-create an Eden: a garden of perpetual fruits and blooms. At Padua, as in other early botanical gardens, paths symbolized the four rivers of the world (Euphrates, Tigris, Phison, and Gihon), and the resulting sections of the circular garden represented the four continents (Europe, Asia, Africa, and America).

The idea of the garden as a microcosm of the world predates the 16th century. Persian Paradise Gardens were typically divided into four sections to represent the four "corners of the world." With the exploration of the New World, the "corners" became continents and places to discover and collect God's creations. Explorers actually looked for the mythical tree of life, which some believed was the banana tree of the Caribbean. The plants were located in the garden according to both their genus and their geographic origin, and additional displays of fauna and minerals created a sci-

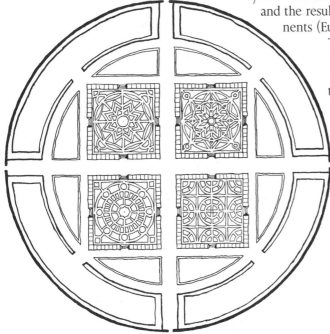

Above: The botanical garden at Padua, plan redrawn by Jennifer Miller.

Right: Jens Jensen's council ring is intended to recall the Native American's place for story telling. (Courtesy Robert Grese)

entific microcosm of the natural world. As part of this allegory, individual plants embodied the virtues and teachings of the Old and New Testaments, as noted by John Prest in his book the *Garden of Eden*:

> Everything in this garden was then, in its turn, enveloped in allegory. Each individual flower illustrated some aspect of the Christian faith, reminding the observer either of some simple virtue, or some more sophisticated theological truth. Thus the rose, whose bud opened and whose blossom fell in a single day, put one in mind of the modesty of the Virgin.
> (Prest, 23)

In this gathered and constructed world, scholars of religion, medicine, and botany found complete knowledge invested in the creations of God—nature.

As a book collects and compresses information within its binding, the garden gathers knowledge and experience within its walls.[1] Many other gardens since the early botanical gardens have created microcosms. Even the vast mid-17th-century garden of Versailles represented the larger universe. Louis XIV, aptly named the Sun King, created a garden with Le Notre that placed his Royal Palace, and him, on the central east-west axis of his universe, where the iconography and naming of rooms, fountains, paths, and pools beyond related to the planets and Gods of the solar system. In a contemporary instance, Parque Tezozomoc, created for Mexico City in the late 20th century, reconstructs in miniature the ancient lakes that were obliterated by the development of the world's largest city and so gathers the history of the city's development and culture into one recognizable place.[2] These and many other gardens and parks bring through the language of metaphor and synecdoche the vast and indecipherable world into a coherent, memorable, and recognizable form.

Gathering is a significant means of making narratives and landscapes. Any narrative, no matter how simple, is more than just a scattered series of events, but a "grasping together" of events, characters, processes, and place into meaningful configurations. Likewise, the configurations of landscapes reflect the interconnection of natural and cultural processes. Any valley, watershed, island, or coastal plain gathers. As stories create boundaries and compress time into beginnings, endings, returns, and cycles, so too, gardens, parks, and neighborhoods create a focused "story space." We use narrative as a means of tying together events to make sense of both experience and place. Memory is critical in this process. By definition, memory, as re-collection or re-membering, is also a gathering. To the degree that it is shared, it becomes a collective gathering linked to common experiences between family, community, region, or nation.

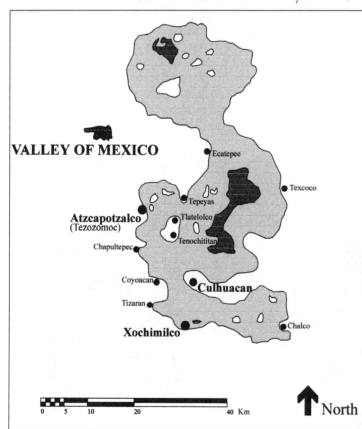

VALLEY OF MEXICO

Ecatepee

Texcoco

Tepeyas

Atzcapotzalco
(Tezozomoc)

Tlatelolco

Tenochititan

Chapultepec

Coyoacan

Culhuacan

Tizaran

Xochimilco

Chalco

0 5 10   20   40 Km

North

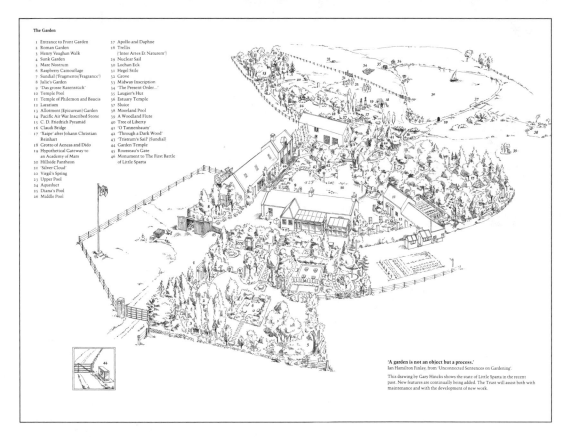

The Garden

1 Entrance to Front Garden
2 Roman Garden
3 Henry Vaughan Walk
4 Sunk Garden
5 Mare Nostrum
6 Raspberry Camouflage
7 Sundial ('Fragments/Fragrance')
8 Julie's Garden
9 'Das grosse Rasenstück'
10 Temple Pool
11 Temple of Philemon and Baucis
12 Lararium
13 Allotment (Epicurean) Garden
14 Pacific Air War Inscribed Stone
15 C. D. Friedrich Pyramid
16 Claudi Bridge
17 'Xaipe' after Johann Christian
     Reinhart
18 Grotto of Aeneas and Dido
19 Hypothetical Gateway to
     an Academy of Mars
20 Hillside Pantheon
21 'Silver Cloud'
22 Virgil's Spring
23 Upper Pool
24 Aqueduct
25 Diana's Pool
26 Middle Pool

27 Apollo and Daphne
28 Trellis
     ('Inter Artes Et Naturem')
29 Nuclear Sail
30 Lochan Eck
31 Hegel Stile
32 Grove
33 Midway Inscription
34 'The Present Order...'
35 Laugier's Hut
36 Estuary Temple
37 Sluice
38 Moorland Pool
39 A Woodland Flute
40 Tree of Liberty
41 'O Tannenbaum'
42 'Through a Dark Wood'
43 'Tristram's Sail' (Sundial)
44 Garden Temple
45 Rousseau's Gate
46 Monument to The First Battle
     of Little Sparta

'A garden is not an object but a process.'
Ian Hamilton Finlay, from 'Unconnected Sentences on Gardening'.

This drawing by Gary Hincks shows the state of Little Sparta in the recent past. New features are continually being added. The Trust will assist both with maintenance and with the development of new work.

This chapter discusses three manifestations of gathering—the *miniature,* where larger ideas and places are compressed into smaller contained and identifiable spaces; the *souvenir,* where a piece or a part acts, much like a synecdoche, as a reminder or representation of a larger event or place; and the *collection,* where many pieces are assembled in an ordered way, revealing narratives of the collected and collector. Although these three concepts will be introduced separately, they often occur in the landscape together. For instance, a souvenir may be represented in miniature and as part of a collection.[3] Gathering is a way of regaining, remembering, preserving, and re-creating what is desired or lost, as well as a way of creating a more coherent world.[4]

THE MINIATURE GARDEN AS ALLEGORY

The poet, artist, and gardener Ian Hamilton Finlay condenses in his private Scottish garden, Little Sparta, a personal and philosophical thesis related to liberty and revolution, all embodied by the work of past philosophers, poets, and artists and their landscapes of origin. As with previous emblematic gardens, such as Stourhead and Rousham, he quotes, footnotes, and retells history within the geographic setting of Lanarkshire and the context of art and literary traditions. Miniature representations—fragments of text, pieces of other landscapes, and visual excerpts from classical paintings and sculpture—all evoke the past while creating a new world of their own.[5] Little Sparta appears as an island, set apart from the open and bare Lanarkshire moorlands. Within this island garden is an ensemble of smaller "memory gardens," including Roman Gardens,

Above: Plan of Little Sparta.

Opposite top: Aerial photograph of Parque Tezozomoc in Mexico City. (Courtesy GDU)

Opposite bottom: The plan of Parque Tezozomoc in Mexico City re-creates the 15th-century geography of the valley of Mexico. Drawing by Paul Fritz.

Above: Looking out at the moorlands over Lochan Eck.

Below: "THESIS fence ANTITHESIS gate SYNTHESIS style" at Little Sparta.

the Temple of Philomen and Baucis, Woodland Garden, the Grotto of Aeneas and Dido, Lochan Eck, and Julie's Garden. Each small garden is a tiny place made large by metaphor, metonymy, and poetic associations.

At Little Sparta, Finlay has cultivated and cultured a whole world that he is completely attached to. In thirty years, he has scarcely left this place. Ann Uppington, who gardened for Finlay, describes his garden as "a cocoon, sheltered by the trees from brutal weather, a sacred grove—not a clearing in the woods but a woods in the clearing" (Uppington). A series of boundaries defines this distinct garden. The first directional sign for Little Sparta is located along a local road, then next at the foot of the driveway is a monument to the first battle in 1983 that Finlay and his supporters waged with the local government. It establishes a militant stance and also marks and defends the territory of the garden, as does the flag flying in the corner of the garden. The site also marks an ecological boundary between the lowlands and the moorlands. A stile inscribed with the poem "FENCE Thesis, GATE Anti-thesis, SYNTHESIS style," separates these landscape types, yet at the same time suggests a joining of ecosystems. It is both a fence that delineates and a gate that allows for passage. At the farthest edge of the garden and in the moorlands, the one-word poem "Fragile," reveals the relationship between Finlay's world and the outside world and the fragility of this ecosystem.[6] Paradoxically, the garden's boundaries and Finlay's own need to stay close to home enlarge this highly imaginative and richly interpretive world. While this garden absorbs him, he extends its bounds through the metaphorical and multiple association of miniature representation. His son Alec Finlay expresses how his father imaginatively creates a "little kingdom":

> The garden is a secret place, a place chosen, bounded, set aside: a little kingdom, as Virgil says, or as Finlay calls his garden, Little Sparta—a Raspberry Republic, where Capitals and watering cans are crowned in place of Kings. Like Stuckeley, or Shenstone, or Jefferson, his garden becomes also his world. A little world, within the greater world, to retire to. One of his Detached Sentences reads: "A garden, being less a place than a world, is a proper work for an exile."
> (Eck 1995)

His garden is both a refuge and a revolutionary battleground, for Finlay writes in an "unconnected sentence on gardening" included on the visitor's map: "certain gardens are described as retreats when they are really attacks" (Finlay). The name of his garden also evokes the idea of the garden as a battleground, emphasized again at the entrance, where the "Monument to the First Battle of Little Sparta" marks February 1983 as the date that local bailiffs attempted to take works of art from the Garden Temple in exchange for contested "unpaid rates."[7] In the same place, the garden evokes the history of an ancient Greek city that served as the training ground for young soldiers, a militant city set apart from Athens. French Revolutionary heroic leaders such as Robespierre and Saint-Just figure prominently in the garden's overall narrative,

of fighting for justice and liberty.[8] In the smallness of a title, Finlay conjures whole worlds and spans centuries.[9]

By playing with differences in scale, Finlay also connects Little Sparta to faraway places and plays with the double meanings of being in more than one place. For instance, cast models of aircraft carriers located adjacent to the pond transform the pond into the battled sea waters of World War II. The fighter birds land on and take off from the aircraft carrier, which like toys transform the everyday world into fantastical associations. The aircraft carriers, called *Homage to the Villa D'Este,* refers to that Italian villa's miniature depiction of the aqueducts and the Tiber River.[10] The pond, as synecdoche, refers to the larger sea, and the large boat, as metonym, refers to appropriately deeper waters. When Finlay first arrived at the site, then named Stonypath, in 1967, he described his farmyard pond as an "excerpt from a longer stretch of water," revealing his way of seeing the landscape in terms of a language with its rich potential for metaphorical associations (Bann 1995, 70).

Finlay employs poetic metaphors and visual associations that transport the reader back and forth between the sensorial experience of the landscape and conceptual ideas. Finlay's son Alec describes how metaphors radiate in and out from the microcosm to the macrocosm in the poem "Sea Poppy":

Above: The Rometta at Villa D'Este is a miniature replica of Rome.

Top left: Aircraft carrier at Little Sparta

Below: "Mare Nostrum" at Little Sparta.

> In the first version of "Sea Poppy" the words, "Day Star," "Bright Star," "Universal Star," and their shape, create a visual and metaphorical rhyme between the flower, the ocean, and the circling universe. The metaphor carries us on a journey through different forms of experience and perception: from the lyrical beauty of a single flower, through the social world of work, the lives of the fishing community, to the eternal universe, represented by the "Universal Star" which lies at the poem's center.
> (Eck, Finlay, 1995)

The metaphorical associations of text placed in the garden expand the geographic and conceptual boundaries of Little Sparta. The tree plaque "Mare Nostrum," translated as "Our Sea," the Roman expression for the Mediterranean, placed upon an old ash tree in the Front Garden, transforms the sound of the wind blowing through the leaves of this inland garden tree into the sounds of the Mediterranean winds and waves. The association of the sea is multiplied by the poem on a bench beneath the ash that reads: "the sea's waves / the wave's sheaves / the sea's naves." As the writer Stephen Bann wrote, the text acts as "a relay between past and present" (Bann 1993, 106), and also between here and there.

Finlay also reworks picturesque traditions by creating miniature representations of faraway landscapes painted by Dürer, Poussin, and Claude Lorrain within the small gardens of Little Sparta. These paintings were also replete with allegorical classical references. As the artists once represented a landscape in their picturesque paintings, Finlay represents their paintings in this landscape and so creates a chain of associations. Finlay also gathers together multiple and ambiguous interpretations of the landscape:

> *See Poussin/Hear Lorrain* is thus the ambivalent "signature" of an elegiac classical landscape, perceived in miniature across Finlay's constructed pond: according to the degree of serenity of the prospect, we can interpret what we see through the medium of Poussin's calm stillness or Claude's more animated atmospheric effects.
> (Bann 1995, 75)

Above: Claude Bridge at Little Sparta.

Below: Miniature boats in the window of Ian Hamilton Finlay's studio.

Little Sparta is an extraordinary poetic and personal example of a miniature landscape, yet miniatures are commonly found in both designed and vernacular, public as well as private spaces. The layout of the typical suburban home, for example, often represents in miniature a large estate. The stunted circular drive connotes an elegant long driveway with a carriage dropoff, a short fence connotes a pasture for horses, while gateposts refer to the gatehouses providing security for the wealthy.

The many and varied miniature landscapes share three important ideas that will be discussed. Miniatures create a *fantasy world*, an imaginary place entered and synthesized by the reader and his or her imagined characters. Miniatures *frame and control the narrative* within definite bounds and differences in scale. Boundaries such as Finlay's fences and hedges, the gates to a housing development, or the wall of a Chinese garden define the story space and control the meaning within a closed system of signification. Finally, the miniature controls not only the story space, but the story time, for the miniature world enables the narrator to condense, collapse, and continue time.

FANTASY

Miniature worlds such as Little Sparta enable the reader to travel conceptually through time and space into an imaginary world.[11] Whether it is James entering a peach pit in *James and the Giant Peach*, Alice entering a rabbit hole in *Alice's Adventures In Wonderland*, or Mary Lenox and her cousin Colin passing through the gate in *The Secret Garden*, the miniature world is a place controlled and expanded by the imagination. Susan Stewart, in her book *On Longing*, discusses how the miniature object, in particular the toy, transforms the everyday world into a world of possibilities. As Finlay's miniature aircraft carrier transforms the role of a bird in the landscape, a Matchbox (a one inch) car can transform a sandbox into a desert, an anthill into a mountain, or a puddle into a lake. Stewart writes that "the toy is the physical embodiment of the fiction: it is a device for fantasy, a point of beginning for narrative" (Stewart, 56).[12]

Top left: A backyard in Oriskany Falls, New York, tells an idyllic version of the town's history by placing miniature icons such as the church and a mill in a pastoral setting.

Top right: Marcia Donahue's garden stone faces.

The miniature landscape is often experienced by characters such as James or Alice who imaginatively and privately discover a world of their own; in contrast, the gigantic landscape, also a fantastical creation, works its powers on the viewer. Monumental sites such as the Grand Canyon or Niagara Falls, as well as enlarged landscape creations like Coney Island or Bomarzo in Italy, inspire fear, excitement, awe, and a sense of the unknown, while miniature landscapes tend to tame and make coherent the unfathomable.

FRAMING AND CONTROLLING THE NARRATIVE
The gates, walls, streets, and fences that form the boundaries of these miniature worlds frame the interpretive space for the story to be told. Within the bounds of Little Sparta, Finlay creates a utopia partly in reaction to the disorder and injustices of the outside world. The early walled botanical gardens also re-created Eden in response to the idea that Eden had fallen. As Prest writes, the botanical gardens arose out of the belief that after the Fall, Eden had "scattered" into chaos but the pieces of the "jig-saw puzzle" could be recollected in the discoveries of the Americas to make again a "completed picture" (Prest, 39) within a defined space.

Miniature gardens often share the desire to re-create what has been lost or to redefine the world within controlled bounds. In relation to the miniature, humans become giants who can move and mold the small pieces of a created world. Places like Disneyland or Sturbridge Village in Massachusetts control the telling of history by creating a miniature scene of selected parts of history, a storybook version perfectly choreographed and

In a small backyard lot in Berkeley, California, Marcia Donahue created "a garden of abundance." The diversity and lushness of flowering and fruiting plants envelop this small garden and create a separate world that imaginatively expresses Donahue's philosophy of life. "She leads me through the acanthus and azara and a 'tunnel of climbing roses' to an enlarged wooden gate with a handle shaped like a hand. Upon the gate and at our feet reads the metal inscription: 'Also, Also and Plus &'. This poem marks the entrance into a world of abundance. Donahue writes, 'This is the garden that wants it all and then some. I ask a lot of this small space. My choices must be clear and disciplined. I have to keep up with the pruning. Everything left is essential, yet it is full and overflowing.' She leads me to 'The realm of Flora,' a memorial grove with trees dedicated to her parents, brother, and friends; 'The Mars Garden,' 'a collection of astounding plants that convinced me that they were essential to my well being'; 'lots of bamboo,' 'a jungle and an oasis,' 'a gravestone path to the compost heap littered with stone skulls,' 'a narrow but not straight path of righteousness,' 'Daphne's fence,' and lots to eat—'kiwis, persimmon, apples, tamarillos, berries, figs, and vegetables.' In her garden, Donahue celebrates the diversity of life, 'vegetal and imagined,' with ongoing work and open parties."

(Donahue)

oasis · *desert*

Gardens are essentially abstractions/extractions of nature and the larger landscape. Pamela Burton's Oasis/Desert Garden in Venice, California, distills the essence of two landscapes, the "desert" and the "oasis," into abstract fifteen-foot-by-fifteen-foot cuts in a driveway where one plant or stone represents a whole environment and climate. In the "oasis," she planted a ficus tree, a California pepper tree, Gardenias, grasses, liriope, and bamboo. In the "desert," she laid a base of somis sand where sculpture could be exhibited. This extreme abstraction of the garden as a microcosm creates a larger commentary on the constructed California landscape. What landscapes are being re-created and why?

Top left: The Oasis/Desert Garden by Pamela Burton and Company recreates microcosms of both a dry and a wet landscape. (Courtesy Pamela Burton)

Top right: Condensing time: The final garden of the Ocean Park Boulevard Parkway Series by Pamela Burton and Company uses drought-resistant and native plants of the chaparral-covered hillsides to represent current and future trends in Californian garden design. Live oak, bougainvillea, blue wild rye, Carmel creeper, California sagebrush, Our Lord's Candle, and yuccas are planted in this garden. (Courtesy Pamela Burton)

Bottom: The Mississippi River in miniature at Riverwalk *in Memphis, Tennessee.*

perfectly formed. Because we normally feel that the surrounding landscape and the course of history are beyond our control, the miniature landscape is a way of exercising control.

CONDENSING TIME

Miniature landscapes condense the events of a long period of time into clear and coherent spatial moments. Little Sparta gathers philosophical and art history from the past, as Ross's Landing gathers four centuries of the history of Chattanooga onto one plaza, or the Crosby Arboretum gathers the natural history of the Pearl River Basin onto sixty-four acres, or Pam Burton represents the landscape history of California in a series of small plantings along Ocean Boulevard in Santa Monica. All these spatial representations freeze time, create a series or storyboard of events, and create a continuous narrative where events over time are juxtaposed in one place. Like speed photography, which collapses time so that change is perceivable, these landscapes distort and condense time to create clear ideological constructs and associations. What is unique about visual narratives is their power to compress time in space.

As expressed by Christine Boyer in *The City of Collective Memory*, the physical form of the city gathers and absorbs the memories of the many purposes, ideas, and traditions of those who have shaped and lived in it:

The demands and pressures of social reality constantly affect the material order of the city, yet it remains the theater of our memory. Its collective forms and private realms tell us of the changes that are taking place; they remind us as well of the traditions that set this city apart from others. It is in these physical artifacts and traces that our city memories lie buried, for the past is carried forward to the present through

through these sites. Addressed to the eye of vision and to the soul of memory, a city's streets, monuments, and architectural forms often contain grand discourses on history.

(Boyer, 31)

As centers of social and cultural activity, cities also tend to express the narratives of the greater regions that they represent. For instance, in the Plaza de Espana in Seville, Spain, the culture and history of the provinces and cities throughout Spain are represented in seating areas defining a crescent-shaped plaza. Each sitting or gathering area includes a reference map in the pavement and a painting that depicts a regional event of national importance. Similarly, in Memphis, Tennessee, the city expresses its connection to the regional landscape in a ¾-mile scale replica of the Mississippi River and its major tributaries. Visitors can walk along and across the river and swim in a pool that represents the meeting of the river with the Gulf of Mexico. Here Memphis is imagined/understood as part of a natural system of drainage, and as a discovery and transportation route connected to its related cities up- and downriver.

Top left: Landscape architecture students in the "Barcelona region" of Plaza de Espana.

Top right: Condensing space: Overall view of Plaza de Espana in Seville, Spain. (Courtesy Gabriela Canamar)

Below: Aerial view of Place Berri looking up from the plaza toward the woods of Mount Royal in the background. (Courtesy Peter Jacobs)

The design of Place Berri, a public park in Montreal's Latin Quarter, also expresses in miniature the identity and character of the region's topology, topography, and morphology. Although a region's distinctive environmental processes become a part of the history and daily lives of people who live and work in the landscape, often the processes are not consciously articulated or are forgotten and erased by urban development. In fact, Place Berri's successive development from grassy plateau, to farmland, to hospice, to a manufacturing site, to a parking lot, to the public park it is today marks a series of forgotten and remembered histories. Place Berri distills the large-scale geologic processes of Montreal into coherent forms and serves to remember what has been forgotten and fragmented.

Located in the "core of the city and at the heart of the Latin quarter," it has a sloping topography that parallels the growth of Montreal as a series of *côtes* or successive rings, first established along the river's shore, then extended to the plateaus of the city and later to the foothills of the Laurentian and Appalachian Mountain ranges. These layers of shore, plain, mountain, and plateau are expressed in miniature: the

active Saint Catherine Street as the river shore, the granite plaza as the gridiron of the city on the flat river plain, the lawn as the *côte placide,* fountains emerging from the terraced slope as the streams that flow into the Saint Lawrence, and the trees as the higher reaches of the wooded Mount Royal. Upon this formal structure the designer, Peter Jacobs, in collaboration with Philippe Poullaovec-Gonidec, layered activities associated with the regional landscape upon recognizable forms. For instance, in the winter the granite plaza turns into a skating rink in the shape of the Montreal Forum, and benches along Saint Catherine enable people to watch the flow of pedestrians. Peter Jacobs describes the nature of Place Berri's narrative:

> The narrative of the plaza is not expressed explicitly nor is it spoken of in any explicit terms. It is sensed, however, and the users recognize that it is a place that invites occupation in a manner that is typical of the rites and rituals of Montreal. It is of Montreal, its history and its geographic structure. It celebrates the memory of the mountain, the city and the river yet seeks to re-interpret these places and the events that have occurred within these landscapes in light of the potential for new stories in the future.
>
> (Jacobs 1996)

THE SOUVENIR

As the miniature landscape controls or contains the past or outside world, the easily grasped souvenir enables its holder to transport a memory of a place or an event to the everyday present world. A miniature replica of the Eiffel Tower or a bag of sand from Daytona Beach captures and "brings home" in its smallness the totality of a remembered experience.

The narratives of the souvenir are tied to the stories of its owner: How did she find this object? What happened on his trip or during that event? The souvenir frames the experience of whole landscapes, historic events, and cultures through the personal narrative of the owner. The Battle of Gettysburg is captured in the toy soldiers acquired on a fifth-grade school trip, the Eiffel Tower is remembered in a snapshot of a romantic rendezvous, or a home landscape is remembered by a Polish American immigrant who brings a seed from a parent's garden. The souvenir also represents a claim to an experience, of having eaten in that ancient city, hiked that mountain, floated on that river. The bumper sticker "This car climbed Mount Washington" claims a personal victory over a daunting landscape. Stewart discusses how the tourist "tames" exotic cultures by acquiring the souvenir, which becomes a sort of "trophy" (Stewart, 147).

Residential landscapes often communicate the stories of their owners through the display of souvenirs. Fragments of farm equipment, for instance, conjure the stories of the family that once farmed the land, while transplanted oddities such as a bowling ball, lobster pot, wheelbarrow, or memo-

Top: The touring boats *(trajineras)* in the *chinampas,* floating islands, of Xolchomilco.

Center: Model *trajineras* for sale at Xolchomilco

Bottom: The souvenir trajineras in Matthew Potteiger's truck in upstate New York.

rial tree displayed in the yard connect the landscape with the lives of its owners. The meaning and details of these stories are often held privately with the owners, but the souvenir as a displaced object poses questions that initiate the sharing of these stories. A bathtub sitting empty in a backyard may seem strange, for instance, except to the family that remembers using it to chill champagne for a daughter's wedding.

Like so many other Victorian gardens, Naumkeag, designed in the early 20th century by Fletcher Steele for Mabel Choate, includes souvenirs gathered by the owner and designer during their trips throughout the world and brought back to the Massachusetts Berkshire Mountains. Steele and Choate traveled extensively, independently and together, visiting Europe, Africa, the Caribbean, and Southeast Asia. The house is filled with souvenirs, including Chinese roof tiles and figurines, Waterford crystal chandeliers, Egyptian water carriers, walking sticks from around the world, venetian glass lamps—a pastiche of cross-cultural trophies collected by a wealthy and educated family. In the landscape, their trips to Germany, Italy, France, Spain, England, and China figure most prominently.[13]

Over time and with more traveling, the garden became a collage of different landscapes that meet unexpectedly and abruptly. The designer did not try to blend these captured scenes of faraway places with the Berkshires, but instead let each souvenir stand on its own, like a postcard on a shelf. For instance, the famous blue steps, which were influenced by Steele's visits to grand Italian villa gardens, seem strange and fanciful in relation to the local apple orchard and meadow. In another instance, a trip to Paris influenced the development of the design for Naumkeag's South Lawn. As Robin Karson writes, Naumkeag exemplified the Victorian's love of collecting:

> Piecemeal design and construction at Naumkeag had resulted in complexity and richness rare in any garden. But it also had exaggerated Steele's tendency to conceptualize garden areas separately....In truth, he rarely considered the aesthetic experience of movement in a garden, or the effect of areas upon one another when experienced sequentially. Concern with circulation was particularly lacking at Naumkeag in favor of an emphasis on a Victorian love of diversity.
> (Karson, 285)

The Chinese Garden and the Chinese House at Naumkeag were influenced by Choate's and Steele's trips to China. A marble slab from the actual Old Summer Palace in Peking, blue roof tiles from the same factory that manufactured tiles for the Temple of Heaven, a stone railing from a garden in Soochou, pink brick as seen in the Forbidden City, a wall and a moon gate based on photographs Steele took at Chieh Tai Ssu, and rocks and statues collected by Choate all gather in the Berkshires (Karson). As Robin Karson wrote, Steele "freely decorated the landscape" with imagery from China to "bring a recollec-

Elizabeth A. Boults, assistant professor at the University of Kentucky, made these jars to represent and remember her travels in Italy. The journal entry in the lid reads:
"25vi96: bologna: miles of arcade confine the landscape to a single aspect that changes—city to the right, country to the left, reverse. many votive chapels line the arcade and offerings accumulate as we visit san luca greeted by a framed view of a wooden crucifix at our final ascent and a bright ochre paisley of agrarian geometry. I light candles and say prayers for my mother; I sign a book with my name and hers, not knowing if it is a visitor's log or a prayer book."
(Boults)

Top: Boults road jar

Below: Steele's design for the blue steps at Naumkeag were based on his visits to Italian villa gardens.

Right: The Chinese Garden at Naumkeag.

Far right: Photograph from Fletcher Steele's trip to China. (Courtesy SUNY ESF Archives)

Below: Mabel Choate and Fletcher Steele's view from their Paris hotel window. (Courtesy SUNY ESF Archives)

Bottom: Ronde Point, named in memory of a trip to France, was sketched by Choate and Steele from a Parisian hotel window overlooking the Place d'Etoile.

tion of the atmosphere and appearances of places seen in China" (Karson, 223). This "Traveler's Garden" is a garden of recollections rather than a re-creation of sites visited.[14] As Steele wrote in a 1949 letter to his sister[15]: "Of course it is no more Chinese than an old parlor in Salem filled with Chinese Objects" (Karson, 223).

In the late 1950s Naumkeag ceased to be a family home, associated with the personal stories of its owners, and became instead the property of the Trustees of Reservations, a collection landscape valued more for the shared cultural and aesthetic worth of its contents than for the personal memories of Choate's and Steele's travels. The collection of souvenirs at Naumkeag relates to a tradition of 19th- and early 20th-century English and Victorian landscapes of the wealthy, travel narratives told through the eclectic mix of souvenirs, plants, artwork, and furnishings gathered from many cultures. Many of these garden estate collections became anthology landscapes and today's arboretums and botanical gardens.

THE COLLECTION

Although collections are often organized systematically by chronology, material, geography, or some other classification, their narratives lie in the life of the collector, stories of acquisition and the life of the object collected. As Walter Benjamin writes in his essay "Unpacking My Library," "the period, the region, the craftsmanship, the former ownership—for a true collector the whole background of an item adds up to a magic encyclopedia whose quintessence is the fate of its object" (Benjamin, 60). While unpacking his library, Benjamin remembers the rooms and landscapes where he found or kept his books. The collection triggers the telling of his childhood stories.

Now I am on the last half-emptied case and it is way past midnight. Other thoughts fill me than the ones I am talking about—not thoughts but images, memories. Memories of the cities in which I found so many things: Riga, Naples, Munich, Danzig, Moscow, Florence, Basel, Paris; memories of Rosenthal's sumptuous rooms in Munich, of the Danzig Stockturm where the late Hans Rhaue was domiciled, of Sussengut's musty book cellar in North Berlin; memories of the rooms where these books had been housed, of my student's den in Munich, of my room in Bern, of the solitude of Iseltwald on the lake of Brienz, and finally of my boyhood room, the former location of only four or five of the several thousand volumes that are piled around me.

(Benjamin, 67)

In a project titled *Mnemonics,* a collection of four hundred glass block reliquaries are randomly dispersed through the New Stuyvesant High School in New York City. Collectively they refer both to the history and lore of the school and to the wider world's mysteries and resources. Letters, sports equipment, reports cards, and school photos, for instance, give glimpses of the past life of students; while rocks, insects, melted snow, tree boughs, and more artifacts, gathered from places around the world, convey a more worldly view. Eighty-eight empty blocks are left to be filled by each graduating class until the year 2078. According to the artists, Kristin Jones and Andrew Ginzel, "the experience of viewing *Mnemonics* was conceived to be slow and revelatory, of four year's duration, an experience of questioning and discovering the enigmatic" (Jones and Ginzel).

Narratives also lie in the system of classification. Arboretums, for instance, are often organized around a plant classification system that tells of the evolution and discovery of plants, while a cemetery may be organized around genealogies that tell of the continuity and interruptions in the lives of families. The collection of names on the Vietnam Veterans Memorial wall in Washington, D.C., seems chaotic until the underlying order—dates of death—is understood. Unlike the souvenir, which stands alone as a sentinel of memory, objects fit into the order of the overall collection. The value of the collection lies in the relationship between its parts and its state of completeness, for most collections are in a state of becoming complete.

The village of Yorkville Park collects the Canadian landscape of northern Ontario into a one-acre lot in the fashionable Yorkville neighborhood of Toronto.[16] Plants naturally located hundreds of miles apart in landscapes with differences in temperature, elevation,

Top: A glass block reliquary in the Stuyvesant High School cafeteria. (Courtesy Jones and Ginzel)

Above: The jars contain water from the Yellow River and loess soil which gives the river its name and nickname, "China's Sorrow." Sent by the Embassy of United States of America Beijing, People's Republic of China. (Courtesy Jones and Ginzel.)

Left: Cleveland, Ohio's downtown Central Market was destroyed with the building of the new Jacob's Field Ballpark. To preserve memories of the marketplace, the artist Angelica Pozo, in collaboration with Penny Rakoff, created a terra-cotta glazed planter that gathers historic photographs and castings of market fruits and vegetables. (Courtesy Angelica Pozo)

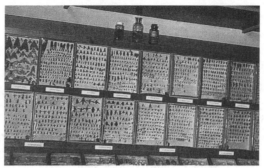

Top left: Aerial view of the Village of Yorkville Park. (Courtesy Ken Smith)

Top right: The Village of Yorkville Park appeared like a Victorian collection box to the landscape architect Ken Smith. (Courtesy Ken Smith)

Above: Project partner David Meyer with a segment of the bedrock formation that is being moved to the Village of Yorkville Park. (Courtesy Ken Smith)

Below: The Canadian Shield bedrock formation as a place to meet and gather. (Courtesy Ken Smith)

and moisture here lie within a few feet, sharing the same grid line. The context of an architecturally Victorian neighborhood suggested to the landscape architect, Ken Smith, the idea of creating a collection box of the Canadian landscape, in keeping with the once-popular Victorian collection boxes of insects, fossils, or bones. The historic lot lines are extended from the adjacent blocks across the park to define circulation and the distinct ecotypes. Although located on a level urban lot, the sequence through seventeen ecological zones conceptually moves vertically through the lowland and upland ecological zones of Canada. The zones—"Amelanchier and fern," "mixed herbaceous border garden," "bedrock formation," " willow border," "alder grove," "wetland garden," "crabapple grove," "rock/herb garden," "birch grove," "prairie garden," and " pine grove"—are depicted by representative plant species. The grid creates a unified framework that gives each zone equal space and location, much like a scientific classification system.

Set within this ecological collection is a major specimen, the Canadian Shield bedrock formation, which was transplanted from the Muskoka region of Canada. It is a gigantic souvenir with shared associations, for the Muskoka region is a popular vacation destination and a scenic place made familiar by the Canadian Group of Seven Painters. At the Village of Yorkville Park, the rock has become a gathering place to meet friends, sun, and read the paper over cappuccino. Its extraction and disassembly from a remote "natural location" and its relocation to an urban center represent a taming and commodification of nature. Ken Smith, who intended the park to comment on the idea of nature as commodity, remarked, "It is contextually correct in a boutique shopping and entertainment district that nature is dealt with as a specimen which is collected and brought into the city for display and entertainment" (Smith). Once extracted from its original context, nature becomes a captive and possessed object, much like a zoo animal.

By fitting nature into a formal system—a collection box—the individual narratives behind each part are superseded by the whole entity (Stewart, 153). Like trees lost in a forest, the collection of nature marks its disappearance and removal from the events of everyday life. Yet a tree in a forest still retains its individual identity for those who choose to see it. Collections do, however, have the power to resonate with the public. The Canadian Shield bedrock, for instance, evokes a personal experience with Canadians who remember vacationing in the Muskoka region. It is challenging to find shared experiences that allow each viewer to "disappear inside" the collection, as Benjamin does at the end of his essay (Benjamin, 67).

COLLECTIONS AND DISPERSIONS
Although the movement to preserve cultural landscapes has been influenced by the tendency to collect the landscape into identifiable places

(such as Plymouth Plantation or Sturbridge Village), another approach is to preserve and leave dispersed historic sites in their places. Heritage Parks preserve sites within broad cultural and environmental regions, defined by natural collective forms such as a watershed, a river, a valley, or a mountain range, yet allow the dispersed sites to be interpreted within their local place of origin.

Two landscape architects, Terrence Harkness and Mira Engler, have differed in their approaches toward the preservation of the rural midwest agricultural landscape. Although both are interested in preserving the meaning and collective memories of this landscape, Harkness has gathered remnants and souvenirs of the landscape into newly created gardens, while Engler proposes leaving its remnants in dispersed "rural reliquaries."

Harkness compresses and collects the scenes and forms of the regional agricultural landscape to create a new assemblage of real and faux fragments. In a plan for a residence, a "remnant orchard" aligns the driveway, a "lowland garden" forms the formal lawn, a "levee dike and hedgerow" edges the lawn, and a "remnant prairie on a railroad right of way" shapes the backyard. The pieces appear as remnants removed from their whole. Harkness even makes the seam between pieces apparent, a strategy common to postmodernism. In the East Central Illinois Garden, the form of two separate farm ponds are joined, yet do not fit together.

By exhibiting these parts together in a new context, the meaning of the otherwise ordinary landscape changes. What was once part of a working agricultural landscape becomes part of a leisure, residential, or commercial landscape. The agricultural pieces/remnants are also organized in the tradition of classical residential design, attaching yet another layer of association. As in a museum, the pieces become objects of visual interest disassociated from their original function. What would be a hedge in a traditional formal garden is instead a simulated volunteer hedgerow associated with but separate from an agricultural landscape. Yet as Harkness states, the act of "splicing, sewing and bringing together" these pieces reveals "shared histories and aspirations" about the development and life of the Midwest (Harkness). Reassembling the pieces of the landscape history acts as a metaphor for making what is fragmented whole again.

Mira Engler's proposals for "rural reliquaries" also preserve the remnant buildings and agricultural machinery of the agricultural Midwest as social "memory boxes" and gathering places. Instead of gathering the forms and transplanting them to a new site, as Harkness does, she works with actual artifacts in their original site. She proposes that these fragments be connected by pedestrian and bike trails that utilize abandoned dirt farm roads along a "continuous cultural-natural network of public paths and nodes" (Engler 1996, 1). Her proposals vary from restoration to adaptive reuse to creating grave sites, ruins, or wildlife preserves. For farm number 3474 in Clear Lake Township, Iowa, she proposes to tear down the abandoned Samuelson family farmhouse and replace it with a reflection pool. This memorial gesture addresses the tragedy of the loss of a farm for the Samuelsons, the Midwest, and greater North American society. Other exist-

Above: This collection of tea bags marks the passing of days with each morning's cup of tea. (Potteiger)

Below: Pond fragments in Harkness's East Central Illinois Garden.

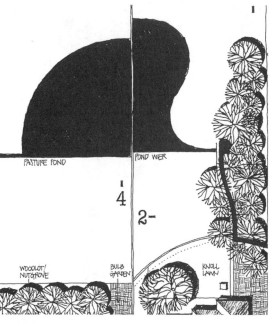

Right: The *horizon garden, lowland garden,* and *prairie remnant garden* by Harkness, are composed of abstracted parts of the midwest landscape. (Diagram by Terry Harkness)

Below: The designs for the *horizon garden, lowland garden,* and *prairie remnant* garden.

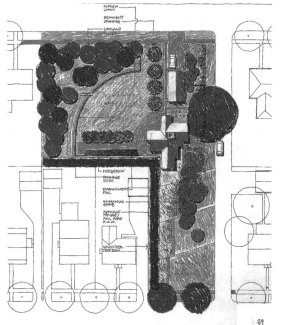

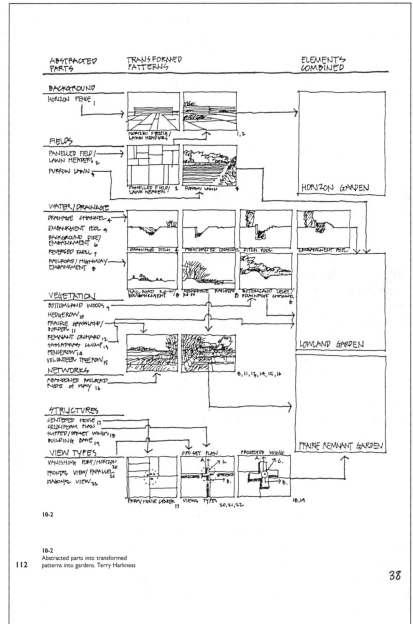

10-2
Abstracted parts into transformed patterns into gardens. Terry Harkness

112

38

ing remnants will be transformed for new uses, such as the round mesh wire corn bins that will become gazebos for viewing the site. Engler thinks it is important to engage the public in difficult memories such as the loss of a family farm, memories that are glossed over in themed town landscapes that emphasize progress or romanticize farm life.

Places such as the Samuelsons' farm are the locus of layers of personal and shared memories. These clustered buildings and fields, which evolve over time in response to the cycles of farming and the life of the family, are rooted, gathered dwellings. The extraction of pieces like this farm from their original sites potentially creates a loss of memory, experience, and meaning. Preserving history in one frozen moment also represents the death of a site that would otherwise evolve as a "continuous compendium of natural and cultural processes" (Engler, 97).

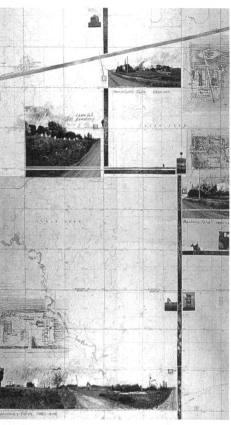

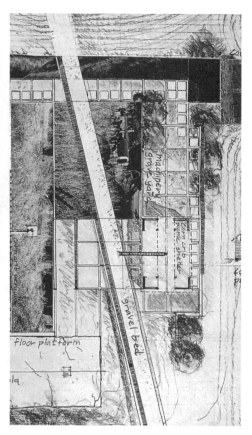

Heritage Parks and Regions—such as the Michigan National Heritage Corridor, the Blackstone River Heritage Park, the Lowell National Historical Park, and the Southwestern Pennsylvania Heritage Parks—all represent efforts to preserve remnants of the past within the context of the formative and evolving landscape.[17] Remnants, fragments, and glimpses are interpreted as part of a whole landscape of change, without controlled distinctions between what is part of the museum and what is the diverse lived-in landscape. At one of the first Heritage Parks, in Lowell, Massachusetts, for instance, visitors take a boat ride along the Merrimac River, crossing environmental changes and adaptive reuse. Traveling through the urban park and the city, the visitor learns that an old factory that once made luxurious fabric for trains now dyes yarn for automobile upholstery or that another company is planning to relocate in the Carolinas because the growth of their company plant is too limited by the physical constraints of the canal system.[18] Unlike at Disneyland or Sturbridge Village, people live and work in this landscape to become a part of a dynamic history and ongoing narratives.

Memories take place, and remembering the events of life is often triggered by associations with the sense of a place, its rhythms, seasons, light, sounds, activities. If what gives a landscape its character is removed, the collective memories that evolved with the landscape may be forgotten. Interested in the preservation of both the character and the memories of place, Mary

Top left: Mira Engler's prairie paths connecting the "rural reliquaries" for the Samuelson family farmhouse.

Top right: Mira Engler's Rural reliquary for the Samuelson's family farmhouse near Stanhope, Iowa.

Bay : Marsh

Top left: Harry Shourds, of Seaville, blending in with a bank in his sneak box at Beesley's Point. (Photograph by Dennis McDonald)

Top right: The New Jersey Pinelands "seasonal round" for the bay/marsh. (Photograph by Dennis McDonald)

Bottom left: The New Jersey Pinelands "seasonal round" for the woodland.

Bottom right: Dusia Tserbotarew gathering mushrooms in a pitch-pine and oak forest near Cassville. (Photograph by Joseph Czarnecki)

Huffard, a folklorist working with the American Folk Life Center, researched the culture of the New Jersey Pinelands by noting the regional and subregional life/work cycles linked to the landscape. From observations and interviews, she surveyed the location and timing of activities, such as gathering pinecones or collecting wild mushrooms in the woodland landscape, and found that each landscape—the bays, the marshes, or the agricultural landscapes—generated its own distinctive cultural activities. In other words, the culture of the Pinelands gathered in the landscape around seasonal cycles. Because landscape and culture are so interconnected, the conservation of a place requires more than simply collecting and preserving its pieces.

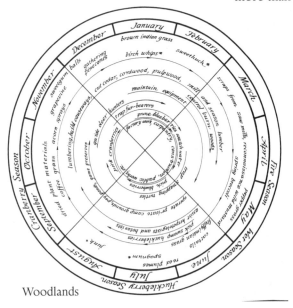

Woodlands

By and large, we protect ecosystems by understanding the relationships between parts and their wholes. The Pinelands National Reserve safeguards its natural resources not simply by preserving a cedar swamp here and a tree frog population there, but by protecting the enormous body of water that sustains all swamps and all amphibians in the region. . . . Along the same lines, we cannot effectively protect the living landscape by recording a boat pattern here and restoring a forge there without paying attention to the wellspring that animates them—the collective memory.

(Huffard, 107)

SUMMARY

The *casitas* in New York City's South Bronx provide a vivid illustration of a garden as the gathering place of social activity, culture, and memory. *Casitas,* meaning "little houses" in Puerto Rico, encompass the miniature, the souvenir, and the collection. They are tiny reproductions of Puerto Rico filled with memorable souvenirs from a shared childhood landscape. Their active members collectively create a place that visiting Puerto Ricans describe as more like Puerto Rico than Puerto Rico.[19]

In the late 1970s, José Manuel "Chema" Soto and his friends began one *casita* named Rincón Criollo, meaning "Creole Corner, or Down-home Corner" (Sciorra, 20), on a former abandoned lot on East 158th Street and Brook Avenue by cleaning out debris.[20] Loads and loads of illegally dumped appliances, auto parts, and construction debris were dug up and carted out of the lot. They cleaned up the site to re-create a place that would remind them of their childhood homes and the rural landscape of the central mountainous region of Puerto Rico, a place associated with beauty and a relaxed lifestyle lacking in New York City.

Rincón Criollo would become a home away from home with a small wooden house, a vegetable garden, pecking chickens, and a barbecue pit. As

Bomba on a Friday evening at Rincón Criollo.

Luis Ramos describes why he joined Rincón Criollo:

"When I came here, oh my God. . .It reminded me of Puerto Rico. I was like reborn. This place motivated me to produce. Here people really practice their traditions. We share. We bring ideas, we get involved with the churches, the community. The people here feel that they are part of the community and that gives them an identity."
(Ramos)

Top: Luis Ramos, inspired by the celebration of Puerto Rican culture at Rincón Criollo, began to carve pistachio and walnut shells and make other crafts with materials native to Puerto Rico.

Bottom left: Luis Ramo s and founder Jose Manuel "Chema" Soto in the fall with their ripening *calaeazo.*

Bottom right: Luis Ramos and the current president, Norma Cruz, with a *chequera* made from the *calaeazo.*

Luis E. Ramos said: "Chema wanted to create a place to socialize. People were hungry for it. Before you knew it, lots of people came here. Norma taught girls how to dance, Chema how to make instruments, Benny taught people how to make drums." Anyone could join as long as they respected one another: "There is a code here. Here you have got to respect each other: the women, the men, the children" (Ramos).

Rincón Criollo, bounded by a chain-link fence, is cherished despite the difficult urban surroundings. A single apple tree, transplanted about twenty years ago from an adjacent construction site, is regularly inspected for damaging insects, paths are carefully swept, and gardeners compete to make the most productive, well-weeded vegetable patch. The level of control within the fence contrasts drastically with the world beyond the fence, where the streets are marked by illegal dumping, fires, and vandalism. Not only are the physical elements of the *casita* cared for but so are the members. Some of these members have been rescued from problems with drugs, gangs, and broken families and offered a haven to relax, contribute, and learn about drum carving, cooking, gardening, *bomba,* and *plena.*

Unlike the privately purchased souvenir, this *casita* belongs to a shared memory, kept alive by the difficulties of living in the Bronx and the desire to make a community. Like a souvenir, Puerto Rico comes to New York in the form of an imported seed or drum or the sharing of traditional culture. Unlike a souvenir, which may be shelved into a state of forgetfulness, the active social club of Rincón Criollo functions in the present and creates an ongoing life that extends beyond memories of the past. The City of New York threatens this lively cultural center with its plans to build new housing on this site and to relocate the *casita* so that it becomes an exhibit that would be part of an official community center. But like any home, Rincón Criollo is an irre*place*able landscape bonded to the memories, pride, and culture of a self-formed and unofficial community. Its meaning cannot be substituted with comparable but relocated square footage or maintained by reducing its use to an exhibit.

Rincón Criollo connects its members to the ongoing seasonal cycles and celebrations to create a shared group identity. On the last day of December, the New Year is celebrated in a parade where someone dresses as the *moula*. *Calaeazo* becomes ripe in the fall and once dry, the gourd is cleaned out to make a rattle for *bomba* and *plena* and the seeds are saved for the following spring. Soto and Ramos describes the fall season:

> We give out food to everyone. This year we gave tomatoes, peppers (hot and sweet), apples....For the first crop we take a little bit of everything and make a big pot of beans, tomatoes, peppers and then everyone comes to eat together.
> (Ramos)

NOTES

1. Medieval cathedrals such as Chartres similarly gathered in the iconography of their art and architecture the comprehensive teachings of history and life, and became learning centers and pilgrimage destinations.

2. Parque Tezozomoc was designed by Grupo de Deseño Urbano and built in 1984.

3. Souvenirs and collections can also fragment and disrupt the very whole that they intend to represent by geographically dispersing parts. The collection of heads of endangered species clearly represents the destruction of habitat and loss of species.

4. Susan Stewart's book *On Longing* provides an analysis of narrative in terms of the objects of the miniature, the gigantic, the souvenir, and the collection. Her book provided valuable insights and useful ideas for structuring this chapter.

5. According to Ann Uppington, Little Sparta is a "resetting of already existing places either in the mind or from other places such as Ermenonville."

6. Finlay is one of the formative concrete poets who combine the meaning of text with its visual representation and its placement in the landscape.

7. The local tax authorities considered the Temple of Apollo to be commercial and taxable space; however, Finlay believes that the temple is a sacred space to experience art.

8. Finlay associates Saint-Just with Apollo because of his bravery. Saint-Just spent the night before his public hanging writing on the importance of liberty.

9. Gavin Keeney and Alec Finlay note that the name Little Sparta refers to the geographic and political relationship of Stonypath to Edinburgh, popularly referred to as the "Athens of the North."

10. This reference multiplies the cultural/geographical analogies between Stonypath and Edinburgh, Tivoli and Rome, Sparta and Athens.

11. In Roald Dahl's story *James and the Giant Peach,* James escapes his abusive aunts by entering the magical world of a peach pit. Within the fuzzy soft and edible world of the peach, he gains the support of a group of insects and overcomes the challenges posed by their journey together across the sea.

12. Ian Finlay made small toys before he made his garden and now makes model boats for pleasure.

13. In 1913, Steele visited Villa D'Este, Villa Lante, and Villa Aldobrandini—all landscapes that influenced his design for Naumkeag.

14. The Corot souvenir landscape paintings were considered "poetic evocations" or "invented landscapes which conjure up the particulars of a place and a set of emotions" (Metropolitan Museum of Art exhibit).

15. Steele also expressed his concern for the increasing accumulation of objects/souvenirs. In a letter to Choate he wrote: "we must hunt for things to throw out" (June 13, 1949).

16. The Village of Yorkville Park was designed by Ken Smith with Schwartz Smith Meyer and Oleson Worland Architects.

17. These Heritage Parks also represent efforts to revitalize the regional economy and encourage tourism. This intention influences what stories are told, and how they're told. The ingeniuty and perseverence of the community, for instance, are often emphasized.

18. Alexander Demas led our tour through the Lowell National Park. He plays the fiddle during the boat ride in order to tell the stories of the early Irish immigrants who dug the canal.

19. The folklorist Joseph Sciorra inspired us to visit Rincón Criollo in the Bronx through his article on *casitas* published in *New York Folklore*.

20. Prior to Rincón Criolla, Soto had established a popular club on the corner across the street called La Parade, "the great stop." He found that simply a shelter and a television on the street would create a gathering place.

REFERENCES

Abrioux, Yves. 1992. *Ian Hamilton Finlay: A Visual Primer*. Edinburgh: Reaktion Books.

Bann, Stephen. 1993. "A Luton Arcadia: Ian Hamilton Finlay's Contribution to the English Neo-Classical Tradition." *Journal of Garden History* 12 (1 and 2):104–112.

———. 1995. "Ian Hamilton Finlay: An Imaginary Portrait." In *Wood Notes Wild*. Edinburgh: Polygon. Pp. 55–79.

Benjamin, Walter. 1976. *Illuminations*. New York: Schocken Books.

Boults, Elizabeth. 1997. Letter to author regarding 1996 journal entry.

Boyer, Christine. 1996. *The City of Collective Memory: Its Historical Imagery and Architectural Entertainments*. Cambridge: MIT Press.

Donahue, Marcia. 1996. Letter to authors and interview with author in Berkeley, Calif.

Dorst, John D. 1989. *Written Suburb: An American Site An Ethnographic Dilemma*. Philadelphia: University of Pennsylvania Press.

Eck, Finlay. 1995. "Memory Gardens." Harvard Lecture Series in Boston, fall.

———. 1997. Interview with authors by telephone, spring.

Engler, Mary. 1996. "The Necessity for Ruins: Rural Reliquaries." Brunnier Museum Lecture, February 18.

———. 1997. E-mail to authors, May.

Finlay, Eck, ed. 1995. *Wood Notes Wild: Essays on the Poetry and Art of Ian Hamilton Finlay.* Edinburgh: Polygon.

Finlay, Ian Hamilton and Gary Hincks. 1994. *A Book of Wildflowers.* Edinburgh: Wild Hawthorn Press.

Griswald, Mac. 1993. "Box Set: Cumberland Park, Toronto." *Landscape Architecture.* April.

Harkness, Terrence. 1995. Project files. Unpublished.

Hertz, Betti-Sue. 1989. "Unfinished Displays: Casita Decoration and Embellishment." Unpublished version of paper given to authors by Hertz.

Jacobs, Peter. March 30, 1996. Letter to authors.

Jones, Kristin, and Andrew Ginzel. 1992. *Mnemonics* project description sent to authors.

Karson, Robin. 1989. *Fletcher Steele, Landscape Architect: An Account of the Garden Maker's Life, 1885–1971.* New York: Abrams/Sagapress.

Keeney, Gavin. 1995. "A Revolutionary Arcadia: Reading Ian Hamilton Finlay's Un Jardin Revolutionaire." *Word and Image.* 2(3):237–255.

Marling, Karol Ann. 1984. *Colossus of Roads: Myth and Symbol along the American Highway.* Minneapolis: University of Minnesota Press.

Prest, John. 1981. *The Garden of Eden: The Botanic Garden and the Re-Creation of Paradise.* New Haven, Conn.: Yale University Press.

Ramos, Luis. 1996. Interviews with authors at Rincón Criollo in the Bronx, August and October.

Rincón Criollo members. 1995–1996. Authors interviewed Luis Ramos, Norma Cruz, Pedro Figuera, Miguel Sierra, and José Manuel Soto at Rincón Criollo.

Robertson, Iain M. 1988. "Design Principles for the Creation of Regional Landscape Gardens and Exhibits." Paper presented at the National Meeting of the AABGA, Scottsdale, Arizona.

Smith, Ken. 1995–1996. Interview with authors in New York City.

Stewart, Susan. 1993. *On Longing: Narratives of the Miniature, the Gigantic, the Souvenir, the Collection.* Durham, N. C.: Duke University Press.

Sciorra, Joseph. 1994. "'We're not here just to plant. We have culture.' An Ethnography of the South Bronx Casita Rincón Criollo." *New York Folklore* 20(3–4):19–38.

Uppington, Ann. 1996. Interview with authors in Byfield, Mass.

CHAPTER SEVEN

OPENING

INTRODUCTION

THE idea of open landscape narratives, places with multiple stories shaped by a plurality of voices, is particularly important in the context of a growing trend to create closed narratives: theme parks, theme restaurants and malls, and gated communities. Controlled and scripted by developers or other authorities, these places can silence or displace diverse voices, erase layers of history and complexity of associations, and draw distinct boundaries between them and the living, changing, growing places they simulate. Although the themed mall that replaces the downtown street, or the commercial waterfront that replaces the working waterfront, may be more marketable, cleanliness, safety, and predictability may erase the subtle, layered, and less marketable narratives that evolve over time. While we can question the distinction between the authentic and the simulated, what is important is the issue of control.

A public street is a place where a diverse group of people participate in the ongoing narratives of place. On Twelfth Street in Manhattan, for instance, a stoop is an active gathering place where people meet, talk, and relax. Peter Peterson, who lives in a Twelfth Street apartment building started a curbside garden. His efforts represent a means of taking care of this public space, yet it is difficult to control this space. The garden is open to anyone passing through; some contribute plants, others express gratitude, yet others destroy or disregard the plants by picking flowers, tearing branches, or leaving trash. Unexpected encounters and random events punctuate routine acts. Although the street is controlled, cleaned, and maintained by the City of New York, it is constantly affected by the political and social changes of a varied group. The street changes as people move, businesses change, and traffic fluctuates. Stories are made every day by those who freely come and go.

The street is often simulated because it represents democratic ideals of free expression and open marketing. In the Hollywood Hills of Los Angeles, Universal Studios

Bottom left: One morning a man was found sleeping in a cardboard box on Twelfth Street.

Bottom right: In the past June Cash would take her mother, Ida, to the beach, but since her mobility has been limited they have decided on sunny days to bring the beach chairs down to Twelfth Street.

Above: Hollywood narratives are a part of the main street of Universal City Walk.

re-created a fantastical Main Street designed by Jerde Partnership called Universal City Walk. Visitors pay a fee to enter this private property at a controlled vehicular entrance. Everyone arrives by car and no one lives there. From the parking garage, visitors ride down a central escalator to the main street. The architecture of the street, including its advertisements, facades, and signs, refers to Hollywood narratives of adventure and exploration within the real context of commerce and private control. Facades simulate buildings from different periods yet are made of the same material and built at the same time. The twist in the street replicates an old city street, but this street was twisted not by geology, waterways, time, or culture.

Comparing a street such as Twelfth Street with a themed main street like City Walk reveals contrasting qualities that define open and closed places and narratives.

closed	open
represented experiences	lived experiences
determined	indeterminate
commodified	participatory
private	public
separately framed	integrated
selected time frames	layering of multiple times
scripted	nonscripted
intended and encoded meanings	possible and decoded interpretations
author controlled	reader interpreted
story space	discourse and intertextual space

The idea of open narratives derives from contemporary theories that stress the importance of the role of the reader in producing meaning; means for denaturalizing established ideologies; and the multiple, contextual, and changing nature of meaning.

Opening shifts the production of meaning from the author to the reader so that the vitality of the work is created by the active and multiple engagement of the reader. In a sense a work is always opened by a reader who brings new life to the text. An entire field of audience-oriented criticism, following the modernism of the 1950s, sought to redefine the work of writers and artists in terms of the active involvement of the reader or viewer. Jonathan Culler in "Stories of Reading" describes how readers engage with texts by filling in the gaps, solving a puzzle, struggling to understand, and projecting their own experiences and stories into the text. Umberto Eco described any "text as a lazy machine" that required the contribution of the reader (Eco 1994, 13).

Much of contemporary art and design integrates these concepts into the very production of work. Umberto Eco in an article titled "The Open Work" uses the example of music to define the meaning of *open.* He describes scores written so that performers would choose combinations, rhythms, or sequences in their interpretation of the music. With each playing and with each player, the meaning of the work evolves and expands. In these open works, the performers may rearrange the music like "a stack of filing cards," creating a range of possibilities (Eco 1979, 48). Lawrence Halprin applied the idea of open scores and closed scores to landscapes. He differentiated open and closed in terms of the level of choice, ambiguity, and potential for exploration (Burns, 53). The water features in Halprin's urban parks are predominantly open because they encourage people to engage with the water in diverse ways, and to explore, despite the dangers.

Opening is a strategy for denaturalizing ideology that appears natural, inherent, or closed to interpretation. Finding and negotiating the multiple and interrelated stories of place is a way of challenging privileged points of view and questioning what is taken for granted. The landscape too may be taken for granted, and opening is a means for challenging conventional notions about its value and use. Too often designers attempt to attach meaning to place through naive symbolism that uncritically perpetuates naturalized ideology. Circles, for instance, are frequently meant to represent unity, peace, and harmony, yet do they necessarily mean this?

The landscape designer does not solely make meaning, for meaning resides in and evolves with the layers of personal and social experience attached to a place. Thus opening landscapes begins with understanding the site as an intersection of layers of stories connected to other stories. It is not only the people who live in, work in, experience, and remember the landscape that create ever-changing and multiple meanings, but also the medium itself, which is constantly shifting due to natural events and processes. Although closed narratives may be unified, they also exclude aspects that make landscapes so vital—the messiness and risks of ordinary life, the diversity of social experience, the incompleteness of history, and the dynamics of nature.

This chapter presents ways that artists, planners, and landscape architects trigger an active exchange of stories and memories. Some of the work evolves out of listening and understanding without predetermined ideas, while other work is ideologically motivated to denaturalize existing narratives that serve certain power interests. Both forms of work question how meaning is encoded, whose stories are represented, and what means of representation are used.

EXCHANGING STORIES

In a direct yet symbolic act, the artist who pioneered "happenings," Allan Kaprow, inspired a dialogue about the ordinary garden by trading a bucketful of dirt from his garden with dirt from other people's gardens. Each exchange of dirt initiated a different dialogue about the exchange, dirt, gardens, and knowledge of the earth. The process brought him into conversations with people he had never met before in private backyards he had never seen. After three years, he finally put the last exchanged bucket of dirt into his garden. Trading Dirt illustrates how context and activities affect the exchange of stories, for stories about places are more likely to be heard

Right: Beating the bounds in Buckland Newton, Dorset. (Courtesy Common Ground)

Bottom left: Storytelling in Durant Mini Park. (Courtesy Walter Hood and Space Maker Press)

Bottom right: Walter Hood's design for a theater in Durant Mini Park. (Courtesy Space Maker Press)

People communicate their desires for the way they want their environment to be through their everyday actions and patterns. In *Urban Diaries,* the landscape architect Walter Hood documents what people are doing in Durant Mini Park in Oakland, California, in order to inform his redesign of the park. In the entry for "Day One" Hood writes:

"They are there all day—the shuck/jiving flows like liquid from the mouths of the old. Their faces show signs of time-aged copper, each line bears a story, a tale, an adventure. The wheelchair man moves back and forth from store to corner. The bag man is always at the bench playing cards. The young hustlers try to play, but it is the storytellers who have lived: they've heard the angels."
(Hood 1997a, 26)

This observation inspired him to design three differently shaped theaters for lingering and telling stories. By improvising, or using what is already happening or what is at hand, Hood reshapes a park that responds to the community's desires. (Hood, 1997b)

over shared activities or in a familiar environment than in arranged formal meetings or distant professional offices (Lacy, 248).

Common Ground, an English not-for-profit rural action group formed in 1983, found that reviving a British tradition of "beating the bounds on foot," like trading dirt, initiated the exchange of "all kinds of wisdom between people who had never met before" (Clifford and King). Historically, when maps were unavailable to small villages, the tradition of walking the boundaries of a village communicated knowledge to the younger generation about their territory so that it could be better known and protected. Recently towns such as Aveton Gifford, Great Berry Pomeroy, Torrington, Uplyme in Devon, and Rydycroesau in Shropshire have revived this tradition. Through the experience of walking, communities talk about the specifics of fences, walls, streams, topography, and buildings, and share stories about their common landscape. It is the expressed hope of Common Ground that this knowledge effects an awareness and an interest in protecting local distinctiveness:

Our wealth of parish paths needs constant care; there are many ways of raising interest and activity to keep them in use, which is the best way of ensuring their survival. Some encouragement to walk again, especially locally, may help to reintroduce people to things they have forgotten and give others confidence to explore.
(Common Ground)

Opening the interpretation of landscapes to a wider perspective changes how a site is understood. The stories of the lesser known are more often found through hearing oral histories, reading personal diaries, and spending time exploring a place and listening to people than in looking at published maps and history books. Ann Chamberlain, an artist from San Francisco, became familiar with a street in Staten Island through the memories and personal archives of its residents. When she first visited Jersey Street in 1994, the physical traces of the once busy main street had disappeared. In the 1950s and 1960s, much of the declining main street was replaced by several HUD high-rise housing projects. While no images of the street existed in the Staten Island Historical Society archives, many Staten Islanders remembered their "Main Street."

Jersey Street attracted Chamberlain because it was alive with pedestrians despite the surrounding automobile-dominated suburbs. Clearly a community existed, and she sought it out by interviewing residents door to door. Through this "on the street" research she discovered a set of 1935 photographs of the street kept by the Diodati family. She rephotographed this archive and mounted the photographs end to end to create a thirty-foot-long image of the street that she carried with her to interview the older members of the community. Those who had grown up on the street were able to literally walk her through the vanished neighborhood, describing their personal knowledge of delicatessens, bakeries, beauty shops, gro-

Reflecting on the diversity of the neighborhood, Ann Murphy said, "Jersey Street was a league of nations: there were great people on Jersey Street." Norman Nunn added: "Jersey Street was social: your father was my father, your sister was my sister. Everybody was like a family. In my neighborhood there were half a dozen black families on the block and you went in and out of everyone's house like it was your own; in and out, up and down, no problem. Everybody could tell the next one don't do this, and it was the end of the story. It was an ideal community: the Italians, and the blacks, Irish, Polish, and Jews completely mixed."
(Chamberlain, 1994)

Left: Jersey Street in Staten Island, New York, by Ann Chamberlain.

Junebug Productions is a southern theater arts group that uses "story circles" as a means of creating greater unity and awareness among community groups. The circle makes a good space for telling stories because everybody in the circle is equal, sees one another, listens to one another, and has a chance to tell their story. As John O'Neal, of Junebug Productions, writes in his suggestions for running story circles, "That the key to making a good story circle (like so many other things in life) is honesty, care, respect among the people in the circle and the stories they share." (O'Neal, 1)

The sharing of stories is a significant part of Junebug's community based projects, Adella Gautier, Junebug's associate artistic director, emphasizes, "When people have a chance to witness their collective stories, they get energized, more critical and more powerful as a group." (Schwarzman, 10)

Children in the community having their photo taken during "photo opportunity night" in one of the local housing projects. (Courtesy Ann Chamberlain)

ceries, synagogues, and other shops and social clubs. The photographs elicited stories that had been buried for sixty years and revealed the memories of an integrated working-class neighborhood.

Next Chamberlain photographed Jersey Street as it appeared in 1994 and interviewed local businesspeople and residents. Like the old photographs, the current photographs inspired narratives of the street. Sara Richardson, an elderly woman who routinely walked the street and acted as a watchful caretaker in the context of tough social and economic problems, described her experience:

> The best thing about the community is taking care of the children. We see that kids stay out of trouble and out of drugs. I have spent my whole life on this street. In 1988 my grandson got killed, no reason: being in the wrong place at the wrong time. He was 15. I can remember the day like it was right now and that took a lot out of me.
> (Chamberlain 1994)

To get to know the families and friends who currently lived in the housing projects, Chamberlain set up a "photo opportunity night" in one of the community rooms. Here she photographed for free anyone who was interested and rephotographed the old photographs that they brought with them. Cleo Banks, who assisted her with the photographs, told her both of his pleasurable memories as a boy playing with his friends on the street and his current fears and worries of trying to "survive" on the street. Many project residents described a racially and economically segregated community and feelings of powerlessness against the difficulties of poverty and isolation.

In a final exhibit, Chamberlain overlaid the thirty-foot-long image of Jersey Street with the stories and photographs of the individuals who lived and worked on the street. Staged in the midst of the projects, the exhibit was about "affirming and celebrating the community that continued to exist on Jersey Street, giving them a way to picture themselves, and giving a voice to their own stories" (Chamberlain).

Ann Chamberlain wrote in her diary, "There is no product that will solve the problem of how to go about telling a story, for stories are like gifts, they take time and confidence and care in the giving and receiving" (Burnham, 44). Taking the time to listen to the stories of a place is not typically part of the site research and analysis process of sketching, photographing, sending out questionnaires, or interpreting the place through the designer's eyes. Listening requires time as well as an attitude of responsiveness. Too often the experiences of people who live in a place are overlooked by planners and landscape architects trained to consider official documents and their professional interpretation as primary. Learning that Sara Richardson lost her grandson on the street expands the understanding of what it means for a community to have a high incidence of crime or violence. The gesture of exchanging something basic such as dirt, the simple act of walking, or fully listening to the community's personal knowledge of their landscape all represent ways of stepping out of the single perspective of a designer, and so reveal meanings not evident in more official versions.

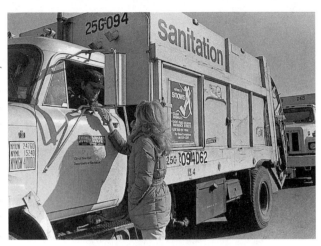

ASKING QUESTIONS

Asking questions is a way of finding stories and engaging communities with their own understanding of places. Questions not only ferret out information, but also challenge assumptions and initiate discourse. Who asks the questions, and how the questions are directed, affect responses and what will be found.

"Whose history?" is the core question of the work of a collaborative group of artist called REPOhistory. By asking questions about history, REPOhistory (Repossessing History) seeks to "demystify the official version, and insert the stories, peoples, and events that have been omitted." Their intent "is not to substitute 'our version' for 'their version' but to provoke critical and multiple readings" (REPOhistory 1992/1993). In its 1992 and 1993 Lower Manhattan Sign Project, REPOhistory positioned thirty-nine signs in the financial district of lower Manhattan. Many of the signs "repossessed" the history of this area by asking questions about the meaning of lesser-known people such as three homeless people, an anonymous soldier, Rose Schneiderman (union activist), and Madame Restell (19th-century abortionist) or retelling forgotten events such as "Nelson Mandela's Visit to New York City," "Stock Market Crash, "Subway Fire," or "Office Workers Eat Their Lunch." REPOhistory's standard 18"-by-24" metal street signs attached to lampposts appeared to be like all the other official historic markers of the American Express Heritage Trail or the Landmark District Signs; however, their signs asked the viewer to critically question given history and actively construct other versions of history. The back of each sign included questions such as "Is this an historic site?" or "Is this part of your history?"

One of the REPOhistory artists, Jayne Pagnucco, included an image of the potter's field burial ground on Hart's Island on

Simply contacting the ordinary people of a place and learning their perspectives enriches understanding of place. Mierle Laderman Ukeles, in a piece titled *Touch Sanitation*, spent nearly a year shaking hands with every one of the sanitation workers in New York City. In the act of shaking their hands and making direct contact with every worker, she learned of their personal experiences of cleaning the streets and their feelings about being treated as garbage men. "Ukeles recounts the stories of workers who never told their neighbors what they did for a living, or those who would never dry their uniforms on outdoor laundry lines for fear of castigation" (Felshin, 183). "The Handshake Ritual" gets in touch with the stories of the everyday and routine process of maintaining the landscape, stories that are typically overshadowed by the more dramatic events of discovery, design, and construction.

Above: Mierle Laderman Ukeles, "Handshake Ritual" for *Touch Sanitation*. (Photograph by Marcia Bricker, courtesy Ronald Feldman Fine Arts Inc.)

Left: In REPOhistory's *Lower Manhattan Sign Project:Whose History* asks "Is this part of your History" (Photograph by Mark O'Brien)

What is all-inclusive history?

Potter's Field, Hart's Island, The Jacob A. Riis Collection

Above: REPOhistory sign located on 17 Battery Place by Jayne Pagnucco titled *Potter's Field/Ellis Island* questions the detaining, the subsequent death, and the method of disposal of an immigrant woman named Rose who arrived at Ellis Island in 1904.

Right: The columns of the Boston Holocaust Memorial evoke multiple meanings. (Photograph by Richard Purinton)

a sign that asks "What is all-inclusive history?" The back of the sign describes the incident of "Rose," who was detained on Ellis Island and subsequently died. The sign was located on the northern side of the WhiteHall Building at Battery Place, where immigrants once arrived on the shore of Manhattan from Ellis Island. The story of Rose challenges naturalized notions about the United States' openness to immigrants within view of a democratic icon, Ellis Island.

Questions evoke response and engage readers to become aware of their own views and experiences. Questions do not always take the form of literal text; they may be implicit in the ambiguity, choice, or incompleteness of a form. Stanley Saitowitz, the architect for the Boston Holocaust Memorial, hoped that the form of the six steaming columns would continue to illicit many associations such as "candles," "a menorah," "towers of spirit," "six million Jews," "six pillars of breath," or "six chambers of gas." These kinds of discourses bridge political and personal experiences by asking people to make their own sense of historical events.

In the Story Garden in Portland, Oregon, designed by Doug Macy and Larry Kirkland, the visitor is also asked to construct his or her own narrative based on given images and questions found in the context of a maze. Four sculptural elements—a "King of the Mountain" throne, a building block gateway, a granite tortoise, and a granite hare—surround the central maze and correspond conceptually to the 150 or more images found along the maze pathways. Although the designer correlated ideas and images (such as power and the throne, childhood and the gate, wisdom and the tortoise, and youth and the hare), it is up to the visitor to make the assorted imagery coherent. The visitor refers to common fables and stories such as "The Tortoise and the Hare," "Little Red Riding Hood," and "Jonah and the Whale" to construct his or her own story. Imaginings, beyond the given references, are also elicited. One parent, for instance, found that her children imagined one figure in the pavement to be a spaceman and then used the tortoise and the hare as spaceships for "blast off." In many games, the throne becomes a power seat won by making it through the maze.

In the middle of the maze, the path wraps around itself without a defined center. Here questions inscribed in the granite ask "What is your joy?" "What is your strength?" "What is your sadness?" and "Why is there evil?"

Through questions and the puzzle of multiple imagery, the designers intended that the visitor discover his or her own meaning:

> The maze is a metaphor for life's journey. It is a place for the child in everyone, a place to ask questions, share conversation with a family member or friend; an environment for learning and playing. It is rich with discoveries, whether one happens upon it or returns to the experience again and again.
> (Walker & Macy)

The Story Garden maze.
(Courtesy Walker & Macy)

LOOSENING CONTROL

Even in "participatory design" processes, designers often filter the input of others through their voice to make an authored or "master" plan. This role can exclude possibilities that occur when designers or artists expand to be facilitators, catalysts, collaborators, or supporters. Instead of univocally retelling stories, designers can potentially open places to a dialogue between diverse narrators. When voice is given to the community, the traditional division between artist and viewer, or designer and community, blurs. Places have a greater potential of being sustained when more members of a society consider themselves participants and when professionals become more aware of the potential everyone has in shaping their landscape.

The English rural action group Common Ground inspires communities to get more involved in the ongoing changes of their own landscape. The group developed from the idea that decisions made by planners and designers are not sustained without ongoing community support and involvement. Furthermore, for Common Ground, the experts are the people who live in a place and who have the greatest understanding of how a place should evolve.

The Parish Map projects throughout England were launched in 1985 with the "purpose of encouraging people to share information about their localities and to record aspects they cared about" (King, 31). The maps trigger the sharing and telling of stories by opening up the process of constructing representations of place to the whole community. In their many projects taking place in rural parishes and urban neighborhoods, residents who intimately know a place gather to construct maps of their landscape. Civic societies, tenants' groups, artists, parish councils, schools, sewing circles, garden clubs, or 4-H clubs work together sewing, painting, patching, or sculpting a map while exchanging knowledge about the ordinary landscape. During the mapmaking, information typically held by city officials or planners, such as tax values, watersheds, and property maps, becomes accessible so that everyone can become an expert about their home landscape. And, more important, the particular character of a place is revealed through unofficial information and personal experiences. Regarding a map made for Muchelney Somerset, Clifford and King write:

> The question "What do you value in your place?" turns everyone into experts. From the smallest of details to the most enduring stories, no one else can dictate what is important to you—the

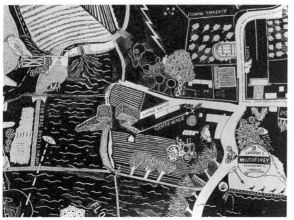

Parish map of Muchelney
by Gordon Young.
(Courtesy Common Ground)

lovely doors along the row, Geoff's hedge and how he keeps his holly trimmed, the pollarded willows, the sluice gates, orchards and wandering chickens; seasonal things such as where the best blackberries or mushrooms can be found, Jim ploughing that way, where the toads spawn, the floods; events that have become stories: "Do you remember when lightning struck the holm oak?" All of these and many more are captured by Gordon Young's Parish Map of Muchelney. It could not be anywhere else. (Clifford and King, 2)

In the process of making the parish maps, decisions are made about what form a map will take and what to include in it. Differing opinions about the location of boundaries, the prominence of landmarks, the naming of places, and other features of place lead to a discourse so that "tensions are revealed or sometimes healed," according to Sue Clifford, cofounder of Common Ground (Clifford and King). Although the completed map may represent resolutions of certain agreements or disagreements, the responses to the exhibited maps are ongoing and "become an influence that continues in the life of the people around it" (Clifford and King, 62). Maps, writings, photographs, and other representations of place are means for expressing knowledge and power so that when communities (as opposed to only professionals or authorities) gain access to representing their landscapes, they also gain important knowledge and decision-making power. Loosening control over who represents and shapes the landscape is therefore a key means of opening narratives.

OPENING DISCOURSES

As more voices participate in the interpretation of landscape, complexity, conflict, and the potential for dialogue increase. The memories of the former inmates in the United States' World War II concentration camps for Japanese Americans conflict with the government's version of what happened; the parish mapmakers disagree about what is valuable or important to their village; and the individual memories of Staten Island's Jersey Street each evoke a different street. When the telling of stories is opened up to a wider range of perspectives, the meanings of place do not cohere into a unified view but branch off and overlap with each association. Where the stories of ordinary or less powerful people such as coal miners, migrant workers, servants, crop pickers, and battlefield nurses combine with the stories of company owners, landowners, military officers, and war heroes, the designer must decide whose story is told and how it is told. By asking these sometimes difficult questions and realizing that there is no one version to tell, designers are more apt to make places that connect in meaningful ways to the community around them.

The design for the Charles J. Loring Memorial in Portland, Maine, transformed the story of an individual war hero into a broader community discourse about courage and commitment. This project was presented to the designer by the sponsor group, the American Veterans Post #25. As with many other memo-

Left: Sewing a parish map.
(Courtesy Common Ground)

Maps and models of places often reconnect people to their memories and experiences of place. This happened at the Japanese American National Museum in Los Angeles in an exhibit titled "America's Concentration Camps: Remembering the Japanese American Experience" curated by Karen Ishizuka and designed by Ralph Applebaum Associates. At the entrance to the exhibit, visitors and former inmates could pick up a model of the barracks they once lived in that they would then place in a model of one of the eleven wartime camps. By finding the location of their own block and barracks number, they could retrace their paths through the camps and remember the location of latrines, mess halls, and baseball fields and the sounds and smells of being there. Former inmates would return to the exhibit many times to show family and friends where they lived and to express the reality of a much erased history. According to Ishizuka, on many occasions the exhibit space became a spontaneous reunion for visitors and docents, who were also former inmates. Visitors could add their photographs, stories, and names to "Camp Albums" and respond to other entries. One entry read:
"There was a deep sense of anger that my government put all of us in concentration camps. This was something I could not talk about for many years—not even to my son. This sort of humiliation should never happen to any group of people."

In the model and albums, the narratives of many individuals, laid over official government blueprints of the campsite plans, represent a repossession of the power to tell one's own story.

rials that commemorate local heroes, the veterans sought to commemorate their comrade Charles Loring. One of the designers, Todd Richardson, recalled that the assignment at first did not immediately resonate with his own ambivalent sentiments about war. This personal dilemma led him to find ways to connect the biography of Charles Loring with the community of Portland, Maine, the home of Loring, and the site of the memorial.

As design began, Loring's friends and family, as well as local residents and schoolchildren, gathered in a workshop to talk about Charles Loring's life and his heroic, yet suicidal, act of dive-bombing his fighter plane into attacking enemy troops to save U.S. troops during the Korean War. Alfred DePew began the workshop held at the Valle Steakhouse with two major questions: "What makes a hero?" and "What would you die for?" People privately wrote their responses to these questions and then shared them in a discussion that extended into a wider context to include the heroic acts of Loring's everyday life, his childhood, and his relationship with family and friends. A boyhood friend and football teammate of Loring described Loring's final moments as a "reenactment of things he had been through in his younger life a number of times" and his "supreme generous self-sacrifice" as integral to his everyday life.

As more stories were heard, the content of the memorial began to relate to the everyday life of the people living in Portland. One man shared a story about his wife's fears and courage, which generated the design concept of relating heroic acts to the events of everyday life:

I would like to talk about courage too....Sometimes you find yourself—maybe you are out hiking or on a canoe or something with your family and something adverse happens, a gale picks up or something that you didn't expect and you are not really prepared to deal with what happens. That's when I see courage in my wife, who is generally wimpy in these situations except when I get into them, and probably wiser for that. But when the thing happens that she is

Below: The words developed for the Charles J. Loring memorial came from the participation of the community during the workshop.

One woman and teacher who spoke about the importance of the "heart" inspired Richardson and Uppington to include this word in their "vectors" relating to Charles Loring's life:

"As I was listening, . . .I was really taken by the word heart because it is a word that. . . this is what I wrote: 'A mystical word that describes the indescribable, about the depth and breadth of the living being potential of a feeling animal...he (Loring) is the kind of teacher, he is the kind of person that I wish could help all my kids understand what that means and strive for that because it represents a fullness of being that I would touch and understand. It is hard for me to find words that express that; that is why heart is a really important word.'"

(Richardson and Uppington)

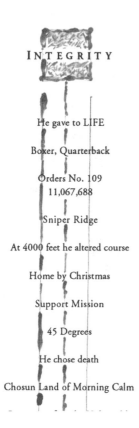

afraid would happen, rather than panicking or freaking out or telling me I told you we should not be here, she deals with the adversity at the moment....When the gale is blowing or when the situation appears to be at its worst and you don't have time or you don't have the luxury of being able to complain, you really have to just deal with it. I have seen that in a number of surprising instances.
(Richardson and Uppington)

Others responded with their own stories, stories about the young boy who rescued children swimming in the local dam and stories of local politicians who fought for difficult issues.

How would the many voices, stories, and views about bravery and the life of Loring translate into a physical form? The landscape architects Todd Richardson and Theo Hortwijck, and the artist Ann Uppington wanted to find a way to express both the diversity and complexity of these ideas as well as the flow and rhythm of their discussion with the community. The community gave them the structuring concepts. The center would represent Loring's heroic act and, as described by one veteran in the workshop, "the moment you bring all of your history, all of your skills, everything into a real defining point, where all of your life experiences sort of converge and all things you have been taught, all things you have experienced, all come to one point where you do that thing that you never thought yourself capable of or prepared to do before." Other key ideas, from the community's testimonies and discussions, were represented by five granite sentinel posts positioned at the periphery of the memorial and titled "Integrity," "Presence," "Spirit," "Heart," and "The Untold Portion of His Life."

They collected and laid out other fragments of phrases and stories from the workshop and newspaper clippings along the five vectors that radiate from the center. The placement of text embedded in the pavement allows for multiple readings so that phrases such as "Home by Christmas," "he kept his word about everything," "Anderson Street, Munjoy Hill," "45 degrees," and "what you are most afraid of" connect to other phrases depending on your movement through the space. In this way references to war, love, family, and Portland are collected and collaged by the reader's movement. The fifth vector includes Charles Loring's birth and death dates and "represents the untold portion of his life" (Richardson and Uppington) in keeping with the concept that knowledge and understanding are found partially in this waterfront park but predominantly, where the vectors point, beyond the park, in the community.

COUNTER NARRATIVES

Countering popularly accepted narratives with a conflicting version opens a discourse about what happened and encourages a critical evaluation of any "given story." By placing unfamiliar stories in the familiar landscapes, for instance, REPOhistory's Lower Manhattan Sign Project challenges conventional notions about the meaning of places. There is a tendency for designers to strive to make landscape seem more coherent, consistent, and unified, yet disparate forms or ideas and debate are ways of encouraging

Gloria Bornstein,
Shore View Points and Voice Library.

people to make up their own minds. In a work titled Shore View Points and Voice Library on Seattle's waterfront, the artist Gloria Bornstein countered the official historical information with signs that posed questions about given history. Stories of the homeless or the working people who once resided on the waterfront, for instance, were placed next to historic markers locating scenic landmarks. Or, information about the displacement of native populations was juxtaposed against the settlers' version of successfully establishing communities in Washington State.

Bornstein's signs stirred an ongoing dialogue about the waterfront recorded in a "Voice Library," a voice-mail system that allowed people to listen to recorded messages or leave their own messages so that views were shared through questions and responses. Hundreds of messages were left, including one by Carl Nordstrom, who stated:

> I saw the signs alongside the historic markers on the waterfront today, and I have a question as to how long they are going to be up. I don't think they should be there very long. My ancestors were part of the building of early-day Seattle, and we wrested the land from nature and the Indians and we don't want to give it back.
> (Bornstein 1996)

Another person identifying himself as a Cherokee Indian left a message about how people are custodians of the land and do not own the lands. Bornstein believes that the Voice Library and other work that encourages an exchange of differing opinions help to heal wounds of conflict (Bornstein 1996). Both *Shore View Points* and the Lower Manhattan Sign Project explicitly reveal contrasting versions of the history of places and illustrate ways that places can be more open to ongoing discourse. Although encouraging the expression of differences does risk the potential for dangerous conflicts, that can be disguised by harmony and unity.

LEAVING SPACE FOR ONGOING DISCOURSE

Stories are kept alive by their retellings, retellings that do not necessarily follow the script of any known author but that take on new life with the interpretation of each teller. In the same way, places without scripts become vitalized by the unplanned events and ongoing claims of a changing community. Unprogrammed places, which act as settings for activities rather than scenes with regulated and programmed activities, attract people to participate in their own way. In *Discovering The Vernacular Landscape,* J. B. Jackson writes about the early history of parks and the popularity of the unstructured "terrains vagues" versus formally planned parks for sporting events. He advocates retaining more informal groves and unstructured places in urban communities so that children have places to play without supervision (Jackson, 127–130). Roger Hart also believes in leaving unplanned spaces where more interesting activities are apt to happen. For instance, he writes that the street is a place where children can "create their own settings for play rather than having them defined for them" and goes on to say that "it is for this reason that a single tree can often satisfy the same child's climbing aspirations for many years" (Hart, 4–5). In the street or in a tree, children can establish their own goals without adult supervision.

Designers are trained to program spaces and add corresponding forms, although sometimes the existing activities of a place happen because that place is empty and flexible. For instance, for the fisherman using the Portland, Maine, waterfront, the unobstructed dock space gives room for stacking lobster pots, fish, and equipment. The competing interests of tourism and the conversion of fishing warehouses into condominiums and commercial and office space has jeopardized the working waterfront. However, the landscape architect Terry Dewan, in collaboration with Terrian Architects, found a way to accommodate the expressed concerns of the lobstermen as well as the changing roles of the waterfront as a place for commerce, tourism, and offices. They refrained from decorating the waterfront with the typical site furnishings of bollards, benches, and light poles, which would inhibit the maneuvers of the fishermen. Instead, concrete boxes serve as both a work table for loading and a bench for tourists and office workers. Tough cobble and asphalt pavement enables the trucks to pull up close to the docks. The designers considered the Portland waterfront as a setting for the activities of the local fishermen rather than merely a scenic stage for tourists. Their restrained design respects the ongoing life of fishing instead of delegating fishing to a sentimental past.

Leaving space or leaving silence welcomes the voices and actions of others. The designer who busily fills the space is analogous to someone who incessantly talks without listening to others. The silence of unstructured space allows for emerging dialogue and response. In the Washington, D.C., Holocaust Memorial Museum, pads of paper and pencils are left out so that anyone can tell their own story in response to the exhibits. This opens a semipermanent exhibit of ongoing stories. Rather than conveying an idea that the exhibit is complete, left space respects the many private and untold stories that lie beyond the museum walls.

The Portland, Maine, waterfront. (Design by Terry Dewan and Terrian Architects)

Space is often conceived as a container of shared memories and experiences. The Canadian architect Richard Henriquez included "memory wheels," wheels on which each family member could put objects or words of memory, in the design for his family's house. Andy Leicester's design for a coal miner's museum in Maryland included "memory rooms" where the personal artifacts of coal miners were stored. And time capsules have been included as a part of projects that intend to preserve the memory of distinct years or events. The base of the Vietnam Veterans Memorial wall in Washington, D.C., has been a memory ground where thousands of artifacts have been left to remember stories of loss, grief, love, and admiration of soldiers who died.

A MEMORIAL TO

VICTIMS OF GANG VIOLENCE

Left: Gang war memorial. Design by Sue Ann Ware.

The idea that space contains memories, along with the African-American tradition of leaving spirit objects at cemeteries, inspired Sue Ann Ware's design for a gang war memorial intended for either downtown Oakland or Tyrone Carey Park, California, the "heart of gangland." In interviews with gang members and families who had lost a friend or a family member from gang war, she learned how families value "signature artifacts" such as Rico's hat, Nathan's walking stick, and other objects that were part of an individual's life.

By giving an open framework for the constant addition of these objects, families could grieve and "offer the individual comfort in their journey to the afterlife" (Ware, 13). To do this, Ware designed a maze of coffin-shaped cubes and voids, which would receive the "spirit objects." The shapes developed out of experiences with burial ceremonies and the natural life cycle. The longest shadow at noon on winter solstice determined the length of the void so that the shadow of the cubes would "bury the voids" (Ware, 39).

It took a trip to another graveyard to inspire my design for the voids. Unfortunately I had to attend a funeral for one of the gang members I had interviewed. It was a sunny day for mid-February, even in northern California. I watched them lower the coffin into the ground. The earth's precedents had proclaimed it the abode of the

As Ware discovered in her interview with Beatrice, objects that "embodied the spirit of the dead" needed a place in the memorial:
"Beatrice was the first woman I interviewed, and she had lost one of her sons in 1988 during a drive-by shooting. I asked her about what her son liked to do. She said that he was seventeen when he died, and by that time he was really not around much. 'He did love ball games; on Saturday afternoons he would go to the A's games. After he got shot the first time, he would sit in the damn chair and watch ball games instead of doing his knee exercises.' Her son had been shot previously in an attempt to rob a local store. He was only fourteen; consequently he spent a year at a juvenile detention center and was released on parole. Beatrice elaborated on this: 'My boy Nathan, he had a limp ever since that first shot. His friend G.T. made this walking stick for him; he said he carved it out of one of them tree branches in the park where Nate used to hang. Nate thought that the stick was lucky and he used it all the time.' She showed me the walking stick and it felt worn. I kept thinking about the African-American graves in the rural South and how the people believed that the objects last touched embodied the spirit of the dead. This stick was Nate. The memorial has to have individual artifacts that represent the loss of life."
(Ware, 30)

dead. I thought about the sweet-smelling soil. "We return unto once we came." The minister's words fell heavily on my mind. The memorial must respect the simplicity of a grave. The simple excavation of soil to form a space, the idea of using a void to create a new space, was aligned with the masses...With this in mind I began drawing...
(Ware)

Each solstice, the accumulated objects would be removed and stored in a protective place to empty the crypts and begin a new cycle. "The collection of objects would grow until the violence stopped or the space ran out" (Ware, design presentation).

Left: James Drake's sculpture of the attack dogs used by Police Commissioner Eugene "Bull" Conner at Kelly Ingram Park.

Far left: Sculpture by James Drake of the fire hoses used by "Bull" Connor on the African-American children at Kelly Ingram Park.

Below: Andy Warhol, *Birmingham Race Riots.* (Courtesy Syracuse University Art Collection)

Even an ordinary park can be part of naturalized ideologies such as racism. The recent redesign of the Kelly Ingram Park by Grover and Harrison in Birmingham, Alabama, revealed some of the inherent racism as it proposed physical changes and a retelling of Birmingham's history. For instance, the central commemorative rock with a historic plaque noting the importance of Kelly Ingram, the first sailor killed in World War I, was replaced with a central reflecting pool to represent peace and harmony between the races. The decision to tell the story of violence and repression directed toward the black community in the 1960s stirred louder debate.

The controversial new sculpture in the park by James Drake realistically portrays white policemen gunning African-American children with fire hoses, and police dogs attacking demonstrators. In fact the visitor must pass through these violent and vivid scenes to circulate through the park. Some members of the Birmingham community voiced their opposition to the sculpture because they do not want to remind the public of their "past history," believing that it might rekindle conflict within the community. Others do not want to believe it happened or don't think this story should be told in a municipal park. Others want to remind the public of the racism that continues to exist or that may reappear if forgotten. The opening of this park to a dialogue of different views potentially bridges communications between separate views as stated by Horace Huntley of the Civil Rights Institute: "We grow through dialogue. We don't grow by hiding things under the rug" (Elliott).

Opening this park to debate is particularly significant given the political history of Kelly Ingram Park, which was socially closed to blacks, who lived in a nearby neighborhood, prior to the late sixties. In the same way that debate has ensued during the park renovations, people from different communities have been brought together in the use of the renovated park to picnic and attend cultural events. As noted by Colonel Johnson, the civil rights activist, union representative, and bodyguard for Reverend Fred Shuttlesworth, simply walking black and white together along the new circular "freedom walk" that surrounds the park is meaningful to someone who has witnessed inequalities, segregation, and political activism through the eighty years of his life.

Below: Overlay of points, lines, and planes at Parc de la Villette by Tschumi. (Courtesy Bernard Tschumi Architects)

Bottom: Explosion *folie* at Parc de la Villette by Tschumi. (Courtesy Bernard Tschumi Architects)

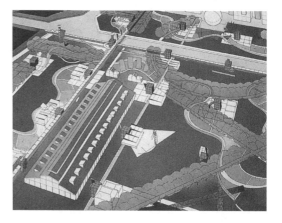

BREAKING THINGS UP

Breaks in the unity of structure can become openings for interpretation. Deconstruction challenges concepts of a composed, unified, and ordered world and provokes more complex and contradictory conceptions of the world. Although the philosophical underpinnings of deconstruction can be nihilistic, given the intentions to make no sense and no coherent meaning, the ideas ironically illustrate constructive means for making places more open. There are very few built projects that present a deconstructivist approach, partly because the idea of creating a disjointed place does not appeal to most clients and partly because the ideas are more vivid in theory than in physical actuality. In a pure sense, the constructed work is not really deconstructed. Despite this paradox, Tschumi designed the Parisian Parc de la Villette so it would open a landscape to diverse uses and interpretation by superimposing discordant information and leaving things in an unfinished state.

An underlying grid structures Parc de la Villette and creates an open plan that evens the ground plane and removes traditional formal hierarchies, hierarchies that typically give greater importance to a central axis, major intersections, or chosen key locations. The grid was randomly placed over the landscape, intentionally disregarding the existing "semi-industrial" context so that chance intersections happen. For instance, a *folie* falls half on an existing historic industrial building, or new bridges meet the existing canal

Concert event in front of a *folie* at Parc de la Villette by Tschumi. (Courtesy Bernard Tschumi)

at odd angles. The grid responds to the surrounds in unanticipated ways, and the independent layers of surfaces, points *(folies),* and lines within the grid combine in unusual ways. The new relations don't intend to make sense in conventional terms. For instance, an athletic track intersects a cafeteria so that runners exercise next to people eating lunch. This unexpected juxtaposition of activity, although not uncommon in dense urban spaces, is more the result of chance than a rational programmatic analysis that evaluates relations between activities. In a paradoxical phrase, Tschumi describes the principle of superimposing disassociated, confrontational, and heterogeneous elements as an act of "calculated discontinuity." Such chance configurations engender events that are not controlled or scripted by the designer. Unexpected events occur: "the football player skates on the battlefield" (Tschumi 1987, 22). As with the Charles Loring Memorial, *Shore View Points,* or the Parish Maps, Parc de la Villette encourages a dialogue between different users, and finds formal architectural means for constructing a disruptive discourse.

UNFINISHED AND EVOLVING WORKS

Parc de la Villette is also meant to be in a state of constant change—never finished and always open to innumerable interpretations. The folies or "points of intensity" in the grid mark locations for possible future constructions by other designers that will recombine to create new interpretations and in Tschumi's words "semantic transformations" (Tschumi 1987, 26). Although Tschumi uses the French interpretation of *folie* to mean madness or insanity, the plan for future construction is more rational than the theoretical claims. Again the theory is incongruous with the built work. A grid will expand or contract over time into the surrounding context and so create a park boundless in time and place. Both movable pieces and a shifting game board create a place in constant flux.

But the constant flux of natural processes is not engaged at Parc de la Villette in any remarkable way. The park is more of a technocultural architectural construct than a place where nature openly evolves. In fact, Tschumi conceived of this park as "the largest building ever constructed" (Tschumi 1987, 1). Rather than working with all the contingencies of a site's layers and ongoing processes, the designer imposed a formal diagram of points, lines, and planes that were not conceived as interacting with the ongoing dynamics of nature (Meyer,). The park's openness happens in terms of cultural and human activities. Forces of nature can, however, be agents of change and transformation for landscapes in the making.

For George Hargreaves, nature, experience, history, and context are all agents of change in landscapes with multiple and unstable meanings. His forms often collect these many and ever-changing associations. For instance, the mounds at the top of the former landfill of Byxbee Park refer to the Ohlone Indian refuse shell mounds, the garbage heaps dumped by the trucks that continue to fill the adjacent landfill, and the ongoing shaping of the landscape caused by erosion and deposition. Superimposing these references and any others found in the interpretive experience of being at Byxbee creates a place that evolves through dialogue. The surrounding natural and cultural context of highways, waste, industry, and estuarine systems provokes an intertextual exchange beyond the designer's control.

All landscapes are in a state of change affected by forces that erode and detain and grow and decline, yet few designers engage these forces in an open-ended way. Hargreaves Associates uses the processes of nature to create places of indeterminacy. Natural processes add to and transform the initial construct, countering the notion that there exists a particular ideal state. The often-heard designer's complaint that "the project has gone downhill since it was first built" or that "changes ruined its original intent" differs from an approach where the designer establishes a framework that reveals the evolutionary processes of nature and culture. By working with the medium of landscape itself (earth, industrial materials, water, wind), the changes made by the ongoing processes become indecipherable from the original construct. In fact, many of the natural processes may erase Hargreaves's physical constructs yet reveal his approach. For instance, the retaining weirs at Byxbee or the sculpted mounds at Guadalupe River Park will be in the former case hidden by deposition from the eroding slope or in the latter case eroded by the force of the flooded river. Rossana Vaccarino finds a paradox of openness in Hargreaves's design. She writes that "the details themselves determine indetermination" (Vaccarino, 92).

Above: Byxbee Park earth mounds shaped by wind erosion. (Courtesy Hargreaves Associates)

Where the designer is silent other voices may be heard, what the writer leaves unfinished the reader may complete, what the designer deconstructs the visitor may imaginatively construct. Like the performers in Umberto Eco's example of the open score, cultural and environmental processes create "fields of possibilities."

REFERENCES

Bornstein, Gloria. *Shore Viewpoints and Voice Library*. Unpublished video description sent to authors.

———. 1996. Telephone interview with authors, April.

Burnham, 1994. "Linda Frye Abroad and at Home." *High Performance* 17(2).

Burns, Jim. 1986. "The How of Creativity: Scores and Scoring." Lawrence Halprin: In *Changing Places*. San Francisco: San Francisco Museum of Modern Art.

Burton, Pamela, and Richard Hertz. 1995. *The Language of Scripted Places*. Unpublished paper sent to authors.

Chamerblain, Ann. 1994. Jersey Street Project Documents. Unpublished.

———. 1995. Interview with authors in San Francisco, November.

Clifford, Sue, Angela and King, ed. *From Place to Place Maps and Parish Maps*. London: Common Ground. Common Ground can be reached at 41 Sheldon Street, London, UK WC2H.9HJ.

Common Ground. 1990s. "Celebrating Local Distinctiveness." Pamphlet by Common Ground, 41 Sheldon Street, London, UK WC2H.9HJ.

Cox, Thomas Hughs. 1995. "Reflections on a Place of Revolution and Reconciliation: A Brief History of Kelly Ingram Park and the Birmingham Civil Rights District." Paper produced for the Birmingham Civil Rights Institute.

Culler, Jonathan. 1982. *Stories of Reading*. Ithaca, N.Y.: Cornell University Press.

Eco, Umberto. 1979. *The Role of the Reader: Explorations in the Semiotics of Text*. Bloomington: Indiana University Press.

———. 1989. "The Open Work." Cambridge: Harvard University Press.

———. 1994. *Six Walks in the Fictional Woods*. Cambridge: Harvard University Press.

Elliott, Debbie. 1996. National Public Radio news report, March 12.

Felshin, Nina. 1995. *But Is It Art: The Spirit of Art and Activism*. Seattle, Wash.: Bay Press.

Hart, Roger. 1986. "The Changing City of Childhood: Implications for Play and Learning." The 1986 Catherine Molony Memorial Lecture.

Hayden, Dorothy. 1995. *Power of Place: Urban Landscapes as Public History*. Cambridge: MIT Press.

Hood, Walter. 1997a. *Urban Diaries*. Washington, D.C.:Spacemaker Press.

———. 1997b. Interview with authors in Rome.

Jackson, John Brinckerhoff. 1984. *Discovering the Vernacular Landscape*. New Haven, Conn.: Yale University Press.

King, Angela. 1993 "Mapping Your Roots: Parish Mapping." In *Boundaries of Home: Mapping for Local Empowerment*. Gabriola Island, B.C.: New Society Publishers.

Lacy, Suzanne, ed. 1995. *Mapping the Terrain: New Genre Public Art.* Seattle, Wash.: Bay Press.

Meyer, Elizabeth. 1991. "The Public Park as Avant-Garde." *Landscape Journal* 10(1):16–26.

O'Neal, John. 1996. "Junebug Productions: Suggestions for Running Story Circles." Unpublished paper.

Register, Richard. 1996. Interview with authors in Berkeley.

REPOhistory. 1992, 1993. "The Lower Manhattan Sign Project." Pamphlet published by REPOhistory.

———. 1996. Interviews with Lisa Maya Knauer, Tom Klem, Greg Sholette, Neill Bogan, Betti-Sue Hertz and authors.

Richardson, Todd, and Ann Uppington. 1994. The Charles Loring breakfast tapes. Valle's Steak House. Working tapes, September 10.

Schneekloth, Lydia H., and Robert G. Shibley. 1995. *Placemaking: The Art and Practice of Building Communities.* New York: John Wiley & Sons.

Schwarzman, Mat. 1996. "Drawing the Line at Place: The Environmental Justice Project." *High Performance.* Summer:8–12.

Tschumi, Bernard. 1981. *The Manhattan Transcripts.* New York: Academy Editions.

———. 1987. *Cinegram Folie, Le Parc de La Villette.* Princeton, N.J.: Princeton Architectural Press.

Vaccarino, Rossana. 1987. "Re-Made Landscapes." *Lotus International* 87:82–107.

Walker and Macy. Story Garden Project Description. Unpublished.

Ware, Sue Ann. "A Monument in Death: A Theoretical Memorial to Victims of Gang Violence." Unpublished design presentation.

Young, James E. 1993. *The Texture of Memory: Holocaust Memorials and Meaning.* New Haven, Conn.: Yale University Press.

PART THREE
STORIES

The three chapters in this section tell stories about stories. They bring together narrative theory and individual practices and projects to tell larger "cultural stories": of refiguring culture's relation to nature in chapter 8, "The Wasteland and Restorative Narrative"; retelling traditions of community design in chapter 9, "Writing Home"; and negotiating cultural differences in chapter 10, "Road Stories." As cultural stories, these are collective works that extend beyond individual design projects and places into other areas of narrative production. Investigating New Jersey's Meadowlands, for instance, we found a poet's elegy for a vanished ecology, an artist fascinated with narratives of entropy, and a duck hunter turned advocate for preservation, as well as landscape architects establishing vegetation succession on landfills. Their stories are produced and shaped in art, projects, daily practices, and collective memory, by negotiations with clients or government mandate, and in varied contexts.

Each story is also linked to a discrete type of place: the wasteland, the home, and the road. And each place serves as both setting and organizing metaphor of the stories. A landfill, for instance, embodies the declensionist plot of the wasteland, a tangible record of loss, consumption, decay, crimes, and indeterminant futures. In the chronotope of the idyllic home, generations are "rooted" in place and linked to cyclical processes of nature. We use Mikhail Bakhtin's concept of "chronotope" to name this fusion of space and time, plot and place. In the figure of the chronotope, "time, as it were, thickens, takes on flesh, becomes artistically visible; likewise, space becomes charged and responsive to the movements of time, plot and history" (Bakhtin, 84). Thus, to go on the road initiates change, and a journey becomes the very metaphor of narrative sequence. Bakhtin concludes: "The chronotope is the place where the knots of narrative are tied and untied. It can be said without qualification that to them belongs the meaning that shapes narrative" (Bakhtin, 250).

The three stories and sites interrelate in various ways. On one level each is a narrative of creating fundamental spatial relationships: creating a center around home and community, reworking the marginalized sites of wastelands, and crossing spatial and cultural boundaries on the road. Yet, there are also inversions and crossovers. The wasteland is most poignant when it is found not at the margins but under the very ground of home and communities. And while the road and strangers are often threats to the security of home and community, these same qualities can also be found on the road. In addition each demonstrates fundamental relationships of storytelling and place. Walter Benjamin, in an essay entitled "The Storyteller," identified two complementary figures and their relationship to place: the person who brings tales from travels on the road to far-off places and the person who stays home in touch with the accumulated layers of history and memory in one place. To this we add the very modern figure attempting to "re-story" what has been lost, restoring the wasteland and retelling traditions.

All the stories are works in progress. Old tales are revised by very contemporary imperatives, and the same story may be interpreted in different ways. The intent is to track the ongoing processes of selecting, designing, revising, negotiating, and interpreting landscape narratives.

Bakhtin, Mikhail, M. 1981. "Forms of Time and of the Chronotope in the Novel." In *The Dialogic Imagination: Four Essays by M.M. Bakhtin*, ed. Michael Holquist, trans. Caryl Emerson and Michael Holquist. Austin: University of Texas Press. Pp. 84–258.

Benjamin, Walter. 1968. "The Storyteller." In *Illuminations: Walter Benjamin, Essays and Reflections*, ed. Hannah Arendt, trans. Harry Zohn. New York: Schocken Books. Pp. 83–109.

CHAPTER EIGHT
THE WASTELAND &
RESTORATIVE NARRATIVE

ON the night of January 1, 1990, just one year after the Exxon *Valdez* spill in Alaska, 567,000 gallons of number 2 fuel oil leaked into the Arthur Kill[1] from an underground pipe at an Exxon storage and refinery facili-

Above: A ship graveyard in the Arthur Kill.

Below: One of the heron rookeries that had developed on a *dredge spoil* island.

ty. However, unlike in Alaska, the Arthur Kill, which separates Staten Island from northeastern New Jersey, is not known as a pristine wilderness. Flanked by the world's largest landfill at Fresh Kills, it is a working river plied by a dense traffic of tankers and barges transferring oil and chemicals to the bulkheads lining its shores. Spills are endemic (Burger, 1–15).

This time, however, there was a twist in the plot of the Arthur Kill. While many had written it off as a defiled industrial wasteland devoid of any ecological value, photographs of injured birds revealed the presence of significant rookeries established on old "dredge spoil" islands. The ecologists who had been studying these habitats for years were able to make exact measurements of the impact of the spill on habitat and wildlife, providing the basis for a successful settlement with Exxon for fifteen million dollars toward reparations and future prevention.

Just five years after the event, marsh grasses were thriving on the most heavily impacted shore across from the refinery. The grasses had not come back on their own. They were planted by New York City Parks Department staff who gathered seeds from the local spartina in October of 1992, grew them in greenhouse beds, and then planted four thousand of them per day, twelve inches on center.[2]

These six acres of restored salt marsh holding on to a shore buffeted by waves from constant river traffic compete not only for space amid the industries, but also for a vision of the future of the river. The plots of different stories intersect in the scene of marsh grass juxtaposed against industries. Between them is a sequence of events, characters, motives, causes, and ends yet to be determined.

But this is just one scene in a series of similar scenes that combine to tell a much larger "cultural story"—restoring wastelands of the late 20th century. From reestablishing the wetlands of the upper Mississippi Basin, to "daylighting" culverted streams in California or planting small patches of prairie natives in backyards, restoration practice cuts across a spectrum of scales, contexts, and

Above: Restored salt marsh and power plant face each other downriver from the oil spill site.

Below: Gathering spartina seeds, Old Place Creek Marsh Restoration. (Courtesy Soleditions, Antonia Pisciotta Goldmark)

institutions, going head–to–head with the diverse ways that landscapes have been damaged, fouled, beat up, abandoned, and left for dead. Going beyond the sacred aura of preserved natural areas to muck about a profane mix of nature and culture, restoration has emerged as one of the more compelling stories being worked out in the contemporary landscape.

PART I: THE WASTELAND

Restoration is quite literally built on wastelands, and much of the power of this narrative derives from transforming land with tragic pasts. Practically every community has its dump, waste beds, derelict sites, and other wounded places at the margins, interstices, and even centers of communities. Separated by fences enclosing strange artifacts and effects, these are curious sites inviting speculation and explanation. Traces, fragments, and abnormalities point to unnatural causes. Much is beyond immediate perception, however, as radiation inhabits benign forms, heavy metals sink into layers of sediment, and toxins accumulate in food chains. What is most provocative are the absences. These are the enigmas that raise questions and generate stories about wastelands. What happened here? Why? What are its effects?

Uncertainty and repressed horrors make wastelands uncanny sites. According to the architectural critic Anthony Vidler, the experience of the uncanny is an outgrowth of the horror story or the grotesque, both related to the Romantic experience of the sublime. However, unlike the awe and respect before the overwhelming, unattainable power and otherness of nature, the theme of the uncanny is a sickening estrangement from self, home, and nature. Its power comes from the inversion of what has been repressed and distanced. Like the horror story read in the comfort of home, the uncanniness of the wasteland is most palpable when it strikes home, when it comes back to haunt the pleasant streets of suburbs such as Love Canal, New York, or the small town of Centralia, Pennsylvania. In this coal region town fires smolder in a labyrinth of underground mining tunnels and smoke issues from the ground around the homes of the few remaining residents, who know no other home and have resisted a government buyout. The real threat, however, is invisible, odorless carbon monoxide.

These now familiar scenes are at the center of the modern narratives of alienation resulting from industrial growth, which severed ties of local traditions, as well as from nature. Romantic artists and writers warned of the consequences of estrangement in the 19th century. The scenes of this narrative were made explicit in Thomas Cole's five panels of *The Course of Empire* (1836). The last two scenes in this moral allegory of imperial ambition foretell "destruction" and "desolation."

In the 20th century these wasteland narratives are known from an equally familiar set of stories evoked repeatedly in film and literature. In 1922, T. S. Eliot's poem, *The Waste Land,* spoke for a generation who witnessed the mechanized death of the First World War and urbanization of the eastern seaboard of North America. He described emblem-

Clockwise from above left: Thomas Cole, *The Course of Empire:* "Savage State,"
"Pastoral State," "Consummation," "Destruction," "Desolation."
(All collection of the New-York Historical Society)

Thomas Cole's *Course of Empire,* 1836,
is a narrative cycle, a story that moves
through a series of pictures. To grasp
their meaning, however, the spectator
has to move through the sequence of
five stages[3] which show eons of change
occuring in one place. The sequence
begins in the American wilderness of the
"Savage State," which is transformed into
an ideal garden (English in character)
of the "Pastoral State," and reaches a
degree of opulence and civilization in
"Consummation" (as a climax, it is the
largest canvas in the series). The next
phase, "Destruction," marks the beginning of a declensionist plot where the
monuments of pagan ambition are
wrecked by storms, pestilence, and war.
In the last scene, "Desolation," nature
returns as a heron makes its nest on top
of a column fragment. Throughout the
series a mountain stands as a constant,
timeless witness in the background.

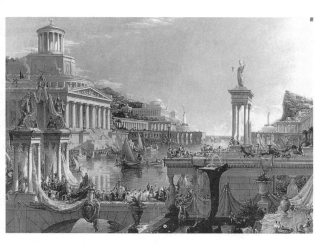

atic elements of what has become a very modern narrative topos—dead trees that give no shelter, stony rubbish, a river that sweats oil, and gray fog descending on a mass of commuters. This topos is not limited to a literary canon, its elements are known through commonly shared stories: elegies of loss; counter-narratives of the downside of industrial growth, failure and abandonment; crime and victim stories; the new narratives of ecological history; and personal experience and memory. Wastelands also give tangible form to the popular fear in science fiction of a familiar world gone alien.

In all these narratives wastelands appear as a setting caught in a tragic plot, a fall from some ideal relationship with nature. The environmental historian William Cronon identifies this downward course of events as a "declensionist plot." As in Cole's *Course of Empire*, the declensionist plot is a reversal of how human history, at least in the West, has typically been constructed as a story of improvement, achievement of will, or the perseverance of pioneers to create a civilized world out of brute nature. Since the plot of these dominant narratives is ascending to an end better than the beginning, Cronon calls it a "progressivist plot." The difference between the beginnings and ends of each plot establishes the criteria for judging the morality of actions in each narrative. Each story reflects its historical and political contexts as well. The progressivist plot continues the project of the 18th century Enlightenment and its notions of progress, while the declensionist plot derives from Romantic reactions to progress.

THE WASTELAND AS CHRONOTOPE

The effects of time of the declensionist plot become palpable, visible in wasteland scenes. In this way the wasteland is a "chronotope," the materialization of time and space that becomes the organizing center of the narrative events. In wastelands we see the belligerent disruption of the natural course of events either through a disaster or the gradual wasting that effaces the luster of progress. The temporal dimensions are often geologic in their scale. The growth of a landfill forms layers and epochs, and its future can seem limitless. When the deposition on landfills stops, and they are capped for indeterminate afterlives, the wasteland becomes a sublimated and buried history. Fenced and removed from the center of daily life, many waste sites, in a sense, exist out of time.

The fear associated with wastelands results from the anxieties of time and the difficulty of comprehending the effects over time. Looking at the eroded hills of ancient Attica, Plato used the metaphor of an aging body: "...what now remains compared with what then existed is like the skeleton of a sick man all the fat and soft earth having wasted away, and only the bare framework of the land being left" (Glacken, 121). Even though much of the wasting of the American continent has occurred within living memory, as opposed to the centuries of change wrought on ancient landscapes, it is still difficult to comprehend. The monumental landfills are deceptively inert. How long does it take for toxins to travel in the groundwater, for pesticides to accumulate up the food chain, for incidents of cancer to indicate a cause?

Location of the New Jersey Meadowlands.

THE MEADOWLANDS, NEW JERSEY

From the New Jersey Turnpike just north of the Arthur Kill, the New Jersey Meadowlands appears as a jumble of refineries, tank farms, office towers, chemical plants, rail yards, landfills, giant sports arenas, and warehouses that stretch several football fields in length. None of it rests on solid ground. Set against the escarpment of the New York City skyline, these displaced pieces too massive or too noxious to fit within the city or in the backyard of suburbia, rise up from a glacial fen. The complex meanders of the once wild Hackensack River, the streams, points, and sluiceways have been crisscrossed, cut, filled, pushed, dredged, drained, and diked into irregular green pieces now dominated by the common reed—*Phragmites.* Looking at the reedbeds in light of their surroundings raises speculation on the history of toxins that are buried in the mud, what assaults this urban estuarine system endures daily, and the irony of the transformation of New Jersey's Meadowlands into a wasteland. As a wasteland it evokes multiple and interrelated narratives.

These questions mark the beginning of the narratives of the wasteland as elegy, ecological history, progressivist narrative, crime story, and entropic narrative.

WASTELAND AS ELEGY

Amy Clampitt describes the common denominator of the Meadowlands, the *Phragmites,* in her poem "Reedbeds of the Hackensack." These "uncultivated reeds" are actually reminders of something that has been lost. The theme of loss in this poem can be regarded, as Clampitt says, "as a last ditch effort to associate the landscape familiarly known as the Jersey Meadows with the tradition of elegiac poetry" (109). An elegy is a narrative that attempts to reconcile grief and bewilderment of loss by recapitulating the life of the individual or in the case of wasteland elegies, the life of species, places, ecosystems. The resolution hinges on a declaration of belief in immortality, some essence, idea, or memory that lives on despite apparent loss (Tract, 19). Many residents of the Meadows also recall its former life in an elegiac manner.

The opening and closing stanzas from
"Reedbeds of the Hackensack,"
by Amy Clampitt:

Scummed maunderings that nothing loves but reeds,
Phragmites, neighbors of the greeny asphodel
that thrive among the windings of the Hackensack,
collaborating to subvert the altogether ugly
though too down-to-earth to be quite fraudulent:
what's landfill but the backside of civility?

that actual, unlettered entity the asphodel,
may I, among the channels of the Hackensack—
those Edens-in-the-works of the irrevocably ugly,
where any mourning would of course be fraudulent—
invoke the scrannel ruth of a forsooth civility,
the rathe, the deathbed generations of these reeds?

WASTELAND AS ECOLOGICAL HISTORY

To the ecologist and environmental historian, the benign–looking reedbeds of the Hackensack also represent a story of loss and degradation of what had been a more complex estuarine ecosystem—the final scene in a declensionist plot. If you know where to look from the vantage point of the New Jersey Turnpike, the low tide reveals the stumps of cedar trees out beyond the *Phragmites* on the mud flats, remnants of the Atlantic White Cedar swamp, which once covered a third of the area of the Meadowlands.

The ecological history of the Meadowlands reconstructs a creation story of natural history, beginning with the gestural actions of advancing and receding ice sheets, on through epochs of evolutionary change producing an ideal, a pristine functioning ecosystem of marshland and cedar swamp. From this beginning human intervention, in the form of European settlement, initiated a series of crises and a process of decline ending in a compromised system. The cedar swamp was cut down, and after centuries of altering the hydrologic patterns through draining and filling and severely compromising the water quality with pollutants, the native grasses of the salt marsh died. Only a vast lawn of *Phragmites* persists, marking if not a dead end of the Meadowlands ecology at least the dull demise of a diverse marsh that still lives on albeit in debauched form. However, the environmental history is only a very recent and revisionist interpretation of the Meadowlands and other such wastelands. In fact the environmental history is a counter–narrative to progress and its effects.

WASTELAND AS PROGRESSIVIST NARRATIVE

To European settlers, the Meadowlands, like other swamps, barrens, or deserts, appeared as a useless, unproductive, unhealthy impediment in the narratives of progress. From their point of view, the ideal scene at the beginning of the ecological history was a natural wasteland. The moral connotations of such wastes were reinforced by their location beyond the margins of society, the preferred habitat for criminals, the location of noxious industries, and the depository for the poor and the diseased. The rock outcrop known as Snake Hill looms in the background of Meadowlands scenes much like the mountain in Cole's *Course of Empire*. But rather than as some timeless, sacred presence, Snake Hill has served as the site for a sequence of prisons, an asylum, and a quarantine for tuberculosis patients. To reform such a natural waste was an act of improvement that often had heroic or even pious overtones.

The first reformation of this waste took advantage of the fertile soil of the high salt marsh, extracting the native grass, *Spartina patens,* known as salt hay, a high–grade feed for cattle as well as an excellent insulator and packing material. All the salt hay farmer needed to do to "improve" the land for production was to dig ditches to allow the flow of the tide to escape.

Don Smith, a lifelong resident of the Meadows, recalls what it was like when he was growing up. It was through hunting and trapping that he first learned the ecological relationships of the wetlands.

"We had a ditch, it was called the 'riser ditch,' in my backyard. It was the headwaters of Losen Slote Creek. I started catching frogs and turtles, bringing them up in the bathtub. Then I started trapping muskrat and the creek took me further into the Meadows, and as you got older you followed it a little further. As you kept seeking out muskrat it took you to new areas, creeks that you'd never been to before. Then you learned that you found the most muskrat in what we called when we were kids, 'punks,' narrow leaved cattails that were a preferred food for the muskrat. So when you got to an area like that there were a lot of muskrat huts and the trapping would be good. Unfortunately, that part of the Meadows is all gone today, silted in; the *Phragmites* took it over." (Smith)

"MEADOWLAND DEVELOPERS:
THE WIZARDS OF OOZE"
So proclaimed a headline for a 1966 article in *New Jersey Business* that sought to dispel the "myths" that the Meadows were unsuitable for building. According to the author, you did not have to watch your "dream factory or warehouse" sink into the ooze: "few people want to hear the prosaic fact that anything can be built anywhere on the meadows. A fifty-story skyscraper could rest securely on the bogland..." (Cunningham 1966, 19)

"Swamp lands are blurs upon the fair face of nature; they are fever breeding places; scourges of humanity; which instead of yielding the fruits of the earth and adding wealth to the general community, only supply to the neighboring places poisonous exhalations and torturing mosquitoes. They are, for all practical purposes, worthless; and the imperative necessity for their reclamation is obvious to all, and is universally conceded." *Frank Leslie's Weekly*, Nov. 16, 1867 (Cunningham 1959, 18)

Through the efforts of farmers as well as larger scale speculators, the swampland was transformed into a meadowlands. Martin Johnson Heade, who painted similar salt hay marshes in Massachusetts and Rhode Island, also spent time in the Meadowlands. He depicted a pastoral interlude in the narrative of progress (the second phase in Cole's *Course of Empire*), a place of stillness and retreat from the economic enterprise of the city.

But ever larger scale efforts were ventured to "reclaim" areas for salt hay production and farming. The New York Iron Dike and Land Reclamation Company promoted a scheme in the 1860s to build a dike protected by iron plates that were supposedly more economical, less labor–intensive, and muskrat resistant. The claims proved false when the iron cores settled into the underlying peat while muskrat burrowed holes underneath. Draining and diking continued in the early decades of the 20th century, though, this time in the name of health. The Oradell Dam, built upriver to provide drinking water for northern New Jersey, cut off the regular flushing of freshwater to the marshes. Meanwhile, to desiccate the breeding ground of insects, considered to be the carriers of malaria, which afflicted one out of four people in the

Above: Stumps of former cedar swamp revealed at low tide.

Bottom left: Martin Johnson Heade, *Jersey Meadows*, ca.1875–80. (Spencer Museum of Art, University of Kansas, Edith Clark bequest)

Bottom right: The New York Iron Dike and Land Reclamation Company at work on the Meadows. (Used with permission from Robert B. Burnett, ed., *Pictorial Guide to Victorian New Jersey* [Newark: New Jersey Historical Society, 1986]; original in *Frank Leslie's Weekly*)

Above: Fifty-acre landfill in Kearney Marsh (site of Nancy Holt's Sky Mound).

Below: Map of the pattern of landfills, transport corridors, and wetlands in the Meadowlands. (Source: HMDC 1995)

▨	Wetland
■	Solid Waste
░	Hackensack R
⋯	Railroads
╱	Roads

↑ North

area, the Bergen County Mosquito Commission dug over 1,500,000 feet of ditches. In addition, it sprayed 30,000 gallons per year of #2 fuel oil and used crankcase oil on the marshes to control the breeding of insects (Secura).

Despite all these efforts, the Meadowlands appeared on maps as a distinct gap in development, resistant to the progress that had transformed the areas around it. Here, the progressivist narrative was complicated by failures and setbacks that might still be overcome by technology. "Frustration dogged the footsteps and clogged the shovels of every builder and Meadowlands dreamer until recent times, however" (Cunningham 1959, 19). After World War II, with larger earth-moving equipment and an expansive economy, the gaps were filled in by the New Jersey Turnpike, distribution warehouses serving much of the East Coast, Giants Stadium, and the unself-conscious monuments to growth—landfills.

The truncated pyramids of landfills rise in some cases fifteen stories above the *Phragmites* to dominate the Meadows. Built by the garbage of one generation, they displace three square miles of Meadowlands. Unproductive marshland could at least become a useful sink disposing of waste. At its peak in 1968, the Meadowlands received thirty thousand tons per week from over a hundred surrounding communities and out-of-state (New York City). On many of the "dump and push" operations, the garbage was routinely deposited directly into the water, and the piles on top were often burned at the end of the day (Zurn II-2, II-4). As the mounds grew before their eyes, many saw them as the inevitable future of the Meadowlands.

Curiously, the landfills do not appear on topographic maps or they are designated as "park and recreation" zones on land-use maps. There is also no fully documented history of exactly when the dumping began, who was responsible for it, and what the consequences were.

WASTELAND AS CRIME STORY

With illegal dumping and negligence, wastelands can also be told as crime stories—crimes against property, against individuals, and against society and nature. They have always been suspect, but with clear correlations between pollution and disease, growth abnormalities, and death of humans, formerly acceptable behavior is now punishable. Wastelands have victims and perpetrators.

Ecological guilt is defined in federal laws that spell out conditions by which civil and criminal claims can be sought. In the case of the Arthur Kill oil spill, Exxon was found to be criminally negligent, and a civil liability suit to claim natural resource damage was also successful because the impacts could be clearly documented. Through a technique of "fingerprinting,"[4] the oil found in the river and on the birds could be matched with the oil leaking from the pipe, as opposed to all the other suspect oils floating in the river (Burger, 36).

In most cases the culprits and correlations are harder to pin down and the perpetrators are too numerous or have left town. In the Meadowlands there were hundreds of landfill operators, many with alleged links to organized crime. They paid minimal fees to local authorities, who provided virtually no oversight of the operations. There were also hints of collusion. As the dumps were rising, Snake Hill was being leveled, sold for rubble and road material. Anthony Just, the mayor of Secaucus, questioned the ethics of the deal: "The county politicians were responsible for demolishing it...I'll tell you what they did. They said: 'Go ahead and knock it down. Just make sure you see us at the end of the week'" (Stover).

Many landfills remain fenced off in legal limbo as past owners, new owners, or municipalities attempt to shed liability. Information that might be in the public interest is often suppressed. In the Meadowlands a public agency acquired the liability for most of the major dumps. However, numerous "orphan landfills," sites that ceased operation before 1983 and are therefore exempt from regulations, continue to pose unknown threats. These unsolved mysteries add to the uncanny nature of the wasteland.

WASTELAND AS ENTROPIC NARRATIVE

The barren, hacked-at remains of Snake Hill, the uniformity of the *Phragmites*, the rubble of landfills—these are the paradigmatic scenes of entropy. Like the other wasteland narratives, entropy is also a narrative of loss—the loss of energy as it breaks down from more complex organizations into inert unavailable forms. Like ecological history, it can be a critique of progress.

The environmental artist Robert Smithson was fascinated by these sites of entropy, especially as they appeared in science fiction. While Thomas Cole and other 19th—century artists traveled to remote wilderness areas and warned against their destruction, Smithson traveled to New Jersey and scaled fences to explore quarries and dumps. On Saturday, September 30, 1967, he took a bus from New York City to Passaic, New Jersey, which borders the Meadowlands. The trip is described as a tour in an article titled "The Monuments of Passaic," published in *Artforum*. Along the way he skimmed through a paperback science fiction, *Earthworks*, and stopped to photograph a series of ordinary things—waste pipes, dredging derricks, etc.— as monuments in a narrative of a self-destroying world. He later returned to New Jersey for one of his mapping projects, *Entropic Pole*, in which he located the center of an entropic form in the Meadowlands.

From a natural waste that frustrated attempts to improve it to a few tattered remnants of a debased ecosystem, the story of the Meadowlands illustrates a series of wasteland narratives—elegy, ecological history, progress, crime story, and entropy. These narratives, available in many sites, are cumu-

Robert Smithson, *Entropic Pole*, 1967. (Courtesy the estate of Robert Smithson and the John Weber Gallery, New York)

lative, diverse, and interrelated. They are critical for explaining causes, assigning responsibility, influencing actions that shape the landscape, and evaluating the rightness or wrongness of those actions.

PART II: RESTORING THE WASTELAND

By the 1960s, the various forms of destruction accellerated to such a pitch that it looked as if the fate of the Meadowlands would be a final wasteland. However, the extreme magnitude of the problem catalyzed opposition. Scenes of landfills, poisoned waters and loss of wildlife, and frequent fires that shut down the turnpike and rail lines became visible icons in a counter-narrative of the emerging environmental movement which recast the progressivist narrative as the cause of, not the solution to, the problem of the Meadowlands. The attempt to inscribe the wrong story in a landscape that could not sustain it (Cronon) created a scenario for ecological crisis that galvanized reactions for change.

The concerns were not just environmental, however. Even in the 1950s, proponents of development criticized the haphazard, piecemeal development and warned against "offensive industries" that could kill more prosperous enterprise. They called for coordinated planning and regional cooperation that could overcome the limitations of environment (Cunningham 1959).

The impressionable Meadowlands bears the marks of a great diversity of wasteland actions, including dumping, digging mosquito ditches, and filling in for warehouses and transportation corridors. (The site of the HMDC Environmental Center is at the edge of the landfill to the lower left center.)

In 1969, just as a coalition of local groups was forming, the New Jersey legislature established the Hackensack Meadowlands Development Commission (HMDC), the first of only two regional planning authorities in the state, and equipped it with a broad array of powers to change the fate of the Meadowlands. The official mission was threefold:

- To oversee the orderly development of the 32-square–mile Hackensack Meadowlands District
- To manage the flow of solid waste within this district
- To maintain the ecological balance of the district

Efforts to control the dumping ran into significant resistance. Don Smith relates: "In the early days when we went to control them, we had .45s pointed at us. I was turning trucks around at the landfill coming in from New York illegally. Then they want to know where you live. They don't want to know where you live because they want to send you a Christmas card." (Smith)

The HMDC began as a watchdog agency enforcing new environmental laws, pinpointing and monitoring effluent outfalls, closing twenty–four of twenty–five active landfills, cutting the proposals to fill wetlands by two–thirds, and reducing the number of sewage facilities while upgrading the remaining ones. It also took steps to preserve significant acreage of wetlands and wildlife habitat with the 1,400–acre Sawmill Basin Preserve.

These efforts effectively ended the most flagrant excesses of the wasteland practices. However, the Meadowlands had been so damaged that regulation, cleanup, and preservation were not enough. In the 1980s HMDC initiated a series of experiments to put together new ecosystems on the lumpen wastes of landfills, the dredge spoil islands, and the degraded wetlands covered by acres of *Phragmites*. In effect, it began the new narratives of restoration, narratives as vivid and diverse as the wastelands they engaged.

The 110–acre site of Richard W. DeKorte Park at the HMDC Environmental Center focuses the varied scope of restoration[5] efforts in the Meadowlands. To begin with, the selection of this site and the placement of the center were strategic. Located up against the edge of a 200–acre landfill, the center is a literal barrier to the expansion of the dump and a symbolic gesture declaring the end of the history of wasting (HMDC 1993). With its back to the dump, the center looks out over a series of restoration experiments: a tidal mud flat edged by a shore of restored spartina grass, a marshland impoundment resulting from dikes that cut the area off from tidal flow, the "garbage island" reclaimed with several created habitats, and a park on the edge of the landfill with upland successional growth. All of this would have been covered by the landfill.

At this site, throughout the Meadowlands, and in countless other contexts beyond, restoration has become a cultural story with significant import. As an alternative to continued progress that ends in a wasteland and environmentalism that preserves separate enclaves beyond human habitation, restoration offers a mediating role. It reverses the declensionist plot of the wasteland while remaking natural systems in various contexts through direct human manipulation and invention. Since restoration is the goal of an increasing number of projects affecting the future of small communities as well as larger regions, involving significant sums of money, it is important to look at how restoration narratives are told. What metaphors and strategies are invented, sanctioned, and employed, and what values inhere in them? In short, what makes restoration cogent and convincing in response to the long history of forces that have created and continue to create wastelands?

Built literally on wasteland sites, restoration generates new meanings from the remains of the old. By definition, then, it is metaphorical. However, the scientific language of ecology and practical trial–and–error experience often "naturalize" the central metaphor of restoration.

The negative scene at the end of the declensionist plot of the wasteland is transformed, through sophisticated reconstructions, into a healthy, functioning ecosystem resembling the original as much as possible. Nature bears much of the symbolic workload. Associations of death and corruption of wastelands are countered simply by the reappearance of nature, which comes precoded with associations of life, health, morality, history, origins, and local identity. The interlocking of metaphors of wasteland and restoration, death, nature, and life is critical for linking the natural with the moral. The title of the multimedia program at the HMDC Environmental Center, "This Ressurected Land," alludes to this connection.

However, the critical question is, Which nature to restore? Not just any nature, not just

Restoration ecology is defined as "the full or partial placement of structural or functional characteristics that have been extinguished or diminished and the substitution of alternative qualities or characteristics than the ones originally present with the proviso they have more social, economic or ecological value than existed in the disturbed or displaced site." (Cairns, 3)

Richard W. DeKorte Park at the HMDC Environmental Center consists of a series of restoration projects: Kingsland Overlook on the edge of the landfill, Tidal Impoundment with Marshland Discovery Trail linking old dredge spoil islands, Transco Trail, and the Lyndhurst Nature Reserve ("Garbage Island").

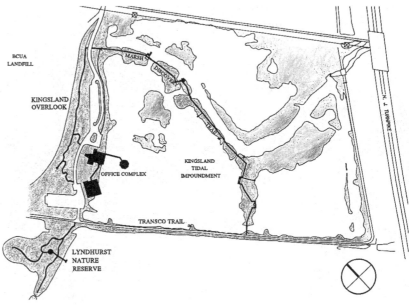

anything green, or the conventions of a pastoral park can be called restoration. Rather than a fallen nature of *Phragmites,* or eastern poplar, restoration seeks a nature before the fall—spartina grasses and Atlantic cedar—native, local, diverse, and healthy ecosystems. It is a selected, manipulated, and in some cases reinvented nature. The choices are as practical as they are ideological. Gathering seeds from local genotypes within a 100-mile radius is necessary in certain cases for successful revegetation, and it also reinforces the ideology of the local versus the exotic. The various types of restoration practices—mitigation, synthetic ecology, regeneration—signify differences in approach, degree of historical authenticity, and models of ecological order, as well as different ideologies of nature and culture. The negotiation and discourse between these differences make restoration a vital work in progress.

The remarkable innovations of just the past decade in restoration should be seen against the backdrop of previous efforts to create a cogent narrative. Restoration is closely linked to preservation as a counter-narrative of progress, pointing to the impacts of what have normally been hailed as human achievements. Through the early warnings of 19th-century romantic artists, such as Cole, and documentations of human impacts on nature by George Perkins Marsh, preservation began to rewrite the progressivist plot. In this context Olmsted worked extensively in the blighted margins of growing industrial cities, restoring Boston's Fens, for example, to replicate the contours, hydrology, and vegetation of a natural salt marsh, which would also slow runoff and reduce groundwater pollution. At about the same time, in 1892, and on a much larger scale, New York State drew a line around an area that had been denuded by lumber barrens, causing major erosion on steep mountains, silting, and flooding, which threatened water supplies to major cities. The line defined the Adirondack Park, an area larger than Glacier, Grand Canyon, Yellowstone, and Yosemite National Parks combined, a mix of public and private land—not a park preserve—that Bill McKibben declared as the world's largest-scale, longest-running experiment in ecological restoration (McKibben 1995b).

Restoration is also closely linked with the advance of ecology. In the 1930s and 1940s, Aldo Leopold and ecologists at the Wisconsin Arboretum searched roadsides and old railroad rights-of-way for remnants of prairie species, which they used to systematically re-create a specific ecosystem (Cairns, 16). In the course of their work they discovered the importance of fire in prairie ecology. Thus, instead of only studying undisturbed systems, repairing disrupted sysems became an important tool in ecological research. Restoration, like all narrative, became a means of knowing.

The status of restoration today as a major cultural story is reflected in the diversity of people engaged in telling it, from professional consultants to artists, biologists, farmers, government agencies, local grassroots organizations, and corporations. It is also practiced at a range of scales from the backyard to the continental. In the case of "daylighting" streams in urban neighborhoods, the metaphors of restoration extend to the social sphere of "revitalizing" communities. Certain consulting firms focus almost exclusively on ecological design and restoration, such as Andropogon in Philadelphia, which

Aldo Leopold writes that we should regenerate the land through "the creative use of the same tools which have heretofore destroyed it." (Game Management, xxxi)

"The same intelligence, energy and ingenuity with which humanity subdued the earth is needed now to heal it." (Berger 1990, xxxiii)

gets its name from a species of native grass first to begin succession on disturbed sites. However, because the restoration narratives are constructed through the interaction of cultural and natural processes, there is no single author, but many narrators.

In the Meadowlands there are a variety of groups that have a stake in restoration, ranging from the Audobon Society, to hunting and fishing groups, to fourteen different municipalities, as well as the chamber of commerce, which links restoration to issues of quality of life for attracting businesses. The HMDC, however, is the central planning authority. Within this agency a range of disciplines, including planning, economic analysis, public relations, and education, along with engineers, naturalists, a host of environmental specialists, and landscape architects are involved in the restoration efforts. Thus the restoration narratives are diverse, and localized, and sometimes offer alternative and competing versions.

RESTORING TIME

Like the wasteland, restored sites function as chronotopes, the visible representation of events and time in a new narrative plot. Restoration begins by retelling the history of the wasteland. The necessary site histories assess what has often been sublimated or ignored. A mix of archaeology, ecological history, and forensics, these site histories begin to give a narrative order to the chaos of waste, categorizing jumbled debris, distinguishing red stack slag scraped out from the inside of smokestacks from blue popcorn slag deposited from fly ash, mapping toxic "hot spots" as well as "habitats," and organizing it all into chronological and causal sequences. Out of this emerge stories of unique hybrids and miraculous adaptations, such as vernal pools rich in life caused by the compression of soil by truck traffic or the heron rookery established on the dredge spoil islands of the Arthur Kill. "The imagined wasteland becomes something new and unexpected" (Jordan, 2).

The Kingsland Overlook initiates a sequence of vegetation succession on the edge of a landfill.

RE–SEQUENCING

On these dead–ended sites, out of the stasis of the wasteland entropy, restoration initiates a new sequence of events most legible in the form of vegetation succession. On the six–acre side slope of the landfill at the HMDC, staff landscape architect Katy Wiedel, with landscape architect consultant Helen Heinrich, began the first in a series of experiments of restoring through vegetation succession. The slope follows the classic narrative of ecological succession which proceeds in distinct stages: "pioneer species" quickly "colonize" disturbed ground, building nutrients and establishing conditions that eventually lead to a "climax" condition. It is natural history in the making, a creation story repeating what happens after the disturbances of violent storms, the retreat of glaciers or volcanoes. Only now it follows in the wake of human impact. The wasteland of progress is replaced by the progressive development of nature moving from entropy and simplicity toward greater cohesion, diversity, and stability.

However, as Lisa Cameron, a landscape architect with the HMDC, points out, old landfills if left alone simply do not return to an ideal state of nature. Exposed to wind, dry conditions, shallow soils, and a lack of habitat for song-birds that bring seeds of fleshy-fruited plants, they often remain weedy hills with mugwort and artemisia, which are of little value for habitat and wildlife. On the Kingsland Overlook, the successional process was carefully directed, re-sequenced, and made more legible with five representative communities: two early succession meadows, a late woody field, a young woodland, and a mature forest. These temporal phases of a natural sequence were re-present-ed as a spatial sequence along a trail. Certain successional relationships were set in motion by, for example, planting white clover to fix atmospheric nitro-gen and act as a "nurse cover" for slow-to-establish grasses. In other ways succession was simulated and accelerated. The soil for the woodland section, for instance, which takes decades to develop the necessary organic matter, was simulated with recycled municipal leaf compost. Because it was an early experiment, native plants or seeds were difficult to obtain and some non-native species had to be substituted. Soil depths under each stage vary from 6 inches under the meadow areas to 3 feet in the woodland. The whole project is underlain by a special impervious synthetic cap spun from recycled soda bottles bonded with a standard chlorosulfonated polyethylene liner to pre-vent slippage on the steep side slope (Cameron).

RETELLING ORIGINS

The clear story line of ecological succession gradually effaces the evidence of the wasteland and proceeds toward a representation of a state of nature prior to human disturbance—a return to an original state. This is one of the most compelling narratives of restoration. Philosopher Mircea Eliade has shown that the desire to return to origins whether childhood, historical, or ecological is a powerful story and one that reappears in various cultures. The restored site has particular appeal because it is a point of beginning that can be reinhabited. Describing one restoration, a designer explained that visitors would be immersed in prairie, visually isolated from intrusions so "they will feel they are in native America" (Krohe, 47). Here, nature is metaphorically substituted to represent a former place or time—Eden, Arcadia, a golden age, precontact America, the prairies of the pioneers, childhood.

However, many find the narrative of returning to origins, to a precon-tact, pre-Columbian moment, problematic for several reasons. First of all, there is a degree of nostalgia for an unattainable past as a hedge against the anxieties of the present. More important, the question "Restore to what?" begs questions of humans' place in natural order as well as the very question "What is natural order?" Setting up a nature of pre-European contact as pris-tine ignores the often significant role of Native Americans in shaping land-scapes, even if their changes were of a different magnitude than today's tech-nology (Hanford and Nash, 5). It may also have a nationalistic or ethnocen-tric subtext. In his argument for the restored prairie at the Wisconsin Arboretum, Aldo Leopold described it as "a sample of what Dane County looked like when our ancestors arrived here" (Sachse, 27).

In addition, ecologists who once emphasized the stability of ecosystems and the clear narratives of succession and climax conditions now talk of multiple contingencies and disruptions as the norm. To them there is no fundamental balance of nature, no ideal set of conditions at one point in time or in timeless stasis, only constantly changing mosaics resulting from constant disturbances of different magnitudes (Hanford and Nash, 5).

This question of origins is not just an academic or symbolic issue. The question of "Restore to what?" has social and environmental consequences, not to mention significant implications for the cost of restoration. When nature becomes a measure of health and morality of these actions, it is important to know whose nature and what nature is restored. Frank Kermode's distinctions between different approaches to narrative applies equally well to the different approaches to restoration: "There are those who seek to restore something authentic but lost and those who conclude that the nature...of narrative in general is to be 'open'—continuously modified, indeterminate, provisional" (Kermode, 82).

The issue of origins is especially challenging in the Meadowlands, where the alterations have been extreme, making it next to impossible to bring back the original wetlands and cedar swamp. One of the largest attempts at restoration in the Meadowlands highlights the controversies over a return to natural origins as opposed to restoration adapted to present needs. Few get a chance to see this landscape since it can only be explored by boat. Heading into the Chromakill Creek, the tunnel–like effect created by the *Phragmites* ends abruptly and the meadows take on a more open look. Spartina grass covers a low brackish marsh with a series of channels, islands and mud flats exposed at low tide. Passing under the New Jersey turnpike, additional elements explain the scene further. A billboard aimed at the highway above shows a hand holding an egg–shaped globe with the quote: "Because it should be handled with care...we've donated $5 million to the improvement of the wetlands. Hartz."

This is the "wetland mitigation" site known as Harmon Meadow. Behind the restored marsh is the backside of a $1 billion mixed–use development created by the Hartz Mountain Corporation, one of the largest land developers in the area, which has a less than altruistic reputation. As a condition of approval for filling in 123 acres of wetland, the developer agreed to restore 158 acres of "low–quality marsh" (Smith).

Over the years the HMDC has been successful not only in restoring a certain level of environmental quality, but as its name suggests it has also continued the progressivist narrative by maintaining the economic competitiveness of the region with new development. The Meadowlands sports complex was built in 1976 (not under jurisdiction of the HMDC, however) on top of 3.5 million cubic yards of sand dredged from Ambrose Channel off New York Harbor. The complex has brought national as well as international attention to the area with events such as the 1994 World Cup and a visitation by Pope John Paul II. Because of its proximity to New York City and the infrastructure of roads and rails, the Meadowlands became a real estate hot spot in the 1980s spawning corporate

At the mitigation site of the Harmon Meadow, behind commercial development, the *Phragmites* have been cleared and the land lowered by several feet so that tidal action interacts with a more complex series of islands, channels, and mud flats.

parks with street names like Wall Street West. The HMDC sees this development as necessary for funding ecological restoration of the wetlands, which is too expensive to be supported by the state or federal government.

For those who want to see more protection of what marshland exists, the Harmon Meadows is a questionable site since a low brackish marsh probably never existed there in the first place. From their preservationist perspective, they question any further development that continues to fragment and intrude on the integrity of the remaining marshes. Without a baseline measurement of what is natural, restoration goes down a slippery slope of relativism, where anything might be justified. As Michael Soule points out, such relativist arguments have been assimilated by the Wise Use and Social Ecology and Justice movements to justify further exploitation of the environment (Soule, 160, 161).

But much of the future restoration of the Meadowlands is constructed around this scene. The new master plan (Special Area Management Plan, SAMP) calls for more mitigation and wetland banking as a way to reassemble the critical components of the Meadowlands ecosystem through development. The strategy is to trade low−quality marshland for developer-sponsored mitigation, remaking common reedbeds into higher−quality wetlands. The goal of restoration shifts from one of returning to an authentic past to restoring an ecological system that will function in a dramatically different contemporary context. However, even this is not a simple task. In the summer of 1993 the spartina grass in the Harmon Meadow mysteriously died off.[6]

The substitution of ecological systems for disturbed sites would seem to be a simple plot of reversal working toward closure, like a well−configured story, and in many cases it is just that. The temporal sweep of the transformation is often grand, redressing centuries of abuse and changing the trajectory of history. When asked to comment on the design life of the Wisconsin Arboretum, Aldo Leopold envisioned something that would last "for a thousand ages" (Sachse). Yet, restoration, which weaves cultural time and natural time, remote pasts and indefinite futures, takes on twists and turns, multiple layers of time, and different trajectories. Possibilities and choices arise between many different pasts and possible futures. As the metamorphosis takes time, it is also open to events of indeterminate natural processes creating anything but a linear narrative sequence. In practice restoration becomes a complex narrative.

JUXTAPOSING

These fragments I have shored against my ruin.
    T. S. Eliot

In *The Waste Land*, T. S. Eliot experimented with juxtaposing fragments of dialogue—descriptions of post−World War I cityscapes with images of old pastoral landscapes, and Alpine resorts with deserts, sacred places, and hell. This strategy not only registered the shock of the new, but questioned the relevance of the old order of idealized, traditionally good places (Conron, 5, 6). Abrupt contrasts and jarring sequences are commonplace in the Meadowlands, as well. A train may suddenly wisk through a gap in the *Phragmites*, and above the horizon of salt marsh the sun reflects off silver cars passing silently in the distance on the New Jersey Turnpike.

Juxtaposition is also an effective strategy for staking out the metaphorical route from wasteland to renewal, from where we have been to where we might go. When processes of succession and transformation are so gradual, juxtaposition brings change into clear moments of contrast, as in the view of the wildflower meadow positioned against the scene of the active dump in the background. Likewise, a series of recycled PVC pipes rise up from a restored shoreline of spartina grass to pinpoint landmarks of the Manhattan skyline in the distance.

Juxtaposition opens the discourse of boundaries between nature and culture, past and future, in restoration narratives. In some cases restoration repeats the tendency of preservation to create a separate preserve, a closed ideal realm protected from cultural change. The juxtaposition of restored shoreline with a distant Manhattan repeats the common motif in posters and other popular images—a view from inside nature looking back. Wildlife—a heron or other numen of the marsh—stands silhouetted against a city skyline. However, the distance between the two is so great that it reinforces a discourse of separation or even opposition between culture and nature more indicative of preservation.

The interplay and negotiation with context make restoration inherently different from preservation. Often by necessity restoration sites require connections to context. To begin with, that is where seed sources for new species come from. In restoration nature is rewoven into the stuff of ordinary, real places where it can have critical impact. For this reason, the HMDC has tried to influence the local office parks to replace their manicured lawns with more diverse and adaptive wetland habitats. Bill McKibben, who wrote *The End of Nature*, describes the significance of restoration throughout the settled portions of the East Coast: "Nature's grace in the East offers the most important kind of hope to a world in terrible need of models. For the East is a real place—not a Yellowstone, with clear boundaries to separate people from nature" (1995a, 80).

As habitat reemerges on closed landfills and rights-of-ways, the boundaries begin to be blurred. This ambiguity is evident in the Meadowlands, where a long–distance natural gas transmission line is transformed into a linear island with an undulating restored shoreline (made with biodegradable coconut fiber rolls) and truck turnarounds are remade as distinct habitats: high salt marsh, upland plant communities, and two sand beaches.

In sites such as this, restoration occupies a middle ground between the blunt opposition of nature and culture (an opposition responsible for all the troubled wastelands in the first place). It is a narrative of finding "a more complicated and supple sense of how we fit into nature," according to Michael Pollen (Mckibben 1995a, 80). People play a necessary and positive role in understanding, manipulating, directing, selecting, and in various other means of intervening in the course of natural process. This

Above: PVC pipes on Garbage Island pinpoint landmarks on the surrounding horizon.

Below: Biodegradable coconut fiber rolls help establish an irregular shoreline edge for an existing utility pipeline. In the background a portion of a truck turnaround doubles as a restored high salt marsh.

anthropogenic nature can be one of degrees, rather than an either/or proposition between pristine or paved.

GATHERING

Because the spatial and temporal connections of the wasteland are fragmented, dislocated, and scumbled, restoration is often about gathering fragments to re−create a sense of wholeness, albeit in miniature form. In a manner reminiscent of what others did for the first Renaissance botanical gardens, which recollected remnants of a shattered Eden, researchers at the Wisconsin Arboretum searched along roadsides and railroad rights-of-way for species that they reassembled in the first large−scale systematic prairie restoration.

Above: The Lyndhurst Nature Reserve, also known as Garbage Island, gathers and miniaturizes several regional habitats in the restoration of what was once an illegal dump.

At the HMDC center a similar strategy of gathering and reassembling remnants was used to restore what was a dump. The Lyndhurst Nature Reserve, or "Garbage Island," as it is known, compresses a restored brackish wetland ecosystem along the island's edge, two sand beaches, a northeast woody plant community, a high salt marsh fringe, an eastern coastal prairie, a bayside shrubland, and an ephemeral freshwater pond onto 3.5 acres of a former illegal landfill. Each of these habitats is a synecdoche, a piece of what has been reduced to remnants in the larger landscape but brought together here in a unified microcosm.

The island makes an especially pertinent symbol for ecosystem unity and fragility. Islands have become the spatial synecdoche for explaining what is happening to ecosystems on the larger scale. Ecologists warn that continued development that subdivides and fragments ecosystems, in effect making them islands, exposes species to predation and other stresses and interrupts the movement of populations. Fragmented ecological islands are also more exposed to greater levels of pollution and noise.

A TREE STORY

Don Smith, long time resident and naturalist for the HMDC, found the trunk of a 254−year-old Atlantic white cedar. The tree is now located at the edge of a restored salt marsh shoreline on Garbage Island, where it serves as a relic of the original cedar swamp, a witness to change, and as he imagines, a character in a children's story.

"Well what I thought I'd do is start it out by the big cedar log I dragged over to the park. It was stuck in the mud for a long, long time, and the turnpike came along and unearthed a lot of them and made them available to float. This one was in the tidal flats. I had my eye on it for a year, but then a storm washed it up to a spot near the turnpike where I could get at it with the boat.

"I thought a story might start out when I was leaning over the log, tying a rope on it, and I hear a voice from the log, telling all the history it had locked up inside it, starting back from when it was a seedling underneath the parent tree about the time Columbus sailed.

"One day a deer approaches it and just as it's about ready to nibble on it, there's a thud and the deer falls to the ground with an arrow in it." This episode leads to a description of the Lene Lenape who lived an idyllic existence in nature. A storm knocks down the parent tree and "things are disrupted for a while. The eagles return that year but can't nest in the tree and have to go to another place. But the light that's let in allows this tree to become larger than all the others around. It's in the right place, the lucky spot, and it grows eventually to take the place of the old tree. The cycle's completed in its growth when the eagles return to nest.

"Then there are strange noises and voices. The trees are being cut by European settlers who show no respect for the land. They actually attack the cedar forest. They set the trees on fire in dry years because outlaws hide there, not too far from New York City, where there is wealth and money.

"It comes down to there being very few cedars left. Because it was so big and the farthest one out there, this one was hard to get to. It wasn't cut, it fell— the roots are still intact. Cedars on the edge of a forest are subject to wind damage and blowing over because they are shallow rooted. This tree was exposed because all the trees are cut down around it, so it's vulnerable to the wind. I suspect it fell 250 years ago. It lay buried in the mud until some guy who was digging for the turnpike pulled the tree up, and the tree, after being buried for so many years—the light hits it again and it is exposed to all the changes that have taken place.

"I have a lot of true stories... that's the only fictional one."

Recognizing similar patterns throughout the Meadowlands and the failure of isolated, piecemeal mitigation projects, the new HMDC master plan has as one of its principal goals limiting the fragmentation of habitat and reconnecting areas, to create whole systems. The plan gives figural unity and ecological connectedness to what was only ambiguous space sliced up by random vectors of freeways and railroads and pushed to the margins by office parks, warehouses, and dumps. In an interesting reversal of current planning trends, the goal of restoring the unity of the natural systems precludes the development of a traditional town center. Instead, the master plan calls for clustered nodes of development.

REVEALING

In the attempt to restore ecological systems and create narrative unity, there are inevitable erasures and maskings of the wasteland. The revegetated slope of the edge of the landfill at the HMDC center hides views of the massive landfill, concealing this essential part of the site's history. The gardenlike quality of these six acres is perhaps a cheerful but misleading scene given the enormity of the problem on hundreds of other acres and orphan sites. The anomalies of vent pipes and collection troughs for leachate peek through the successional vegetation, but they are not explained. Instead of exposing the encapsulated layers of landfill, a difficult and risky engineering task, the HMDC developed the "trash museum" to reveal the contents. However, it does not display the accurate proportions of paper and other kinds of waste, nor does it depict the ooze and decay.

Some restorationists argue for acknowledging and telling the whole tragic history of wasteland sites, rather than concealing them under a mantle of green. Landscape design is too often used to wipe out technological guilt rather than raise awareness (Engler, 24). To restore yet reveal the wasteland is a more complex narrative of both reversal and reminder. Perhaps because the Meadowlands is so filled with reminders, the HMDC center offers a necessary escape and respite. Still, there are traces of memory. The Marsh Trail connects a series of dredge spoil islands and reveals the course of an "extinct" creek, which disappeared when the area was impounded and submerged as a result of a dike built for a utility right-of-way.

THE WASTELAND NARRATIVES OF GEORGE HARGREAVES
The work of the HMDC is part of a larger dialogue in other projects and contexts across the country. The work of George Hargreaves in particular offers an approach to the complexity of the narratives with no intention of completely concealing wastelands or regaining a lost Eden. In the mid–1980s his office took on a series of typical derelict sites, two landfills and a neglected urban river. This trilogy, Candlestick Point Park, Byxbee Park, and Guadalupe River Park, is accessible from the freeway system that runs from South San Francisco, which bills itself as the Industrial City, southward around the bay to San Jose and the heart of "Silicon Valley."

These three projects are topographic narratives about the making and remaking of land, a hybrid interaction of cultural and natural forces. The landforms tell of genesis from wind and water, yet boldly display human abstraction, intentions, and use. At Guadalupe River Park, for instance, the forms and patterns are derived from sandbars typical of braided western rivers with their narrow ends pointing upstream, which are abstracted and engineered to both magnify their reference to natural process and serve as a "deconstructed levy," a practical flood–control device dispersing and slowing floodwaters, similar to how braided rivers work in the first place. The landform at Byxbee Park reflects the deposition of garbage as well as the action of wind. A series of hillocks on the tops of the mounds reflect wind erosion with their steeper lee slopes pointing in the direction of the prevailing wind. They also refer to various human–shaped landforms, from the shell middens of the indigenous cultures to the repetitive patterns of mine tailings or the still active process of dumping and piling of garbage and fill immediately visible on the active landfill adjacent to the park.

The landform sets up the elemental conditions for new processes to emerge from the interaction of water, wind, and land. At Byxbee a series of concrete weirs cross the swale line to capture moisture, collect sediment, and create conditions for differences in plant succession. Likewise on the lee sides of the hillocks different wind and moisture will favor certain species and patterns of growth. There are no precise controls, no invidious distinctions to select and encode only the native or the original. The boundaries are not predetermined, they happen. "I'm setting up a framework on the land. Then vegetation, people and water wash over it" (Beardsley, 50). Rather than composing and controlling a representation of some original, historic nature, this landscape of events happens in the present, in the given disturbed conditions of the wasteland, and works toward an indeterminate future.

Natural process is not simply opposed to the cultural but emerges within and out of the cultural story of the wasteland. The palimpsest of cultural memories comes through and is readable in the signatures of landforms, fragments, and design interventions. At Candlestick Park there is an area of concrete rubble, twisted rebar, and unidentifiable debris that has not been covered by a legible geometry or smoothed into streamlined forms. In this domain of feral cats, the uncanniness of the wasteland still haunts such sites. What lies beneath the surface is revealed rather than glossed and sublimated. At Byxbee a keyhole shaped gravel area next to the methane gas disposal unit catches the shadow of the flame, otherwise invisible by daylight, produced from the decomposing trash underneath. The references point not only to buried histories but to current realities of the immediate context. The "Jersey Barriers" at Byxbee line up in a chevron, referring to the Southshore Freeway audible in the near distance, and align with the landing route of the adjacent airport. In aeronautical language the chevron say "Do not land here."

Against these fragments of an industrial history, Hargreaves encodes reference to a time before, with landforms as icons of prehistoric time. The monumental inclined plane of Candlestick implies a fixed time resistant to ephemeral change. Likewise, a large spherical mound rises out of a miniature representation of a braided flow at the center of Guadalupe Courtyard Park. These monumental earthworks add another cultural reference and an expanded sense of time commensurate with the scale of the wasteland.

Top: Candlestick Point Park.

Center: Jersey Barriers used as a folly in Byxbee Park.

Above: Accentuated forms of a braided river at Guadalupe River Park.

INTEGRATING WASTE

In many respects Hargreaves' work owes many of its themes and strategies to that of the early earthworks artists; in particular Robert Smithson's monumental–scale earthworks and use of prosaic icons of wastelands (Jersey Barriers). Nancy Holt,

Above: Nancy Holt, Sky Mound, Sun Viewing Area with Pond and Star Viewing Mound, 1986. A 57-acre 100-foot-high landfill. (Courtesy John Weber Gallery)

Below: View of Methane Wells on Sky Mound.

married to Smithson at the time of his death, engaged wastelands in her artwork as well. Before Hargreaves began his work in the Bay Area, she was invited by landscape architect Cassandra Gates of the HMDC to develop a plan for the 1-A landfill, which became known as Sky Mound.

Holt substituted the landfill vernacular of methane wells, vents, and earth mounds for the megalithic alignments of prehistoric cultures. Like some neo-Stonehenge, Sky Mound is oriented to cyclical events of the sun, moon, and stars as well as spectacular views of Manhattan, Newark, and the rest of the meadows. The second phase (which has not been funded) will reveal the inner workings of the mound. A steel measuring pole will mark the original height and gradual settling of the mound as organic matter decomposes.

RECYCLING

Sky Mound celebrates the common vernacular forms of methane "mining" of landfills, expressing another restoration strategy—recycling. Sky Mound is part of a network of three sites on 400 acres of landfill that produces enough methane to supply the energy needs of some 10,000 homes. Plans are to double the amount of production. It recycles the waste in various systems to control air emissions from the landfills and reduce the effects of gases on vegetation. This also provides revenue to the HMDC that supports other restoration projects (HMDC fact sheet, 1994).

Recycling transforms restoration. Rather than re-creating nature, it integrates with ongoing human activities. Other recycling efforts include a vegetative composting program and a proposal for a Recycling Industries Complex to make end-use products that recycle material from the region instead of importing and consuming products from other places. Recycling reconnects the rupture between consuming and wasting, often disguised by restorations or parks, so that restoration not only heals the past but reconnects cultural practices with natural processes of energy flows and decomposition, for mutual benefit.

RE-VISIONING THE WASTELAND

The view from Garbage Island recapitulates the primary scenes of the Meadowlands' story and the narratives of restoration. Against the backdrop of the Manhattan skyline, the New Jersey Turnpike arcs above what's left of Snake Hill. In the immediate foreground, low tide reveals the stumps of the original cedar swamp. In the effort to inscribe the narratives of progress on the very impressionable marshland, the Meadowlands remained a constant challenge, a frustrating zone of resistance. Uncared for and apparently unproductive, it became a logical site for depositing the wastes that everyone wanted to distance themselves from. The Meadowlands became a counter-arcadia, "Manhattan's moat of stinks" (Clampitt, 79). Both respons-

es, to reform a perceived natural waste into a productive land or to fully waste unproductive marsh, denied the ecological realities of the place.

Garbage Island re–creates a vision of the ecological realities that have been lost. Here is a well–told story with snapshots of remnant ecologies gathered and organized into a clear sequence. It is a necessary fiction, however, that serves as tangible reminder of what was and feeds the imagination with the potential to reverse what seemed impossible only a few years ago.

Surrounding the imploded scene of the island is the panorama of the Meadowlands and the larger challenge for creating an effective restoration narrative. Out there the picture does not have a clear beginning, middle, and end. After hundreds of years of abuse, it is impossible to restore the past. Rather than creating carefully contrived images, the task is one of experimenting and inventing a future script negotiated in the particular social realities of the Meadowlands. Places like the Meadowlands are critical in developing new narratives that not only restore ecological processes but reconfigure the human relationship to nature. It is precisely because the Meadowlands is at the margins that it offers a freedom to experiment with new metaphors and rework old stories, beyond conventional restraints of the city center or the suburbs. Here, in this lacuna, restoration engenders a range of possible stories: preserving remnants, retelling origins, revealing and critiquing the wasteland, reworking the ends and beginnings of the cultural narrative of progress, integrating processes of decomposition and decay, or inventing new stories of interdependence. All these stories effectively end the wasteland not by denying it but by lifting the cordons of fear and shame and engaging it (Engler). As Bill McKibben concluded, restoration in places like the Meadowlands is a narrative of hope in a world desperately in need of new stories (1995a, 83).

NOTES

1. *Kill* derives from the Dutch word for river or creek.

2. Karl Alderson was responsible for organizing, designing, and implementing the planting program for the Parks Department.

3. The idea of cultural history as a sequence of stages goes back to classical antiquity and spans centuries of writing from Hesiod to Varro and Seneca. Hesiod defined five stages of human history beginning with the golden age, followed by the silver and bronze ages. As in Cole's work, the plot becomes declensionist, beginning with the race of demigods and ending in the contemporary iron age (Glacken, 132).

4. Fingerprinting oil is based on comparing chromatographic patterns of oils (Burger, 36).

5. We are using *restoration* in an inclusive sense, as any action that seeks to reverse the plot, conditions, actions, and meanings of wastelands. The distinctions that various professionals make between restoration, mitigation, reclamation, rehabilitation, and so on reflect important differences in ideologies and discourses concerning nature, culture, and history.

6. Restorationist Dan McHugh believes the death of the spartina could have resulted from hydroseeding without using local genotypes. He recommends instead planting with spartina seedlings and establishing habitat for mussels.

REFERENCES

Analysis of Alternative Solid Wastes Management Systems for the Hackensack Meadowlands District. 1970. Trenton, N. J.: Zurm Environmental Engineers.

Bakhtin, M. M. 1981. "Forms of Time and Chronotope in the Novel." In *The Dialogic Imagination: Four Essays by M. M. Bakhtin,* ed. Michael Holquist, trans. Caryl Emerson and Michael Holquist. Austin: University of Texas Press. Pp. 84–258.

Beardsley, John. 1995. "Poet of Landscape Process." *Landscape Architecture* 85(12):45–51.

Berger, John, ed. 1990. *Environmental Restoration: Science and Strategies for Restoring the Earth.* Washington, D.C.: Island Press.

———. 1992. "The Hackensack River Meadowlands." In *Restoration of Aquatic Ecosystems: Science, Technology and Public Policy,* ed. Committee on Restoration of Aquatic Ecosystems. Washington, D.C.: National Academy Press.

Burger, Joanna, ed. 1994. *Before and After an Oil Spill: The Arthur Kill.* New Brunswick, N. J.: Rutgers University Press.

Cairns, John Jr., ed. 1988. *Rehabilitating Damaged Ecosystems.* Vol. I. Boca Raton, Fla.: CRC Press, Inc.

Cameron, Lisa G. 1995. "Experimental Park Grows on a Landfill." *Public Works,* June, pp. 48–51.

Clampitt, Amy. 1985. *What the Light Was Like.* New York: Alfred A. Knopf.

Conron, John. 1973. *The American Landscape: A Critical Anthology of Prose and Poetry.* New York: Oxford University Press.

Cronon, William. 1992. "A Place for Stories: Nature, History, and Narrative." *Journal of American History* (March):1347–1376.

Cunningham, John T. 1959. "Reclaiming the Meadows." *Newark Sunday News,* Feb. 22.

———. 1966. "Meadowland Developers: The Wizards of Ooze." *New Jersey Business* 12(8):19.

Douglas, Mary. [1966] 1980. *Purity and Danger: An Analysis of the Concepts of Pollution and Taboo.* Binghamton, N. Y.:Vail-Ballou Press.

Eliot, T. S. 1934. *The Waste Land and Other Poems.* New York: Harcourt, Brace and World.

Engler, Mira. 1995. "Waste Landscapes: Permissible Metaphors in Landscape Architecture." *Landscape Journal* 14(1):11–25.

Epstein, Nadine. 1995. "The Mysterious Meadowlands: A Secret Garden Amid Urban Sprawl." *America West Airlines Magazine,* August.

Glacken, Clarence. 1976. *Traces on the Rhodian Shore.* Berkeley: University of California Press.

Hackensack Meadowlands Development Commission. 1993. ASLA Awards submittal.

———.1994. Fact sheets.

———. 1995. Draft, Environmental Impact Statement for SAMP.

Hanford, Jim and Linda Nash. 1995. "Cosmopolitan Nature: Environmental Restoration and Design in the Urban Context." *On the Ground.* 1(2):5,6.

Harker, Donald, Sherri Evens, Marc Evans, and Kay Harker. 1993. *Landscape Restoration Handbook.* Boca Raton, Fla.: Lewis Publishers.

Hayles, N. Katherine. 1995. "Searching for Common Ground." In *Reinventing Nature? Responses to Postmodern Deconstruction,* ed. Michael E. Soule and Gary Lease. Washington, D.C.: Island Press.

Jordan, William R. 1991. "Editorial: The Pastoral Experiment." *Restoration and Management Notes* 9(1):2-3.

Kermode, Frank. 1981. "Secrets and Narrative Sequence." In *On Narrative,* ed. W. J. T. Mitchell. Chicago: University of Chicago Press. Pp. 79–97.

Krohe, James Jr. 1992. "Return to Native America." *Landscape Architecture* 82(2):44–47.

Leopold, Aldo. [1933] 1986. *Game Management.* Madison: University of Wisconsin Press.

Lynch, Kevin. 1990. *Wasting Away,* ed. Michael Southworth. San Francisco: Sierra Club Books.

Mason, Doug (principal, Wolfe/Mason Assoc. Berkeley, California). 1995. Telephone interview, July 22.

Matilsky, Barbara. 1992. *Fragile Ecologies: Contemporary Artists' Interpretations and Solutions.* New York: Rizzoli.

McKibben, Bill. 1995a. "An Explosion of Green." *Atlantic Monthly*, April.

———. 1995b. "Letter to Editor." *New York Times*, November 17.

Melosi, Martin. 1981. *Garbage in the Cities: Refuse, Reform, and the Environment 1880–1980.* College Station: Texas A & M University Press.

Miller, David Cameron. 1982. *"Desert Places": The Meaning of Swamp, Jungle and Marsh Images in Nineteenth Century America.* Ph.D. diss., Brown University, Providence, R. I.

Nabham, Gary Paul. 1991. "Restoring and Re-storying the Landscape." *Restoration and Management Notes* 9(1):3–4.

"Narrative of Landscape Forum." 1994. In *Tract.* Published by Department of Landscape Architecture, Ryerson Polytechnic University, Toronto.

Oakes, Baile, ed. 1995. *Sculpting with the Environment: A Natural Dialogue.* New York: Van Nostrand Reinhold.

Rainey, Ruben. 1994. "Environmental Ethics and Park Design: A Case Study of Byxbee Park." *Journal of Garden History* 14(3):171–178.

Rathje, Williams, and Cullen Murphy. 1992. *Rubbish! The Archeology of Garbage.* New York: HarperCollins.

Register, Richard (founder, Ecocity Builders, volunteer coordinator for restoration of Codornesis Creek, Berkeley, California). 1995. Interview with authors, November 22.

Sachse, Nancy D. 1974. *A Thousand Ages: The University of Wisconsin Arboretum.* Madison: Regents of the University of Wisconsin.

Sebold, Kimberly. 1992. *From Marsh to Farm: The Landscape Transformation of Coastal New Jersey.* Washington, D.C.: GPO. U.S. Department of the Interior.

Secura, Robert (environmental educator, HMDC). 1995. Interview with authors, August 7.

Smith, Don (naturalist, HMDC). 1995. Boat tour of the Meadowlands with authors, July 20.

Smithson, Robert. 1967. "The Monuments of Passaic." *Artforum,* December.

Soule, Michael E. 1995. "The Social Siege of Nature." In *Reinventing Nature? Responses to Postmodern Deconstruction,* ed. Gary Lease and Michael E. Soule. Washington, D.C.: Island Press. Pp. 137–170.

Stover, Mark. 1996. "Snake Hill, Mountain of Memories." *New York Times* (New Jersey ed.), April 7.

Tsai, Eugenie. 1991. *Robert Smithson Unearthed: Drawings, Collages, Writings.* New York: Columbia University Press.

U.S. Environmental Protection Agency, Region II, and U.S. Army Corps of Engineers, New York District. 1995. *Draft Environmental Impact*

Statement on the Special Area Management Plan for the Hackensack Meadowlands District, New Jersey.

Vaccarino, Rossana. 1996. "Re-made Landscapes." *Lotus International* 87:82–107.

Wiedel, Katy (landscape architect, HMDC). 1995. Interviews with authors, June, July, August.

Worster, Donald. 1993. *The Wealth of Nature: Environmental History and the Ecological Imagination.* Oxford: Oxford University Press.

CHAPTER NINE

WRITING HOME

HOMElessness, the loss of stable place-bound identity, is a pervasive theme of modern experience. While periodic displacements by war, famine, and economic fate have occurred throughout history, critics of industrialization, and its decline, point to more fundamental conditions of homelessness resulting from mobility, alienation, and destruction of shared memory. In this narrative the advent of the railroad, steam power, and banking systems in the 19th century shattered the heterogeneous landscape of distinct villages, and regions differentiated by climate, food, language and custom (Nash, 7–10). Local power, authority, and distinctiveness were superseded, absorbed, and homogenized by a new network of mass-produced goods and labor, controlled by long-distance capital.

This now familiar story of displacement from home provides the foundational ideology for a significant number of 19th- and 20th-century movements in the allied design professions, most notably regionalism, preservation, and the urban parks and City Beautiful movements. The themes continue to resonate through books such as Michael Hough's *Out of Place* or James Howard Kunstler's *The Geography of Nowhere*, which enumerate an expanded list of threats including: information technology and the collapse of space and time, international-style modernism, tourism, Disneyfication, museumification, and utopianism. Their design proposals attempt to negotiate a difficult course, trying to establish a sense of identity, continuity, and rootedness of the premodern while avoiding a nostalgic return or postmodern simulation.

In the face of these circumstances, the attempt to maintain or re-establish home is one of the more compelling stories being worked out in various contemporary projects. People in search of the small-town ideal "discover" the backwater places, forgotten by the mainstream of progress, such as Pocatello, Idaho, or Metamora, Indiana, and in so doing significantly remake these places. The strategies of the historic preservation movement and the recent development of heritage regions address notions of historic continuity from the scale of the house to Main Street and the vernacular region. Meanwhile, designers reinvent the past in major new projects of New Regionalism and neotraditionalism. In the related movement of Bioregionalism, the desire to reinhabit nature draws on the metaphors of home in such titles as *Boundaries of Home* and *Home! A Bioregional Reader*.

Four Letters Home, written by Wilfred E. Holton, Ph. D., professor of sociology at Northeastern University, tells how a sequence of groups (New England farmers, Irish, Polish Jews, southern blacks), from the early 1800s to the present, made the Roxbury part of Boston their home. The letters are inscribed in granite outside of the Ruggles Station transit station as part of a series of projects along the Orange Line coordinated by UrbanArts, a nonprofit agency. The following excerpts tell of changes wrought by transportation technology.

(Continued overleaf)

Above: Karen McCoy, *Uprooted*, 1994; Krakeamarken sculpture park, Randers, Denmark.

(Continued)

April 30, 1834
To Wendell Jones
Vassalboro, Maine
Changes are coming to our small town.
The big news these days in Roxbury is
that a railroad from Boston to
Providence, in Rhode Island, will be
started within a year. The plan is to
have a trestle across Back Bay marsh
and run the rail south through the
Stoney Brook valley. It will come near
our farm and perhaps force us to move.

July 16, 1886
To Patrick Kelley
Kilcogan, County Galway, Ireland
We try to take the family on a horsecar
ride some Sundays after Mass. Recently
we went up to Franklin Park, which is
now being finished at the edge of
Dorchester.
....More telephones are being put in
all the time. Many new 3-family houses
are going in on farm land.

February 2, 1960
To Albert and Hattie Robinson
Pleasant Hill, Georgia
Change is coming. We hear that two big
highways will be built and join at the
corner of Ruggles Street and Columbus
Avenue. Our building will probably be
torn down in a few years for the Inner
Belt Highway.

THE CHRONOTOPE OF HOME

The narratives of home are about identity sustained over time, in place, and between a group of people. Just as the storyteller in oral tradition embodies the collective memory, home is both the container and the content of the narratives of identity and continuity. And the scale of this container is elastic. As geographer David Sopher noted, home in English and Germanic languages extends the familiarity, security, and sentimental associations known at the scale of hearth and home to the street, neighborhood, hometown, region, homeland, and for some the biosphere. At each scale it contains different social institutions, family, kin, community, folk, nation (Sopher, 130, 131).

Home is also a center. As mentioned, the hearth is a primary metonymy of home and all its associations. The *fire* of the hearth is also the root of the words *focus* and *foyer*, and in a sense the home is a focus, a center around which the experiences of a person's life, family, or community gather (Paulson, 85, 86). In this manner, Jens Jensen's council rings attempt to recall the ideal of a Native American community gathered around a campfire. Other metonyms of home such as the table, the church spire, the plaza, or the family farm mark organizing centers of experience.

The practices of making a home attempt to anchor the dissipation of time to the stability of place. The suffix of *homestead* has archaic origins for making a stand (steadfast) not only in place but in time. The metaphor of rootedness signifies the notion of an organic connection with soil, environment that grows and deepens over time. It takes time to establish the boundaries of home, and they persist often longer than built forms. It also takes sufficient time to come to know the multilayered and densely textured stories of the home place. Making a home, therefore, establishes a unique set of geographic and temporal circumstances, which are not always easily replicated or exchanged.

Home often tends toward the conservative, toward time as a cycle enforcing a return to a center, as opposed to progressing away. And the desire to return, the journey home or "nostos," is an ancient story, forming the root of nostalgia. It is also reenacted every time a baseball player circles the bases and returns....to home. For these same reasons home can also be the place to leave, to escape. Home is also where one starts from.

HOME TRUTHS, CONTESTED TURF, AND NECESSARY FICTIONS

This chapter examines the narratives of home as they are constructed and told in a series of three sites: a small town preserving its sense of history, a new town replicating traditions of home and community, and a community resisting displacement from their home. Since so many relationships of personal identity, ethnicity, class, and gender inhere in the notion of home, it is imperative to examine how the different narratives reflect and shape these values. The narratives of home attempt to ground values in fundamental terms such as nature, biology and history. The continuity of home naturalizes ideologies, or to use the colloquial, they appear as "home truths." However, as much as anything, home is about the very process of creating boundaries between self and other, inside and outside, center and not-center. Therefore, it becomes a privileged place, but also a contested place.

Despite these challenges, home is a necessary fiction that makes the world habitable. The stories of home are not only *about* shared identity and continuity but they contitute these qualities. The very act of making stories reinforces, challenges, and shapes the notion of home. As Barbara Johnstone writes, "A person is at home in a place when the place evokes stories.... In an important sense, a community of speakers is a group of people who share previous stories, or conventions for making stories, and who jointly tell new stories" (Johnstone, 5).

A GOOD PLACE: THE IDYLLIC NARRATIVES OF CAZENOVIA, NEW YORK

Standing on the village green of Cazenovia, in central New York, twenty miles from Syracuse, the leader of a walking tour, a retired history teacher, asks the group from the Newcomers Club to look down the main street and note what is missing. Besides the lack of neon or a McDonald's someone finally notices the lack of overhead wires. The tour guide explains that the wires were always underground, part of a traditional concern for an aesthetic unblemished by modern technology. And the neon signs? They were removed in the 1960s in one of the first preservation efforts of that decade. This moment of introduction presents Cazenovia as a distinctive place, a place of history and tradition, resistant to forces that have destroyed other such places. It is these qualities that have attracted these newcomers from Atlanta, Chicago, New Jersey, a suburb of nearby Syracuse, and a small rural town just down the road to buy a home and a piece of this community heritage.

Most introductions to Cazenovia ask, rhetorically, what makes it a special community.

> Cazenovia, New York, is an unusual community. To the casual passerby it is notable for its lack of fast food stands as well as many other detractions of modern strip development....
>
> The Township of Cazenovia is an enigma. Similar communities have existed elsewhere but most have either been absorbed into anonymous metropolitan areas or withered away from lack of economic sustenance. (Grills 1986, 5)

IDENTITY TOLD IN LOCAL, NATIONAL AND ANCIENT STORIES

For Cazenovians the explanation of the village's unique identity lies in a tradition of three interrelated narratives: history, community, and nature. First, the ideal home is often imagined to be located somewhere in the past, and this narrative has influenced the preservation of Cazenovia's historic landscape. Much of the village and surrounding landscape is officially designated as a historic district by the National Trust for Historic Preservation or by local recognition. This history is actively produced by a not-for-prof-

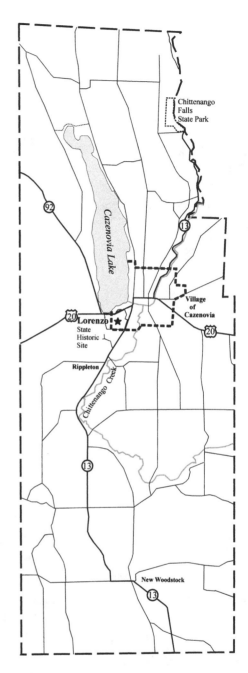

Location map. The village is situated to the east of the lake in the Town (township) of Cazenovia (Fritz 1996; SUNY CESF).

Above: The Fourth of July parade past the village square.

Below: Milo Stewart, *View of Cazenovia from the West Hill.* Oil on canvas, 1848. The village spires are visible in the middle ground, and the Lorenzo mansion is to the right of the road. The road is now Federal Highway 20. (Courtesy Lorenzo State Historic Site)

it organization, the Cazenovia Preservation Foundation (CPF), legal and political powers, several local historians, books by amateur and scholarly authors, and artists, as well as in festivals and enacted narratives. Second, the distinct identity of the landscape is considered a reflection of a distinctive community. "Cazenovia has...been blessed throughout its history with *concerned citizens,* who have worked as individuals and in groups to plan its future development and promote the appropriate while fighting the undesirable." As we will describe later, community, here, is largely an extended narrative of family genealogy. Third, Cazenovians protect their natural heritage as vigorously as their history. As a former town supervisor summarized, "Together our environment and our community create a quality of life which is unique" (*Land Use Guide,* ix). The historic village is set in nature, next to a picturesque lake, rolling hills, and a spectacular waterfall—all of which figure prominently in Cazenovia's identity. The lake in particular has been a constant source of uniqueness. Its Indian name, Owaghena, refers to a variety of yellow perch found only in these waters.

These foundational narratives of history, community, and nature establish a sense of distinct local identity and they continue to influence the shape of the landscape. It is difficult to separate them into distinct strands because they cross and weave so, nature, for instance, becomes historicized and community is thought to be both a product of history and at the same time an organic extension of the environment. It should be noted that nature, history, and community are also aestheticized, and contribute to the appreciation of what is often described as a beautiful, picturesque, and charming landscape.[1]

Cazenovia is important to look at not only as a set of local narratives but for how it localizes landscape narratives of national and even Western cultural tradition, including the New England village and the more ancient topos of the idyllic landscape. Visitors can easily mistake Cazenovia with its white church flanking a green, a small college, and pastoral surroundings for a New England village, and they are not far off in historical or ideological terms. The town is a part of upstate New York, which geographers refer to as "New England extended" to describe the westward settlement of people from Massachusetts and Connecticut in the first decades of the 1800s. Besides a geographic connection, Cazenovia also evokes the symbolic power of the New England village imagined as the archetype of an American place-based community, the origin of American democracy, and an ideal combination of city and country (Wood).

The New England heritage and the narratives of history, community, and nature connect Cazenovia, as well, to the traditions of the idyllic landscape. This is a landscape narrative with a long history extending from Theocritus's *Idylls* of ancient Greece to 19th-century romanticism and the contemporary imagination of suburban commuters. Bakhtin describes the idyllic as a narrative of escape from the complexities and fragmentation of city life to a domestic landscape, close to nature, bound and sufficient unto itself, where the continuity of generations can be sustained (Bakhtin, 224–242). Books on Cazenovia with titles such as *Upland Idyll* or *Upstate Arcadia* refer directly to this tradition, and much of the landscape embodies this tradition.

In Cazenovia, then, we can examine a set of culturally dominant narratives—history, community, nature—critical in creating the stability, centeredness, and continuity of home. These narratives are not only important in Cazenovia, but are taken up within professional and academic discourse, from the professional designs of Downing or Olmsted to projects of preservation, neotraditionalism, and regionalism. Since these design ideologies evoke places similar to Cazenovia as models to emulate or translate, it is important to examine how the stories of this place are constructed, as well as critique the values at work in the process.

SYNOPTIC HISTORY: BLURRING TEMPORAL BOUNDARIES

Continuity over time, where the past lives on in the present, is the principle theme of tradition in a place like Cazenovia, and it is continuity that you can see in the landscape. Because the synthesis of past and present is visible in the landscape, we refer to this as a "synoptic narrative." It is an effective strategy repeated in the fabric of daily life of the place. However, one site, the Lorenzo mansion, takes precedence. It occupies a commanding position terminating the view on the long axis of Cazenovia Lake. Built by the town's founder, it also occupies a central position in the local narratives, bringing together historic origins, community memory, and the particular role of nature. Residents advise newcomers that they must visit Lorenzo to understand what the whole of Cazenovia is about.

As one walks through the carefully restored house and grounds of Lorenzo, the site is both text and context (Hugill, 3–10) for recounting the foundational narrative of Cazenovia:

The Lorenzo mansion.

John Lincklaen, a Dutch naval officer representing the interests of Dutch bankers known in the 1790s as the Four Houses, and later as the Holland Land Company, explored, evaluated, and purchased a vast tract of land in upstate New York. This long strip of land resulted from a surveying error and was known as the Road Townships, because sale of these lands was to support the building of roads (Hugill 1995, 33–38).

Given a significant share of land for himself, Lincklaen returned the following spring as chief land agent. "On May 8th. he arrived at the foot of Cazenovia Lake.... Trailing closely behind were an oxcart

Above: Dwight Williams, *Cazenovia Lake from Lorenzo*. Oil on canvas, 1874. (Courtesy Lorenzo State Historic Site)

Below: Contemporary views out to the lake from Lorenzo are now protected by easements and public ownership.

of supplies and a crew of axemen, some of whose descendants, including Freeborns and Sweetlands, still reside in the community" (Grills 1986, 10).

He set himself up not only as land agent but founder and proprietor, reserving the fertile bottom lands at the end of the lake for himself[2] and purchasing significant amounts of land from the state and neighboring landowner (3,475.75 acres) in order to direct the growth of the village and control access to the lake. He built an infrastructure of roads, mills, a distillery and brewery, a store, a potash works, and a church to attract settlers, a practice known as "hothouse" development. With visions of a great city in the wilderness, he wrote to his assistant "...I am now master, and will try to make something handsome of Cazenovia" (Grills 1986, 12). Ten years after he first set foot here, he began plans for building his own permanent home, Lorenzo.

Lorenzo also links this story of origin synoptically with the present story of preservation. The site was "rescued" from subdivision plans in the 1960s when New York State purchased it and "the heirs agreed to donate the entire contents of the mansion to the trust and to sell it a scenic easement to the lake to ensure that both the furnishings and the view would remain unchanged." (Grills 1986, 96). Thus, the visitor can take in Lincklaen's original view of the lake that inspired him to make his home here in the first place. The site is very much a part of ongoing activities and the staging of events that are part of the historic community identity. Throughout the town, history is integral to the fabric of daily life, and the strategies of a synoptic history foster the elision of past and present.

Any change in a synoptic history only reinforces the continuity over time. Lorenzo not only frames the origin and the present but is connected to the other defining moment of Cazenovia's identity, the late 19th century, when some of the East Coast's most wealthy industrialist families came to establish estates, or "cottages," on the shores of the lake in what was known as Summer Colony. As one brochure recounts:

Founded in 1793 on the shores of beautiful Cazenovia Lake, the village first prospered as the economic crossroads of the region. Following the Civil War, the village was discovered by wealthy coastal families who made it their summer retreat.

Today Cazenovia remains a popular summer retreat...

Even when closer readings of history might reveal disruptions, the framing of beginning and end as being similar enforces a sense of continuity. The site manager of Lorenzo, a historian, wrote a more complex tale of change, adjustment, decline, and restoration. Yet, despite all the change, he reasserts the synoptic tradition by ending with the present-day accomplishments of the CPF and other organizations as consistent with the founding vision of the place. In fact, when home is presented as a narrative of sustained resistance to forces of change, it survives the challenges and appears even stronger and more authentic.

Beginning	Origins	Origins	Origins
•	Preservation	Summer Colony	Growth
•		Preservation	Summer Colony
•			Automobile and decline
•			Present threats and recovery
Ending			Preservation

increasing number of events - - - - - - - - - - - - - - - - - ->

Different versions of Synoptic Histories. In each case the ending creates a continuity with the beginning. The story can be expanded by numerous events in between or collapsed, but when framed by the same beginning and end it still tells a narrative of continuity.

The effect of this strategy is to create a sense of historic identity that is stabile over time and inherent in place. It is something essential, inevitable, given. The same strategy applies to the narratives of community and nature. The Cazenovia *Land Use Guide* goes to great lengths to establish a necessary and deterministic link between environment and community. "There is an intangible connection between people's enjoyment of Cazenovia's physical resources—natural, historic, recreational, and scenic— and the strong community spirit that exists, which is evident in the numerous volunteer organizations dedicated to helping the community." While this link is intangible, it was perhaps more visible in the past when the 19th-century community "remained mainly dependent upon its own resources" (*Land Use Guide*, 1). This reflects notions of an organic community often cited in Regionalism.

Also evident in the writing, the brochures, and the tours is an aestheticization of history, nature, and community. As in a synoptic tradition, to the aesthetic gaze these qualities appear unmediated, self-evident, given. As Duncan writes, "To aestheticize something then is to render it naturalized, enchanted or in some cases an object of unquestioned and unarticulated beauty" (Duncan and Duncan, 4).

CONSTRUCTING A DISCURSIVE HISTORY
In effect when these narratives anchor identity to essentialized categories they appear as given or natural. However, identity is never complete in and of itself but is figured in relation to constantly changing circumstances and contexts. Rather than something given, the identity of home is actively conceived, constructed through stories. And it is important to open up the dis-

cursive realm of these stories to see how they structure values, to see what purposes they serve. Rather than just presenting a critique or a means of undermining the authority of these narratives, the intent here is to establish the necessary role of storytelling in the process of forging identity of home and community.

While the identity of Cazenovia is hitched to the certainties of history, community, and nature, one could argue that the strength of its identity comes rather from successful invention, reinvention, or authorship of these narratives. The story of the founding of Cazenovia, for instance, reads like the plot of an idyllic narrative in which, according to Bakhtin, out of an alien and indeterminate world the hero establishes a well-defined place—a local, secure, stable world of family and community where nothing is foreign (Bakhtin, 232). In contrast to closure, a discursive history reveals how the sense of continuity is maintained by selectivity and smoothing over disjunctions. It also contextualizes the narrative. Cazenovia's foundation, for instance, rests less on the influence of an ideal environment or the moral purpose of its founder than on a global system of investment and imperial expansion. Lincklaen, a foreigner who spoke four languages, represented a consortium of some of the world's most powerful bankers speculating in the resources of a new nation (Hugill, 33–35). In this "developer's frontier," tradition was constantly, sometimes radically, reinvented. When Lincklaen's early industrial-based village was bypassed by the Erie Canal, the next generation actively invested in the aesthetic creation of an idyllic landscape that attracted wealthy summer colonists. Whereas the Industrial Revolution

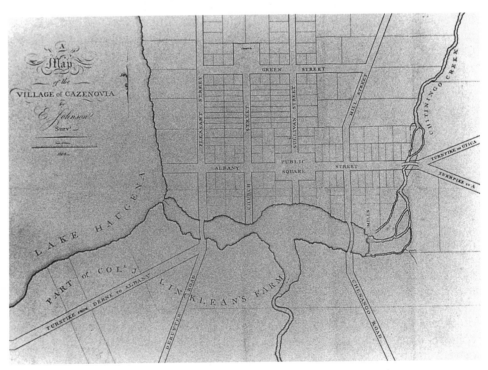

An 1808 plan of the Village of Cazenovia as established by John Lincklaen.

Early on, the scenic quality of the lake was defined, contested, and ultimately controlled by the Lincklaen-Ledyard family. In the 1850s when Henry Ten Eyck planted trees that would have blocked the view of the lake from Ledyard Lincklaen's estate, The Meadows, Lincklaen filed a lawsuit. Lincklaen won the suit, which helped to establish the lake as an aesthetic domain over which his family had control (Hugill, 110–113). (Courtesy Lorenzo State Historic Site)

broke up families and destroyed so many traditional places, here, the summer colonists found a picture of stability, which had actually undergone significant economic and symbolic change. Traditions were reinvented again after World War II, yet to the new commuters Cazenovia appeared a stable vision of the past.

Looked at discursively, the history turns out to be full of discontinuities and contests, rather than a seamless synopsis. Even contemporary debate over the proper style of benches for the main street or about the Victorian additions to Greek Revival homes continues to reconstruct histories. Some attend to very specific historical references, others conflate the town into the general category of "historic." Instead of passively received or simply protected, history is actively made within a social context, often to legitimize the present identity of the community.

(Courtesy W. Chard)

To open the narratives of home nature, history, and community, then, one needs to ask, Whose history is told, how and for what purpose? Whose authority and power are constituted in the telling?

COMMUNITY AS NARRATIVE OF FAMILY GENEALOGY

History, nature, and even community in Cazenovia are linked to one particular family. In a very literal sense, Cazenovia is a "master-planned community," and the authority established by Lincklaen was maintained through a narrative of genealogy for two hundred years. Constituted around the desire to perpetuate the family, genealogy provides the sense of temporal continuity of the idyllic chronotope. But it depends on the metaphors of land-

A view of an Olmsted design for a formal garden with the lake in the distance. (Courtesy W. Chard)

The following oral history is by someone who grew up on one of the largest estates and model farms in Cazenovia. Like many of the other estate owners, this family had genealogical connections to Boston and other parts of New England. The Olmsted office was employed to design the estate.

"The reason they decided to build here was my father's brother was living here at the Barkley estate, and they suggested we look Cazenovia over and pick a nice site and build a home. Katheryn —— was a great friend of Mother's, and they lived next to them outside Boston in Chestnut Hill.

"They called it [this estate] Meadowwood because it was where the meadows met the woods.

"I remember my father saying they had forty Italians from New York digging the cellar hole and they set up a little town of their own down on the flats. It was the first all-fireproof house built in Cazenovia. The front porch and living room looked over the lake, but I don't think you could see the lake now with the trees.

"I remember going down to the Meadows as a little kid. I remember Ethel—and the little theater productions in the barn. They all had French governesses. Tommy spoke French till he was four years old.

"Later on in 1914, my dad had always played polo and he wanted polo ponies, so we bought two. They also imported French Percheron horses and bred them.

(Continued)

scape to locate and root the sequence of generations in place. Since these claims genealogy makes on time and place are hard to replicate, it is a narrative of distinction and differentiation (Hugill 1984). The power invested in genes maintains boundaries between long-term resident and newcomer, elite and other classes, and one ethnic group and another.

In Cazenovia, genealogy served the differentiation of social class and ethnic origins. In his book on Cazenovia, *Upland Arcadia: Landscape, Aesthetics, and the Triumph of Social Differentiation in America*, geographer Peter Hugill meticulously charts how the narrative of genealogy encoded in landscape became a critical means of social distinction. As Hugill notes, Lincklaen became American, native, and regional through a shrewd marriage to Helen Ledyard, a member of an elite New England family. The alliance with old New England stock created a web of kinship that would be a consistent source of identity and power in subsequent generations (Hugill 1995, 42–53). This New England connection also links Cazenovia to an elite that has shaped landscape tastes and design traditions at the national scale.

The necessity to change names, make new alliances with social competitors through marriage, and adopt children to maintain the family line indicates the instability of genealogy and the potential for disruption each new generation brings. Therefore, the landscape was a critical means of encoding stability. From the beginning, Lincklaen made the lake the domain of distinct social status, and for a century only members of the family could purchase land in this realm. Inheritance practices reinforced place bound identity in that the benefits of the family's fortunes were often restricted to those who remained in Cazenovia. After the Civil War, with more fluid capital and the rise of a wealthy industrial class, the summer colonists who came to Cazenovia to build their estates on the lake were accepted and sold land only according to their family status (Hugill 1984).

Despite a decline in numbers and political power, the old elite successfully translated the narrative of genealogy and its goal of social differentiation into a community story. After 1950 the old families formed a new alliance with a class of professionals who commuted to Syracuse. Together they formed the CPF, and through community action they revitalized a distinctive heritage that had started to erode. They created a broad base of support and "democratized" many of the elite concerns (Hugill 1984, 28). Now newcomers and longer-term residents who were never connected to the old elite speak of "our heritage." Yet, this heritage is often a memory trace of the old families. The town offices, for instance, occupy an Alexander Jackson Davis building known as the Gothic Cottage. It was saved from the bulldozer in the 1960s by a descendant of the Lincklaen-Ledyard family who happened to be born there. Family memory becomes town history, and today, traffic court, planning board meetings, and other business takes place in rooms with restored carpets, and furnishings and the portraits of Lincklaen-Ledyards peering from the walls.

Two different landscapes developed on the east and west sides of the lake. On the east were the large estates such as Ormonde *(top)* designed by the well-known architect Frank Furness, for a Philadelphia banker. On the west side, "tenters" from Syracuse spent the summer in more rustic settings. The McClure family, shown *(below)* at their Kosy Kamp also had their picture taken in front of many of the large estates. Those are actually the McClure children appropriating the lawn of Ormonde *(above)* for their picture. (Courtesy Lorenzo State Historic Site)

(Continued)

"There were 300 acres. Five thousand chickens at one time and quite a few farmhands. My father never did any farm work, but I did. I loved working with the horses. I used to drive a pair, then I graduated to the tractor.

"I sailed for a good many summers. We had races on Wednesdays and Sundays. We used to race all around Cooperstown, Skaneateles....

"I worked twenty-five years. I was away so much. I would get up for vacation or week-ends. I would fly up for a weekend myself, and land on the farm. You landed downhill on a little tiny field and you made your approach over Chittanango Gorge.

"I graduated from Harvard Engineering school in 1933 and finally got some money together with the help of the family and got into the auto business. I retired in 1955. I was losing money and had two daughters to put through college. When Mother died in 1963, she left the cottage to Chester. He didn't want the house; he was living on the West Coast so he sold it to me.

"Then B—— bought Meadowood and immediately covered the walls with carpet. He closed the open porch, which looked over the lake. He had nine children and he put in pinball machines and things. People have warned me never to go up and look at the house."

CAZENOVIA'S OTHER

Saving the Gothic Cottage and other preservation efforts are described as the efforts of "concerned citizens" or "thoughtful town residents" (Stokes et al., 90). However, in most cases the projects were defined and spearheaded by members of the elite. Use of "community" here smooths over the social and ethnic diversity of other people who claim this place as a home—descendants of Yankee farmers, working-class villagers, Irish who came as domestic servants, "tenters" who became year-round residents on the lake, commuters from different income classes, and students from a wide range of backgrounds. Many of these Cazenovians do not have the same story or landscape as the elite. Just as this rhetoric renders them invisible, much of their landscape narrative is gone, invisible, or subordinate to the dominant themes.

The sense of a coherent identity, a center, is not complete without the perception of the other, what is not-center. Rather than conceive of otherness as directly opposed to self or community identity, they are in dialogue with each other—every construction of identity implies the other. To para-

Tony is a second-generation Italian who came to Cazenovia and made a living as an upholsterer working for many of the estate owners. He lives alone now at the very southern border of the township. His house is filled with every issue of *National Geographic* since 1909, although he has no intentions of leaving this home.

"My wife came here when she was about seven in 1919. She grew up in what was called Hell's Kitchen in New York. See, you heard of the Fresh Air Fund? Well, she could come up in the summer to a farm near here. She kept coming every summer after. She loved it up here.

"After the war my brother and I decided to go into a partnership in the upholstery business. We came up here and I bought this place and moved in the spring of '47. I started a garden that year and I've had one every year since. This is going to be my fiftieth garden. Not many can say that, so I said I'm going to make it a good one, went all out. I told my daughter to take a picture of me here with a big 50 sign.

"I planted these lilacs thirty years ago, but they got destroyed last winter. They'll grow back, but I won't see it.

"I don't want to go in one of those nursing homes as long as I can live here.

(Continued)

Tony working in his fiftieth consecutive garden.

phrase anthropologist Clifford Geertz, landscapes are stories people tell themselves *and others* about themselves (Duncan 1990, 19).

What is important is the architectonics of the relation between identity and otherness: how the boundaries between them are drawn, the nature of connections, and the ratios of power (Holquist 1990, 29). Cazenovia happens to skew this relationship toward the dominance of an elite group.

Transportation technology played a key role in selecting and controlling who had access to this arcadia. In the 1880s the elite invested heavily in a railroad line that connected Cazenovia to the East Coast cities, the source of wealthy, well-bred summer colonists. However, a competitor and social rival of the Lincklaens built a line from nearby Syracuse that brought "daytrippers," primarily immigrant groups, out to picnic grounds by the lake. These were the very people the elite had abandoned in the city, and these crowds, typically characterized by their loud music, public drinking, and an apparent disregard for nature, represented a moral threat to the idyll. In just a few years this scene was effectively shut down by passing noise ordinances and buying and clearing the campgrounds and building estates in their place. The barge Lakeview was scuttled, and remnants can still be seen in the shallow waters.

Today this is not a gated community. Rather than building a wall, the most effective means of preserving identity is by enlisting participation and consensus on a strong heritage. Since ownership in this place is a mark of social status, many are willing to belong and participate in maintaining its distinctive qualities. Even many Irish who have achieved economic and political status in cooperation with the elite families identify with rather than contest the dominant discourse. Thus, identity is hegemonic; it selects certain narratives and discourses over others. And these are made to seem natural: "there is no need to explain, we all agree" (Duncan and Duncan, 5).

Revealing and concealing boundaries negotiates relationships between others within the community. A designated historic district encompasses 344 properties on the west side of the village, but excludes the working-class homes and remnants of industries of the east side associated with the memory of Irish families. A recent main street design initially extended only to the entry on the west side, not to the east entry, where gas stations, convenience stores, and the fire station have been allowed to develop. The homes on this side do not reflect distinct historic styles, they are not named, but they are connected with other expressions of identity nonetheless. As a parody of the historic markers on the west side that name original 19th-century occupants, one resident on the east side hung out a sign with his own name and date of construction, 1948.

TALE OF TWO PARKS

Two parks, Lakeland Park and Gypsy Bay Park, reflect the issues of otherness, boundaries, and social differentiation. Both occupy key visual positions in the landscape, but their names suggest very different histories of use, preservation, and social position.[3]

Lakeland Park

The first thing the visitor notices entering the park is the long stone wall topped by a wrought iron fence and a sign stating "For Cazenovia Residents Only," along with a list of use restrictions. Inside, despite an extensive lawn, activity gravitates to the water's edge. There are no paths across the interior lawn. The southern edge is defined by a private club and the northern edge by one of the original estates, Willowbank.

How residents use and remember the park reveals differences in social history and the power that the elite tradition has in interpreting and inscribing its memory in the landscape. Long-term residents of middle and lower-middle income remember active summer use along the water's edge. They comment negatively about restrictions throughout the rest of the park forbidding picnicking and ball playing. For these people, who do not belong to either of the two private clubs along the lake, the park is an important recreation space. Other long-time residents, members of the upper income groups and those involved in preservation, remember Lakeland as the name of the old estate that stood on this site (Maroun, 3–5). According to local legend, Samual Foreman, John Lincklaen's assistant, built the house exactly one foot larger in every dimension than his employer's house, Lorenzo—a reproduction of an elite landscape, plus one. However, the owners in the 1930s fared poorly in the Depression and sold the place to the village. Several attempts to save it failed, and the village officials, at this time of Irish descent and not interested in preserving an estate tradition, razed it in 1937. The texts on Cazenovia, produced largely from historic and preservation points of view, not surprisingly, emphasize the estate history of the park and describe the loss of the house and the willows along the water's edge in mournful tones (Maroun, 7–9).

The park serves as a memory landscape of the estate era, a cemetery of sorts, filled with traces and clues to its former life. Some of the pieces of this mnemonic landscape are barely visible to the uninitiated observer, such as the level mound that was once the estate's tennis court. The stone wall with the wrought iron fence, however, is the most telling (and problematic) piece of the past. The fence inscribes the name Ten Eyck, the name of the prominent family that once owned the house, in an arch against a background of trees and sky. The stone wall extends from the park and joins the wall of the adjacent estate, Willowbank. This metonymic relationship joins the now public park directly with a private estate. The wall, the fence, and the old family name not only refer to the history of a "gracious" era, dedicated to enforcing a distinct boundary, they underline the discourse of social exclusion inherent in that history (Maroun, 6–7). Is this a public park in the guise of an estate or the other way around? Even though the creation of the park represents a moment when the elite lost economic and political power, the control of the interpretation and design of the landscape comes from an elite position. As James Duncan notes: "Authority lies with those

Named buildings in the historic district and one parody on the east side of town.

(Continued)

"I lived in the Bronx, but I grew up on Second and Seventy-eighth Street. We were everything, Italian, German, Polacks. Chinese had a laundry on the corner. We played stickball or boxball on the street. The street was always full of kids, just full of kids. I went back to the Bronx about '78 it was devastated. Too bad, it was a good place to live.

"Do you know the Meadows? I used to do curtains and furniture for Mrs. Oakman. She was a gracious woman, always took time to talk to you. This one room they called the book room was lined with books, and it was where they schooled the children. I used to sit and talk to her there in that book room. I liked working for her. These people who get rich who never had any money before...not like people who grew up with money.

"The people who bought the Meadows painted the room all white and filled it with modern furniture."

(Interview with author May, June 1996)

who control interpretations of the great texts and have the responsibility for defining the society's identity" (Duncan 1990, 22).

Gypsy Bay Park

If Lakeland Park is a site of memory of an estate landscape and the discourse of social exclusion, Gypsy Bay is a place on the margins for Cazenovia's Other. There is almost no mention of its history, and the origins of the name are vague. (There are photographs of Gypsy camps in the area.) For years it has been an undeveloped site where anyone could pull off Rte. 20, take his or her dogs or a six-pack of beer and hang out or swim in a shallow unsupervised cove. It has a different crowd than Lakeland. There may be a familiar face, but it is not the more closely knit group of people who see each other every day in the high school or village. Some Cazenovia parents advise their children against going to Gypsy Bay.

Cazenovia would like to forget a piece of recent history that happened at the local-fire-company-sponsored circus staged at Gypsy Bay on July 4, 1993. That night the teenage son of one of the long-time residents took a short-cut through a wooded section to meet his parents for the evening fireworks at the park. He never made it, and was found the next day in the lake, becoming the first in the history of the town to be murdered. It has been hard to accept; such things do not happen in a rural idyll. That it happened during an event at Gypsy Bay, however, reinforces a fear of outsiders and otherness. The following year there was no circus, but a small community-focused event took place inside the wall of Lakeland Park. Now Gypsy Bay Park has a landscaped parking lot and a wooden rail fence along the road, perhaps not directly related to the tragedy but still reflecting a desire to enforce boundaries and authority.

LOCATING HOME IN NATURE: THE ESTATE WRIT LARGE

Despite the notion of an organic community bound and determined by nature, nature has been framed, miniaturized, managed, and encoded with stories. To begin with, the repeated comparison with an idyllic or arcadian landscape evokes a narrative of return not only to the historic past but to a past relationship to nature. The estates encoded this narrative of rural escapism and search for ancestral roots. Naming estates after trees, the Oaks or simply Old Trees, not only describes key features but makes the metaphors of genealogy tangible and natural. Farming, in the rural idyll, reestablishes the spatial unity of life, labor, and nature, as well as the temporal unity of cyclic, timeless repetition. Architectural styles were emblematic of this lifestyle. Stanford White's Colonial Revival design for the Hickories interpreted an American agrarian heritage emblematic of "domesticity, dedication, difficult yet satisfying labor and a nourishing connection with nature" (Wood, 42). Some owners enacted the rural idyll by managing their own model farms, but more often they re-created an English pastoral landscape and depended on surrounding farms as a scenic backdrop. The *Land Use Guide* translates this tradition into present practice, defining a "Farmland, Open Rural" character zone critical to many farm-

Top: The gate to the park with the former owner's name, Ten Eyck, inscribed in the ironwork.

Above: Public access at Gypsy Bay

ers and nonfarmers' sense of identity. It also defines a "Greenbelt" character zone around the village that prohibits suburban sprawl, preserving the vision of an organic village integrated with the countryside, a scene very much from the 19th century.

Today, like many rural areas in the East, Cazenovia appears much wilder than it did a hundred years ago. It is easy to forget that this nature, which resonates with the myths of wilderness, emerged out of a cultural context of "second growth" forest and old fields. Likewise, the preservation of this changing nature is rarely examined as a cultural practice. Again, we can return to Lorenzo to see the precedent and present efforts to preserve the more wild parts of Cazenovia. In 1852 Ledyard Lincklaen created a frame around Lorenzo's formal garden with a grove of spruces and native plants, which became known as the Dark Aisle. It functioned in miniature in the same way that a kind of wild nature did on the larger scale as a picturesque frame around the cultivated landscape. For Lincklaen, an avid genealogist, this miniature forest recalled the ancient origins of his Anglo-Saxon ancestors. In 1976 the Syracuse Garden Club completed the restoration of the Dark Aisle as a bicentennial project. One member described the process:

> We went to the books he [Lincklaen] had in the library on wild gardens and consulted the description of the garden. Rather than replanting, wild gardening, instead, is about eliminating root competition. We got rid of all the public enemies like poison ivy, choke cherry and ostrich fern. It was wall to wall ostrich fern. And wouldn't you know it, but baneberry and other native plants started to reappear.
> (Interview by author, June 1996)

Therefore, nature appears much like synoptic history, as a constant, something given, when in fact, on both the microscale and the macroscale it is tended, managed, and shaped by stories. Despite the rhetoric of shared public good, nature is a product of property relationships, privatized and linked to social class (Duncan and Duncan). What passes for wild is often land of marginal economic use that has been abandoned. This economic discourse appears in the metaphors of "scenic value" or "investment for future generations."

BLURRING SPATIAL BOUNDARIES

The shaping of nature is critical in the narrative of social differentiation. The desire to see a low-density pastoral landscape requires both exclusion and the concealing of boundaries to extend symbolic possession and control over a larger landscape that even the wealthiest individuals could never purchase on their own. Lorenzo employed the uniquely English device of the ha-ha to conceal boundaries and give the illusion of continuity with the context. Meanwhile, estate owners set about improving their view of the surrounding landscape, passing ordinances enforcing aesthetic values, funding improvements, and exhorting citizens to participate in kind. By the 1880s the parklike vision of the whole landscape started to come into focus: "It will not be long

Above: Enacted Narrative. The landscape of model farms was important as a setting for enacting the narratives of the rural idyll. Here, the daughter of one of Cazenovia's wealthiest families loads shocks of wheat. (Courtesy Lorenzo State Historic Site)

Below: Volunteers at work maintaining the Dark Aisle.

before Cazenovia in all parts will be a great park, with few visible lines to divide private grounds from public possession" (Lorenzo archives, broadsides collection).

Subdivision threatens the unity of the idyll. So many people want a piece of this landscape, and how this landscape is parceled out for newcomers in large-lot horse farms or minimum-lot developments or divvied up internally among estate heirs is a critical means of shaping identity. The *Land Use Guide* uses topography as a means of determining boundaries that "reinforces, rather than homogenizes, the differences between the areas," thereby maintaining a discourse of distinction. Within this framework each subdivision request before the planning board reactivates and continues to shape the identity of place.

Enacted Narrative: the Upland Idyll and the Lorenzo Driving Competition. The route of the competition crosses properties that are owned by the state (Lorenzo), the Cazenovia Preservation Foundation, or heirs of the Lincklaen-Ledyard family, or properties that have easements placed on them for scenic, agricultural, and recreational uses.

1. The start at Lorenzo, State Historic Site. 2. View of Fairchild Hill, CPF property. 3. Smith's Clearing, private park with easements. 4. Water hazard on property owned by Lincklaen-Ledyard descendant and the designer of trails. The CPF holds an easement for the trails. 5. Trail through the woods with easement. 6. The Meadows Farm, formerly run by the Lincklaen-Ledyard family, preserved by means of a limited development with agricultural and scenic easements held by the CPF. 7. The Meadows Estate, formerly owned by the Lincklaen-Ledyard family. Sold. The CPF intends to purchase easements.

PIECING TOGETHER AN UPLAND IDYLL
Directly to the south of Lorenzo, the Cazenovia Preservation Foundation and descendants of the elite families have been working to patch together a vast upland domain. To counter new subdivision, dispersion of generations, and property taxes, they have employed a compendium of preservation strategies, from outright purchase to easements and limited development. However, the practice that gathers and commemorates the various pieces of the upland idyll is the enacted narrative of the Lorenzo Driving Competition.

At 8:15 in the morning on the third weekend in July, antique carriages and carts, with their tack all polished, trot past the Lorenzo mansion and the "concour d'elegance" judge, before heading off on a timed marathon. This part of the Lorenzo Driving Competition follows the patchwork of old lanes, trails, hedgerows, woods, and fields of the upland idyll. As an enacted narrative, it recalls a pre-automobile past and the image of a rural landscape romanticized in the model farms of the estate era. This is not just a vague, generalized history, but one connected to specific memories of specific individuals who still play a role in the event and in the landscape. The founder and organizer of the competition is a descendant of the Lincklaen-Ledyard family who from an early age enjoyed driving carriages on trails, many of which she designed herself.

The course's sequence of sites reveals the discourse of Cazenovia's narratives.
• Lorenzo—Provides the main staging ground for all the events and the start and finish of the marathon.
• Nature preserves—The trails also cross lands purchased by the CPF for their scenic and natural values.
• Trail easements—The course picks up a series of trails on private land owned by a group of interrelated families. These trails are part of an evolving system put together by easements and purchases by the CPF,

funded by grants from the New York State Council on the Arts, and assisted by landscape architects, planners, and a committee of citizens (preservationists). The owners of large estates have sold only large parcels of land in areas that are the least visible, preserving a private rural domain.

• The Meadows Farm—Listed on the National Trust for Historic Preservation, this site was operated by Linklaen's descendants. The CPF preserved the farm through a limited development plan. With $300,000 it purchased the farm and 80 acres of land identified as critical to forming a "Greenbelt" around the village. It placed restrictive covenants on the land to ensure agricultural use, designated a conservation area along the creek, defined scenic viewsheds for protection, and established a procedure for architectural review of any changes to the exterior of the buildings. Once these were in place, it subdivided the property into two lots and sold them to "sympathetic" buyers.

• The Meadows Estate—Built by Lincklaen-Ledyards in 1826 as a replica of Lorenzo and lived in continuously by descendants of the family until 1993. It is a remarkable vision of an English landscape garden that preserves open space at the very southern edge of the village. From here the drivers return to Lorenzo.

With connections to Lincklaen, the town founder; the scenic qualities; the "Greenbelt Character Zone"; the nature preserves; the agricultural context; and living memory, it is easy to understand why the upland area immediately south of Lorenzo has become a target for preservation. From outright purchase to limited development, trail easements, and enacted narratives, preservation transforms what was essentially a private domain to one with a degree of public access (countering charges of elitism). The ritual of the driving competition reinforces the notion of an unbounded pastoral landscape, resisting the constant threat of subdivision.

On the larger scale, the creation of this separate nature conceals the connections to environmental problems elsewhere. Those who live in this privileged nature deny their dependence on an ecologically destructive economy (Duncan and Duncan, 20). In fact, some of the families who helped create this idyll also created the Solvay Wastebeds which contributed to the pollution of Onondaga Lake in Syracuse 20 miles away. The wastebeds and the lake are now the focus of a multimillion-dollar cleanup by the county, state, and federal governments.

Top: View near Fairchild Hill (#2).

Above: Smith's Clearing (#3).

SUMMARY: A MODEL COMMUNITY

Despite its elite nature, Cazenovia has broader relevance in the narratives of home. First, it represents an ideal, much like the New England village, of a small community, stable over time and rooted in place. Even the discourse of social differentiation has broad appeal in American culture. The dominant narratives of this place also prevail in professional practice, and Cazenovia has had sig-

Karen McCoy, *Considering Mother's Mantle.*
Stone Quarry Hill Art Park,
Cazenovia, 1990. (Courtesy
Courtney Frisse)

The recently established Stone Quarry Hill Art Park has become a space where artists and the community can engage discourses of nature, history, and identity. For the opening show "Re-claiming Land," one of the artists, Karen McCoy, revealed the discourse of boundaries. She started by aligning arrowhead plants in a pond to create a grid that followed the same orientation of plants growing in the north-south lines scored into rocks by glaciation. By extending these lines into the field by inlaying sod, bleaching, and weaving grasses into a spiral cul-de-sac, she represented the history of land division. She also revealed alternative and forgotten histories of the area by uncovering the overgrown traces of the first owner of this land who was a woman and a weaver in the early 1800s .

nificant help from the National Trust for Historic Preservation, the Natural Resource Defense Fund, the Nature Conservancy, landscape architects, artists, and architects.

What is at issue is the sense of closure of "home truths," which are established when certain relationships become so familiar, tangible, and close to home that they appear natural. While certain notions of history, community and nature have helped to preserve a quality of architecture and encourage a better ecological fit in Cazenovia, there are certain hidden consequences. In their study of Bedford, New York, a community very similar to Cazenovia, James and Nancy Duncan point out that ideologies of local "home rule," and the aestheticization of nature, history, and community, hide the social inequalities of services and affordable housing options. (1988, 124).

Given the cogency of home, it is important to develop a critical practice that opens the discourses of these narratives. Even in a place like Cazenovia with a strong identity and sense of place, these qualities develop through processes of negotiation, contest, interpretation, and change. And they have very real consequences in the ongoing life of the community. The purpose in arguing for the storied nature of home is not to dismantle the construction of one group to validate claims by others, or to lose the whole notion in relativism. Home and community may be unstable and multiple, but their very purpose is to define limits, conventions, and identity through shared stories. A critical practice recognizes the necessity of home and the importance of establishing and fixing identity in place, as well as its provisional and storied nature.

RETELLING TRADITION: KENTLANDS, MARYLAND

By all accounts neotraditionalism, also referred to as the New Urbanism, is one of the most successful contemporary challenges to the loss of home and community. As its name describes, neotraditionalism looks back to traditional places like Cazenovia as models to emulate in new community design. In fact, one of the leaders of this movement, Elizabeth Plater-Zyberk, spoke at Cazenovia, noting its strengths and recommending ways to maintain it.[4] It is important to ask, however, what kind of cultural practices are involved in reinventing and retelling tradition. Are there certain ideologies embedded in the promotion of the physical form of traditional towns? And what are the implications of adapting places like Cazenovia as models for contemporary communities when much of their strength comes as a consequence of essentialized notions and a history of exclusion?

Developer Joseph Alfandre cites another upstate New York community, Chautauqua, as his model for the neotraditional town of Kentlands in Gaithersburg, Maryland. In the 19th century Chautauqua started from a single tent where people gathered in the summer to hear orators, educators, and musicians, and grew into a town and a traveling institution that gathered communities across America around its program of arts and education (Schlichting). Alfandre, on the other hand, started by restoring the existing mansion of the Old Kent Farm and initiating a comprehensive planning process for this tract of land in a rapidly developing suburban region just outside the Washington, D.C., beltway.[5] After the first master plan failed to satisfy his vision for a traditional village, he invited Andres Duany and Elizabeth Plater-Zyberk (of DPZ Architects) for a one-week design charette to generate the plan (Shoshkes, 228). He recognized that the success of the venture depended not only on a plan but on creating a convincing social narrative. Alfandre wrote a town charter, established a town newspaper, and produced numerous promotional brochures.

One of the first brochures (1989) for Kentlands tells a story in pictures and words. The cover image of an old estate is framed by ragged black matting suggestive of photographs from the 19th century. Inside, the next picture, labeled "Town parade" (the period framing no longer matches the era of the photograph, which is ca. 1940), shows a community lining the streets of a small town with a church or town hall in the background. The text poses a rhetorical question, "Where have all the small towns gone?" and the following pages locate the blame with a picture captioned "Detroit assembly line." The text under the title "The Road the Automobile Led Us Down" tells of technological determinism in which "neighbors drifted apart" because "the automobile actually reshaped the physical design of our communities." On the last page we return to the Kent home with a historic picture of two children on the porch (in period dress) and a text describing the restoration of home and community through design: "Kentlands. A sense of belonging." This return to home repeats the synoptic narrative structure so implicit in Cazenovia. In fact, the estate house depicted on the cover is similar in style and period to Lorenzo, and the scene of the town parade is enacted in Cazenovia every Fourth of July. The question posed here is also similar to that posed for newcomers by the tour guide, except that now Cazenovia offers an answer, a model for reversing rather than preserving history.

Neotraditionalism is told against the background of post-World War II suburban development that census data show is now the home of a majority of Americans. From this point of view, suburbia is the metaphor for the loss of place-based community and all the problems, social and environmental, that result. To reproduce the traditional model of a Cazenovia or other traditional forms for new communities, then, is not just a nostalgic return, according to Duany and Plater-Zyberk, but a major counter-narrative that addresses the foundations of social life, issues of public space, democratic values, and political power.[6] Leon Krier, a major influence on DPZ, calls for a nationwide program of community building. "The small-town philosophy of the TND [Traditional Neighborhood Development] is not just an architectural paradigm, but a social synthesis which, if applied nationally, will allow a much larger range of people and talent to become active citizens in the full meaning of that phrase" (Krieger and Lennertz, 119). Thus, every detail, curve radius, proportion, and setback of the neo-traditional town speaks against "suburbia" and helps to build an effective critique and alternative.[7]

Top: Brochure cover showing the Kent Mansion.

Center: "Where have all the small towns gone?"

Bottom: The last image of the brochure, the porch of the Kent Mansion.

(Courtesy Joseph Alfandre Company)

The generation gap.

"Forty years ago, a walk through a typical American neighborhood would be quite different than it is today." (Alfandre)

When Joseph Alfandre was in his late thirties he began to develop Kentlands. In a *Time* magazine article he spoke of how this new development recalled his memories of growing up in Bethesda, Maryland, in the early 1950s: "It is the kind of place I grew up in, that I have always dreamed of re-creating. When I was five years old, I was independent—I could walk into town, to the bowling alley, the movie theater, the drugstore. Duany just reminded me of it." (Andersen, 53)

Above: Kentlands master plan. (Courtesy DPZ Architects)

Below: Aerial sketch of the Old Farm Neighborhood designed to appear as if it grew from the original farmstead at the center (courtesy DPZ Architects).

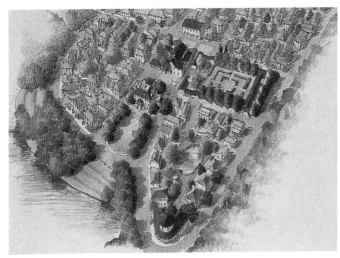

As a whole, the neighborhood or village serves as the metaphor for the restoration of the traditional place-based community. A setting from the past is substituted to reform the present. Advertising appeals to the desires for what has been lost. "A community is more than someplace you live. It's a place that gives you a sense of belonging" (Alfandre). Given this desire, the design delivers something complete, not partial, something stable and bounded. Thus, in neotraditionalism we see the anchoring of identity to certain essentialized notions, history, community, and nature, as described in the case of Cazenovia. Only, now there are important differences in who constructs the narratives, what values inhere in the telling, and who inhabits the story.

STRATEGIES FOR RETELLING TRADITIONS

CONCEALING TEMPORAL BOUNDARIES

The vision of unity and seamlessness in space also represents a narrative of seamlessness in time. The TND, developed in the mid 1980s, mends a forty-year gap in time that is the history of the last forty years of suburbanization. The forty-year span is also significant because it is the conventional time frame of a generation. As the brochure recalls: "Past generations of families used to live and work in small towns just like it all across America. And they understood something that younger generations need to learn once again." By evoking a generational connection, the story becomes family memory, not just history. The goal of the TND design is to repair the rupture in time, and ultimately, as in the pastoral idyll, create a sense of continuity that blurs boundaries across generations. As Duany claimed in a presentation, "Many people will not know it [Kentlands] was built in the latter half of the 20th century" (1996).

Even more remarkable is that it appears to have been designed in seven days. In this and other projects, DPZ use a design charette, a Beaux-Arts tradition that relies on knowledge of shared design typologies, as an effective means of not only generating the concept plan but also forming a kind of temporary community with the shared vision and momentum to take it through the protracted approval process. The race against time and the interplay between the principal actors—designers, officials, and developers—provide tension and a sense of drama that also play well to media accounts. Despite a significant amount of earlier work, in effect the charette becomes *the* founding event in the history of the community that will take shape.

INSCRIBING ORIGINS

Amid the rapid and mass initiation of a new community, selected remnants of the past play a key role in creating a sense of continuity. The existing 1852 manor house serves as a synecdoche of the past. It embodies a family memory, a genealogy, in the same manner that the Lorenzo mansion marks the origins and authorship of Cazenovia by Lincklaen and his heirs.

The Kent mansion could have been treated in several ways: demolished, preserved as a house museum, saved as a home, or set off as a monument at the end of a formal axis. The alternative chosen created a small green and court around the building, extended its low walls, and created small-scale enclosures in the design of the surrounding "Old Farm Neighborhood." The developer and designers chose this because it implied a narrative of "historic evolution—how old farms become the seeds for towns that grow up around them" (Shoshkes, 242). The result is a resonance between what is original and what is reproduced, what is old versus what is new, what is surface and what is inscription. John Dorst identifies this kind of inscription as a "vignette," a term from graphic arts, where an image merges with the materiality of the surface, and the surface gradually becomes the inscribed image (Dorst, 119). It is a strategy of undecidability, blurring the distinction between image and its referent. Unlike interpreting the changes around Cazenovia's green, where one deciphers what has been inscribed on the past, here one tries to interpret how the past is inscribed into the surface of the present. The actual history becomes the beginning of an "as if" story used to shape the present.

GATHERING THE REGIONAL LANDSCAPE

The neotraditional town is a collection of references to the regional history told in building types, styles, architectural details, and town form. The process begins with measuring and documenting the prosaic elements of regional form—roof lines, lot sizes, window proportions, setbacks, street corner radii, as a kit of parts for the charette and a codified typology of forms. The appeal to regionalism evokes an established ideology in the design professions. In the ideology of the regional vernacular, every decision makes sense as part of a tra-

Top: The Kent mansion.

Above: The historic vignette flanking the Kent mansion.

"History has always played an important part in the overall feeling of Kentlands. Originally a sprawling family estate called 'Wheatlands' dating from the mid 1800s, its main mansion still stands high above a lake at the center of the property. Along with the mansion, the estate's old brick barn and fire house will be refurbished and used as a cultural center for the greater community." (Alfandre)

dition that evolves and adapts to the local environment. This has definite practical benefits, as in DPZ's design for Seaside, Florida, where the houses weathered Hurricane Andrew significantly better than other newer homes because they employed framing and roofing techniques derived from vernacular tradition of the area. But it also evokes an image of a close-knit premodern or preindustrial community that shared common building traditions. These conceptions of the vernacular often conflate culture with nature. For instance, in *Out of Place*, Michael Hough uses metaphors from evolutionary biology to describe the vernacular as resulting from "an inherent drive to fill a niche, to seize an opportunity to flourish, or to enhance one's chances of survival or success...vernacular landscapes, whether urban or rural, are the product of necessity and limitation" (Hough, 57–58). Thus it evokes the authority of nature as well. This linkage of community and nature in the regional vernacular is an integral part of the ideological project of neotraditionalism.

Regionalism is closely aligned with an ideology of contextualism. The common vocabulary of forms and the emphasis on a total ensemble imply a community of builders very different from the modernist pursuit of pure objects in space or the individual "showpiece" house. To simulate the contextual narrative in the absence of such a community, DPZ substitutes a formal code (not zoning) for what were once oral traditions or implicit social agreements governing form. This is probably one of the firm's chief accomplishments—rewriting the code of suburbia. It is variable by region and allows many architects to be involved, producing a sense of diversity that normally evolves over time. The designers describe this simulation where "in the absence of historical time, the Codes encourage authentic variety while ensuring the harmony required to give character to a community" (Duany Plater-Zyberk & Company, 3). Whereas Cazenovia developed idiosyncrasies and a mix of styles as a result of fires, rebuilding, cycles of economic change, etc., at the Kentlands diversity is simulated by involving a mix of architects, primarily local practitioners.

INVENTING TRADITION

Neotraditionalism, as the name suggests, is an "invented tradition"—it uses historically loaded symbols, repetition, rules, and codes to create a sense of continuity with a largely invented past (Hobsbawm and Ranger, 1–5). It is similar to the invention of the New England village-as-tradition in the 19th century, by social reformers and landscape architects who sought to "replicate landscapes which they believed had worked in the past to foster domesticity and community in the present" (Wood, 44). It also shares intentions with schools of regionalism in art, literature, and design such as the Prairie School of Hamlin Garland and designers like Wright and Jensen, or the California Mission heritage created by Lummis and the Ramona stories. Created out of historical fact, experience, myth, physiography, and new imperatives, these regional stories serve various purposes, from reform to boosterism.

COMMUNITY VERSUS CONSUMPTION OF COMMUNITY

The "tradition" at the Kentlands is invented within social contexts of professional design and corporate development, mass media and sophisticated lifestyle marketing, very different from the small-town or vernacular image evoked in the plans. Though neotraditionalism is thoroughly explained in common-sense terms and revolutionary rhetoric directed against development and planning practices that have created suburbia, the success of the movement has been in persuading private developers and investors, not to mention town planning boards, risk managers, engineers, and ultimately buyers, to risk their capital in a radical alternative. While the ideal is some vision of face-to-face neighborliness, it is an image that has market appeal.

Regionalism is also a marketing strategy. In the case of neotraditionalism the two should not be separated, but must be seen as mutually supportive (despite the contradiction with the ideology of regional design). The distinctive house styles represent targeted lifestyles for niche marketing (Till, 719). They respond to and encourage a late 20th-century search for difference and self-conscious identity. The threat to regional identity is not so much homogenization as it is difference, albeit one of surface images, freely simulated and exchanged. The eclecticism and lack of historic specificity in neotraditionalism is actually one of its greatest marketing assets.

CONCEALING A MALL
The design of the regional mall/main street at Kentlands demonstrates the conflict and collusion between design ideology and market ideology. Controlled by an "outside" entity, not the developer, the shopping component had to be "regional" rather than local in its clientele (Shoshkes, 235). With this comes certain formulas for parking, visibility, etc., that cut across the texture of a traditional town (as if a Walmart were inserted in Cazenovia). The designers negotiated various ways of fitting it in but ultimately choose concealing it under a veneer. The design packaged the large retail outlet into a building that on the surface appears to be several smaller ones.

PUBLIC/PRIVATE
Neotraditionalism is positioned against the privatization of America and the sacrifice of public space to the private automobile and the patterns of suburban isolation. Civic symbols figure prominently in all the plans—town halls terminate vistas; "instant monuments" of parks, squares, and other forms of public space orient and organize experience of the place. The neotraditional development also attempts to forge the institutions of a democratic community by publishing a newspaper and writing a town charter as opposed to forming a homeowners association. The difference, of course, is that these elements are provided by a private developer. Duany blames the public sector planners for losing this vision while at the same time exhorts developers to become "town founders" (like Lincklaen).

A sense of public life is ingrained in details, dimensions, and typology. Retooling the geometry of town form, pulling things closer, remixing housing types, adding porches, and enclosing public space bring physical cohesion out of the atomized suburban patterns. According to an ideology of spatial determinism, closeness means more chance for encounter,

This description of the first family to move into the Kentlands on December 10, 1990, is excerpted from the second edition of the *Kentlands Exchange*, a newspaper published by Joseph Alfandre and Company (winter 1990/'91):[8]

As Texans, Tim and Brenda —— know what it's like to live through a real estate slump. They were living outside San Antonio when the bottom fell out of the real estate market.

"When we came up here it was clear this area was going to go through a slight decline," said Tim ——, "but we figured Kentlands was the best place to weather the storm."

On December 10th, the ——s moved into the new home they bought from Rocky Gorge Communities, becoming the first family to move into Kentlands. "We were looking for the charm of an old home and the convenience of a new one," said Tim.

"We scoured this area," he said. "We looked everywhere but downtown D.C."

Then Tim read about Kentlands. "I saw it somewhere...a picture of all the architects gathered in the old barn and I thought 'that looks really interesting...'"

Because the real estate market appeared to be stalling, the ——s did consider leasing for a year, but they wanted to put down roots and make a home somewhere.

"That was one of our concerns, protecting our equity," said Tim. "But the location, the concept, the point it is in in the development cycle...we felt our money would be safe here."

"Our daughter hasn't seen it yet, but our son is wild about the place," laughed Brenda. "He's already claimed the garage guest suite as his own."

exchange, and therefore neighborliness. It is the ideal of a community based on face-to-face encounters. This type of encounter is considered more immediate and therefore unmediated and direct. Again, a common-sense argument is used to attach identity to something essential, unchanging, natural. However, more than simple spatial determinism is at work here, since simple proximity, which can be found in the big city, can also produce alienation and violence. Instead, the ideal face-to-face community is considered an attribute of the urban village, or small town (Young). Thus, community is not determined by the dimensions of the TND, rather the picket fences (wood, no chain link), the porches, and the "instant monuments" all act as signs of a sense of community already imagined.

KENTLANDS' OTHER

Kentlands collapses social distance into face-to-face encounters on the neighborhood scale but maintains social differentiation on the larger scale. Such a community appeals to the suburban fear of the other, the stranger, the poor, and crime in the city. While there is no guarded gate, the TND is still a separate enclave. Kentlands still has a wall, a fieldstone terrace with vegetation set back from an arterial road. There is an inviting gate with two arches for unlikely pedestrians. Set beyond Washington's beltway, Kentlands offers a vision of Georgetown, or Annapolis, but without the crime or low-income and minority groups.

Despite its elite heritage, which is part of its marketing appeal, DPZ believes the new urbanism can rectify the miserable failures of public housing and solve the social problems of segregation and affordable housing. "Poverty is not the problem, concentration of poverty is," Duany explains. They propose to mix affordable housing in with community, 10 percent according to the code. But it would be disguised: "It should look like middle class housing type, the poor actually prefer that" (Duany, 1996). However, Duany warns that porches, romanticized by the middle and upper class, are stigmatized in lower economic class experience. And in a reversal of the modernist tradition where the best of the avant-garde devoted itself to designing public housing, Duany believes affordable housing should be done by the very best "conventional designers."

As opposed to maintaining spatial separation of class and other differences, the narrative here is one of assimilation and upward mobility. Affordable housing should take on the mass and proportion of a single-family house but serve as a duplex. Another strategy in the code puts small affordable flats in the back alley above garages or uses small "granny flats," spaces commonly adapted for family members or for additional income of a boarder. The hierarchy and relationship of control become very direct. Such a strategy for making lower income groups invisible by incorporating them into a dominant aesthetic has been suggested in Cazenovia and in design guidelines for Shaunessey, Vancouver. Instead of allowing apartments and other housing options in the midst of a near crisis housing shortage, architects proposed to maintain the "Estate Scale Legacy" of

Above: The wall and entry gate (vehicular and pedestrian) to the community.

Below: A remnant of the former landscape directly across from the gate to the Kentlands.

Shaunessey by converting existing coach houses and related outbuildings into affordable housing (Duncan, "Shaughnessey," 13–19).

SUMMARY

The neotraditional community is, to use Umberto Eco's term, a hyperreal place. Modeled on a community ideal that never really existed, nevertheless it comes to be regarded as "realer than real." Returning to a past or recovering an original is easier than ever to simulate, and the simulation supplants the real (Ellin, 108–9). Here the narrative of tourism, which Dean MacCannel identifies as the defining experience of the age, applies. Dissatisfied with ordinary life which seems inauthentic, disconnected, the ideal community is thought to exist elsewhere—usually in the past or places coded as embodying the past (MacCannel, 3). Neotraditionalism provides a vision of this that can be reoccupied. Indeed, Duany uses such points of reference, pointing out how people will drive to places, like Georgetown, just to walk for entertainment in a place emblematic of times past. The neotraditional place seeks to create something authentic that has been lost in ordinary life, and this is what makes it so desirable and so ironic.

Kentlands and its variants replicate not only the form of the traditional home of places like Cazenovia, they also naturalize some of the ideologies and discourse of social differentiation. What then are the prospects for creating a more open narrative of home that satisfies the legitimate needs for continuity without erecting exclusionary boundaries? How can notions of stable, essentialized identity be replaced with a recognition that identity is multiple, negotiated, and necessarily flexible? These questions are part of an ongoing discourse in a place most people would not consider as an ideal model of home, the South Bronx.

NOS QUEDAMOS (WE STAY) IN THE BRONX

In just one night, on November 12, 1992, after a decade of developing a plan, planners found out that, despite statistics and appearances that seemed to signify a "ghetto," the South Bronx was a place that people called "home."[9] The city was proposing an urban renewal plan of a thirty-block area of the South Bronx known as Melrose Commons. This would mean, according to the city, displacing 78 private homes, 400 tenants, and 80 businesses and replacing them with 2,600 new middle-income housing units, 250,000 square feet of commercial space, a centrally located 4-acre park, and a realignment of streets in one portion to a ninety-degree grid system (Bautista, Garcia, and Stand, 4). However, the numbers and the impacts were underestimated. Seeing this proposal for the first time at the presentation, normally quiet residents became vocal, peacefully shouting down the planners, halting the meeting, and forcing them to reconsider what they had thought was a good plan and a fait accompli.

The problem stemmed from certain assumptions about this place, about the "inner city," and about the kind of ideal home to replace it with. During all the time of preparing these proposals, however, the planners and the city never attempted to find and listen to the stories of the community. As a result, the

The President of Nos Quedamos, Yolanda Garcia, recounts the recent history and residents' commitment to this place. "I have lived in the area for thirty-five years. We were here when this area of the Bronx was beautiful and we saw the downfall of the Bronx. The city abandoned us with the necessary municipal services, like the police, sanitation, and fire departments. I once had forty fire extinguishers in my store; if there was a fire, we would go out and take care of it. We still have to clean up the area because the sanitation trucks don't come around here very often. But now that the Bronx is coming back, the planners of the mapping action wanted to throw us out just like garbage, without taking the time to include the community in any form or way, as if no one who lived here had any substance or meaning. The city should have taken into consideration that those who remained here were survivors. I decided that I did not want to get out and started to fight; soon after that Nos Quedamos was born."
(Bressi, 1994, 5) (By permission of Municipal Art Society)

Children from Melrose Commons drawing images of their place. On the wall behind them is the working plan developed block by block on 11" x 17" photocopies.

city had to withdraw the plan, and the community group that had formed to oppose it entered into a ground-breaking collaborative design process to create an alternative for Melrose Commons. The name of the group, Nos Quedamos, We Stay, describes their mission.

ASSERTING HOME

Nos Quedamos had to counter the ghetto narrative of the area, and tell their own story. Planners assumed that if offered money, people would leave and they could develop a middle-income, home-ownership-based community. Even Senator Daniel Patrick Moynahan assumed that this was not a home: "People don't want housing in the South Bronx, or otherwise they would not burn it down" (Vergara, 40). Yolanda Garcia, who became president of Nos Quedamos, steadfastly questions these outsider assessments: "Would you burn your own home? People own this place. It's a social place. Look at the level of finish of private homes. And this is the poorest congressional district in the United States. People here don't dump garbage. They come from over the borders." Yolanda Garcia and others shared a common experience of protecting their home through adverse times. They survived the worst period of disinvestment by the city, lack of basic services such as fire protection, impacts of building the Cross Bronx Expressway,[10] and flight of the middle class. In spite of these conditions, many residents resisted offers to buy them out. They were not so much opposed to the new prosperity envisioned by the plan, but rather to the idea of being displaced by what they had sacrificed and waited so long for. In their estimation they deserved to be an integral part of this vision.

RENEGOTIATING HOME

The story of Nos Quedamos is not just another case of scrappy local resistance to an outside development scheme; rather, it has turned into an extended, open-ended experiment in community authorship of its own sense of identity and control of a place that they call home. Unlike with other schemes to reclaim ghettos, at Melrose Commons the residents did not seek to dissolve difference by building middle-class housing and making it another zone of exclusion. They intended to draw identity from existing and future diversity. Value was granted to and gained from existing residents who, through their time and investment in the place, had acquired tenure (equity) within the community (Bautista, Garcia, and Stand, 7). The goal was to "buy people in" rather than buy them out; residents asserted that "no involuntary displacement should occur." In a collaborative process the community worked with experts, the local authority with the city, the marginal with the mainstream. They moved from opposing to renegotiating the very structures of power built on difference that had created the ghetto in the first place.

The shift in power came first of all in numbers and direct contact with the diversity of the community. The group that had attended the meetings and opposed the plan went house to house to canvass residents to see if the greater community shared their resistance. They did to an overwhelming degree. This also served as a local census revealing a population of 6,000, almost three times the official count. To sustain the support of politicians, Nos Quedamos translated the new numbers into political power with a voter registration drive. They carved out a political space, however tenuous, for their voice to be heard.[11]

The time and place for developing the plan were localized by shifting planning from the city to the neighborhood and opening a storefront office. Here, community members, many too self-conscious to speak before authorities, could participate in an open process in familiar surroundings. Every Tuesday night they met to to develop the alternative plan in the allotted six months, and they continue to meet to realize it (168 times in one year). It took this time just to get past the neighborhood skepticism of planning, to develop local expertise, to find the means of representing ideas, etc. The community was wary at first of working with designers, Petr Stand of Magnusson Architects and landscape architect Lee Weintraub, who had been consultants for the city. They offered their assistance pro bono, and the community demanded their commitment to the place over a long period of time. Strand and Weintraub demonstrated a willingness to walk the blocks, listen to the stories, and stay with it for the duration. Lee Weintraub relates, "You can't have a charette and walk away. Doing tricks is rather unfortunate. It raises expectations that may never be met." In this regard, the name Nos Quedamos aptly describes the community's vigilance. "We want to make sure all the promises are kept. If the project takes 10 years to complete, we'll be around for 20" (Gonzales).

On the wall at 811 Courtlandt, the 11" x 17" photocopies taped together to form the Melrose Commons Plan indicate the lack of money for large-scale maps and reproduction, but also chart a detailed, incremental, highly interactive process that proceeded issue by issue, block by block. "Rather than gazing from above, it was conceived in a cauldron, with a great mix of ingredients" (Weintraub). Even though 60 percent of the area appears as a blank slate of large vacant lots, the plan was crafted from the physical remnants of built form rewoven by memory of residents, many who had stayed for over thirty years and knew the neighborhood before the abandonment, fires, and demolitions. It also reflects the local "infrastructure of daily life," the details and patterns of living in this place as the residents know it. Petr Stand describes the approach: "If someone, a family or even one person, wanted to stay in Melrose, that level of commitment represented a significant investment, a threshold that was more than enough

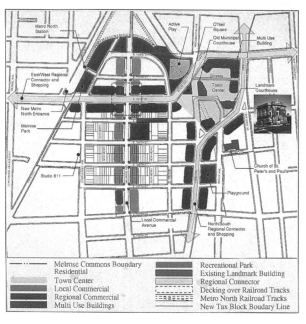

Above: The alternative plan developed by Magnusson Architecture and Planning, P.C. with Nos Quedamos. (Courtesy Magnusson Architecture & Planning, P. C. with Nos Quedamos. Funding for this design study was provided by the New York Council on the Arts.)

Bottom left: A Rock and a House.

Lee Weintraub and Petr Stand originally proposed to build on this site, but they were told "no way" by neighborhood teenagers who considered the rock an important memorial to "Ron," who died there on his wedding day.

There is also a pattern of existing houses, many of which were slated for demolition. The proposed plan weaves 1,700 new units into this existing pattern. Retaining the existing houses produces smaller, less monumental, and more diverse development sites.

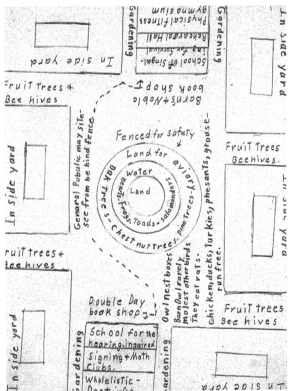

Above: A Tree. This sketch by Albert Messiah, a gardener, which depicts housing around a tree and a common courtyard, became the inspiration for the pattern of "midblock pedestrian mews."

Opposite: Context and plan of a block (center) with a mix of town houses, cooperative housing for single mothers and children above a day-care center, and five-story residential units above commercial space in one block. The town houses are organized around an internal courtyard/parking area and midblock pedestrian mews through the center of the block. This pattern is adapted to existing houses on the block. The co-op housing is at the bottom right corner. (Courtesy Magnusson Architecture and Planning, P.C. with Nos Quedamos. Funding for this design study was provided by the New York Council on the Arts.)

to plan a block and develop a community around" (Cary, Stand, and Weintraub, 4).

The design and location of the common space of parks reveal the clearest difference between the city plan and the community plan. The city plan located a four-acre, four-block park in the geographical center of Melrose. Residents foresaw a bleak future for this scheme. Too big to see from one end to the other and without city money and manpower to maintain it, the park would become a haven for vandals and drugs, not the community. Like other aspects of this plan, it displaced residents. Raphael Negrone refers to himself as "home plate" since his home would have become the baseball field.

The community plan, instead, creates a series of parks of different sizes and identities: a one-acre park at the town center; community gardens, which are a tradition in the neighborhood; and small parks, "midblock pedestrian mews," in the middle of residential blocks. While the smaller, integrated parks reflect a concern for "defensible space," they are not exclusionary. Petr Stand recalls, "One [resident] brought in a sketch of a block with a path and tree in the center and the community grew around it." This became the basis for a pattern they called midblock mews. When residents were asked if these spaces were public or private, one woman said there was a gate but everyone else said no, they wanted to keep the sense of public access.

Petr Stand, who once designed spec housing, opened the process by asking residents: "How do you live? What is home?" This helped to generate affordable housing types for multigenerational families and the great diversity of cultures. In the existing housing stock it is not uncommon for families to double, even triple up in small apartments. As in much of America, in Melrose the family is no longer a nuclear unit. Here, though, the numbers are skewed toward 70 percent single-woman heads of households, and in the context of low wages, unemployment, drugs, crime, and prison; this means the maintenance of home is a difficult struggle. One design prototype offers an adaptable floor plan for changing family configurations, much like the flexibility of a loft. Nos Quedamos and designers also proposed two-family housing, "mother/daughter" condos with two units on two floors so that a family could buy both. They looked for existing cases of shared responsibilities in apartments that could be the model for a co-housing alternative, a "women's co-op."

The most controversial recommendation is for six to eight story apartment towers with commercial use at ground level. To achieve this critical urban density, they have first had to challenge city requirements for parking that consumes land and reduces density.[12] But more significant, these apartments are not the American vision of home, and planners warn that developers will not take the risk to build such forms. The residents and designers disagree and point out that they work here, that people choose them over single-family home ownership. They prefer the affordability, the

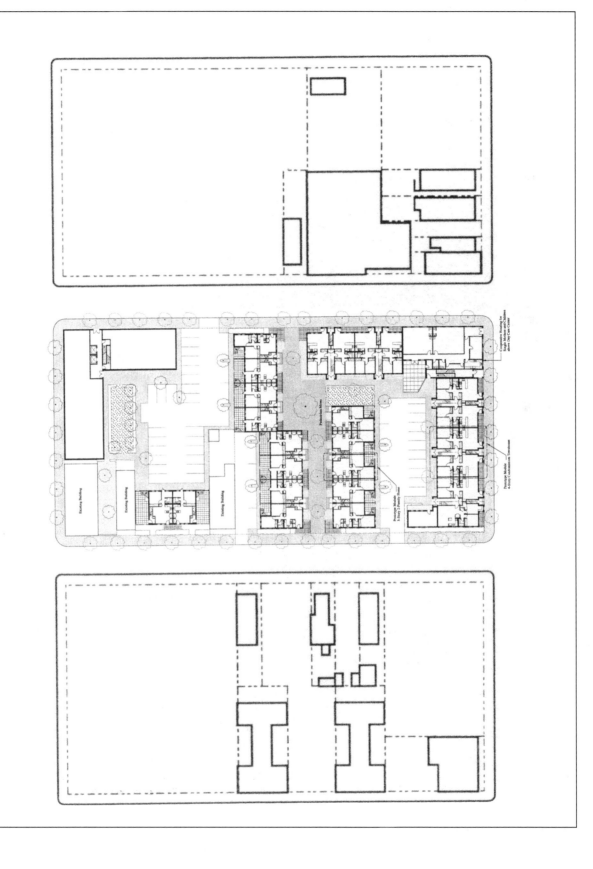

Cooperative Housing for
Single Mothers and Children
above Day Care Center

Prototype Module
4-Story Condominium Townhouse

Prototype Module
3-Story 2-Family Home

Pedestrian Mews

Existing Building

Existing Building

opportunities for shared resources, and the service of public transportation that such urban density offers. The Bronx borough president, Fernando Ferrer, supports the idea: "There's a segment of the development community that believes that all you can do in inner-city neighborhoods is single- and two-family homes, because the poor people can't deal with anything different. Not only is that bigoted, it happens to be wrong and pretty stupid" (Rothstein, 8R).

The Melrose plan is different from the "suburbanization of the ghetto" that has taken place in other parts of the Bronx. Camillo Vergara documented the abandonment, fires, and demolition of a five story substantial brick apartment building in the South Bronx that was replaced by three colorful town houses made of wood and plastic, "too flimsy to last." He also photographed the changes on Charlotte Street, once a national symbol of urban decay, and now a tree-lined street with suburban ranch houses, picket fences, and yards. In an odd inversion, here the narrative of the rural idyll replaces the landscape that so many fled. While it is a desired home that people protect, it actually exacerbates the problems of the Bronx. Large tracts of urban land are given to or sold cheaply to developers who build middle-class housing that requires incomes of $40,000, in an area where the median income is $12,000. The existing landscape is further destabilized, and as more apartments are demolished and replaced by low-density houses, the options for affordable housing diminish. Meanwhile, the suburban street becomes a safe but separate enclave, repeating the narrative of exclusion in the very heart of the landscape that has been marginalized to begin with (Vergara, 72–75).

A key challenge for the designers and Nos Quedamos was how to include the diversity of ethnic, racial, and income groups in the Bronx, yet develop a common identity of place. Ethnic and racial identity, in particular, have been sources of strength, maintaining communities in difficult circumstances. Within the area, however, that strength varies between groups, and there is competition for scarce resources. The Puerto Rican community, for instance, displays a strong sense of identity with their casitas built as miniature homes, and gardens as memories of rural Puerto Rico, complete with music, food, and dancing. Yet, here identity is produced within and for one group, separated from the mainstream. Another challenge was how to avoid the transformation of cultural difference into a commodity, marketable to the mainstream in search of a romanticized otherness.

One response has been to incorporate the different forms of local knowledge as a source of original solutions. The idea for a storm water retention and recycling program within the Bronx, for instance, was suggested from the experience of a Jamaican immigrant. Since most groups are from "the South"—the American South as well as the Caribbean and Central and South America—the plan includes a preference for open, sunny space, and rooftop solaria.

While recognizing diversity, the designers also sought a common architectural language that could be appropriated by different groups. They found that people valued neoclassical buildings such as a landmark brick

A Tower and a Garden. Many residents prefer apartment living to single-family home ownership. James lives in the tower to the left, where he can observe the community garden he tends below. His T-shirt, "Abraham Linclon, 1992," is from a reunion for a housing project in Harlem where he lived most of his life. In the background on the right, Puerto Rican men build a wooden house for a social club. Instead of these fifteen story towers, the apartments proposed by the new plan are only six to eight stories.

courthouse in the northeast part of Melrose. The value of this style derives less from some inherent universal principle than the global history of colonization. Many residents displaced from former colonies of western Europe share a memory of this one style. As Petr Stand reiterates, "If you're from Cambodia, you've seen it. If you're from Jamaica, you've seen it..." The difference now is that these postcolonial cultures will occupy and adapt forms that once represented a dominant power. The street names and architecture of the Bronx attest to a sequence of occupants who have left their mark, and the area is expected to continue to receive peoples from different places. Rather than erasing these names and styles, the plan seeks to retain these layers of experience against which contemporary change is registered.

BRINGING IT ALL BACK HOME

Many of the design elements of Melrose Commons would also be endorsed by proponents of neotraditionalism. However, the design and process of Melrose Commons shows that the notions of home and place-based identity need not be derived from elite models. In fact, here the metaphors of home, rootedness, and continuity over time were used to claim space within the city by groups that have been marginalized at the local, national and global levels. Their narratives of home were critical in a political struggle for place and power. Their claims to identity are as socially constructed as those in Cazenovia, or the Kentlands, but the process and the ethics of the deployment of identity are very different.[13] In the Bronx identity was critical for surviving in difficult circumstances and resisting displacement. In turn, the planning process used the sense of home in an open, inclusive discourse. Rather than stressing static inheritance, Nos Quedamos acknowledged the negotiation of identity ("...So began the transformation process of each other's determination of reality" [Nos Quedamos 1993, 3]) between different groups within the neighborhood, between the community and the city, and with the designers. They created a hybrid identity, not just in the physical plan, but in the melding of local power with that of the city, developers, and even a global postcolonial world.[14] Finally, they established one of the most common traits of home, the sense of security. This was derived not from essentialized constructs of community, history, or nature, but by the security that comes from claiming the means of defining themselves and their home (Revill, 137).

Rincón Criollo, one of several *casitas* that have transformed vacant lots into gardens and social centers, re-creating memories of home for the Puerto Rican community.

NOTES

1. The elite community of Cazenovia is very similar to Bedford, New York, studied extensively for over ten years by geographers Nancy and James Duncan. We have found their approach and critique to be particularly relevant to understanding Cazenovia. See Duncan and Duncan and their forthcoming monograph on Bedford.

2. Lincklaen named the scenic reserve at the end of the lake Helensburg, after his wife. The name appears on a 1798 map of the town. (Russell Grills, manuscript, Lorenzo State Historic Site).

3. The discussion of Lakeland Park is based on interviews and text completed by Patty Maroun, a master's student in landscape architecture at the State University of New York, Syracuse, during the spring of 1991. Maroun grew up in the village.

4. In her talk she recommended that a painting depicting Cazenovia's vision of the town's future be displayed in the town offices, a recommendation that recalls Pope Sixtus V's plan for Rome hanging in the Vatican Library.

5. Lake Helene at Kentlands is named after the former housekeeper and adopted daughter of Mr. Kent. He adopted her on his death bed, November 29, 1973.

6. It should be noted that neotraditionalism synthesizes and makes a coherent narrative out of a varied set of existing design practices and ideologies. Duany and Plater-Zyberk make references to the City Beautiful movement, the work of specific designers such as Elbert Peets and Raymond Unwin, and regionalism and contextualism. They have also responded to early criticism of their work from an environmental standpoint. The names Andres Duany and Elizabeth Plater-Zyberk, however, have become so synonymous with neotraditionalism that a broad range of other contemporary designers (William Rawn, Randall Arendt, etc.) working with similar ideas are often overlooked.

7. Duany, however, insists that their work is not ideological. If something else "works," they will adapt and use it (Duany 1996). He uses *ideology* as synonymous with *dogma* or *distortion* rather than to mean a system of beliefs implicit to any design practice.

8. The *Kentlands Exchange* newspaper originally served as an advertising device. It is now the *Kentlands Town Crier*. It is controlled by an independent community group and contains accounts of changes, opinions, a regular column by the traffic engineer or designers, and editorials. Admonitions to drive slower on the streets, not park in the alleys, and

uphold the design codes come not only from the designers and developers but also from the residents.

9. We originally began this section: "The South Bronx would seem an unlikely place to find the ideals of home and community. It is referred to more often as a 'ghetto,' a home by lack of any other choice for the poor, immigrants, drug addicts, the incarcerated..." followed by various statistics and the visible features (razor wire, barred windows, burned-out buildings, vacant lots, and garbage) that signify "ghetto." The intent was to repeat a very prevalent conception that was then immediately countered. However, community members who reviewed the draft reacted strongly to the typical beginning of a predetermined story so often told by outsiders, a story they have had to contest to save their homes. Someone made the comment that by portraying the area in this way, "the very notion of civility has been placed beyond possibility." Despite our self-perceived good intentions, we got it wrong. Following this, we went through a process of listening, adjusting, and engaging in a dialogue similar to that of the designers, but nowhere near the scale of their time and commitment. This points to the importance of beginnings and raises issues concerning the ethics of storytelling and designing.

10. See Marshal Berman's discussion of how the Cross Bronx Expressway impacted his own home in the Bronx in his conclusion to *All That Is Solid Melts into Air* (New York: Penguin, 1982).

11. The structures of city planning and state urban renewal laws did not provide for this degree of community involvement and public review. The community had to constantly assert their voice and guard against attempts by City Hall to control the process (Bautista, Garcia, and Stand, 16).

12. Requirements for parking .5 cars for every unit (or one car for every two units) to be provided on site mean that large areas must be reserved for apartment buildings. Subsidies for affordable housing do not permit construction of parking garages. The community was able to reduce the requirement to .4 which they consider still too high (Bautista, Garcia, and Stand, 9).

13. To simply say that every identity is socially constructed is not enough. There are ethical issues to deconstruction and its uneven ideological impacts. To simply deconstruct the fictive nature of the stories of those who have been marginalized becomes problematic because of the uneven structures of power, and geographies of advantage and disadvantage (Jacobs, 163).

14. In fact, they have begun a dialogue and shared experiences with people visiting from Russia, Jamaica, and those who once lived under apartheid in South Africa.

REFERENCES

Alfandre. 1989. *Kentlands.* Promotional brochure.

Andersen, Kurt. 1991. "Oldfangled New Towns." *Time,* May 20.

Bakhtin, M. M. 1981. "Forms of Time and Chronotope in the Novel."
In *The Dialogic Imagination: Four Essays by M. M. Bakhtin,* ed. Michael
Holquist, trans. Caryl Emerson and Michael Holquist. Austin: University of
Texas Press.

Bautista, Eddie, Yolanda Garcia, and Petr Stand. "Melrose Commons: A Case
Study for Sustainable Community Design," ed. Barbara Olshansky,
Environmental Defense Fund. Unpublished manuscript.

Benjamin, Walter. 1969. "The Storyteller: Reflections on the Works of Nikolai
Leskov." In *Illuminations,* trans. Harry Zohn. New York: Schocken Books.

Boyer, Christine. 1994. *The City of Collective Memory.* Cambridge: MIT Press.

Bressi, Todd W. 1994. "There is a Tomorrow That Will Favor Us: An Interview
with Yolanda Garcia." *The Livable City* 18(1):5.

Brown, Patricia Leigh. 1988. "In Seven Days, Designing a New Traditional
Town." *New York Times,* June 9.

Cary, Catherine, Petr Stand, and Lee Weintraub. 1994. "We Stay: How Melrose
Hopes to Build Its Future." *The Livable City* 18(1).

Cazenovia Community Resources Project. 1984. *Land Use Guide.* Cazenovia
Preservation Foundation.

Dorst, John. 1989. *The Written Suburb: An American Site, an Ethnographic
Dilemma.* Philadelphia: University of Pennsylvania Press.

Duany, Plater-Zyberk & Company. 1996. "Traditional Town Planning Practice."
Unpublished compliation, Miami, Washington, Charlotte.

Duany, Andres. 1996. "New Urbanism," Presentation at Syracuse Convention
Center, April 18.

Duncan, James S. 1994. "Shaughnessey Height: The Protection of Privilege." In
Neighborhood Organization and the Welfare State, ed. S. Hasson and D.
Ley. Cambridge: Cambridge University Press. Pp. 52-82.

———. 1995. "Deep Suburban Irony: The Perils of Democracy in Westchester
County, New York." In *Visions of Suburbia,* ed. R. Silverstone. London:
Routledge.

Duncan, James S., and Nancy G. Duncan. 1988. "(Re)reading the landscape."
Environment and Planning D: Society and Space 6:117–126.

———. Forthcoming. "The Suburban Wilderness." Baltimore: Johns Hopkins
University Press.

Ellin, Nan. 1996. *Postmodern Urbanism.* Cambridge, Mass.: Blackwell
Publishers.

Garcia, Yolanda (president of Nos Quedamos). 1996. Interview with authors,
June 28.

Girling, Cynthia L., and Kenneth I. Helphand. 1994. *Yard-Street-Park: The Design of Suburban Open Space.* New York: John Wiley & Sons.

Gonzalez, David. 1993. "Revolution of People Power Wells Up in the Bronx." *New York Times,* June 8.

Grills, Russell. 1986. *Cazenovia: The Story of an Upland Community.* Cazenovia Preservation Foundation.

———. 1993. *Upland Idyll: Images of Cazenovia, New York, 1860–1900.* Louisville: Harmony House.

Guterson, David. 1992. "No Place Like Home: On the Manicured Streets of a Master-Planned Community." *Harper's,* November.

Hobsbawm, E., and T. Ranger, eds. 1983. *The Invention of Tradition.* Cambridge: Cambridge University Press.

Holquist, Michael. 1990. *Dialogism: Bakhtin and His World.* London: Routledge.

Hough, Michael. 1990. *Out of Place: Restoring Identity to the Regional Landscape.* New Haven, Conn.: Yale University Press.

Hugill, Peter J. 1984. "The Landscape As a Code for Conduct: Reflections on Its Role in Walter Firey's 'Aesthetic-Historical-Genealogical Complex.'" *Geoscience and Man* 24(April):21–30.

———.1995. *Upstate Arcadia: Landscape, Aesthetics and the Triumph of Social Differentiation in America.* Lanham, Md.: Rownam and Littlefield.

Jacobs, Jane M. 1996. *Edge of Empire: Postcolonialism and the City.* London: Routledge.

Johnstone, Barbara. 1990. *Stories, Community, and Place; Narratives from Middle America.* Bloomington: Indiana University Press.

Knack, R. 1989. "Repent, Ye Sinners, Repent." *Planning* (August):4–13.

Krieger, Alex, and William Lennertz. 1992. *Andres Duany and Elizabeth Plater-Zyberk: Towns and Town-Making Principles.* New York: Rizzoli.

Luymes, Don T. 1996. "Scripting the Landscape of Privatopia and the Closing of Open Space." *Selected CELA Annual Conference Papers* 7:49–60.

MacCannell, Dean. [1976] 1989. *The Tourist: A New Theory of the Liesure Class.* New York: Schocken Books.

Mack, Arien, ed. 1993. *Home: A Place in the World.* New York: New York University Press.

Maroun, Patricia. 1991. "Cazenovia's Other." Unpublished research paper, State University of New York, Syracuse.

Nash, Suzanne, ed. 1993. *Home and Its Dislocations in Nineteenth-Century France.* Albany: State University of New York Press.

Nos Quedamos. 1993. "Melrose Community Resident and Business Owner Petition." April 26.

———. 1994 "Outline for Proposed Melrose Commons Standards and Guidelines," October 24.

———. 1996. Interviews with authors, June 28, November 12 and 23.

Paulson, William. 1993. "Hearth and Homelessness: Place, Story and Novel in Flaubert's Sentimental Educations." In *Home and Its Dislocations in*

Nineteenth-Century France, ed. Suzanne Nash. Albany: State University of New York Press. Pp. 85–101.

Plater-Zyberk, Elizabeth. 1991. Lecture at Syracuse University School of Architecture and Cazenovia League of Women Voters, February 13.

Revill, George. 1993. "Reading Rosehill: Community, Identity and Inner-City Derby." In *Place and the Politics of Identity,* ed. Michael Keith and Steve Pile. London: Routledge.

Rothstein, Mervyn. 1994. "A Renewal Plan in the Bronx Advances." *New York Times,* July 10.

Schlichting, Eileen, chairman, Kentlands Community Foundation. 1997. "Letter to Citizens Forum." *Kentlands Town Crier,* May 15.

Sciorra, Joseph. 1994. "'We're not here just to plant. We have culture.' An Ethnography of the South Bronx Casita Rincón Criollo." *New York Folklore* 10 (3–4):19-41.

Shoshkes, Ellen. 1989. "Kentlands: New Town Plan." In *The Design Process: Case Studies in Project Development.* New York: Whitney Library of Design.

Sopher, David. 1979. "The Landscape of Home." in *The Interpretation of Ordinary Landscapes,* ed. Donald Meinig. New York: Oxford University Press. Pp. 129–149.

Stand, Petr (Magnusson Architects). 1996. Interview with authors, June 28.

Stokes, Samuel N., with A. Elizabeth Watson (Genevieve Keller and J. Timothy Kellor, contributing authors). 1989. *Saving America's Countryside: A Guide to Rural Conservation.* Baltimore: Johns Hopkins University Press.

Till, K. 1993. "Neotraditional Towns and Urban Villages: The Cultural Production of a Geography of 'Otherness.'" In *Environment and Planning D: Society and Space* 11:709–732.

Tompkins, Kenneth. 1982. "Mystery Resurfaces: Historians Debate Origins of Indian Canoe That Keeps Popping Up in Cazenovia Lake." *Cazenovia Republican,* March 7.

Vergara, Camilo Jose. 1995. *The New American Ghetto.* New Brunswick: Rutgers University Press.

Weintraub, Lee. (chair, Landscape Architecture Department, City College of New York). 1996. Interview with authors, June.

Wood, Joseph S. 1991. "'Build, Therefore, Your Own World': The New England Village as Settlement Ideal." *Annals of the Association of American Geographers* 81(1):32–50.

Young, Iris Marion. 1990. "The Ideal of Community and the Politics of Difference." In *Feminism/Postmodernism,* ed. Linda Nicholson. New York: Routledge Chapman and Hall. Pp. 300–323.

CHAPTER 10
ROAD STORIES

GOING

Crossroads Shrines, Hermes and Interpretation

Crossroads are events in narrative journeys —points of decision, of encounter with strangers, of meeting or nonmeeting. Chip Sullivan and Elizabeth Boults have documented the myths, sacred traditions, and spatial implications of crossroads tabernacles and roadside shrines in Tuscany, Italy. These *Madonnini* have their origin in the Roman and Greek gods of Mercury and Hermes. Hermes' name derives from the word for the stone heaps used to mark boundaries and crossroads. As a god of boundaries and a trickster, he moved between the familiar and the strange. He became a god of the road, of travelers, and of interpreters who translated messages across boundaries of different worlds. (He was also credited by Homer with inventing music, the lyre, and pipes.)

TO get in the car and head out on the road, to "light out for the territory," would seem preferable to sitting down and writing about it. When ideas move only grudgingly across the blank page, going on the road is a way of escaping, as well as making things happen. But even Jack Kerouac, who followed a method of spontaneous prose, a kind of "road of consciousness" pressing onward, nonstop writing—"No periods separating sentences—structures already arbitrarily riddled by false colons and timid usually needless commas—but the vigorous space dash separating rhetorical breathing"—was thwarted in his first attempt to hitchhike "one long red line called Route 6" across the country (Kerouac 1955, 12). Stranded in the rain just beyond New York City at a traffic circle on a picturesque parkway below Bear Mountain, he had to revise the script of his road trip and return to the city to catch a westbound bus. After seven years of travel, he paused for a month and wrote *On the Road* on one continuous roll of paper.

In his story the road is not only the theme and a symbol for *a way of life*, but it becomes an icon that resonates throughout the structural design of the text. It determines the sequence of events, the language, the punctuation, and the very process of writing itself.[1] This synthesis of space and time, theme and symbol, process and structure, exemplifies how the road functions as a chronotope. Bakhtin explains how "time as it were fuses together with space and flows in it (forming the road)." This is the source of the rich metaphorical expansion (the course of a life, the course of empire, etc.) across a great tradition of "road stories" (Bakhtin, 244).

Kerouac's estrangement from his father and search for self-knowledge follow a course similar to that of Oedipus[2], whose fate was determined at the crossroads where he mistakenly killed his own father. The road is an important place for such chance meetings and the encounter of social differences in stories ranging from Chaucer's *Canterbury Tales* to J. G. Ballard's *Crash*. Goethe reworked the themes of fate, chance and social differences into the bildungsroman, a narrative of personal education and self-transformation. The open road has turned out to be a particularly vivid space for exploring the existential dilemmas of freedom and its close counterpart, alienation. In the films of Wim Wenders, including *Kings of the Road, Wrong Moves, Wings of Desire, Until the End of the World*, and *Paris, Texas*, people outside conventional bounds find identity and redemption in movement itself. However, these are primarily male odysseys in which women are obstacles who threaten to end the wandering, and end the story.

On the road, Thelma and Louise cross these conventional gender distinctions, between those who are immobile and restricted to a *function of* domestic space and those who enjoy the freedom to move, change identity, and cross frontiers. As part of a growing subgenre of "road movies," these films fuse motion, change, narrative, and the road.

But what do gender roles or the fitful search for identity have to do with the calculus of the interstate? The metaphorical extensions of road stories seem to only gloss the ordinary road paved and determined by engineering and necessity. However, just as destination and destiny are linked etymologically (Curtis and Pajaczkowska, 199), the very alignments, grades, surfaces, beginnings, and ends of roads inscribe the metaphors and desires of a plenitude of travel narratives—leaving home, returning home, rites of passage, tourism, progress, pilgrimage, exodus, migration, social mobility, research, field trips, wandering, and so on. These narratives and their roads structure *differences* of place and people into binaries of here and there, familiar and strange, home and horizon, center and margin, self and other. These differences in space often become differences in time, and the road becomes a metaphor of time traveling. This is the central trope in William Least Heat Moon's *Blue Highways*. He departed from the freeway, signifier of modernity, fast pace, and alienation, in search of an older, more "authentic" America (and self) still to be found along the backroads or the "blue highways," as they appear on old maps.

Whether it is a back road, Whitman's open road, or the freeway, the road is a primary signifier in narratives of American national identity. All the immigrant roads, the gridded network of rural roads across two-thirds of the continent, the freeways, beltways, parkways, thruways, arterials, strips, bypasses, boulevards, and ultimately the interstates are part of one great bildungsroman of national identity forged through continuous mobility and freedom to constantly reinvent that identity. The wanderings of Kerouac or Least Heat Moon are part of the continuing inscription of *America as a road story.*

Designers travel. Olmsted went on the road, and the experience of differences is still a critical part of design education and professional status. Designers have followed their clients on the Grand Tour and move ever more freely across international borders as consultants for governments and multinational corporations. Yet, despite all this travel, professional discourse on landscape and sense of place tends to celebrate rootedness and local identity. In part this is a reaction to a very modern sense of alienation and placelessness resulting from too much travel, too many highways. According to anthropologist James Clifford, the metaphor of "rootedness" and strategies of fixing cultures to local places reflect the desires of cultures with the power to travel and transcend limits. The emphasis on rootedness also denies the importance of travel even for traditional and vernacular cultures. Clifford's aim is to rethink cultures as sites constructed through and crossed by travel:

> I'm not saying there are no locales or homes, that everyone is—or should be—traveling, or cosmopolitan, or deterritorialized...Rather, I'm trying to sketch a comparative cultural studies approach to specific his-

Road Movies:
The Grapes of Wrath (1940)
Gun Crazy (1949)
Bonnie and Clyde (1967)
Detour (1946)
Wrong Moves (1978)
Badlands (1973)
Easy Rider (1969)
The Wild One (1954)
Something Wild (1986)
Wild at Heart (1990)
Pierre le Fou (1965)
Weekend (1967)
Feeling Minnesota (1996)
Leaving Normal (1995)
Mad Max (1980)
The Road Warrior (1982)
My Own Private Idaho (1991)
Stranger than Paradise (1985)
Down by Law (1986)
Mystery Train (1989)
Highway 61 (1991)
Candy Mountain (1987)
Roadside Prophets (1992)
La Strada (1954)
Endless Highway (1997)
Crash (1997)[3]

tories, tactics, everyday practices of dwelling and traveling: traveling-in-dwelling, dwelling-in-traveling.
(Clifford, 108)

To engage the road stories of identity and difference, we took a road trip, south, to Mississippi, where we would be strangers, out of place, northerners. We followed two roads, the Natchez Trace Parkway and Highway 61. They go in different directions and present distinctly different road stories and different issues for design and interpretation. The old Natchez Trace leads into the otherness of nature and the very origins of roads. The design of the newer Parkway, which follows the Trace, illustrates how conventions of travel narratives, in this case picturesque travel, become inscribed in conventions of roadway design. Highway 61, on the other hand, is a vernacular road that leads into the Mississippi Delta and the encounter of social differences marked by race. Here, the themes of the American road story take on different meanings for African-Americans who have been bound to the land or compelled to migrate, or who have become the desired object of visits by tourists and other travelers. Driving on these roads between Nashville, Memphis, and New Orleans also means listening for the sources of a rich tradition of music—country, blues, jazz, zydeco, swamp pop, ELVIS, rockabilly, rock and roll, to name a few. Highway 61, in particular, leads directly into the land where the blues began and is referred to now as the Blues Highway. With its themes of mobility, escape, and cultural crossover into rock and roll, the story of the blues merges with the story of the road.

Above: The routes of the Natchez Trace Parkway and Highway 61 through Mississippi.

Below: Sunken Trace near Port Gibson.

THE NATCHEZ TRACE PARKWAY

ON THE TRACE

Down in the Trace, you can smell the soil exposed by the worn path. Tree roots hold back walls of the erodible loess soil. Muscadine vines and Spanish moss hang overhead. It is as evocative as a Grünewald painting. A sign nearby tells the particular story of this road:

> Preserved here is a portion of the deeply eroded or "sunken" Old Trace. Hardships of journeying on the Old Trace included heat, mosquitoes, poor food, hard beds (if any), disease, swollen rivers, and sucking swamps.

> Take 5 minutes to walk this sunken trail and let your imagination carry you back to the early 1800s when people walking 500 miles had to put up with these discomforts and where a broken leg or arm could spell death for the lone traveler.

This fragment of the sunken Trace is just a brief stop, a place of imaginative wandering for tourists. Dressed more for a pleasurable drive than the

Excerpts from Englishman Francis Bailey's travel on the Trace, in his 1797 *Journal of a Tour in Unsettled Parts of North America in 1796 and 1797*.

Departure:
"From this place, then, we have to date our departure into the wilderness; and here we have to bid adieu to all marks of civilization till we arrive at the borders of the Cumberland river, in the state of Tenessee[sic]."

Obstacles:
"Sunday, July 16th—We passed that afternoon through an almost impervious thicket caused by a tremendous hurricane which happened in this country some time back. The brambles and bushes had grown up in such quantities between the trunks of the fallen trees, as to render it nearly impassable: but as it extended a considerable way, the Indians had trodden a path through it..."

Indians and accommodations:
"Wednesday, July 19th—(at an Indian settlement)—Picture to yourself a dirty hole of a place, without any other light but what came in at the door, plastered up on each side with mud, with...an iron kettle which had served for all the purposes of life, together with all our spoons dipping into it alternately; imagine us sitting round this kettle, in this filthy hut, and in this manner devouring the homely repast which was set before us, and such as one as we had not experienced since our departure from Natchez; imagine all this, I say, and a thousand other things which at the time tended to heighten the effect, and you will then be enabled to form some idea of our situation."

hardships of a wilderness trek, they seem incongruous on the trace. Returning to their cars, they loop back onto the Natchez Trace Parkway and continue on to other stops along a smooth, well-drained, and graded highway. These two roads, the old Trace and the modern Parkway, parallel, cross, and weave in this way for almost 450 miles from Natchez to Nashville.

In effect the Parkway is a road that tells the story of another road, the Old Trace. The alignment of the Parkway parallels, restores, and reveals this older line, which had become overgrown, fragmented, and forgotten. Driving the Parkway is much like reading a story; new scenes appear around each bend. Proceeding from sign to sign, one marked event to another—Springfield plantation, Grindstone Ford, and so on—conjures the characters and history of the Natchez Trace. The repeated crossings of the two roads open a narrative space between the juxtapositions of past and present, sunken and elevated, Old South and New South, hardship and convenience, decline and progress. The Parkway gathers these disparate sites and stories along a line, transforming space into a coherent text in which the driver can participate.

The purpose of the Parkway, as the sign instructs, is to take the visitor back in time. This trope of time travel, where movement through space becomes a trip through time, is a common metaphor of the road. It takes at least a day to drive the whole length of the Parkway, but the temporal scale of the story it tells is much longer, extending back to vague primordial begin-

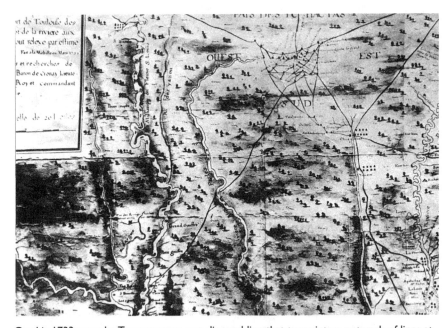

On this 1733 map, the Trace appears as a diagonal line that turns into a network of lines at major settlements of the Choctaws and Chickasaws. Even in the 1800s the Trace deviated from a single line according to the seasons. To avoid dense wet bottom lands in the summer, the route followed low ridge lines. "Map of the territory between the Chattahoochee and Mississippi Rivers, compiled by Baron de Crenay," NTP manuscript files.

Above left: Choctaw Indians touring on the modern parkway.

Above right: Cartoon from the *Times-Picayune*, April 21, 1935, showing the Trace as a historical procession of characters signifying major periods and events of the Old Southwest. (Source: NTP archives. Reprinted with permission of the Times-Picayune Publishing Corp.)

nings. Some argue the Trace originates as an animal track—this inscription *in* nature begins *as* nature. It became an important network of paths linking Native American settlements and was first mapped by the French in 1733. Even without maps the route was a distinct enough spatial notion that a Choctaw Indian could scratch it out on the ground to give directions to the English traveler Francis Bailey in 1797. However, it took the traffic of thousands of travelers in just the first two decades of the 1800s to inscribe the Trace deeply into the soil, as well as into legend and history.

In fact, the Natchez Trace becomes the structure, the plot line for telling the history of the Old Southwest. History becomes a procession down the road led by stock characters ("Kaintucks," Indians, explorers, preachers, armies, post riders, and outlaws), along with the famous and infamous (Andrew Jackson, Aaron Burr, and Meriwether Lewis).

Names and Metaphors

Roads and their stories lead to both actual and metaphorical destinations. At first the Trace was known as *the road to the Choctaw Nation* and later, depending on the direction of travel, it was either *the road to Nashville* or *the road to Natchez.* For the thousands of "Kaintucks" who floated down the Ohio and Mississippi Rivers and sold their goods as well as the logs of their flatboat at Natchez, the Trace was simply *the road home.* For those who traded on the river, established iron mines and forges, as well as agriculture, it was *a road to prosperity and opportunity.* Designated a federal

Eudora Welty's short story "A Worn Path" follows the journey of a nearly blind African-American woman, Phoenix Jackson, on the Trace. It is an enigmatic journey. The reader is left to wonder what motivates her to overcome a series of obstacles and potential catastrophes on the Trace.

"Her eyes opened their widest, and she started down gently. But before she got to the bottom of the hill a bush caught her dress... At the foot of this hill was a place where a log was laid across the creek.

"'Now comes the trial,' said Phoenix. Putting her right foot out, she mounted the log and shut her eyes. Lifting her skirt, leveling her cane fiercely before her, like a festival figure in some parade, she began to march across. Then she opened her eyes and she was safe on the other side.

"'I wasn't as old as I thought,' she said.

"Deep, deep the road went down between the high green-colored banks. Overhead the live-oaks met, and it was as dark as a cave. She walked on. The shadows hung from the oak trees to the road like curtains. Then she smelled wood-smoke, and smelled the river, and she saw a steeple and the cabins on their steep steps. Dozens of little black children whirled around her. There ahead was Natchez shining. Bells were ringing. She walked on..."

(From *The Collected Stories of Eudora Welty* [New York: Harcourt Brace Jovanovich, 1980], pp. 142–149)

Above: Melrose, the mansion where Natchez Pilgrimage began, ca. 1932. The Natchez Trace Parkway is linked to Pilgrimage, a five-week period in early spring when the mansions and gardens of Natchez are opened to the public. In 1932 the women of well-established families planned a garden tour, but it rained on the day so they opened up the homes as well. From then on it grew as a popular event. Over time actual historic and functional elements of the gardens were replaced by images of a southern mythology. Having a modern paved road terminating in Natchez helped to serve the pilgrim tourists. (Collection of Thomas H. and Joan W. Gandy, Natchez, Mississippi)

Below: Mrs. Roan Byrnes, early president of the Natchez Trace Association and leader of the garden club, standing in a sunken portion of the Old Trace.

post road, post riders and frontier newspapers circulated up and down what was an information highway. Armies marched down the Trace three times and it became *a road to war.* When the Choctaw, Chickasaw, Creek, and Cherokee nations were dispossessed from their lands and marched westward, portions of the Trace became part of *the trail of tears* (Davis).

Despite the fact that most used the Trace to travel from Natchez back to the east, all the circulation of people, goods, ideas, and stories served to open territory, cross boundaries of former Indian and European territories, and establish the Southwest as one corner of an expanding American empire. As *a road to the frontier,* the Trace was part of a temporal journey forward in time in the American narrative of Manifest Destiny. Its themes, characters, and direction make up another version of America as a road story.

In this national narrative, mobility also means abandonment. By the 1830s the Trace was bypassed by other roads and by the new technology of steam-powered riverboats. Settlers inscribed new ways through territories beyond the Old Southwest. It is in this period of decline that the road acquired its aura of legend and history as well as its name The Natchez Trace, referring to an ancient track through the wilderness. It was the notion of the road as the trace of historical process that the Daughters of the American Revolution used in the early 1900s to justify memorializing the Trace, first with monuments and then in the form of another road, the Parkway. The Trace as parkway would serve the beginnings of heritage tourism in Natchez known as Pilgrimage, a five-week period in early spring when the antebellum mansions and gardens are opened to the public. Yet, the Parkway did did not only go back in time. For the local people who contended with the obstacles, backwardness, and time it took to travel on poor rural roads, the Parkway was a modern super-highway that led to progress and opportunity for a New South.

Congress appropriated $50,000 in 1934 to make a preliminary survey of the Trace and study the possibilities of a memorial parkway. On May 17, 1935, members of and advisers to the National Park Service met to discuss options for the Natchez Trace. Those present were John Nolen, H. J. Spelman, Thomas Vint, V. E. Chatelain, Herman Kohn, E. S. Zimmer, and George Albrecht. The following are some excerpts from their discussion.

The options:

Mr. Chatelain. The people who introduced this survey had in mind the construction of a memorial highway along the Natchez Trace. We must keep in mind their purpose, but if we are justified in plunging beneath their purpose and if we knew the Natchez Trace never existed it would not be proposed in this way.

Mr. Vint. There seems to be no doubt about marking it....The next step is how far should we go about letting people on it. One extreme is build a parkway very closely paralleling it to give a person a route over the old route. The other extreme is to map out our marking and not depend on the local road systems. The tourist would have to go through and do some exploring like we had to. The third extreme would be to build a modern type parkway or highway through that country without being too closely dependent on the Trace.

Who travels:

Mr. Nolen. The Governor points out that a road like this for his white population would let them get to the State Capitol.

(National Park Service 1935)

ON THE PARKWAY: THE TRACE OF PICTURESQUE TRAVEL

The story of the Old Natchez Trace seems to resolve into the smooth, coherent medium of its telling, the Parkway. However, the syntax of the Parkway, its smoothness contrasted with the wild edge, its fluid alignment, sequences, and avoidance of cities, is a trace of another road story, picturesque travel. At about the same time the cast of frontier characters set out to open a way *through* the wilderness, romantic writers and artists were making long rambles over the countryside *in search of* ideal forms of nature. The gentry took the grand tour across the Alps back to the origins of Western culture in Italy and Greece. Wordsworth, Gilpin, and other English Romantics advocated tours of native scenery of the Wye Valley, the Lake District, or the Scottish Highlands (Andrews, viii). The travel narratives, guides, and images of these prototourists established the practices and conventions for others to follow. In America, A. J.Downing toured the picturesque realms of the Hudson Valley, and as a child, Olmsted went with his family on tours of the picturesque through New England. By the 1930s with the affordability of automobiles, diversionary travel to scenic destinations of America could be enjoyed by the majority of America's middle class.

These daily rambles and extended journeys in search of the picturesque were quest narratives. What they sought in the "outer" journey, in changing scenes and sensations, in nature, in the ruins of history and other cultures, was an expanded sense of the contours of their own "inner" consciousness and identity. The physical journey was both means and metaphor in this narrative search for identity.

The scenes of landscape not only impressed and influenced the travelers, but over time their collective travel also shaped the landscapes they passed through. Besides the physical traces of worn roads or the need for accommodations, picturesque travel also mapped out an ideal landscape. It authenticated sites, defined sequences, and created whole areas for pilgrimage. The writings of Sir Walter Scott or Washington Irving filled picturesque areas with stories. The traveler also remade the landscape via the sketch, the Claude Glass[4] or the journal entry to make it fit the ideal. The desires of the picturesque traveler could also be miniaturized in garden design. The overland journey becomes an afternoon perambulation around the garden, structured by a sequence of follies or ruins that refer to other places, other times, and other tours. In effect the picturesque garden mediates, as Sydney Robinson explains, between what was a static world of "estate culture" and the increasing mobility of ideas, people, and resources, "by having the estate tell us about mobility" (Robinson, 143).

The Natchez Trace Parkway is a 450-mile-long synthesis of picturesque travel and garden design. While the Trace marks the physical route of the boatmen, post riders, and other travelers, the Parkway inscribes the desires and practices of a long line of picturesque travelers. The Parkway also reflects a long tradition of park and garden design that translated the picturesque travel narrative into physical design. Olmsted's innovations of separating traffic in Central Park and establishing urban parkways set precedents for merging the park with the road. Landscape architects with the National Park Service became adept at harmonizing the demand for automobile access with scenic values. Rather than agents of destruction, roads became one of the primary means of revealing and presenting nature, as well as controlling millions of park visitors (McClelland). The Natchez Trace Parkway is also part of a design tradition of grand scenic parkways that include the Mount Vernon Memorial Highway, the Blue Ridge Parkway, the Foothills Parkway, the Rock Creek, and the Potomac Parkway.

A PARTIAL GUIDE TO THE PARKWAY
The existing interpretive literature for the Natchez Trace Parkway focuses almost solely on the history of the Trace. The history of the Parkway is tagged at the end in just a few lines. It remains the medium of the story, not the message. What follows is a partial and unofficial guide that tells the story of the Parkway. It adopts and adapts a guidebook format, a genre typically associated with picturesque travel and a primary tool for formalizing the conventions of seeing and reading the landscape for the tourist. Barthes, however, calls a guidebook "an agent of blindness" because it focuses on a limited range of features and even "masks" much more of what is potentially "read" (Duncan and Duncan 1992, 20). The following guide is intended to work in an opposite manner. It aims to unsettle the smooth text of the Parkway by opening and revealing the discourses implicit in the design, recontextualizing marked sites, naming absences, and foregrounding much of what has merged into the background.[5]

Format
The format of this guide follows that of the Official Park Service Guide. Each entry is marked by its mileage from the beginning of the Trace at Natchez. However, the interpretation is more concerned with typical characteristics of the Parkway than individual sites. Therefore, the mark "↳" is used to designate something that can be found all along the Parkway. Also, in the official guide the sequence of individual sites follows the spatial sequence along the road. They function as synecdoches of a generally shared narrative realm of the frontier, nature, Native Americans, and recreation. There is no linear chronology. However, in this guide to the Parkway the sites are organized to

tell a less familiar story. The plot of this narrative takes precedence, resulting in some shuffling of the spatial sequence of sites along the road.

8.1 On-Ramp, Separation. The Parkway begins eight miles outside Natchez. "A parkway is preferably located through undeveloped areas of scenic beauty and interest and avoids communities and intensive farm lands...a parkway *right-of-way* is defined as a strip of land acquired in fee simple to provide the area for the construction of the roadway and an insulating area to protect the natural values" ("General Parkway Policies," Natchez Trace Parkway Archives).

8.1 Sign, "No Commercial Vehicles"

Getting on the Parkway is a departure, not only from the river town of Natchez but from the ordinary traffic, billboards, faux plantation motels, and commercial plenitude of Highway 61. On the Parkway the road merges with its context, arcing from curve to tangent to curve around topographic swells and through rhythmic sequences of pasture and grove, light and dark, open and closed. There are no intersections, local roads, or traffic lights to interfere in this space of pure motion. Like the Mississippi on which Mark Twain made his classic water journey, the road is separated from community and any ties or friction that might impede.

Picturesque travel has no commercial purpose other than the pleasures of scenic beauty, history and travel itself. The remote rural areas of the 18th century provided such a space, as does the Parkway right-of-way that bans commercial traffic, dissuades convenient commuting access, and avoids cities altogether. The Parkway is also separated from the local roads, local trips, local commutes, and local concerns.

8.2 Sign, "Speed Limit 50 mph." "Soon the bustle of the Trace had quieted to the peacefulness of a forest lane." Today the Parkway gives "present-day travelers an unhurried route from Natchez to Nashville" (NPS Official Guide).

Besides separation in space, picturesque travel seeks a realm outside the time of workday schedules, a privileged realm once limited to the leisured gentry but now the universal experience of the tourist vacation (MacCannell, 5). The 50 mph speed limit sets the road apart as well. It requires an attitude adjustment that separates it from the "real time" of other roads. It also sets up the temporal difference between the past and the present by evoking the notion that the past proceeded at a slower pace.

10.3, 106.9, 232.4, 286.7, 308.8 Native American Mounds (Ruins)
The Parkway reveals and links series of Native American ceremonial and burial mounds dating from 1200 to 1600 A.D. The largest, Emerald Mound, covers eight acres.

"The picturesque eye is perhaps most inquisitive after the elegant relics of ancient architecture, the remains of castles and

Parkway: The rules of the road.
A parkway is a designed corridor that treats the road and its context as a whole. In 1935, the National Park Service defined a parkway by eight criteria, which are generally adhered to today:
1. Ban on commercial traffic
2. Ban on unsightly roadside development/signage
3. Ban on frontage and access rights
4. Wide right-of-way buffer
5. Absence of major grade crossings
6. Development on a previously unbuilt site
7. Best use of native scenery and vegetation
8. Well-distanced entrances and exits
(Leach, 3)

Parkway landscape architect Bob Felker describes the leisurely pace of the parkway:
"We talk about parkways being for recreational driving, and the Natchez Trace Parkway is purely that. You can just relax, restore yourself. You don't have to worry about traffic. You don't have to worry about running off the road. The only thing you have to worry about is maybe some wildlife."

Bear Creek Mound, built between 1200 and 1400 A.D.

abbeys. They are consecrated by time; and almost deserve the veneration we pay to the works of nature itself" (Gilpin, 46).

For Gilpin the pursuit of an ideal nature, represented as a woman, was more important than the attainment of the object:

"The pleasures of the chase are universal...And shall we suppose it a greater pleasure to the sportsman to pursue a trivial animal, than it is to the man of taste to pursue the beauties of nature? to follow her through all her recesses? to obtain a sudden glance as she flits past him in some airy shape? to trace her through the mazes of the cover? to wind after her along the vale? or along the reaches of the river?"

(Gilpin, 48)

abbeys. They are consecrated by time; and almost deserve the veneration we pay to the works of nature itself" (Gilpin, 46).

12.4 Loess Bluff, Revealing Picturesque Nature. This fifty-foot exposed embankment of loess soil was blown and deposited here during the Ice Age. The road reveals this ancient process and others as it cuts across several physiographic zones.

40.4 Tornado, May 8, 1995. Debris disrupts the smooth pastoral landscape, revealing a more sublime nature. The modern Parkway cuts through the kind of obstacles that made travel on the Trace such a hardship for Francis Bailey and other travelers in the early 1800s.

Separated in both space and time from the ordinary, the Parkway opens a liminal space for narratives of discovery. The explicit story told in the marked sites and interpretive materials is the discovery of national and regional identity. However, implicit to the picturesque exploration is a journey toward self-identity. As one audio guide for the Parkway suggests, "You may even learn something about yourself." Evolving, changing, mobile identity is best revealed through differences that are clear, coherent, and essential. Therefore, differences of the past, other cultures, and nature become ideal objects for comparison in this narrative.

In Romantic narratives the ideal of Nature, however, becomes an unattainable object of desire. It is an elusive quarry, slipping between expectations and experience, sketch and memory, the ideal and the actual (Whale, 179). Coleridge described a familiar disjunction between the pursuit of the ideal and the actual experience: "Few have seen a celebrated waterfall without feeling something akin to disappointment." The traveler, instead, must add to, reflect, and improve upon nature: "It is only subsequently that the image comes back full into the mind and brings with it a train of grand or beautiful associations" (Whale, 180). This is one of the enduring paradoxes of picturesque travel. While seeking out an ideal nature untouched by culture, the traveler, like the painter, nonetheless manipulates and transforms it through memory or sketching. The Parkway mediates this tension between art and nature by revealing nature, but only through great concealment of its artifice (Whale, 178). It performs the same task that the traveler's sketches and memories did of reassembling an ideal out of the actual. In the process, an English picturesque garden is naturalized into a native Mississippi ecology.

William Least Heat Moon on his journey of self-discovery on America's "blue highways," found the Natchez Trace Parkway to be the paradigm of "the road in Nature." After reciting the history of the Trace, he describes his drive:

"Now new road, opening the woods again, went in among redbuds and white blossoms of dogwood, curving about under a cool evergreen cover. For miles no powerlines or billboards. Just tree, rock, water, bush and road. The new Trace, like a river, followed natural contours and gave focus to the land; it so brought out the beauty that every road commissioner in the nation should drive the Trace to see that highway does not have to outrage landscape.

"Northeast of Tougaloo, I stopped to hike a trail into a blackwater swamp of tupelo and bald cypress...I had a powerful sense of life going about the business of getting on with itself. Pointed phallic sprouts pressed up out of the ooze...For some time I stood among the high mysteries of being as they consumed the decay of old life.

"Then I went back to the Trace and followed dusk around the spread of Jackson highways that had broken open like aneurysms and leaked out strawberry-syrup pancakes, magic-finger motel beds, and double-cheeze pizzas."

(107–108)

Wandering Alignment.
"A parkway aims to make accessible the best scenery in the country it traverses. Therefore, the shortest or most direct route is not necessarily a primary consideration." (General Parkway Policies, NTP Archives).

"Sharp curves as well as monotonous straight-aways are avoided..." (ca. 1937, Malcolm Gardner, land representative, National Park Service, NTP Archives).

The picturesque journey creates a realm for digressive wandering. In a poem by Alexander Pope, a wandering eye swings from "*Here* waving Groves" to "*There*, interspers'd in Lawns and opening Glades... *Here* in full Light the russet Plains extend; *There* wrapt in Clouds" (Andrews, 18). On the Parkway the alignment of the road assumes this same course of the wanderer. Except here, the driver is passive as the scenes change, practically mimicking the same alternating rhythm as Pope's poem. The Parkway is also like the route of the early picturesque boat tours. The tour of the Wye Valley past the famous ruins of Tintern Abbey was the most popular of these river tours, offering a smooth ride on which one could relax and concentrate solely on "the beauties of the ever shifting scenery...appearing, vanishing, and re-appearing, in different shapes and with different combinations of wood and water"

(Andrews, 89).[6]

Old Trace. A Rough Road.

With twisted roots hanging onto eroded earth and snarled with vines, the Old Trace serves as a sign of the picturesque ideal of "roughness." For Uvedale Price, "hollow lanes and bye-roads" were the very model of picturesque beauty. They were not designed but reflected piecemeal change, and registered the

Repton remarks: "It is remarkable that no attempt should have been made to render objects of so much beauty and variety accessible in a carriage, for however interesting the walks in hilly countries may be, they can only be enjoyed by great labour and exertion." He, instead, endeavors to display the scenes from the windows of the carriage, aligning the road with the view instead of making it necessary to glimpse it in passing so that *"the most careless observer may have the leisure to view the delightful scene,"* which will pass before the eye. (Hunt and Willis, 364)

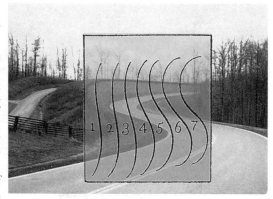

Hogarth's *Line of Beauty*. 1753.

"Though all sorts of waving-lines are ornamental, when properly applied; yet, strictly speaking, there is but one precise line, properly to be called the line of beauty (number 4)...And that the serpentine line, by its waving and winding at the same time different ways, leads the eye in a pleasing manner along the continuity of its variety." (Hogarth, 72, 75, 93)

processes of nature commingled with the actions of humans. He was appalled by the "military style" of the new roads of the late 18th century around London, roads that leveled land, required retaining walls ("palings"), and stranded fragments of nature (Daniels and Watkins, 22). Yet, here again the paradox appears. The effect of this rough nature is best revealed as a surprise or an interruption in a smooth pastoral nature.

↳ Parkway, A Smooth Road.

The Parkway is a smooth pastoral landscape that weaves and alternates with fragments of the rough road of the Trace. "Smoothness" is a means of connection, a way of gathering the mix of picturesque diversions together. It smooths out the hardships of travels as well. In a similar manner the 18th-century improvement of country roads helped to encourage the popularity of picturesque touring in England. Travelers spent less time and ink complaining of their hardships, and more time looking, writing, and sketching. In Barthes's analysis this kind of passive travel was a means of "buying effort" so one could "keep its image and essence without feeling any of its ill-effects" (Duncan, 20). Today the picturesque road is even smoother, and the work of remembering, and reconstituting the journey in writing or drawing can be purchased in post-cards, books and videos.

Smoothness does require, however, its complements of roughness, surprise, interruption, and hardship, if only to keep it from being boring. This is a function of speed, as well. Too many stops and the experience becomes overwhelmed by diversity and plenitude. Too fast and it all blends together. The 50 mph limit keeps it at a regular clip, but not too fast to observe variety.

Top: The Trace (rough road) is on the left, the Parkway (smooth road) arcs to the right.

232.4 Loop Road, Bynum Mounds. Derived from the circular drives of English estates, the loop allows designers to divert traffic for scenic and historic stops without sharp turns or stops (McClelland, 126). In a smooth flow from parkway to parking lot, the visitor can then walk a loop past the Indian Mounds (which merge with the lawn), stopping just a few minutes to read the interpretive sign and arc back to the car and complete the loop back to the road. The side trips rarely present long delays.

233.2 Witch Dance. The story of this site "where bare spots on the ground indicate where witches step," draws more from campfire lore than history.

↳ Old Trace. Southern Gothic.

As Faulkner commented, "The past is never dead; it isn't even past" (Hobson, 16). Sunken and shrouded, the Old Trace evokes ghosts of travelers and stories that have a decidedly Gothic appeal. Names for the Trace, such as "dark road," "haunted highway," or "the Devil's Backbone," conjure a South before the Civil War that had earned a reputation for savagery and violence. Explorer Meriwether Lewis died on the Trace "under mysterious circumstances." Renovations of Kings Tavern along the Trace, revealed a skeleton of a woman with a dagger in her chest behind a bricked-up wall (NPS inventory). The ruthless deeds, disguised identities, and hangings of highwaymen substitute for the *banditti* and gypsies commonly found in picturesque scenes. These images of a visceral, mysterious, or even macabre South were passed on by legend and folktale, by abolitionists, famous visitors such as Charles Dickens, and in the 20th century in work of William Faulkner (Hobson, 15). In some cases they take the milder form of a good scare around the campfire, as at the Witch Dance site.

(© 1938, *The Commercial Appeal*, Memphis, Tenn., used with permission)

Letter from James Neely to Thomas Jefferson, October 18, 1809, describing the death of Meriwether Lewis on the Trace. (Lewis was the territorial governor of upper Louisiana at the time and on his way to Washington, D.C., to answer questions regarding his governance.)

"And on our arrival at the Chickasaw nation I discovered that he appeared at times deranged in mind, we rested there two days and come on, one days journey after crossing Tennessee River. And where we encamped we lost two of our horses. I remained behind to hunt them and the Governor proceeded on, with a promise to wait for me at the first houses he came to that was inhabited by white people; he reached the house of a Mr. Grinder about sunset, the man of the house being from home, and no person there but a woman who discovering the governor to be deranged, gave him up the house and slept herself in one near it, his servant and mine slept in the stable loft some distance from the other houses, the woman reports that about three o'clock she heard two pistols fire off in the Governors' room: the servants being awakened by her, came in but too late to save him, he had shot himself in the head with one pistol, and a little below the breast with the other—when his servant came he says, I have done the business my good Servant give me some water. He gave him water, he survived but a short time, I came up some time after and had him as decently buried as I could in that place."

(NTP Archives)

243.4 Road Kill, Snake. Et in Arcadia Ego[7]

Humphrey Repton:
"It may perhaps be urged that I have made a road where nature never intended the foot of man to tread, much less that he should be conveyed in the vehicles of modern luxury, but where man resides, Nature must be conquered by Art, and it is only the ostentation of her triumph, and not her victory, that ought never to offend the correct Eye of Taste."
(Hunt and Willis, 361)

↪ **Split Rail Fences.** These fences, which recall a rustic past, mark the boundaries to many of the designated sites and have become an emblem of the Parkway.

↪ **Erased Boundary.** Traces of the former fence lines and property boundaries have been removed within the ROW [right-of-way]

There are no visible boundaries along the Parkway. The picturesque eye never likes to see property divisions, because landscapes should belong to nature, and nature, according to Hogarth and others, abhors a straight line (Andrews, 94). Also, a landscape without fences opens up the territory of self-realization and the freedom to wander at will (Robertson, 44). To achieve this requires erasure of any lines of former or existing occupation. In the process the parkway becomes a depopulated landscape. There is no host culture to contend with, to "take" pictures of—there are only split rail fences signifying a distant rustic past, marking the boundaries of the parkway or entrances to designated sites. Those who occupied this land between the pioneers and the present are largely invisible. The traveler becomes sovereign.

Yet, as in the picturesque garden, there is a subtle and complex system of concealed boundaries. The "mow line" makes a subtle transition from road to wilderness, and these trees buffer views of the right-of-way boundary. An overlay of easements blurs the distinction between public and private. In addition, a state statute limits building heights within 1,000 feet of the parkway to less than 35 feet (steeples are now exempted) (Leach, 3).

375.8 Old Trace Drive—Diversion. The romantic desire to get off the beaten path is anticipated in designed diversions: walking trails and even sections of the Old Trace preserved as one-way gravel roads that you can drive on for two miles before returning to the modern motorway.

The Parkway is the product of a tremendous amount of labor in translating the desires of picturesque travel into a designed landscape, walking the centerline, adjusting alignment, blending parkway with nature, negotiating easements for views, and more. Like picturesque travel, it encodes many ironies. It offers a sense of escape and self-discovery through contact with other cultures and nature, but packaged as it is, it removes one from the danger of actually encountering otherness. As the picturesque became conventionalized and part of commodified tourist travel, the more demanding aspects of this mode were left behind (Robinson, 149–50). The effort of travel is traded for ease; it becomes a pleasure drive—stylized motion in a stylized scene (Smith, 79).

↪ **Random Stop, Off the Road.** Stop anywhere (caution: no shoulder makes this unsafe) and walk perpendicular to the parkway, crossing the mow line, and tree line, till you come to the edge of the ROW and the common landscape beyond.

THE TRACE OF PROGRESS: A ROAD TO THE NEW SOUTH

93.0 Road Obliteration. The Parkway is not the Trace, but a new road. Where the Parkway crosses Highway 49 at the edge of Clinton, outside Jackson, the asphalt surface of the Old Trace, which became a county road, will be torn up, planted with grass and protected at either end with split rail fences. Everywhere the Parkway crosses the Trace is also a place where the Trace has been fragmented and erased. When parkway construction began, over 50 percent of the Trace was still used as local roads (National Park Service 1935). Other roads erased by the Parkway are graded to blend with the natural landform.

The Parkway not only leads backward in time to the historic Trace or to a Picturesque nature, it also leads to future progress. Unimproved dirt roads that turned to quagmire in the rain were one of Faulkner's metaphors for the historic backwardness and poverty of the South (Preston, 13). In turn good roads became a symbol of progress, as important as education and industrial development. In fact, these other reforms were expected to follow from the improvement of roads. However, states like Mississippi lacked the tax revenues necessary to match available federal funds for highway building. Conditions only became more pronounced in the Depression.

The proposal for the Parkway offered one route out of the Depression. To begin with, it would put people back to work building a road in rural areas severely devastated by erosion. But there were questions concerning exactly where this progress would lead and who would benefit from the access it provided. For years one group of southern progressives, primarily farmers, advocated for better local roads. In their narrative, improving the farmers' access to market towns also reduced the monopoly of railroads and provided convenient access to city life, making rural life less isolated. Other progressives, businessmen primarily, sought regional connections between North and South for tourism. Another, larger historical concern entered into the decision. White elites (whose interests were served by the railroad monopolies) struggled over the question of how to enjoy the benefits of decent roads, new cars, and the speed and freedom of modernity, yet contain the mobility of their cheap labor supply of African-Americans (Bogan).

The Natchez Trace, with its Southwest/Northeast orientation, limited local access, and historic and scenic themes, ostensibly serves the tourists' desires. But the memory of the Trace in many ways was a pretext for building a modern motor road. In many places, rather than preserving the Trace, the new road obliterated and fragmented it. In the 1930s the benefits of tourism were less tangible than the immediate economic and political effects of distributing road contracts, and the same is true today (Bogan). In the eroded hills of rural Mississippi, an area not dominated by the interests of plantation owners, the new road provided much-needed money and infrastructure. The Parkway became part of the economic and political

Notes from Roadway Obliteration Details:
1. The existing gravel surface shall be scarified before placing topsoil.
2. All other roads shall be obliterated such that the finished surface shall match natural ground contours.
3. Scarification and excavation required for obliteration will not be measured for payment but shall be considered a subsidiary obligation of the Contractor.

Top: Photo captioned in NTP Archives, "Old fashioned use of the Trace," April 1935.

Scenery and Submarginal Land: an excerpt from the 1935 National Park Service discussion on creating the Natchez Trace Parkway:

Mr. Nolen. The big thing is that there is no normal scenery in the country, by retiring the sub-marginal land you develop a more pleasant atmosphere.

Mr. Vint. The Park Service has been kind of spoiled in that it has exceptional areas to work in with all the National Parks. When you get into a thing like these sub-marginal areas then you have to do a little something about it to make them work. In other words this land is going to be a designed sort of thing, just like a State Park instead of a National Park. The thing that would make this national is the glorifying of the Natchez Trace, which is our motive. (National Park Service 1935)

Above: Eroded farmland, March 27, 1935.

Below: Placing a culvert, fall 1947.

process of acquiring some of the most eroded farmland and transforming it into a scenic natural landscape.

266.0 Submarginal Lands and Federal Homestead Program. Much of the Parkway passes through land that was designated in the 1930s as "submarginal land"—erodible soils and other land unsuitable for agriculture, as defined by federal standards. The lower value also reduced costs of acquiring land.

Behind the present Parkway information center and headquarters outside Tupelo is one of three federal homestead projects in Mississippi. This one supplied standard houses with enough land for small orchards and other means of subsistence agriculture.

↳ Smooth Road, Race and Labor History. How are race relationships inscribed in this road? Much of the physical labor was done by an African-American labor force. Even the archaeological digs show black labor and white overseers. While slavery was long gone, one photo caption in the Parkway archives labels two men as "Carter's Negroes."

The road story inevitably reflects the authority of the powers that created it and their way of telling. Race is one of the revealing absences from the interpretation of the Parkway.

↳ Walking the Centerline

The alignment of the motor road was determined by walking and adjusting the centerline in the field. In effect the designers encountered many of the same hardships as the earlier travelers on the Trace.

The building of the modern motor road enacts the narrative of technological progress. Michel Serres, a philosopher of science, saw the building of modern roads as the triumph of a universal space over multiplicity and discontinuity (Serres, 52). The narrative journeys on the Trace, as described by Francis Bailey or Eudora Welty, were once structured by a series of encounters with obstacles—rivers, streams, swamps, Indians—catastrophes of disconnection. Oddly enough, to plot the motorway the designers and engineers had to "walk the centerline" and encounter the original obstacles. In this manner the road grew in discontinuous segments, ten, twelve, fifteen miles at a time. Each new segment required the negotiation of less visible obstacles of political support, funding, and local landowners. Except for a piece around Jackson and the link with Natchez (to be completed early in the next millennium, Leach, 2), the new road systematically erases theses various catastrophes, making a linked homogeneous space. The bridges are key metaphors in this narrative. The early ones are straight spans, but later ones become integral with the roadway alignment, curving effortlessly over obstacles. However, unlike the more heroic scale of the interstate highway, the parkway holds back, diverts to avoid certain features, minimizes cut and fill slopes. This derives from the picturesque strategy Robinson calls subsidence, a "relaxed underutilization of power" (144–45).[8]

↪ **Atomic Highway.** Additional justification for funding the road came with World War II. Before the interstates, parkways were touted as "defense highways" because the limited access ROW could be controlled to evacuate large numbers of people or move troops efficiently. The Natchez Trace Parkway also provided a link between nuclear weapons facilities in Tennessee and Louisiana. Some referred to it as an Atomic Highway.

287.0 Road curve and Beaver Dam.

Marcel Crudel explains one of the influences on the alignment:
We were walking down the center of a ROW on an early stakeout of the alignment and there were a lot of beaver dams in that area. The superintendent was really sensitive about them. We swung the motor road way over right near the ROW line to avoid the beaver dam. But you know beavers are transitory. They come and they go. I was too young at that time; I didn't speak out. Well, by the time we got a contract to even start building the beaver had all moved out. So now we have this real big sweeping curve to the edge of the ROW (Crudel).

438.0 Double Arch Bridge, Rte. 96.

Near the northern terminus of the trace, this bridge marks one of the grandest technological achievements in overcoming discontinuities of space.
It also became the focus of a controversy over whether to provide lighting for safety purposes. This, however, contrasts with the historic policy of keeping the parkway for daytime use and as natural as possible.

Meanwhile, "progress," and change surrounding the Parkway impinge on its distinctive character and fragment its continuity. Views to what was a traditional agricultural South have become increasingly suburbanized or in some cases blocked by dense pine plantations (encouraged by other federal policies). Commuter traffic does not merge well with the journeys of tourists. Growing local communities view the Parkway as a means to solve their transportation needs by adding on-ramps, increasing capacity, and changing alignments and signage. Modern bridges span the Parkway without attention to the classic arched form of earlier overpasses. As context changes and the roadway is altered, the Parkway loses its quality as a separate realm. It "devolves" into a conventional road, which parkways were originally supposed to provide an alternative to (Leach, 4). One alternative is to rethink the narrative of the Parkway in this changing context. Another is to reassert its value through preservation.

In the later sections of the Parkway, curves become integral with bridges.

Parkway landscape architect Marcel Crudel describes the process of "walking the centerline":
"Early on we worked with the Bureau of Public Roads. What they would do, they would put a preliminary line out pretty much down the center of the ROW, and then the park engineers and the landscape architect and even the superintendent would go out and we would walk several miles of line.
"We've done it right in the middle of August and it's brutal. You come walking through the swamp, get to a stream you gotta find a place to cross and we've fallen in. Swinging from a grape vine, a muscadine vine. It was adventuresome. We had some good times, though. We walked all of the 1-B section about fifteen miles up in Tennessee, bustin' our way through the woods. I don't think I've ever been so tired in my life. And it rained the whole time.
"But you found things out. We'd say let's shift it to see if we can save some of these trees. Those things would be put onto the plan and then the Bureau of Public Roads would go back in and they'd start adjusting the line and maybe 8 months later you might go out and walk it a second time. They'd stake it again. We'd walk it. We usually walked it about three times and then you come up with preliminary construction drawings and then we'd walk it one more time."

PRESERVING THE PARKWAY

Because construction began in 1937, the Natchez Trace Parkway now qualifies for National Register status. What began as a memorial to a historic road has acquired its own historic status. This recognition reflects a national movement to preserve scenic highways, park roads, urban parkways such as the Bronx River Parkway in New York, and historically significant routes such as Route 66, the Lincoln Highway, and the National Road, U.S. 40. Preserving the first federally funded cloverleaf on the Mount Vernon Memorial Parkway, for instance, recognizes the role of roads in shaping American identity and landscapes.

Preservation is also rewriting that story. Reasserting the original recreational purposes, slower speeds, integration with context, and other design features of early parkways runs counter to the "natural" expansion of scale and efficiency of roads. California's reclassification of the Arroyo Seco Parkway in 1994 as a historic parkway reversed attempts to make it conform to interstate standards. Preservationists proposed to retain its historic elements and alignment, and, instead, change driver expectations and behavior.

Preservation of the Natchez Trace Parkway brings to the foreground a road that has resolved so harmoniously with its context. One of the first steps, then, is to explicate and document what has been implicit design practice (especially the inscriptions of picturesque strategies described above).

201.3 Closed Picnic Area. Picnicking is becoming an anachronism, and such facilities are being closed to cut budgets.

256.0 Accident, Palmetto Road. Cars askew, contents, papers, vacation provisions strewn about, people consoling and covering those in shock waiting for the ambulance. Chances are this scene is repeated most often at the Palmetto intersection, a juncture of commuters and local traffic running against the stream of the Parkway. Arguments of safety support the desire for separation/exclusion.

267.0 Where Buffalo Roamed, WalMart. On this prairie the Parkway viewshed opens and is vulnerable to the kind of change that vegetation buffers. WalMart now spans almost the whole gap.

The preservation of the Parkway is inextricable from that of the original Trace. But when the Parkway was first conceived and built, there was no systematic mapping of the Trace. The recent multi-listing of all cultural, historic, and archaeological features, however, required mapping the Old Trace. So again, the surveyors walked the Trace. This time, they used the satellite technology of Global Positioning Systems (GPS) to find remnants of the old wilderness road still embedded in the ROW of the Parkway.

MEMORY TRACE

So we return to the original experience and archaic origin of "trace"—a path through the wilderness. This inscription transforms the experience of a wilderness into a text, "a thick tissue of traces and marks" (Butor, 6). We read the Trace as a memory of the passage of people and their journeys, events, and stories. We can also read the inscription of the Trace as a metaphor of writing—continuous marks across the undifferentiated whiteness of a page that trace the passage of meaning (Susan Stewart, 134).

Tupelo is eighteen miles from Fulton. The road that linked these two towns was severed by construction of the Tennessee-Tombigbee Waterway. A bridge was not built over the Tenn-Tom at the site of the old road; rather a new route was established between Fulton and Tupelo.

Trace has an archaic meaning of path or way. The Natchez Trace was such a way. The way between Fulton and Tupelo has become archaic. The memory trace of the old road has become the new trace.

People, having driven the old road countless times, found themselves driving it again only to encounter a dead-end at the levee. Some drivers, comfortable with habit, continued through the barricade, up the levee, over, and into the Tenn-Tom, so strong is the trace.

(Emanuel)

Highway 61

HIGHWAY 61: THE BLUES HIGHWAY

For a stretch of several miles between Natchez and Port Gibson, the Old Trace is now Highway 61. It is a road in the vernacular, exposed to all the road culture that is excluded from the Parkway that crosses above. It is also a federal highway, number emblazoned across a shield, with a great conti-

The Mississippi Delta is an alluvial plain formed by the Yazoo and Mississippi Rivers, and is framed by the Loess Hills to the east. This land of deep, rich soil and vast cotton plantations became the source of the greatest concentration of blues musicians. Each dot represents the birthplace of blues musicians, living and deceased. Source: Mississippi Blues Musicians, Rooster Records and Delta Blues Museum.

nental reach beginning at its northern end in Thunder Bay, Ontario, heading due south, paralleling the Mississippi River, cutting through the middle of America, and ending at New Orleans and the Gulf of Mexico.

Highway 61 traverses an equally extensive landscape of the cultural imagination. Robert Zimmerman grew up in Hibbing, Minnesota, not far from 61, and later, as Bob Dylan, he returned to this road in song. His "Highway 61, Revisited" is no Whitmanesque Song of the Open Road but a song of an alien highway strip, lined with parables ("Oh God said to Abraham, 'Kill me a son.' Well Abe says, 'Where do you want this killing done?'") and a promiscuous social mix (Mack the finger, Louis the King, welfare recipients, seventh sons), as well as a mix of enterprises (religion and sex, entertainment and war), all conveniently located ("But yes, I think it can be very easily done. We'll just put some bleachers out in the sun.") out on Highway 61. Dylan's parable form and theme of alienation, as well as the sound of the bottleneck guitar, are derived from the blues. And the blues comes not from middle America but from farther south on Highway 61 where the road passes through the middle of the Mississippi Delta. Between Memphis and Vicksburg, 61 cuts across this broad, flat alluvial plain revealing the conditions out of which the blues developed. The Delta is often described as a place apart—it has the largest cotton plantations and the densest rural black populations, and was at one time the most segregated, or as author/historian James Cobb once called it, "the most southern place on earth." Highway 61, therefore, links Middle America with an Other America.

This encounter with that which we experience as otherness, in particular with racial differences, is the road story we follow into the Delta on Highway 61. Various travelers have taken this route: tourists, journalists and social critics, and ethnographers, as well as sharecroppers, blues musicians, migrants, and civil rights advocates. The varied road stories of these travelers—the search for the origin of the blues, the witness of social injustice, escape, migration, freedom, return, progress, and heritage—all involve the encounter and representation of cultural difference, at times reinforcing stereotypes and at other times resisting and transforming racial relationships. Many, especially northerners like us, who have traveled this road have "gotten it all wrong." However, trying to set these complex and deeply contested issues straight would be a quixotic journey. Instead, we hope to show, by our own difficulties and doubts, as well as revelations on the road, the problems and responsibilities inherent in any representation of otherness. The goal is not to map a series of "wrong moves," but to affirm the necessity of engaging in the encounter of otherness on the road, but at the same time critically examining the traveler's position, the terms of encounter, and the devices of representation. In this sense these road stories become allegories of landscape interpretation.

Known also as the Blues Highway, 61 leads back into the Delta where the blues began. It is referred to repeatedly in song. Both the blues and the highway are cultural sites visited, collected, analyzed, consumed, and preserved by various travelers. However, the blues has its own road story to tell. The road is a major theme in the blues, and one means of resisting racism, which kept black people in their place. Likewise, Highway 61 also became a road out of the Delta, to the north and other places. In many different ways the blues itself has traveled.

TOURIST-PILGRIMS ON THE BLUES HIGHWAY

When Skeeter Brandon and his band Highway 61 play at Dinosaur Bar-B-Que, in Syracuse, New York, a photograph of the famous crossroads of Highways 61 and 49 in the Mississippi Delta hangs behind the stage. This image, along with the countless legends, histories, and songs, maps out a blues landscape.

When we finally get out of the loop road of the Memphis airport, off of "Rental Road" and then exit the freeway, we make a beeline for Clarksdale on Highway 61, searching vagrant frequencies on the radio dial for WROX or Highway 61, the blues program broadcast from Ole Miss. We are advised to drive with the windows down and listen for the music from porches, churches, and juke joints along the road. Low rolling hills, billboards, and development give way to a straight open highway between flat cotton plantations the size of Versailles. We are in the Delta.

Once the music of rural black people, the blues has traveled well beyond the cotton fields, juke joints, and porches of the Delta, crossing not only spatial boundaries but musical genres, cultures, and racial boundaries as well. The story of how Muddy Waters left the Delta and moved to Chicago, where he helped electrify country blues into urban blues, is now well known, as is the crossover of blues into white audiences via rhythm and blues, Elvis, and ultimately rock and roll. Muddy Waters's song titled "Rolling Stone" was taken to name a group, a magazine, and one of Dylan's songs. As a result, the blues can be found in unlikely places around the world. In Wim Wenders's road movie *Alice in the Cities,* a jukebox in Wuppertal, Germany, plays blues songs while Chuck Berry appears live near by.

Highway 61 is the arterial that collects this world audience of the blues, bringing them back to the sites of origins in the Delta.[9] The blues tourist is not only sightseeing but sound-seeking, and music links sound and lyric to place. The first blues lyrics W. C. Handy heard in 1903, "Goin' where the Southern cross the Dog," locate a well-known rail crossing of the Southern Railroad and the Yazoo-Delta (known as the Yellow Dog) just south of Tutwiler, which also appears on the cover of the set of maps for Delta blues tourists prepared by the former editor of *Living Blues,* Jim O'Neal. The tourist can literally follow songs through the Delta; the itinerary in Robert Johnson's "Traveling Riverside Blues" leads from Friars Point

Defining the Blues.
The blues can be defined by its structure of eight-, twelve-, or sixteen-bar chorus; by its lyric form, usually consisting of three-line stanzas, with the second line repeating the first; by the haunting sound of the "blue note" or "flattening" of the third or seventh degrees of the scale; by its emphasis on the individual guitar; or by an ideology of the outsider. Yet there are many exceptions to these traits, resulting from the great breadth and inventiveness of the folk blues, rhythm and blues, urban blues and so on. When asked, the musicians often define the blues as an emotional state. (Evans, 16)

Travel on, poor Bob just cain't turn you 'round
The blu-u-u-ues is a low down shakin' chill
[speaking] yes, preach 'em now
You ain't never had 'em I hope you never will.
(Robert Johnson, *Preachin' the Blues*)

to Rosedale and Vicksburg. While the music effectively guides, selects, and authenticates the scenes, the context of plantations and sharecropper cabins also authenticates the sources of the music.

Highway 61 is more than a tourist route. It is also a pilgrimage road. On this road, movement structures a narrative of leaving the ordinary, journeying to a place distinguished by a special aura constructed by events, legends, biographies, and other stories, then returning home. While tourism may seem to be superficial, social critic Dean MacCannell, argues that tourism is a secular enactment of the pilgrim's search for a revitalizing center (MacCannell, 14, 43). When much of the modern world seems alienating, or just boring, the tourist-pilgrim looks elsewhere for an Other reality. Black culture and the blues are thought to provide this access to authentic experience, emotion, and the process of re-creation.

While the course of the life of any of the Delta blues artists, as well as birthplaces, places in song, or gravesites, can become the course of a tour, the numen of the Delta blues and the paradigm for blues tourist-pilgrims is Robert Johnson. The 1989 reissue of his complete recordings topped pop charts and inspired another revival of the blues and another wave of scholars and tourists in search of the scant traces of his career (made even more difficult to find by his name changes and frequent moves through the Delta). The search for Robert Johnson began as early as 1938 when John Hammond (who would later sign Dylan to his first record contract) heard the recordings and wanted to recruit him for the "Spirituals to Swing" concerts in Carnegie Hall in 1938 and 1939. However, he learned that Johnson had died a year earlier under mysterious circumstances, probably poisoned (Guralnick, 53). Blues tourist-pilgrims looking for his grave today find two, and the store where he last played and died has since been moved. Even in death he is an elusive figure.

CULTURAL CROSSROADS

"I went to the crossroad, fell down on my knees..."
(Robert Johnson, "Cross Road Blues")

One of Johnson's most famous and most covered songs is "Cross Road Blues." In turn, one of the major tourist sites in the Delta is simply the intersection of two roads, Highway 61 and Highway 49. As so often happens on this road, the mundane is paved with layers of myth and legend. The Delta is referred to as "the land of the crossroads," and in this flat landscape any ordinary meeting of two lines becomes a significant event, a landmark. And "anyone who has ever stood at a little-traveled Delta crossroads out from town at night, with nothing at all for thousands of yards but tall, rustling row crops" can understand why this spot is such a primary metaphor in the blues, a place of fear, a point of decision, and a site of encounter with strangers, usually in the form of the devil (Bogan). Bluesmen cultivated these stories. In legend, Robert Johnson, like other bluesmen, acquired his talents seemingly overnight, through an exchange with the devil (a very significant other) at the crossroads (Palmer, 60). Despite the repetition and clichéd treatment of this idea in movies, the crossroads still resonates. Everyone has his or her own idea of where it occurred; everyone has his or her own crossroads.

The crossroads is also a critical metaphor in the discourse of the Other. At the crossroads the spatial and temporal paths of people who are normally kept separate—outsider/insider, northerner/southerner, white/Black, self/other—intersect. Social distances collapse (Bakhtin, 243). The blues itself is a cultural crossroads, a site crossed by different groups, as well as a medium that crosses over other cultures, from rural to urban, local to international, black to white. While the music has been able to cross social, economic, and racial boundaries, the black people who created the blues in the first place have only crossed with difficulty.

Fable: *How the Fuzz Tone Came to Rock 'n' Roll*
One oft-repeated story purports that the origins of rock and roll's fuzz tone guitar, lie in an incident that occurred on Highway 61. "One March afternoon in 1951, a Delta highway patrolman spotted a flagrantly overloaded sedan wallowing up Highway 61 toward Memphis." Inside were Ike Turner and seven other teenagers who called themselves the Kings of Rhythm en route from Clarksdale to Memphis to record "Rocket 88," one of the first rock and roll songs. "The patrolman...turned on his siren, and as the sedan shuddered to an ungainly halt on the shoulder, several pieces of equipment, including the guitar amp, tumbled off the roof and onto the ground." At Sun Records, rather than fixing the amp, they just jammed some aluminum foil into it, which produced the fuzz-tone on the record. (Palmer, 217)

Stackhouse/Rooster Blues Records, run by Jim O'Neal, founder of *Living Blues* magazine, is one of the first stops in Clarksdale for tourists coming from all over the world. A flag hangs in the window, given to O'Neal from Japanese groups who have made several trips to the Delta.

The *Delta Blues Map Kit,* describes the way to find Mississippi John Hurt's grave: "To get to the headstone marked 'John S. Hurt/July 3, 1893–Nov. 2, 1966,' go east off Highway 7 when you get to Avalon, follow the road (which eventually turns into a gravel road) 3-1/2 miles. You'll come to another gravel road running up the hill; a gate was recently installed across the road but it's probably unlocked. Take this road (which soon becomes a dirt path) one mile, and you'll come to a plot of graves on the left (not always easy to spot from the road; you may have to get out and look). John's grave is at the back of this cemetery. Drivers' warning: a recent visitor who followed the above directions was distressed to find the road to Hurt's grave rough and rutted, and even thought we should warn other pilgrims not to drive their Ferraris up this hill. OK, Ferrari owners, you're warned." (O'Neal, 1994)

Right: Off Route 61 and down Route 49 to Tutwiler, the blues tourist finds a mural depicting one of the first travel encounters with the blues, by W. C. Handy in 1903. Late at night, waiting for a train, he met a guitarist who "as he played, he pressed a knife on the strings," eliciting "the weirdest music I ever heard." (Oliver, 8).

Mara Califf's family operated a crossroads store at Dublin, Mississippi, on Rte. 49 near Clarksdale. Her memory painting of the famous crossing of 61 and 49 combines the current scene with legend and personal experience of the meeting of cultures and the vibrant life at the crossroads.

"My grandfather was Mose Califf. He was a Russian Jew who came to the Delta to meet his brother, who was already in Clarksdale. While selling pots and pans and ice by mule and wagon through the Mississippi Delta, he met my grandmother, Alma Dees. She taught school back over here in one of the fields when he came through here. They met at a card game at a weekend social. They ran off to New Orleans and got married and they came back and opened this store in 1919.

"The people that had the other store right across the street there were Chinese. You had railroad tracks right there, so all the shipping would come in and then everybody would come in from the farm on weekends to buy their food and hang out and drink and play music. On Saturday night, there were no clubs then, though my father ran a honkey tonk sometime in the forties....It's like my Grandfather had this store and, you know those wooden benches you see outside country stores. I can remember even in the sixties when I was a little girl, guys sitting out on the wooden bench, playing those kind of guitars with the string where they nailed it and they had a Coke bottle on their finger. I can remember them playing, people drinking and dancing...sometimes they would have fights and I would get real scared and ask my daddy what was goin' on and he would say 'awh you know, they're just having a good time, it's Saturday night, Dublin Mississippi!'"

Mara Califf, *Crossroads*. Mixed media, 1996. (Courtesy the artist and the Delta Blues Museum)

Why have the blues been able to cross cultural boundaries, and what are the terms of appreciation and appropriation? One explanation is that the blues expressed the common experiences of pain, loss, hard times, or worrying. As Eric Clapton explains, "I think the blues is actually more of an emotional experience than one exclusive to black or white or related to poverty" (Spencer, xvii). While this strategy of universalizing can be seen as a sharing of cultural experience, it also denies the specificity of cultural difference. In other ways the blues has been incorporated into the cultural reality of popular culture. The blues themes of alienation and rebellion in the form of rock and roll were adopted by middle-class suburbanites as well as by the children of some of the most privileged through the folk revival of the 1960s. The blues became their story. Likewise, as Wim Wenders recalls in postwar Germany blues and rock and roll represented the rebellion of his generation against German cultural tradition tainted by association with the Nazi period (Kolker and Beicken, 12–13). The blues tourists returning to the Delta expect to find the source of *their* personal history, expect to freely recross the spatial, social, economic boundaries the music has traveled—boundaries that are still *in place* for many black people in the Delta. By recrossing these boundaries, tourism reenacts the power of one culture to transcend and appropriate certain representations of another for its own purposes.

The blues tourist in the Delta, however, is more often motivated by a desire to recontextualize the blues, to see the cotton fields and sharecroppers' cabins, find the soul-food kitchen, hang out at the juke joints, attend the Baptist church services—all of which affirms cultural difference rather than denies it. In this travel story, going down to the crossroads is a narrative of transformation of personal and cultural identity. However, bell hooks raises the concern that this kind of conversion experience "establishes a contemporary narrative where the suffering imposed by structures of domination on those designated Other is *deflected* by an emphasis on seduction and longing where the desire is not to make the Other over in one's image but to become the Other" (hooks, 25). The desire reflects a longstanding conception of black culture as exotic. In the 1920s white intellectuals influenced by Freud viewed African-American life as a means of stripping away civility, which repressed a more primal, essential self (Hogue 1986, 36). Likewise, Kerouac and other Beats modeled their hip attitudes on an image of "Negritude." For them jazz and the blues held the secrets to a more expressive, more exciting, more rhythmic, more spiritual, more pleasurable, as well as more dangerous life. Thus, racial coding is more subtly embedded in exoticism. Even while tourists may be explicitly critical of racism, their desires can still circumscribe and control (Cantwell, 55).

"Goin' jookin" is a routine way of partying and having fun, but for the tourist it enacts the pleasures and dangers of the exotic (jook is an African retention meaning "evil," "disorderly, wicked" [Francis Davis, 47]). The very look of a joint such as Monkey's Place in Marigold, Mississippi, with its ceiling covered with black plastic garbage bags and laced by Christmas lights, has the inventiveness and edge of "outsider art." Some warn not to go alone, and the tour guide hints of illicit activities ("other activities for the sporting crowd" [O'Neal 1994, 1]). These become the very enticement for crossing the threshold.

Impacts of Tourism

When you actually get down to the intersection of 49 and 61, you find an ordinary highway strip, the modern mass culture of strip franchises instead of the exotic other.

As journalist Mark Jacobson writes, "we came to the crossroads and found McDonald's...'This is the famous crossroads?' I asked a man working at Morton's Service Station on the northwest corner of the intersection. 'That's it,' he said, never looking up from the tire he was patching" (Jacobson, 52).

Goin' Jooking: Tour Guide Planning Tip: "Yes, but is it safe? (General rule of thumb in searching out the real nitty-gritty blues: the places where people will tell you not to go are precisely the places you should want to go.) Incidents do occur but if you don't mess with somebody (or somebody's mate) then they're not likely to mess with you either."
(O'Neal 1994, 7)

The actual crossroads of Highways 61 and 49 in Clarksdale.

The Bobo General Store, known as a place for live blues, burned down in December 1996.

Highway 61 is full of such situational irony. Mass culture starts to make it look like *every other* place, no longer a distinctly different realm for imaginative projections. The traveler gets stuck between the familiar but placeless strip and the imagined place represented in a sanitized or kitsch version. The travel narrative, in turn, takes the form of lament over the perversion of the original and the loss of difference, as well as the indifference by locals as a result of modernization (Pratt, 220).

Yet, farther along, down the side streets, and around the corner, the tourist can still find the juke joints, the Baptist church where Muddy Waters's cousin preaches, and the barbecue places not on the chamber of commerce list of restaurants. Mass culture is not so much about erasing or destroying these "authentic" places. Western commodity culture, especially tourism, actually encourages the search for such differences, for an image of an authentic Other. The problem, then, is not that otherness will be lost, or made inauthentic, but that it will be consumed based on images that encode racial stereotypes. Black people have not had much power in controlling representations of themselves in the media, but in the juke joints, churches, and other such sites throughout the Delta, they have created identities in spaces they control. What happens when tourists cross these thresholds to experience some image of difference, and return home without relinquishing their position in a dominant group (hooks, 23)? What is changed, reinforced, or subverted in the process?

Tourists' impacts on local difference may be resisted if only because of the unpredictability of these places. The weekend visitor may never hear live blues. The bands, which do not clear much money and are made up of people who have other jobs (depending on the season, they may be driving tractors at night), may not show up. Many of the juke joints do not have phones, so you can't find out schedules. What was there last year has closed, or moved, or in some cases burned down.

Reconfiguring the desires of the tourists is a much more difficult task. Rather than assuming tourists should decide the nature of the relationship in these sites, Jim O'Neal's *Delta Blues Map Kit* guide aims at changing tourist expectations and behaviors. It derides souvenir hunters, for instance, for stripping pieces of wood from Muddy Waters's cabin ("—hands off, Bozos!" [O'Neal 1994, 1]). The follower of these guidelines becomes a kind of antitourist, adapting to circumstances rather than requiring them to meet expectations. bell hooks recognizes the potential of an approach "where desire for contact with those who are different or deemed Other is not considered bad, politically incorrect, or wrong minded" (39). If approached critically, tourists' desire for difference can be a means of challenging and reworking the dominant representations of black culture.

THE CRITICAL ROAD INTO THE DEEP SOUTH (TRUTH JOURNEYS)

Highway 61 runs practically straight through the Delta, passing over cane brakes and bayous and through small towns. This vector was constructed between 1936 and 1939, as a new "good road" that brought the Delta closer to New Orleans and Memphis.

The scenes of an Other America by the side of Highway 61 are plainly visible and hard to miss, as photographer Ken Light discovered:

> In my four-and-a-half-year journey along Highway 61 and the smaller, less-traveled roads of the Delta, scenes that I thought had long vanished from this American land were revealed. Nothing had prepared me for this. The cypress-planked shotgun shack still sits on the edge of the plantation. (122)

His is a classic road story of traveling as a witness to another world. The road opens and reveals its truth by the side of the road. Like Stendhal's metaphor of the realistic novel as a mirror held up to the road,[10] the photograph is the record of his witnessing, his presence, his authority, his road story: "Few outsiders would believe what I have seen if not for my camera" (Light, 122). However, few outsiders probe beyond the obvious contrasts. Outsiders' view from the road tends to confirm the view presented in films that reduce the complex and close spatial contact between generations of white and black into simplistic dramas (Klan fright, etc.)—a kind of shadow theater for national racial guilt (Applebome, 27).

Light follows a long retinue of people who have tried to document, explain, and come to terms with this rupture in American identity. Olmsted made this journey before the Civil War. More recently, Light's subject matter, straightforward portraits, stark factual captions, and route follow the precedent of the Farm Services Administration (FSA) photographers of the 1930s (including Dorthea Lange, Edward Weston, Marian Post Wolcott, and Ben Shahn). Traveling through the Delta, the Great Plains, Appalachia, and other places on the margins of America during the Great Depression, their journey was also one of witnessing. For the purpose of documenting the various FSA projects, rehabilitation projects, and integrated farms, as well as the erosion, plight of flood victims, and other themes, Roy Stryker, the project's director in Washington D.C., developed scripts for his photographers' journeys that not only provided background information but outlined routes and stories.

CLARKSDALE

BEVERLY DAVENPORT STATION •

BOBO •

ALLIGATOR •

DUNCAN •

Alignment of Highway 61 from 1939 to the present.

Road Script. A 1939 memo from Roy Stryker to all the FSA photographers included a script for photographing the road (from Keller):
The Highway
Pictures which emphasize the fact that the American highway is very often a more attractive place than the places Americans live
"Restless America"
Beautiful Highways
Elm, or maples at the curve of the road—contrast with rural and industrial slums which highways pass through
Lunch Rooms and Filling Stations
Truckers stopped to eat
Trailers on the road
People walking on the road
Horse and buggy on road
Back view—country road
Signs Large signs
On trees—barns—roofs
Town and village

Marion Post Wolcott traveled alone in the 1930's when this was an unusual and suspect thing to do, especially in the South. Harassed by local officials, pursued by men, and often lonely, she still sought to cross cultural and gender boundaries in search of her own stories. Her experience illustrates the gender coding of travel and the road.

"I always felt envious of the photographers who had wives (or in the case of Lange, husbands) to do their captions, or who traveled with their so-called secretaries as Russell did. I nearly died when I found out about that years later. And I had to be so careful not to meet anybody or see anybody. It was so unfair. If I had ever tried anything like that Roy would have killed me! I'd never have gotten away with it because everyone was so curious about a woman traveling alone in those days and any gossip they could figure out they used." (Hurley, 57)

Bottom left: Photograph by Dorothea Lange. (FSA, courtesy Library of Congress)

Bottom right: Jitterbugging on a Saturday night in a juke joint near Clarksdale, Mississippi, 1939. Photograph by Marion Post Wolcott. (FSA, courtesy Library of Congress)

Marion Post Wolcott recalled, however, that "you weren't bound by the stock scripts" (Natanson, 63), and the photographers, many of whom came from distinctly leftist ideologies, departed from the scripted journey and followed their own convictions. They sent back photographs that revealed the effects of institutional segregation and the servile conditions of field labor (the scratched hands, shoeless feet, evictions). Instead of repeating common racially coded depictions, they used the new, smaller cameras, which required only daylight, to get informal images with a sense of individual differences in dress, posture, and identity (Natanson, 93). Instead of limiting images to cotton labor, a monocultural stereotype, they also showed black people in juke joints, in barbershops, in train stations, on sidewalks, in cotton dealings, and in commissary stores (Natanson, 76). Marion Post Wolcott in particular worked at gaining access to black social life in spaces they controlled, once by persuading the son of a local planter to take her to a juke joint outside Clarksdale (Hurley, 66). This image and many other FSA photos have become emblematic and are often used in books on the blues to underscore the specificity of context.

Many of the FSA photographs have become icons of an era and circulate in the virtual realm of print and electronic media. Sixty years after these historic journeys Karen Glynn with the Center for the study of Southern Culture, retraced the original routes of the photographers. They discovered the man who had escourted Wolcott to the Clarksdale juke joint and located the site of the Sterling well commissary in Dorthea Lounge's famous photograph. This project brought the historic photographs back to the communities and contexts they were taken from.

"In an effort to identify the people and places photographed by Russell Lee in Mound Bayou, Bolivar County, MS, Sarah Torian and I carried two binders of Farm Security Administration photographs to the town and met with a group of elders, brought together by Milborne

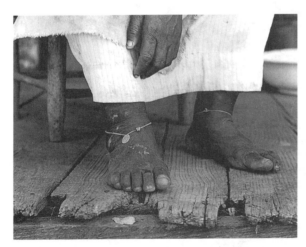

Crowe in City Hall. We arrived early and intercepted Milborne on his way back from the grocery store. He explained that local custom required that he provide refreshments for everyone that attended. While we organized our photographs, Milborne laid out sandwiches and soft drinks.

"We started going through the photographs and folks continued to join us throughout the hour and a half meeting. Room was made around the photograph binders for the newcomers as they appeared. George Spears, an 87-year-old farmer in overalls, was a commanding presence whom everyone deferred to on matters of local history. Mr. Spears turned the pages of the albums for the group, effectively controlling the flow of discussion around each image, identifying people and buildings, recalling addresses and telling stories. People interjected remarks throughout his commentary, agreeing and disagreeing, supplementing, exercising as a group—possession of place—to shape an historic description of Mound Bayou elicited by the photographs .

"This lively interchange took place among people who had lived together in the same community for all of their adult lives. In fact, George Spears might have been the only person at the table who came to Mound Bayou as an adult. For those born and raised there the FSA photographs depicted Mound Bayou as they remembered it during their youth.

"The most powerful story Spears recounted described his arrival in this all black town during the Depression. Russell Lee's photograph of the 'Mound Bayou' sign hanging at the railroad depot stirred his memory. Spears said that he arrived in Mound Bayou following the railroad tracks. As he approached the front depot he saw a 'colored' sign. His curiosity aroused, he walked around the building to the back and saw a 'white' sign. That was the first time he ever saw a sign giving blacks preferential place over whites. He decided, on the spot, to stay.

"The group confirmed his story about the signs adding that blacks and whites generally ignored them and shared the same waiting room area of the depot. (Someone thought that the signs were there because Illinois Central Railroad policy required them in the South.)"

Russell Lee's photograph of the Mound Bayou depot. (FSA, Library of Congress; courtesy Karen Glynn and the Center for the Study of Southern Culture, Univeristy of Mississippi)

In addition to the photographers, sociologists, anthropologists, and folklorists visited the Delta from other federal agencies and academic institutions to record the facts of this Other place. Sociologists Hortense Powdermaker and John Dollard, drawn by the high contrast between black and white, rich and poor, penetrated the social world of black sharecroppers. Folklorists John Lomax and his son Alan took to the road to make field recordings of African-American music. Using the first portable recording machines, they could document the music in place: by the side of the road; in drugstores, cabins, prisons, and fields, to create a great archive of folk

Well well well I wants to ride this new highway: ooo
that the project just completed in a week ago
Well I got to ride this new highway: Lord and I'm
going to cross the Gulf of Mexico
Well well well then I ain't going to stop riding:
well until I park in front of my baby's door
(Sonny Boy Williamson, *Project Highway*; ©
Renewed, Venus Music Corp.)

Bottom left: The commissary of the
Sterlingwell (Hillhouse Plantation)
outside Clarksdale. Photograph by
Dorothea Lange. (FSA, courtesy
Library of Congress)

Bttom right: From another angle of the
same scene, Dorothea Lange created a
more dramatic tableau with the white
owner positioned against the black
workers. This photograph became
emblematic of the place and era.
(FSA, courtesy Library of Congress)

music, much like the photo archive Stryker imagined. The political motivation was similar, to give "voice to the voiceless" and bring these representations, through some form of mechanical reproduction, back to the centers of power (Lomax, xxi). These were landmark journeys across color lines when black people were not considered to have a culture worth studying and such outsiders were seen as agitators. Lomax's recording session with Son House in a crossroads store was broken up by a plantation owner. He was escorted to the local sheriff and told to leave town (Lomax, 16–19). The Lomaxes, however, were themselves southerners. And because their recording of black music suggested that it was part of their identity as southerners and not something completely Other, it was an even greater challenge to dominance (Bogan).

Such direct experience, along with systematic, objective observation supported by mechanical recording of voice and image, makes powerful claims of truthful representation of otherness—Stendhal's mirror to the road. Yet, while they make differences of other places and cultures more visible, they can also conceal the sites (geographical, cultural, political, theoretical) where the representations originate (Duncan, 39). As mentioned, the FSA photo scripts reflected tensions between federal and state power (Lange's proposal for a piece on voter disenfranchisement was turned down) as well as the ideologies of the photographers themselves (Natanson). The sociological depiction of blacks tended to create an image of passive or even pathological victims prone to various health problems and social deviance. Social science that professionalized older tropes of travel imagined itself above or outside its objects (K. Stewart, 25). The observer as stranger, as traveler, actually holds a privileged position, located in the place, yet mobile and relieved of responsibility for that place. The social sciences have since recognized that rather than being outside and neutral, the very presence of the observer influences and changes who and what is observed.

Like the strangers who travel on them, roads also transform the local order. By the end of the 1930s, Lomax, the sociologists, and the photographers were traveling on a newly paved federal highway. The alignment of the new Highway 61 cut a swath through the texture of the Delta, connecting it with New Orleans, Memphis, and beyond. The Greyhound bus company, which began as a local service for miners in the Mesabi Iron-ore Range at the other end of 61 in Minnesota, started running through the Delta, inspiring Robert Johnson to write, "You may bury my body down by the highway side, so my evil soul can catch a Greyhound bus and ride." Johnson and other blues musicians followed the WPA road gangs who had cash to spend at the juke joints. The paved road reworked the relations between inside and out, between the margin and the center, between the Delta and Washington. Both the new road and the New Deal opened the Delta to scrutiny and influenced structural changes in labor and race relations, yet the planters were still able to turn government programs and the new road to serve their goals. Today the radical cut of the new road is masked by strip development. However, travelers can follow the original zigzag route of Old Highway 61 that the first FSA photographers traveled in the early 1930s.

THE PLANTATION ROAD, OLD HIGHWAY 61

Heading north out of Alligator, Old Highway 61 curves along the ROW of the Yazoo and Mississippi Valley Railroad ("the Yellow Dog"), then it strikes due east crossing the railroad, following a section line; after a mile it turns 90 degrees due north to the town/plantation of Bobo, where it makes another turn due east again. Less than a mile later it turns north and realigns with the railroad until the town of Davenport, where it strikes east for three miles, then north into Clarksdale. It proceeds in this manner all the way to Memphis.

This was a plantation highway. Since it was the planters who controlled the land it passed through, its alignment served their economic interests by connecting the plantation headquarters with towns and railroads. The gravel surface and indirect and tortuous route limited outsiders and insulated the Delta. Bypassed by the new road, this back road, now marked as "Old Highway 61," leads directly to the conditions that influenced the blues.

Along this old plantation road there is a certain reciprocity between the visible scene and the voice of the blues. It is as if by looking you can hear the blues, and in turn the blues conjures certain images. Sociologists and blues scholars point to the systems of sharecropping and segregation as keys to understanding this equation between the blues text and its context.

Sharecropping effectively tied black labor to the land. In this system black laborers farmed a portion of land in exchange for a share of the crop.

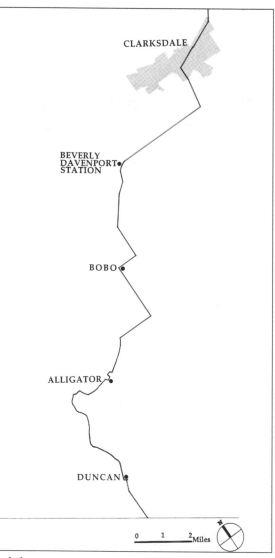

Until the mid-1930s, Highway 61 was a tortuous dirt road linking plantations with railroad depots.

Dennis Jenkins, gas station/grocery store owner, describes travel on Old 61 to Memphis before 1936:
"I would go with my daddy to what they called the stockyards over in West Memphis. Back then Highway 61 went through every little town. It went through every headquarters of every plantation. My daddy had an A Model with them old split rims and all; you had to carry your patches and hand pump because it's all gravel and you'd have flats and all. We could leave in the morning and go into Memphis and it would take us three days and two nights to get back home. It was 167 miles from where we left Skeen to get to the Memphis stockyards. So when they put this straight road through it cut all that off, now it was 80 something miles."

Since the laborers were unable to purchase seed and supplies, or even clothing, food, and housing, they were given these in advance, but the costs were deducted at harvest time. The system served the planters by shifting the risk and burden of interest rates onto the laborers, while creating greater incentive for workers to produce and remain on plantations till harvest. The planters provided the "furnish" of house, food, clothing, and supplies typically in March, and the "settle" between the income of the harvest against deductions came in the fall. For blacks, sharecropping offered the hope of gaining economic freedom, although they rarely broke even, and often ended up in debt. The planters who kept the books also ran the commissaries, which advanced groceries and supplies at very high interest rates. Sociologists Powdermaker and Dollard were surprised at how planters actually boasted of cheating illiterate sharecroppers (Cobb, 55–58). The white planters' dominance extended beyond labor and into all spheres of black life through legally sanctioned practices of segregation. Separate schools meant minimal education for black children, who were more important as field labor. Without legal recourse or access to the ballot box and with the threat and terror of violence, segregation served to keep black labor in place.

THE BACKROADS OF MODERNITY

The Delta offers endless miles of dirt roads for exploring. They cross each other, multiplying choices through a dense ragged grid with spurs reaching back between the bayous and brakes. Roads with names like Dog Bog Road and New Africa Road lead to places such as Booga Bottom. One farmer tells us you can drive from one end of the Delta to the other on the turn roads, the roads at the edges of field rows for turning the tractors. When it rains, however, they turn into thick Delta mud. Traces of gravel in the fields indicate that the network was once even denser.

The great density of dirt roads served one of the most densely populated rural landscapes. Emanual Jefferson, who lived and worked for over fifty years on the Stovall plantation outside Clarksdale, recalls, "This place used to have about four, five hundred children on it. There were so many you could stir "em with a stick. Houses all back in the field, all up the road and everywhere. Yeah, there sure was some labor on this place" The contrast between these poor roads and the modern road only served to underscore the apparent binaries of racism: white and black, progress and backwardness. They structured not only spatial segregation but also separation in time. The dirt roads represented an earlier stage of development, just as blacks were positioned on a temporal hierarchy, developmentally inferior, closer to childhood, the primitive, or premodern—notions used to justify the need for paternalism (Lloyd, 259).

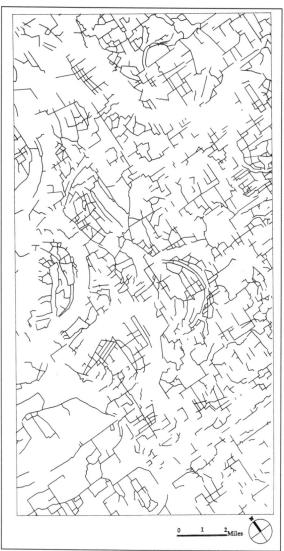

However backward they appeared, these were the back roads of modernity. Like the backstreets to the sweatshops in garment districts or immigrant ghettos near steel mills, the backroads were the infrastructure of a modern industrial underclass. The analysis of James Cobb's history of the Delta refutes the idea that the Delta plantation was a throwback to antebellum or feudal times, but rather an operation based on efficient management. Through sharecroppers' labor, cotton production, which competed on a world commodities market, was made possible. The key was a large, localized labor resource. As Emanual Jefferson says, "There sure was some labor on this place." Small units of production, allotments of twelve to fifteen acres, meant the greatest "hoe power" at peak times...and lots of dirt roads. The poor quality of these roads ensured a condition of underdevelopment for this underbelly of modernism. Jefferson describes the separation and paternalism structured by the dirt road: "If you're sick you go to the boss man's house tell him you need a doctor. If he couldn't get to your house back in the field you had a wagon. The doctor leaves his car at the boss man's house and the man take the wagon and bring him to your house." By limiting access to health care, education, and any other options besides work in the cotton field, the dirt roads helped keep black labor in place.

But the white planter also had to accept the same conditions to a degree as a price for maintaining an immobilized labor force. The desire for decent roads, for new cars, for the speed and travel of modernity, ultimately created tensions and fissures within white elite and middle-class attitudes. Thus, the contrast between dirt and paved, backwardness, and progress is not a simple binary relationship. To simply portray the planters as feudal lords or villains as opposed to rational, modern (yet racist) people with varied self-interests turns them too easily into a caricatured Other as well (Bogan).

Top left: Photograph by Marion Post Wolcott, 1939. (FSA, courtesy Library of Congress)

Above: Pattern of dirt roads in the 1930s.

INTO THE LABYRINTH, NATURALIZING THE BLUES

Heading south toward Alligator, Old Highway 61 follows the arc of Annis Brake, crosses Alligator Lake, and traces the edge of Bland Brake. At the Yellow Bayou the original highway is still unpaved. This gravel track follows the meanders of the Hushpuckena River down to the town of Duncan.

The search for the origin of the blues, as a synecdoche of black culture, leads further back in time to a culture, untainted by modernity, rooted in the land once called "the natural home of the Negroe." The meanderings of the Mississippi inscribed oxbows, high swamps (brakes), bayous, and bogues across the alluvial plain of the Delta.[12] As Shelby Foote describes, it is a backwater labyrinth of "slow, circuitous creeks, covered with dusty scum and steaming in the heat...each doubling back on itself in convulsive loops and coils like a snake fighting lice" (Foote, 242).

In 1941 folklorist Alan Lomax drove out of Clarksdale (built over a former Indian settlement on a high terrace formed by the river) following a dirt road along the arc of the Little Sunflower River to record Muddy Waters at his cabin on the Stovall plantation. Lomax described the early field recordings as a narrative of first contact between modern portable recording machines and an indigenous oral folk tradition: "For me the black discs spinning in the Mississippi night, spitting the chip centripetally toward the center of the table, also heralded a new age of writing human history." Since the notion of "folk" implied culture rooted in place, travel by the folklorists was necessary to discover and document. In 1934 Alan and his father John Loax wrote: "Our purpose was to find the Negro who had the least contact with jazz, the radio, and with the white man" (in Cantwell, 69). The purest source was found in the prison farm camps:

Above: The meanders inscribed by the Mississippi, Hushpuckena, and Sunflower Rivers.

Below: Portion of Old Highway 61 that has never been paved, between Alligator and Duncan.

Here the Negro prisoners were segregated, often guarded by Negro trusties, with no social or other contacts with whites, except for occasional official relations. The convicts heard only the idiom of their own race. Many—often of greatest influence—were "lifers" who had been confined in the penitentiary, a few as long as fifty years. They still sang the songs they had brought into confinement, and these songs had been entirely in the keeping of the black man.
(in Cantwell, 69–70)

Here the representational strategy for confining the Other to a pure, simple, premodern realm becomes literal imprisonment. It is only a more extreme example of common strategies, used not only by ethnographers, but by tourists and designers, of localizing or fixing the identity of some more authentic Other in distant time and space. According to anthropologist Johannes Fabian, it denies the Other "coevalness," or the sharing of the same temporal space. However, it is precisely modernism, mechanization, commercial capitalism, and the factory system that create the desire for the folk or the vernacular (Cantwell, 66). Meanwhile the researcher, tourist, or designer is part of a traveling culture with the power to compare, escape, or find refuge in these other cultures fixed in place.

In 1901 and 1902 Harvard anthropologist George Peabody visited the same Stovall plantation where Lomax would later record Muddy Waters, and wrote down the music of the black laborers he had employed in the excavation of nearby Indian mounds. He found that the songs, "weird in interval and strange in rhythm; peculiarly beautiful," challenged standard musical notation. Peabody lived in a tent, as if in a remote African village, and described how the work songs reflected their "primitive characteristics of patience under repetition." He and others would foster a view of the origin of the blues as part of a racial heritage linked with a primitive, natural landscape. He concluded his piece by calling the objects of his study the "true sons of the Torrid Zone," a reference that recalls Europe's first contact with black Africans and notions of environmental influence on racial character (Duncan 1993). The hot and steamy Delta was easily substituted for Africa as "the natural home of the Negro."

Thus, the metonymy of skin color as *the* indicator of racial difference extends across a whole range of other difference to where it becomes a metonymy of place. It is important, however, to "denaturalize" race, to recognize it not as an essential difference grounded in biology or environment, but as a discourse produced in particular social and historical contexts. Stuart Hall asserts "that racial discourses produce, mark, and fix the infinite differences and diversities of human beings through a rigid binary coding. That logic establishes a chain of correspondences both between the physical and the cultural, between intellectual and cognitive characteristics" (Hall, 290). Ideas of an authentic, pure, and place-bound African-American identity are part of that discourse.

Such distinctiveness is increasingly difficult to find. Emanual Jefferson has lived and worked on the same Stovall plantation Peabody and Lomax visited. He recalls sharecropping, working on the road crews of the New Deal, driving workers to the fields, and the day "that man from Hollywood come up here with his big truck and everything, brought in those big lights and we sat right here on the sofa with him and his guitar between us." Besides being a native of the Delta, he has also appeared in a two-second clip on MTV, part of the John Hiatt music video "Buffalo River Home."

This is an increasingly common trope of postmodern travel—the natives are watching TV and wearing Nike logos. It provides the occasion for an ironic lament of the power and extent of mass media culture. Anthropologist James Clifford calls this the "Squanto effect," after the Patuxet Indian just back from Europe who spoke English when he greeted the pilgrims arriving in the "New World" (Clifford, 97). But rather than lamenting the contamination of the native, Clifford sees this as an imperative to reexamine the notion of pure cultures and fixing strategies. As he proposes, native peoples uncontaminated by contact with some larger world have probably never existed, except in the desires of a very powerful traveling culture. This approach is particularly relevant for the blues. Rather than being a pure isolated form, the blues, including the early form heard by Peabody, incorporates multiple influences from travel and contact with other cultures. Clifford's aim, as mentioned in the introduction of this chapter, is not to deny the importance of locality and home, but to rethink cultures as sites constructed through and crossed by travel, to understand the cultural practices of "traveling-in-dwelling, dwelling-in-traveling."

THE BLUES AND MOVEMENT

Instead of treating other cultures as objects to be illuminated by interpretation, another approach is to engage cultures as creative and productive of their own identities. The blues, like many expressive forms, creates its own richly storied and interpretive space that eludes attempts to encapsulate it. As a form of resistance, the blues takes the experiences of a social predicament and transforms these liabilities into working assets, into lyric music (National Park Service 1996, 28) The rising emotion expressed with the falling pitch of the "blue note" can evoke shared memories of pain and suffering, but it also opens realms of pleasure, power, individualism, community, and alternatives (Griffin, 57).

One of the most important alternatives expressed in the blues is change through movement. In fact, the blues encodes travel narratives in its themes and form. Recent scholarship has shown how the blues retains traces of African oral tradition, including the griot storytelling tradition, polyrhythms, and the call and response pattern that survived the diaspora to America known as the Middle Passage. Robert Johnson singing about meeting the devil at the crossroads, for instance, draws on an African story of a trickster god, Legba, associated with crossroads, mediating the junction between this world and the spirit world. Along the way the blues has incorporated various influences including different instruments and a very American emphasis on the individual.

The Delta was an important site in this travel narrative. After the Civil War, free African-Americans came here from former plantations throughout the South to clear the wilderness, build levees and railroad, open up bayou and bogue, and find new opportunities on the margins. Ironically, their labor and role as pioneer, created the open fields, flood protection, and infrastructure that established the Delta as a successful realm for cotton plantation (Cobb, 69–97). Although there was a brief time when African-Americans enjoyed voting and other civil rights, this ended in the 1880s with the growth of the sharecropping system and the institution of legal segregation. The first generation to taste freedom was also the first to lose it. The blues originates not in the soil but in the frustration of risking all and traveling only to end up someplace worse off than where you started.[13]

In turn, travel and movement became an important theme in the blues. In a system that kept blacks in their place—physically, temporally, and metaphorically—mobility was a significant strategy of resistance. It was common knowledge that one way out of the cycle of indebtedness and abuse was to walk (Nathans). A great deal of local migration—reshuffling of circumstance and debt known as "slipping"—took place after the "settle" in

Tenants being evicted. (Photograph by Dorothea Lange. FSA, courtesy Library of Congress)

Johnny Shines tells of his travels with Robert Johnson:
"We would walk through the country with our guitars on our shoulders, stop at people's houses, play a little music, walk on." From Memphis, to St. Louis or Chicago, "we might hear about where a job was payin' off—a highway crew, a railroad job, a levee camp there along the river... I didn't have a special place then. Anywhere was home..." (Palmer, 120)

the fall and the "furnish" in the spring. Fearing retribution from landlords and criminal charges for breaking sharecropping contracts, blacks often slipped away during the night.

As the Reverend Robert Grant told one researcher, when a man felt like leaving, "you could tell. He sang the blues." And you could hear that voice at night coming across the fields and down the road.

> Gotta mind to move,
> A mind to settle down.
> Gotta mind to move,
> A mind to settle down.
>   (Nathans, 219)

These compact lyrics describe the complexities and ambiguities of movement. The desire to escape, to try out a new piece of land or a different plantation, often met with the realization that the new place only repeated old patterns. The blues persona embodied all the ambiguities of travel. Money and mobility signified that the blues singer belonged to no one, so that was the last person a planter wanted to see coming down the road (Nathans, 221).

THE GREAT MIGRATION ROAD OUT OF THE DELTA

The drive north on Old Highway 61, through Coahoma, Lula, Dexter, Tunica, Robinsonville, passes through an emptied landscape. A mixed pack of dogs roams by as the owner of a crossroads store recounts the former life of Lula: four gins but only one operating, more migrant Mexican labor and casino workers from California. Next door is a Laundromat with a mural of cotton fields and three famous bluesmen who have also left. Up the road we pass the dogs and the idle gins next to the husks of towns, closed stores, and shotgun shacks in various states of collapse. Across a cotton field stands a line of three chimneys. Sometimes it's hard to tell abandonment from inhabitation, since some cabins still lack electricity and other basic features.

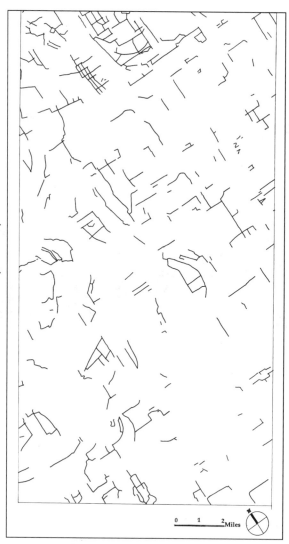

Above: The dirt roads as they existed on 1960s topographic maps.

Landowners demolish them so they can stop paying taxes on the structures. Some guys work at dismantling a cabin but salvage the weathered cypress for custom woodworking.

Oh baby, don't you want to go
Back to the land of California
To my sweet home Chicago
    Robert Johnson

By contrasting freedom and mobility with the harsh realities of Mississippi, the blues prefigured the desire to migrate north (and west) in search of the full benefits of citizenship. In 1943, shortly after Alan Lomax recorded Muddy Waters's lament "If I feel tomorrow, the way I feel today, I'm gonna pack my bags and make my getaway" (Lomax, 417), Waters went to Robert Johnson's suggested destination, Chicago. The way Emanual Jefferson, whose daughter used to dance with Waters at his roadhouse, tells it:

Muddy Waters, he was drivin tractors on this place here. Him and the agent got into it and he left his tractor in the field, come and got his suitcase and went on to Chicago. Got a big electric guitar and got a band and everything. Mr. Stovall had three agents then, now he ain't got but one.

So the migration of Muddy Waters is often cited in the history of the blues as the transformation of country blues into an urban, electrified blues. His move to Chicago, however, is but one of the more famous stories; it only partially accounts for over six and a half million other stories of black people who left the South as part of what has come to be known as the Great Migration. One of the largest internal mass movements of people in history, the beginning of the Great Migration is often explained as a story of modern industry in search of an alternative labor source because European immigration was disrupted during World War I. Yet, here again, blacks are depicted as passive victims buffeted by impersonal forces. But for many blacks it was a significant action, and the journey, framed by biblical narratives, became an exodus. Chicago became the "promised land." Plantation owners initially countered the appealing prospects of Chicago (heavily promoted by the *Chicago Defender,* a popular black-owned newspaper) by arguing that the Delta was the "natural home of the Negro." By the 1940s, however, mechanized cotton pickers, fertilizers, and herbicides reduced the need for hand labor (Lemann 1992). The tractor Muddy Waters was driving replaced the work of several families. Now the dirt roads and cabins scattered through the fields of the Stovall plantation are gone, and along the edge of the road there is just a row of tight little brick homes and what's left of Waters's wood cabin for the tourists.

Above: This mural by Gwendoln Canon (1990) in a laundromat depicts bluesmen Lonnie Shields, Sam Carr, and Bennie Jones, all of whom once lived in Lula, Mississippi.

Below: Picking "pepper grass" along a quiet stretch of Old Highway 61 south of Tunica.

The blues migrated too. What in the South was a music of wandering strangers in the North became a connection to a memory of the South and home. Immigrants would sometimes call out to dance hall musicians "Let's go home," a request for the southern music. In fragmented, changing conditions, the blues provided some narrative coherence (Griffin, 54). But they changed too. The addition of the electric guitar and the transformation of the blues into rhythm and blues, gospel blues, and rock and roll provide a metaphor for what happened to the migrants themselves. The impact of the blues on other musical forms also indicates the impact that the migrants had on the city and American identity.

The migration emptied much of the Delta landscape.[14] Absence, however, does not seem to deter the tourists. As Francis Baker, in his history of the blues, observed, people go to Mississippi "to see things that aren't there anymore." Tourism, as longing and desire, is easily satisfied by representations that mark the absence of the original. The Delta Blues Museum has plenty of photos, books, life-size representations, and artifacts salvaged before collectors could take them away. One of the most popular stops on blues tours is nothing more than the Laundromat in Lula with its mural of a cotton field and three famous local bluesmen, who have since left. And people still come to the site of Muddy Waters's cabin even though in the spring of 1996 the House of the Blues hauled away all but a few rotted pieces of the foundation to its New Orleans venue.[15] Waters has died, but his old cabin is on tour, creating another absence in the Delta. These absences tend to overshadow the blues tradition that is still living and changing in the Delta.[16]

Above: The former location of Muddy Waters's cabin. Only some rotted pieces of wood at the foundation remain. New brick houses for plantation workers line the paved road instead of being distributed throughout the fields.

Below: Russel Lee, "Negro boys on Easter morning on the South Side. Chicago. April 1941." (FSA, courtesy Library of Congress)

Actually, the migration was not a one-way journey in time and space but a multigenerational coming and going between the Delta and points beyond—especially since the search for a freer space ran into different forms of racism elsewhere. One of the traditional strengths that enabled people to leave was a network of extended family. Milborne Crowe, from Mound Bayou, went back and forth between the Delta and school in Chicago where he lived with an aunt. In Chicago he belonged to the Mound Bayou Social Civic Club, one of many "travelers clubs" formed around the towns the migrants had left, such as Clarksdale, Natchez, and Greenville. Highway 61 became the lifeline, the way out of and the way back to the Delta. Crowe's aunt knew 61 "would take them right to their front door." More and more songs referred to Highway 61 in these same terms.[16]

It is important to pay attention to this migration narrative if only because it is one of the most dominant stories in African-American music, visual art, and literature. Also, without these stories, the black

migration remains a statistical graph, an impersonal or "natural" process or an "urban crisis." Instead of passive victims, the migration narrative reveals the complexities of decisions to "uproot" abandon long-denied dreams of land ownership, and reweave social and kinship ties to become urban. Here, the migration narrative denaturalizes the conception of the urban ghetto by speaking within it (Scruggs, 14). It reveals a largely invisible city of "safe spaces," places of identity, and memory within the "ghetto" (Griffen, 100–141). The forging of identity between city and country, past and present is also an example of Clifford's notion of dwelling-in-traveling. Understanding this narrative becomes more important as other migrating cultures insert themselves into new places.

THE ROAD TO FREEDOM: CIVIL RIGHTS

> *In Clarksdale, Old Highway 61 turns into Fourth Street, where it intersects with Issaquena Street, the heart of the "New World" and the once vibrant black commercial district. Day laborers stood out on this corner at six in the morning waiting to be picked up and trucked into the fields. The barbershop of Wade Walton, a blues musician known for working up a rhythm with his razor strap, was also on the corner. As a civil rights organizer in the 1950s, he persuaded friends and others to stay and help instead of leaving. A black business across the street was bombed. Farther on, this stretch of old 61 through Clarksdale has been renamed Martin Luther King Jr. Boulevard.*

Travel on any road has the potential for encounter with social differences. In Mississippi the segregated road made racial differences plainly and painfully obvious. For Milborne Crowe, who grew up in Mound Bayou, driving on 61 revealed the contradictions between American ideals and the realities of race relationships:

> We didn't have to contend with racism and segregation here in Mound Bayou. As I grew up, we learned "The Pledge of Allegiance," but when we ventured out we saw it was really a lie. Traveling on 61 was not really that pleasant between this community and others. When you stopped at a service station to buy gas or use the rest room, you were told to go out back.

Breaking the rules of the segregated road often meant a violent encounter. Crowe recounted an incident at a gas station in Shelby, north of Mound Bayou, where "a young man stopped so that his mother could use the rest room. They told her to go out back. He said never mind about the gas and they shot him. Killed him. That business never really seemed to profit all these years since." One of the first actions of the Regional Council of Negro Leadership, a local civil rights organization, formed in 1951, was to rectify the conditions of road travel by boycotting filling stations that did

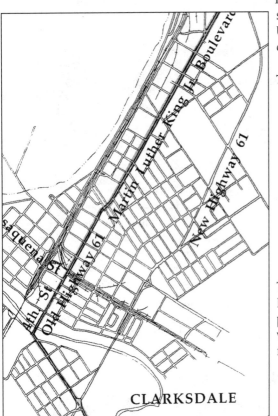

Old Highway 61 through Clarksdale as it turns into Martin Luther King Jr. Boulevard.

not provide rest rooms for black patrons. Milborne Crowe came home from Chicago to participate in these early actions of the civil rights movement.

As a symbol of social mobility, freedom, and a place of social contact, the road became an important site in the contestations of civil rights. "Freedom riders" attempted to ride a bus from Washington, D.C., to Mississippi and cross the boundaries of the segregated road along the way. When their bus entered Alabama, the riders were beaten and arrested, and the bus was burned. The image of the freedom riders resonated so strongly that, as Fanny Lou Hammer recalled, "freedom rider" became a term applied to any of the civil rights workers who came into the Delta (Mills, 23). The Greyhound station in Clarksdale along Old Highway 61 was the site of one of their sit-ins.

The actions on the road became a strategy for unmasking what had become commonplace. The reactions to simply sitting at a lunch counter, as well as the marches and freedom rides, only made the systems of coercion and threats of violence, implicit in the daily life of racial apartheid, more visible to an increasingly national audience. The roads became unsafe for "outside agitators" who had to travel the back roads at night. Freedom riders were matched by "night riders" who asserted their sovereignty on the roads with drive-by shootings and bombings of movement leaders' or sympathizers' homes (Dittmer, 137; Payne, 37). On the ride out of Jackson, surrounded by the National Guard and people who had beaten the freedom riders and burned the bus, one freedom rider observed, "I'm going out of America into a foreign country" (Dittmer, 90).

Music was critical in creating solidarity on the road and in prison cells, and as an organizing tool for meetings and marches. Bob Dylan came down to Mississippi to lend support to organizers and play on the back of a truck in a cotton field. The ideology of the folk revival of the 1960s with its embrace of the blues and black culture, was in sympathy with the causes.

Above: July 8, 1963, Photograph by Danny Lyon. "After giving a concert in a cotton field in Greenwood, Bob Dylan plays behind the SNCC office. Bernice Reagon, one of the original Freedom Singers and today leader of Sweet Honey in the Rock, listens. Mendy Sampstein sits behind Dylan and talks to Willie Blue" (Lyon's caption). (Magnum Photos)

Left: Field workers watched the March to End Fear organized by James Meredith. After he was shot (but not killed) the marchers diverted their route to go through the Delta to hold voter-registration rallies as they traveled. (UPI/CORBIS-BETTMANN)

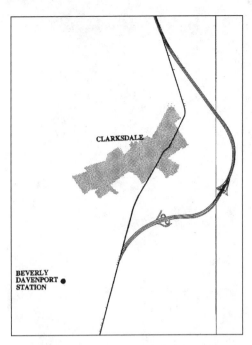

Above: The alignment of the bypass being constructed around Clarksdale.

Below: An earth mound temporarily blocks traffic until all four lanes are opened on the expanded highway.

But it was the gospel spirituals and R & B hits, rather than the individual emphasis of the blues, that catalyzed the meetings and marches.

The music clearly evoked the metaphors of the road, of transformation and change, that where central to civil rights as a *movement.* The experiences on the road also revealed different conceptions of black identity and politics within the movement. After James Meredith was shot (but not killed) as he crossed into Mississippi on his March to End Fear, various leaders convened to continue the march. As they took different routes through the Delta, they also split along ideological lines between Martin Luther King, Jr.'s nonviolence and Stokely Carmichael's more militant ideas of black power, which gained momentum with each stop along the way.

LINKING THE DELTA WITH THE FUTURE AND THE PAST—THE FOUR-LANE HIGHWAY AND THE HERITAGE CORRIDOR

A swath of demolished buildings and recently graded earth runs parallel to the two-lane road, clearing the way for a continuous four-lane highway between New Orleans and Memphis. Some stretches are open, until you come to an earth bulwark and a sign diverting you back to a two-lane stretch of 61 that still passes through the towns of Clarksdale, Merigold, Mound Bayou, Cleveland, and so on. On a Saturday afternoon the smell of barbeque hangs in the air along this old highway strip lined with vegetable stands, flea markets, and variation on the strip vernacular. One man crossing 61 stops, strikes a match on the road, lights a cigarette, and walks on. Soon the new road will bypass these towns. Outside Clarksdale the crossroads of 61 and 49 will become an interchange between two four-lane highways.

I got the key to the highway: and I'm booked out and bound to go
I'm gonna leave here runnin': because walking is most too slow
    Big Bill Broonzy, "Key to the Highway" (Taft, 23)

An enlarged, streamlined, sometimes elevated Highway 61 inscribes the narrative of progress through the Delta. This new highway derives from recommendations by the Lower Mississippi Delta Development Commission (LMDDC, established by an act of the U.S. Congress in 1988 and chaired by then governor Bill Clinton), a regional entity encompassing seven states charged with comprehensive economic planning and development. The commission's reports compare the Delta, with its traditional agricultural base, high unemployment, low levels of income and education, welfare dependency, high infant mortality, and poor housing to the "Third World." This locates the Delta, again, as a place developmentally distant in time and space from the modern world. It also sets up the master narrative of progress in which the highway is a "master key" in moving from poverty to prosperity. Accordingly, shortcomings in the transportation infrastructure have "held back" progress, whereas proposed improvements combat "capital flight" to other regions and encourage economic growth, job creation, and access to a range of social opportunities (Federal Highway Administration, 92). Interestingly, along with poor roads, racism is cited as a factor that holds the Delta back. Improving roads and "facing race" contribute to the goal of transcending boundaries, bringing this Other place into the mainstream, or as one report title declares, "Linking the Delta Region with the Nation and the World."

Tourism is integral to this progress. In a tautological loop, better roads increase tourism, which provides revenues for funding long-term highway improvements. The LMDDC cites the "gaming roads" that lead to the new casinos as one of the "success stories" of tourist road improvements. Old Highway 61 in Tunica County has been widened and repaved; it merges with a gaming road that passes over the threshold of the levee and down to a grand architectural confection on sophisticated floating mechanisms. Yet, these roads that provide access for an exploitive economy hardly lead to progress in racial matters. One local crossroads store owner describes the casino clientele using racial stereotypes of black people as loafers who would gamble away their welfare checks in juke joints or back lots if there were no casinos. So, in his opinion the casino revenues are not a bad way to "pave all the itty-bitty roads around here."

While the new road leads to a progressive future, the commission also recommends developing access to the past through a Heritage Corridor. Toward this goal the National Park Service undertook a comprehensive study, beginning with identifying a framework of stories and sites, evaluating their integrity and importance, and making recommendations that include possible designation of historically significant roads or other routes, Native American as well as African-American Heritage Corridors.

Old Highway 61 near Tunica recently resurfaced to become a "gaming road" leading to the casinos on the other side of the levee.

The Park Service has been an innovator in the use of stories as an explicit means of interpreting place and culture, as well as telling stories in design form. In the Delta the project coordinators used stories told by experts, shared at public meetings or submitted on survey forms, to establish the framework and map the sites of the Heritage Corridor. The participants in the "Stories of the Delta" symposium stressed the need to consider the diversity of Delta stories as well as the complexity of race and how it permeates politics, work, education, food, music, literature... "everything." (National Park Service 1996, 14). They also recommended that there be places where people can tell their own stories. To this end the Park Service staff took a series of extended road trips to hold public meetings encouraging people to tell their stories. Through the familiar activity of storytelling, the public communicated relationships and values of place that are hard to articulate otherwise. At the Clarksdale meeting the audience told stories ranging from those set in the familiar litany of blues sites (W. C. Handy and the crossroads) to those of personal experience (bluesman Johnnie Billington returning home from Chicago in the 1970s to find a lack of local blues), the accomplishments of the black founders of Mound Bayou, and even the anticipated effects of progress (new bridge at Rosedale). However, since not everyone shows up or speaks up in a public forum, other means, such as interviews, are necessary to reveal more diverse, difficult, or embedded narratives of place.

The Park Service was left with the task of analyzing the relative importance of the stories and the integrity of the sites. The blues in particular presents a complex story that is hard to interpret and designate since "the blues exists wherever people bring it, so it is difficult to tie this music to sites" (National Park Service 1996, 14). Beyond established sites such as the Delta Blues Museum, the Park Service evaluated an extensive list of unrecognized but nonetheless significant places, such as the Freedom House in Meyersville (crosses once burned on the lawn, *Eyes on the Prize* was filmed here,), various juke joints, Wade Walton's barbershop, and the small Booker-Thomas

Places such as Boss Hoggs Bar-b-que (owned by a cousin of Jackie Brinson, of Kings of Rhythm fame) on Martin Luther King Boulevard are bypassed by the new highway but have been inventoried as part of the Heritage Corridor.

Museum, containing things left behind by black ancestors who moved north. This site, run by an elderly woman, is typical of the uncertain futures faced by many other sites. The Heritage Corridor offers a strategy of gathering these sites and stories into a coherent set of themes along designated routes, roads, pathways, and waterways.

At first, the roads to progress and heritage would seem to be at cross-purposes. Progress, conceived as a national or even global imperative, makes erasure of local culture seem rational. In support of an argument for the four-lane road, the commission report cites the locational criteria of WalMart, which hastens the demise of small towns. But the two roads, and their two conceptions of time, actually complement each other. As progress moves toward the future, it distances itself from the past. Meanwhile the past, as Other, is studied, selected, storied, and salvaged through heritage sites and routes. Both progress and heritage tend to subordinate the present to opposite ends of a temporal spectrum (Hufford).

What are the implications of these diverging roads for narratives of African-American identity? Many look forward to increased access to opportunities in the workplace, business, housing, and shopping, and other changes. But the new highway also exaggerates the scale of social differences between those who walk and those who ride, and the controlled right-of-way insulates the driver from the local landscape. The crossroads becomes an interchange, a monument to perpetual circulation.[18] The modern road is no longer a place of encountering differences, but a cultural space that unsettles and assimilates what was once a distinct racial identity.

The Heritage Corridor, in turn, can be a means of countering processes of assimilation and alienation, by providing a route back to the source of tradition. This desire for a return is evident in both literature and, since the 1970s, a reverse migration of urban blacks to live in the Delta again. In Arthur Flowers's book, *Another Good Lovin' Blues,* the final chapter, "On Traveling Down Dusty Old Delta Roads," tells of leaving Memphis to search for Taproot, Mississippi, a mythic place of personal origins as well as cultural healing. The author, from Memphis, considers the Delta holy ground, a place to reconnect with spiritual aspects of black experience encoded in the blues.[19] Likewise, Toni Morrison's stories tell of returning to the South as burial ground, as place of cultural origins and home of ancestors (Griffin, 11). This desire for redemption is a common theme in road stories. Travel becomes a means of confronting the places of the past, exhuming what has been repressed, and retelling these difficult stories as a necessary step in moving beyond victimization or nostalgia. A similar role was suggested for the Heritage Corridor at the Park Service's public meeting in Clarksdale: "the Delta's bad history of racism can be a strengthening lesson; we shouldn't deny it."

This demonstrates that an African-American heritage corridor is not simply a matter of substituting black stories or more positive racial images into established tourist formats. There is a politics of interpretation in deciding which stories to tell, who tells them, and where and how they are told. It means reconsidering the common trope of fixing an image of authentic racial identity in another place and time. This practice is especially appealing in the face of modern alienation and assimilation, though it retains traces of racism. A fixed and essentialized racial identity can also be constraining for new identities emerging from new gender, class, and other difference, many of which had been repressed by segregation (Hogue 1996, 23). The first step then, is to critically examine the very practices of representation of cultural difference by tourists, critics, scholars, designers, or other travelers.

How can interpretive practices go beyond this necessary step of denaturalizing to affirm the desire for connection with tradition, identity, and place? One strategy is to recontextualize identity, as in the case of the blues, to chart the intimate but changing relations with landscape, social systems, travel, and tradition. Stuart Hall argues that the end of essentialized racial identity need not negate the importance of tradition. Instead, tradition is constantly reworked, much like the interpretation of any musical form. "What else is any successful blues, any successful jazz standard, or any gospel song but the given ground and the performance that translates it?" (294). Thus, the difficult task of interpreting cultural differences might follow a poetics and politics of engagement with the road story of the blues themselves. The blues clearly demonstrates strategies of dialogue with a changing audience, a situated yet mobile tradition, resistance and hybrid incorporation of influences. In the blues there is always more than what is literally said. Likewise, a heritage corridor need not become a closed narrative, a smooth road for tourist consumption.

These interpretive approaches to Highway 61 recapitulate the sequence of road stories presented in this section. They move from understanding the tourists' ambivalent desires for otherness, to the road of the critical observer and the contextual space of the story. Using the trope of spatialized time, they go further back into a labyrinth to denaturalize the notions of essentialized racial character and place. They then pick up the travel narrative of the blues itself as a road story, as a migration narrative, and as a reworking of traditions and relations of power in the civil rights movement. All these stories, these roads, these interpretations, are brought to the question of the ongoing inscription of Highway 61.

GONE

As travelers on Highway 61, the Natchez Trace Parkway, and back roads through Mississippi, we were constantly aware of crossing many borders— North/South, nature/culture, design/vernacular, white/black—and the issues this raises for interpretation. These transgressions can either reproduce dominant interpretations of others or they can challenge and redefine the borders forged by domination (Awkward, 6). To some degree the road design itself inscribes dominant cultural practices of travel, separating otherness in both distance and time. On a road such as the Natchez Trace Parkway, we were privileged travelers who observed the otherness of nature, history, and cultures in constant motion from a safe distance and within a controlled right-of-way. Lulled into the kinesthetics of this closed narrative space, we could easily gloss over the political, social, historical, and racial discourses that inhere in the very alignments and tropes of travel on the road. However, the desire, the threats, and the negotiations of otherness were all there to be encountered out on Highway 61. For whatever degree of coherence or cogency our interpretation of the blues and black culture conveys, the most telling experiences on this road were those moments of unease upon entering certain places, frustration of not getting access to others, boredom, fun, guilt, excitement, disorientation, and doubt. These were important in revealing the taken-for-granted boundaries of our own knowledge, position, and responsibilities in a discourse of the Other/race. An increasing number of scholars (black and white alike) encourage such "border-crossings" as necessary for renegotiating, reshaping, and repositioning more complex understandings of cultural differences. We are all to some degree shaped by and engaged with cultural crossings and encounters with difference. As Stuart Hall advises:

> The future belongs to the impure. The future belongs to those who are ready to take in a bit of the other, as well as being what they themselves are. After all, it is because their history and ours is so deeply and profoundly and inextricably intertwined that racism exists. For otherwise, how could they keep us apart?
> (299)

Like the traveler who becomes "different," whose broader experience and different position can not be adequately represented within familiar language (Helms, 79), the road exceeds boundaries. It is not just a signifier of difference but an important site for encountering and negotiating differences, which is the story of the road.

NOTES

We made three road trips to Mississippi in March, October, and December of 1996 and would like to thank the people in Mississippi who were generous with their time and help: Sara Amy Leach, Marcel Crudel, and Bob Felker at the Natchez Trace Parkway; Nel Dieterly and Eric Goldsmith with the Park Service mapping services; Jim O'Neal and Mara Califf for introducing us to Clarksdale; the diverse group at the Center for Southern Culture; William Ferris, Tom Rankin, John T. Edge, and especially Karen Glynn for all her leads and sharing her research; Beth and Gerald DeLouch for a driving tour on their back roads; Milborne Crowe; and everyone else we met along these Mississippi roads. Some of the names of those quoted in the text have been changed out of respect for their privacy.

1. Wendy Faris analyzes a similar use of the labyrinth as both symbol and structure of modern literary texts. However, she found no North American equivalent to the extensive use of labyrinths in European and Latin American literature. Perhaps the road is a more significant symbol and structure of North American cultural experience (Faris, 9).

2. Oedipus literally means "swollen feet" and refers to the attempt to disable the young child by hanging him by his feet to keep him from traveling and meeting his fate.

3. We thank Phil Davies, who taught a course called "Road Movies" at Syracuse University (Spring, 1994), for bringing many of these films to our attention and developing a framework for interpreting them.

4. A Claude Glass was a mirror held up to the landscape that compressed the scene and gave it a slight tint, making it conform to the conventions of landscape painting, most notably that of Claude Lorrain.

5. As Robinson describes, the picturesque has come to mean something shallow and conventional, but in its early versions it was complex and undecidable. We use "picturesque traveler" here as a complex reader, an intermediary, one who embodies traces of early romantic intentions as well those of contemporary tourists. The search for the picturesque in the late 19th century was driven by different groups for different motives, but there are traces of a tradition that drew them together (Taylor, 24) .

6. Robinson also notes that wandering and searching are essentially picturesque activities that were formalized for tourists in the 18th century (xiii).

7. *I Too Once Dwelled in Arcady*, is the title of a Nicolas Poussin painting (1639) showing shepherds tracing this same quote inscribed on a sarcophagus, implying that death is also part of the nature of the pastoral landscape. Other paintings by Poussin, such as Landscape with Serpent and Two Nymphs (1651), include snakes in allegories of corruption and purifi-

cation. See Sheila McTighe. *Nicolas Poussin's Landscape Allegories* (Cambridge: Cambridge University Press, 1996), pp. 121–123.

8. The plot of the movie *Thelma and Louise* reverses the sequence of overcoming catastrophes. It begins in suburbia and on superhighways, but as the characters' outlaw status increases and their circumstances become more dire, they drive on increasingly rural roads. They have to wait for cattle to cross at one point. Finally they go off the road. In the end they drive off the edge of the Grand Canyon, a gap not bridged by a road, a catastrophe.

9. The new owners (English and American) of the Crossroads Bar and Grill in Clarksdale are anticipating the beginning of direct flights from Europe to Memphis.

10. Stendahl was a 19th-century novelist, critic, and theorist. Of the novel as a mirror held up to the road he wrote: "Un roman est un miroir qui se promène sur une grande route" ("A novel is a mirror which wanders along a great road" in Kayser, xiii; see also Day).

11. In 1914 a Swedish miner, Carl Wickman, began running a 10 passenger bus between Hibbing (Bob Dylan's home town) and Alice, Minnesota, four miles away. The sleek grey intercity busses of the 1920s were dubbed Greyhounds. See Arthur S. Genet, *Profile of Greyhound* (New York: The Newcomer Society in North America, 1958).

12. The word meander comes from the ancient river in Mesopotamia that twists and turns back on itself, creating a labyrinth.

13. At this same time the Delta produced more wealth per acre than any other part of Mississippi (Hamilton, 44).

14. Days of remembrance were set aside in the Delta to commemorate the migrants (National Park Service 1996, 23).

15. The opening of the House of Blues in New Orleans has contributed to the closing of one of the most famous blues clubs in the city. (Conversation with Professor Peter Ashcoff, Sociology Department, University of Mississippi, February 1997).

16. There is now a program through the Delta Blues Museum for teaching the blues to younger musicians. *Living Blues* magazine, started by Jim O'Neal and now published by the Center for Southern Culture at the University of Mississippi, reports on the ongoing development of the blues.

17. Highway 61 became more of a symbol than a geographic fact, as can be seen in inaccurate representations of its route. It does not go directly to Chicago, as many songs describe. In other songs Highway 61 is said to link New York or Atlanta to the Gulf of Mexico.

That Sixty-One Highway: longest road I ever knowed
It runs to Atlanta Georgia: clean to the Gulf of Mexico

Will Batts, "Highway No. 61 Blues" (Taft, 17)

18. One informal observation we made was the remarkable number of people walking along Highway 61 and along the railroad tracks, mostly abandoned, between towns.

19. Arthur Flowers started to study the blues as an adult, but his army buddies assumed it came naturally with his black Memphis heritage (Flowers 1997).

REFERENCES

Andrews, Malcolm. 1989. *The Search for the Picturesque: Landscape Aesthetics and Tourism in Britain, 1760–1800*. Stanford, Calif.: Stanford University Press.

Applebome, Peter. 1997. "It's Poverty of Imagination to Find Only the South Guilty." *New York Times*, March 6.

Awkard, Michael. 1995. *Negotiating Difference: Race, Gender, and the Politics of Positionality*. Chicago: University of Chicago Press.

Bailey, Francis. [1797] 1969. *Journal of a Tour in Unsettled Parts of North America in 1796 and 1797*, ed. Jack D.L. Holmes. Carbondale: Southern Illinois University.

Baker, Houston A., Jr. 1984. *Blues, Ideology, and Afro-American Literature: A Vernacular Theory*. Chicago: University of Chicago Press.

Bakhtin, M. M. 1981. "Forms of Time and of the Chronotope in the Novel." In *The Dialogic Imagination: Four Essays by M. M. Bakhtin*, ed. Michael Holquist, trans. Caryl Emerson and Michael Holquist. Austin: University of Texas Press. Pp. 84–258

Barthes, Roland. [1957] 1987. "The Blue Guide." In *Mythologies*, trans. Jonathan Cape Ltd. New York: Hill and Wang. Pp. 74–77.

Boddy, Julie M. 1982. "The Farm Security Administration Photographs of Marion Post Wolcott: A Cultural History." Ph.D. diss., State University of New York at Buffalo.

Bogan, Neill (member of REPOhistory; has lived and still has family in Mississippi). 1997. Correspondance, May 5.

Butor, Michel. 1974. "Travel and Writing." *Mosaic* 8:1–16.

Califf, Mara (artist, Clarksdale, Mississippi). 1996. Interview and tour with authors, October.

Cantwell, Robert. 1996. *When We Were Good: The Folk Revival*. Cambridge: Harvard University Press.

Clifford, James. 1992. "Traveling Cultures." In *Cultural Studies*, ed. Lawrence Grossberg, Cary Nelson, and Paula Treichler. New York: Routledge.

Cobb, James C. 1992. *The Most Southern Place on Earth: The Mississippi Delta and the Roots of Regional Identity*. New York: Oxford University Press.

Crowe, Milborne. 1997. Phone interview with authors, January 8.

Crudel, Marcel (Natchez Trace Parkway landscape architect). 1996. Interview with authors, October.

Curtis, Barry and Claire Pajaczkowska. 1994. "'Getting There': Travel, Time and Narrative." In *Travellers' Tales: Narratives of Home and Displacement*, ed. George Robertson, Melinda Mash, Lisa Tickner, Jon Bird, Barry Curtis, and Tim Putnam. New York: Routledge.

Daniels, Stephen, and Charles Watkins. 1994. "Picturesque Landscaping and Estate Management: Uvedale Price and Nathaniel Kent at Foxley." In *Politics of the Picturesque*, ed. S. Copley and P. Garside. Cambridge: Cambridge University Press.

Davidson, J. W., A. Hecht, and H. A. Whitney. 1990. "The Pilgrimage to Graceland." In *Pilgrimage in the United States: Geographia Religionum*, ed. G. Rinschede and S.M. Bhardwaj. Berlin: Dietrich Reimer Verlag. Pp. 229–252.

Davis, Francis. 1995. *The History of the Blues*. New York: Hyperion.

Davis, William C. 1995. *A Way through the Wilderness: The Natchez Trace and the Civilization of the Southern Frontier*. New York: Harper Collins.

Day, James T. 1987. *Stendhal's Paper Mirror: Patterns of Self-Consciousness in His Novels*. New York: Peter Lang.

DeLouch, Gerald (artist and native Delta resident). 1996. Interview and tour with authors, December 13.

Dittmer, John. 1994. *Local People: The Struggle for Civil Rights in Mississippi*. Urbana: University of Illinois Press.

Dollard, John. 1937. *Caste and Class in a Southern Town*. New Haven, Conn.: Yale University Press.

Duncan, James S. 1993. "Sites of Representation: Place, Time and the Discourse of the Other." In *Place/Culture/Representation*, ed. James Duncan and Devid Ley. New York: Routledge. Pp. 39–56.

Duncan, James S., and Nancy G. Duncan. 1992. "Ideology and Bliss: Roland Barthes and the Secret Histories of Landscape." In *Writing Worlds: Discourse, Text and Mtaphor in the Representation of Landscape*, ed. Trever J. Barnes and James S. Duncan. New York: Routledge. Pp. 18-37.

Emanuel, Martin. 1991. *Oostamera*. Atlanta: Nexus Press.

Evans, David. 1982. *Big Road Blues: Tradition and Creativity in the Folk Blues*. Berkeley: University of California Press.

Fabian, Johannes. 1983. *Time and the Other: How Anthropology Makes Its Object*. New York: Columbia University Press.

Faris, Wendy B. 1988. *Labyrinths of Language: Symbolic Landscape & Narrative Design in Modern Fiction*. Baltimore: Johns Hopkins University Press.

Federal Highway Administration. 1995. *Linking the Delta Region with the Nation and the World*. Lanham, Md.: FHWA Research and Technology Report Center.

Felker, Robert (Natchez Trace Parkway landscape architect). 1996. Interview with authors, October.

Ferris. William. 1978. *Blues from the Delta*. Garden City, N.Y.: Anchor Press/Doubleday.

Flowers, Arthur. 1993. *Another Good Loving Blues*. New York: Ballantine Books.

———. 1997. Interview with authors, February.

Foote, Shelby. 1954. *Jordan County: A Landscape in Narrative*. New York: Dial Press.

Gilpin, William. 1794. *Three Essays: On Picturesque Beauty; On Picturesque Travel; and On Sketching Landscape: To Which is Added a Poem, On Landscape Painting*. 2nd ed. London: R. Blamire.

Glynn, Karen. 1996. Correspondance with authors.

Griffin, Farah Jasmine. 1995. *"Who set you flowin'?": The African-American Migration Narrative*. Oxford: Oxford University Press.

Grossman, James R. 1989. *Land of Hope: Chicago, Black Southerners, and the Great Migration*. Urbana: University of Chicago Press.

Guralnick, Peter. 1989. *Searching for Robert Johnson*. New York: Obelisk Books.

Hall, Stuart. 1997. "Subjects in History: Making Diasporic Identities." In *The House That Race Built: Black Americans, U.S. Terrain*, ed. Wahneema Lubiano. New York: Pantheon.

Hamilton, Kenneth Marvin. 1991. *Black Towns and Profit: Promotion and Development in the Trans-Appalachian West, 1877–1915*. Urbana: University of Illinois Press.

Helms, Mary W. 1988. *Ulysses' Sail: An Ethnographic Odyssey of Power, Knowledge, and Geographic Distance*. Princeton, N.J.: Princeton University Press.

Hobson, Fred. 1996. "The History of the Southern Gothic Sensibility." *The Oxford American* (October/November), 15–19.

Hogarth, William. [1753] 1908. *Analysis of Beauty*. Chicago: Reilly and Lee.

hooks, bell. 1992. *Black Looks*. Boston: South End Press.

Hogue, W. Lawrence. 1986. *Discourse and the Other: The Production of the Afro-American Text*. Durham, N.C.: Duke University Press.

———. 1996. *Race, Modernity, Postmodernity: A Look at the History and the Literatures of People of Color Since the 1960s*. Albany: State University of New York Press.

Hufford, Mary. 1996. Presentation to New York State Folklife Society, October.

Hunt, John Dixon, and Peter Willis. 1988. *The Genius of Place*. Cambridge: MIT Press.

Hurley, Jack F. 1989. *Marion Post Wolcott: A Photographic Journey*. Albuquerque: University of New Mexico Press.

Hussey, Christopher. 1967. *The Picturesque*. London: Frank Cass and Company.

Imes, Birney. 1990. *Juke Joint: Photographs*. Jackson: University Press of Mississippi.

Jacobson, Mark. 1996. "Down to the Crossroads." *Natural History* 105(9, 10):48–55, 66–71.

Jefferson, Emanual (lifelong resident and worker on Stovall plantation, Clarksdale, Mississippi). 1996. Interview with author, December 14.

Jenkins, Dennis (grocery store and gas station owner). 1996. Interview with author, December 14.

Kayser, Rudolf. 1930. *Stendhal: The Life of an Egoist*. New York: Henry Holt.

Keller, Ulrich. 1986. *The Highway as Habitat: A Roy Stryker Documentation, 1943–1955*. Santa Barbara, Calif.: University Art Museum.

Kerouac, Jack. 1955. *On the Road*. New York: Viking Press.

———. 1958. "The Essentials of Spontaneous Prose." In *On Bohemia: The Code of the Self-Exiled*, ed. Ce'sar Graña and Marigay Graña. New Brunswick, N.J.: Transaction Publishers. Pp. 618–19.

Kolker, Robert Phillip, and Peter Beicken. 1993. *The Films of Wim Wenders: Cinema as Vision and Desire*. Cambridge: Cambridge University Press.

Lackey, Kris. 1997. *Road Frames: The American Highway Narrative*. Lincoln: University of Nebraska Press.

Leach, Sara Amy. 1996a. "Parkways: More than Low-Profile Parks." *Ranger: The Journal of the Association of National Park Rangers* 12(3):2–7.

——— (Natchez Trace Parkway historian). 1996b.Interview with the authors, October and December.

Least Heat Moon, William. 1982. *Blue Highways: A Journey into America*. New York: Ballantine.

Lemann, Nicholas. 1992. *The Promised Land: The Great Black Migration and How it Changed America*. New York: Random House.

Light, Ken. 1995. *Delta Time: Mississippi Photographs by Ken Light*. Washington, D.C.: Smithsonian Institute Press.

Lloyd, David. "Race under representation." In *Culture/Contexture: Explorations in Anthropology and Literary Studies*, ed. E. Valentine Daniel and Jeffrey M. Peck. Berkeley: University of California Press.

Lomax, Alan. 1993. *The Land Where the Blues Began*. New York: Pantheon.

Lower Mississippi Delta Development Commission. 1990. *The Delta Initiatives: Realizing the Dream...Fulfilling the Potential*.

MacCannell, Dean. 1989. *The Tourist: A New Theory of the Leisure Class*. New York: Schocken Books.

McClelland, Linda Flint. 1993. *Presenting Nature: The Historic Landscape Design of the National Park Service, 1916 to 1942*. Washington, D.C.: National Park Service.

Mills, Kay. 1993. *This Little Light of Mine: The Life of Fannie Lou Hammer*. New York: Penguin.

Natanson, Nicholas. 1992. *The Black Image in the New Deal: The Politics of FSA Photography.* Knoxville: University of Tennessee Press.

Nathans, Sydney. "'Gotta Mind to Move, a Mind to Settle Down': Afro-Americans and the Plantation Frontier." In *A Master's Due: Essays in Honor of David Herbert Donald,* ed. William J. Cooper, Jr. Michael F. Holt, and John McCardell. Baton Rouge: Louisiana State University Press.

National Park Service. 1935. Memorandum, May 17, Natchez Trace Parkway Archives.

———. 1995. Official Map and Guide, Natchez Trace Parkway.

———. 1996. *Lower Mississippi Delta Symposium: "Stories of the Delta."*

Odum, Howard. 1928. *Rainbow Round My Shoulder: The Blue Trail of Black Ulysses.* Indianapolis, Ind.: Bobbs-Merrill.

Oliver, Paul. 1969. *The Story of the Blues.* Philadelphia: Chilton Books.

Olmsted, Frederick Law. [1861] 1969. *The Cotton Kingdom: A Traveller's Observations on Cotton and Slavery in the American Slave States,* ed. Arthur M. Schleshinger. New York: Knopf.

O'Neal, Jim. 1994. *Delta Blues Map Kit.* Clarksdale, Miss.: Stackhouse/Delta Record Mart.

——— (owner Stackhouse and Rooster Blues Records, founder of Living Blues magazine). 1996. Interview and tour with authors, October 24.

Palmer, Robert. 1981. *Deep Blues.* New York: Penguin.

Payne, Charles M. 1995. *I've Got the Light of Freedom: The Organizing Tradition and the Mississippi Freedom Struggle.* Berkeley: University of California Press.

Peabody, Charles. 1903. "Notes on Negro Music." *Journal of American Folk-Lore* 16:148–52.

Percy, William (Delta cotton farmer). 1996. Phone interview with authors, December 10.

Pratt, Mary Louise. 1992. *Imperial Eyes: Travel Writing and Transculturation.* London: Routledge.

Preston, Howard Lawrence. *Dirt Roads to Dixie: Accessibility and Modernization in the South, 1885–1935.* Knoxville: University of Tennessee Press.

Robertson, David. 1996. "The Loneliest Road in America." *Terra Nova* 1(2):41–51.

Robinson, Sydney. 1991. *Inquiry into the Picturesque.* Chicago: University of Chicago Press.

Scruggs, Charles. 1993. *Sweet Home: Invisible Cities in the Afro-American Novel.* Baltimore: Johns Hopkins University Press.

Serres, Michel. 1982. "Language and Space: From Oedipus to Zola." In *Hermes: Literature, Science, Philosophy.* Baltimore: Johns Hopkins University Press.

Smith, Jonathan. 1993. "The Lie that Blinds: Destabilizing the Text of Landscape." In *Place/Culture/Representation*, ed. James Duncan and David Ley. New York: Routledge. Pp. 78–92.

Spencer, Jon Michael. 1993. *Blues and Evil.* Knoxville: University of Tennessee Press.

Stewart, Kathleen. 1996. *A Space on the Side of the Road: Cultural Poetics in an "Other" America.* Princeton: Princeton University Press.

Stewart, Susan. 1996. "Exogamous Relations: Travel Writing, the Incest Prohibition, and Hawthorne's Transformation." In *Culture/Contexture: Explorations in Anthropology and Literary Studies,* ed. E. Valentine Daniel and Jeffrey M. Peck. Berkeley: University of California Press.

Taft, Michael. 1983. *Blues Lyric Poetry: An Anthology.* New York: Garland Publishing.

Taylor, John. 1994. *A Dream of England: Landscape, Photography and the Tourist's Imagination.* Manchester: Manchester University Press.

Whale, John. 1994. "Romantics, Explorers and Picturesque Travellers." In *The Politics of the Picturesque: Literature, Landscape and Aesthetics since 1770,* ed. Stephen Copley and Peter Garside. Cambridge: Cambridge University Press.

PERMISSIONS

Excerpts from *Invisible Cities* by Italo Calvino, copyright © 1972 by Giulio Einardi editore s.p.a., English translation copyright © 1974 by Harcourt Brace & Company, reprinted by permission of Harcourt Brace & Company. (United Kingdom and British Commonwealth rights by permission of Andrew Wylie Agency)

Excerpt from "Introduction to the Structural Analysis of Narratives" from Image/Music/Text by Roland Barthes, translated by Stephen Heath. English translation copyright © 1977 by Stephen Heath. Reprinted by permission of Hill and Wang, a division of Farrar, Straus & Giroux, Inc.

Excerpts from *Course in General Linguistics* by Ferdinand de Saussure, copyright © 1972 by Editions Payot, Paris. English translation copyright © by Roy Harris. Published 1986 by Open Court. Reprinted by permission of Open Court Publishing Company, a division of Carus Publishing Company, Peru, IL. (United Kingdom and British Commonwealth rights by permission of Gerald Duckworth & Co., Ltd.)

Excerpts from *What the Light was Like* by Amy Clampitt
Copyright © 1985 by Amy Clampitt. Reprinted by permission of Alfred A. Knopf Inc.
(United Kingdom and British Commonwealth rights by permission of Faber and Faber, Inc.)

"Four Letters Home" was published by permission from Urban Arts Inc./*Arts in Transit: The Southwest Corridor* as part of a project designed and managed by Urban Arts, Inc. for the Massachusetts Bay Transporation Authority and funded by the U. S. Department of Transporation.

Excerpts from "A Worn Path," from *A Curtain of Green* and other stories by Eudora Welty, copyright © 1941 by Eudora Welty, renewed 1969 by Eudora Welty. Published 1980 by Harcourt Brace & Company, reprinted by permission of Harcourt Brace & Company. (United Kingdom and British Commonwealth rights by permission of Russell & Volkening, Inc.)

"Highway 61 Revisited," by Bob Dylan
Copyright © 1965 by Warner Bros. Inc. Copyright renewed 1993 by Special Rider Music
All rights reserved. International copyright secured. Reprinted by permission.

"Key to the Highway"
Words and Music by Big Bill Broonsy and Chas. Segar
© Copyright 1941, 1963 by MCA-DUCHESS MUSIC CORPORATION, a division of UNIVERSAL STUDIOS, INC.
Copyright Renewed International Copyright Secured All Rights Reserved

"Cross Road Blues"
Words and Music by Robert Johnson
© Copyright (1978) 1990, 1991 King of Spades Music

"Preachin' the Blues"
Words and Music by Robert Johnson
© Copyright (1978) 1990, 1991 King of Spades Music

"Sweet Home Chicago"
Words and Music by Robert Johnson
© Copyright (1978) 1990, 1991 King of Spades Music

Excerpts from *Blue Highways* by William Least Heat Moon reprinted by permission from Little, Brown and Company.

signatures in, 51, 52
  as slow event, 10, 44
  as social construction, 31, 34, 62, 255
Naumkeag, 173–174
Necessary fictions, 235, 242, 243
Neoclassical architecture, 270–271
Neotraditionalism:
  contextualism, 262
  memory versus history, 260–261
  See also Kentlands
Neville, C., 157
New Haven, Connecticut, *9th Square Public
    Art: Path of Stars*, 88
New England village, as archetype, 244
New Jersey Pinelands, 179–181
New Urbanism. See Neotraditionalism
Nicolaisen, W.F.H., 89–90
Nos Quedamos, 265–271
  design process, 267–271
  political organizing, 266–267

Oedipus Rex as road story, 277
Odyssey, 45, 54,
Oley Valley, Pennsylvania, 4, 17, 19, 23, 26, 96–98
Olmsted, F.L., Sr.:
  Cazenovia estate design, 250
  placenaming practices, 93–96
  restoration practice, 224
  travel, 278, 283, 303
O'Neal, J., 297, 298, 299, 301, 302
One Hundred Years of Solitude, 48
Opening and , 58, 59, 187–207
  dialogue, 195, 202, 203
  discourse, 196–198
  ecology and indeterminacy, 59
  landscapes, 187
  means of representation, 195
  narratives of home, 249
  natural processes, 204, 205
  scores, 115
Oral histories, importance of place, 20
Oral tradition, simulated in neotraditionalism, 262
Origins
  of blues, 296–299
  of Cazenovia, 245–246
  retelling, 226–228
  simulating, Kentlands, 261
  New England and American identity, 244
Otherness, 251–254
Other, the
  African-Americans as, 296–322
  crossroads as metaphor of encounter with, 299
  denial of coevalness, 310–311
  desire for, 301
  in dialogue with self, 251,–252
  exoticism, 301–302
  Kentlands, 264
  and mass culture, 302
  nature as, 286
Ovid, *Metamorphoses*, 41, 42, 43, 46, 47, 56, 57

Ovid, New York, 84
Painshill, 137, 138
Palimpsest, 156
Panorama, 115–117
Papago Park, 145, 146
Paradigmatic, 44
Parc de Techniques, 122, 123
Parc de la Villette, 13, 203, 204
Parish maps, 190, 191, 195, 196
Parkway, definition, 285
Peabody, G., 311
Pei, Cobb and Freed, 12
Peoples Park for Guinea-Bissau, 128
Periodization, 121
Personal revelation, 140, 141
Phillips, T., 33
Phragmites, 217, 218, 219 220, 221, 222, 224,
    227, 229
Piazza d'Italia, 153
Picturesque, 113, 136–145, 148, 154, 168
Picturesque travel, 283–290
  as narrative of desire, 286
Pilgrimage:
  Natchez, Mississippi, 282
  and tourism, 298. See MacCannell
Pincote Pavilion, as metaphor, 51
Pine Barrens. See Pinelands
Pinelands, New Jersey, 3, 85–87
Pinto, J., 145, 146
Place:
  importance in memory, 20–21
  scripted, 25
  social construction of, 25
  as time, 35
Place Berri, 171, 172
Placenames, 20, 89, 90
  as cause of stories, 78–79
  classical topos, 83–84
  created by stories, 78
  commodified, 97–98
  Ireland, 101–102
  and memory, 77, 78, 86, 87
  as metaphor and metonymy, 79
  Native American, 85,102
  and racial discourse, 81, 100, 101
  rhetorical, 86
  salvage toponymy 101, 105
  settlements and subdivisions, 96–98
  wilderness, 88
Plater-Zyberk, E., 258, 259, 272. See Duany, A.;
    DPZ
Plaza de Espana, 171
Plot, 7, 45–50, 111–115
  naming, 75–76
  physical space, 115
  progressive, 114, versus sequence, 45
Pope, A., 287
Postmodernism, x, 25
  architecture, 12, 13, 14, 25
  literature, 10

Post-structuralism, *33*, 56, 57, 153
Pottenger, M., 150
Poullaoec-Gonidec, 20, 21
Prague, 11, 14
Price, U., 287, 288
Process, as narrative, 11, 22, 23. *See also*
    Chamberlain, Hargreaves, Long
Progress:
  and heritage, 320–321
  as narrative, 216, 218–220
Project Highway, 306
Propp, V., 48
Puerto Rican community, 270–271

Questions, 135, 193–195, 196–198

race:
  Buttermilk Bottom, 99–101
  denaturalizing, 311, 321–322
  labor history, Natchez Trace Parkway, 292
  Native Americans, 102
  placenames, 81, 99–101
racism:
  binary coding, 308, 309, 311
  and road improvement, 319
  in street names, Atlanta, 100–101
Ramona stories, 262
Reader:
  as narrator, 10
  ideal, 50
  role of, 10, 31, 59
Reading:
  as intertextual practice, 57, 58
  the landscape, 33
  and memory, 58
  multiple, 17
  politics of, 17
  See also Interpretation
Reading the American Landscape, 50
Realism:
  contextualism, 54
  in ecological design, 50
  as mirror to road, 303
  Magic, 39
Reality. *See* Fiction
Reclamation, 219
Recycling, as restoration practice, 234
"Reedbeds of the Hackensack," 217
Reenactments, 117
Regionalism:
  as marketing strategy, 263
  in neotraditional design, 261–263
  placenaming practices, 98
Registering, 53
Relativism, 25, 33, 34, 55–58, 62, 228
  critique of, 57
  of identity, 259
Remnants, 179
REPOhistory, 99–101, 193, 194, 198, 199
Representation: